Creating a
Modern Countryside

The Nature | History | Society series is devoted to the publication of high-quality scholarship in environmental history and allied fields. Its broad compass is signalled by its title: nature because it takes the natural world seriously; history because it aims to foster work that has temporal depth; and society because its essential concern is with the interface between nature and society, broadly conceived. The series is avowedly interdiscplinary and is open to the work of anthropologists, ecologists, historians, geographers, literary scholars, political scientists, sociologists, and others whose interests resonate with its mandate. It offers a timely outlet for lively, innovative, and well-written work on the interaction of people and nature through time in North America.

General Editor: Graeme Wynn, University of British Columbia

Claire Elizabeth Campbell, *Shaped by the West Wind: Nature and History in Georgian Bay*

Tina Loo, *States of Nature: Conserving Canada's Wildlife in the Twentieth Century*

Jamie Benidickson, *The Culture of Flushing: A Social and Legal History of Sewage*

William J. Turkel, *The Archive of Place: Unearthing the Pasts of the Chilcotin Plateau*

John Sandlos, *Hunters at the Margin: Native People and Wildlife Conservation in the Northwest Territories*

NATURE | HISTORY | SOCIETY

Creating a Modern Countryside

Liberalism and Land Resettlement in British Columbia

JAMES MURTON

FOREWORD BY GRAEME WYNN

UBC Press • Vancouver • Toronto

15 14 13 12 11 10 09 08 07   5 4 3 2 1

Printed in Canada on ancient-forest-free paper (100% post-consumer recycled) that is processed chlorine- and acid-free, with vegetable-based inks.

Library and Archives Canada Cataloguing in Publication Data

Murton, James Ernest, 1969-
    Creating a modern countryside : liberalism and land resettlement in British Columbia / James Murton ; foreword by Graeme Wynn.

    (Nature, history, society ; 1713-6687)
    Includes bibliographical references and index.
    ISBN 978-0-7748-1337-2 (bound) ; ISBN 978-0-7748-1338-9 (pbk.)

    1. Land use, Rural – British Columbia – History – 20th century – Case studies.
2. Rural renewal – British Columbia – History – 20th century – Case studies.
3. Environmental economics – British Columbia – History – 20th century –
Case studies. 4. Environmental policy – British Columbia. I. Title.

HD319.B7M87 2007   333.76'0971109042   C2007-902831-4

Canadä

UBC Press gratefully acknowledges the financial support for our publishing program of the Government of Canada through the Book Publishing Industry Development Program (BPIDP), and of the Canada Council for the Arts, and the British Columbia Arts Council.

This book has been published with the help of a grant from the Canadian Federation for the Humanities and Social Sciences, through the Aid to Scholarly Publications Programme, using funds provided by the Social Sciences and Humanities Research Council of Canada, and with the help of the K.D. Srivastava Fund.

UBC Press
The University of British Columbia
2029 West Mall
Vancouver, BC V6T 1Z2
604-822-5959 / Fax: 604-822-6083
www.ubcpress.ca

For my father, who taught me about British Columbia;
my mother, who taught me to look things up;
and for Catherine, who was there for all of it

This war has set its vitalizing hand upon our people.

– Leonard S. Klinck, dean of agriculture and later president of the University of British Columbia, 1918

Only food and drink and, contingently, shelter are absolute physiological necessities that must be gotten, and in general no immense allocation of time has been necessary to get them. The allegations that nature *itself*, the planet as a whole, has been insufficiently generous or unreliable are ignorant and/or dishonest slurs. In those cases where people have gone without, or had to work very hard to meet those needs, they can honestly lay the blame for their misfortune squarely on other human beings.

– Colin A.M. Duncan, *The Centrality of Agriculture*

What we call land is an element of nature inextricably interwoven with man's institutions.

– Karl Polanyi, *The Great Transformation*, 178

Contents

Illustrations

FIGURES

FOREWORD

Soldiers' Fields

by Graeme Wynn

They shall grow not old, as we that are left grow old.
Age shall not weary them, nor the years condemn.
At the going down of the sun and in the morning
We will remember them.

RECITED ON REMEMBRANCE DAY in Canada and England, and on
Anzac Day in Australia and New Zealand, these poignant words
from Lawrence Binyon's poem honouring the dead of the British
Expeditionary Force in 1914, remain powerfully, hauntingly familiar in the
twenty-first century. Engraved on the Cenotaph in London's Whitehall
and on countless smaller memorials to those who fell "in the cause of the
free," they affirm the deep sense of loss felt for the men and women killed
in service of their countries amid the carnage and devastation of World
War I.[1] "We are the Dead" wrote Canadian lieutenant-colonel John McCrae
in an equally affecting commemoration of comrades who fell in the terrible battle of Ypres in 1915: "Short days ago / We lived, felt dawn, saw sunset glow, / Loved and were loved, and now we lie / In Flanders fields."[2]
    From the Canadian Monument at Vimy Ridge in France to the Lib-
erty Memorial in Kansas City, USA, from the Shrine of Remembrance in
Melbourne, Australia, to the War Memorial Carillon in Wellington, New
Zealand and the monument at Delville Wood commemorating South
African troops caught in ferocious fighting during the Battle of the
Somme, moving official tributes to those who died "in defense of liberty
and our country" also offer solemn reminders of the sacrifice made by a
generation of young people: "Their ideal is our legacy, their sacrifice our
inspiration." Few visitors to these sites or to any of the larger cemeteries
constructed and maintained by the Imperial (later Commonwealth) War
Graves Commission remain unmoved by the magnitude of the killing and

the commitment to "preserving the memory of the dead with simple dig-
nity and true equality," in hope of encouraging "future generations to
remember the sacrifice made by so many."[3] Markers in the larger cemeteries proclaim that the names of those buried there "liveth for evermore,"
and Rupert Brooke's familiar sonnet, "The Soldier" paints personal sacrifice bright with patriotic meaning in its best-known lines: "If I should die,
think only this of me: / That there's some corner of a foreign field / That
is for ever England."[4]

Countless other, less obvious, monuments and tributes to those who
fell in the First World War – some of them neglected, others so familiar
that they are taken for granted, their original purpose rarely recognized –
dot the landscapes of the combatant countries. In the years after 1918,
many debated whether commemorative ventures should be ornamental or
utilitarian, whether they should speak to the spiritual values that had taken
men and women to war or provide material means (hospitals, schools, or
museums) to assist the comrades and descendants of those who had died.[5]
Echoing the opinion of the Roman poet Horace – "Dulce et decorum est
pro patria mori" ("It is a sweet and honourable thing to die for one's country") – New Zealand's acting prime minister came down firmly on the
ornamental side in arguing for "something that represents to us duty
done," something to improve the character of generations yet unborn and
make them "realize what it is to sacrifice ourselves for the good of the
whole."[6] Others opted for more directly functional investments. In 1919,
oak trees were planted in an elaborate, extensive design across North
Otago, New Zealand, in honour of each of the four hundred or so men
from the district who never returned from the war. Intended to beautify
the landscape as well as to serve as impressive living memorials to the
fallen, each had a marker post and a bronze plaque; those in rural areas
were surrounded by a protective fence.[7]

Yet the forces of nature, neglect, changing priorities, and fading memories have conspired variously to dull the expression of gratitude inherent
in this and many other commemorative endeavours. Although many of
the North Otago oaks flourished, others surrendered to drought, road
works, and pruning. Today, the Auckland War Memorial Museum is often
referred to simply as the Auckland Museum, and many Canadians are
unaware that Memorial University of Newfoundland was established in
1925 to honour residents of that colony who lost their lives on active service during the First World War. Similarly, few know that when architects
began designing a new sports arena on the south side of Chicago in 1919,
their mandate was to commemorate Americans who died in uniform.

Opened as Municipal Grant Park Stadium on the fifty-third anniversary of the Chicago Fire in 1924, the arena was renamed and dedicated as Soldier Field on Remembrance Day 1925. Much remodeled, it is now more widely recognized as the home of "Da Bears," Chicago's National Football League team, than as the memorial to combatants in a long-ago war that it was designed to be. "Who will remember, passing through this Gate," asked English poet Siegfried Sassoon, in a satirical reflection on the structure erected on the outskirts of Ypres after the First World War to commemorate those missing but believed to have been killed in action nearby, "The unheroic Dead who fed the guns? / ... / Those doomed, conscripted, unvictorious ones?"[8] Memorials, piles of "peace-complacent stone" of any sort, might indeed belie the sacrifice of "the Dead who struggled in the slime" as Sassoon put it, but even as time and circumstance blunt the sharp, sad sentiment that inspired their creation, they give cause to remember (if not always "at the going down of the sun and in the morning") those who died.

But what of those left to grow old after 1918? In contrast with the tributes paid the dead, the fates and fortunes of those who survived and returned to their homelands have been substantially forgotten. Contemporaries recognized that they owed much to those returning from the war. "We owe a great debt of gratitude to these men, and we should be willing to compensate them for the great sacrifices they have made," said one contributor to a parliamentary debate in Victoria (Australia) in 1916.[9] Yet they found this debt of honour far more difficult to pay than that due the deceased. The numbers involved were huge. Of the near nine million people who went to war from Britain and the Empire, almost eight million were discharged. These returned servicemen were a diverse lot. Drawn from city, town, and countryside, from factories, offices, and farms, from relatively affluent, moderately comfortable, and hard-scrabble circumstances into military service, they were generally young and had been affected in various ways by their wartime experiences. Many suffered physical injury – over two million were recorded as wounded in action. More carried psychological scars. "Shell shock," debilitating neuroses, and other afflictions now known as post-traumatic stress disorders (but then largely unrecognized) took their toll. According to the Australian social historian Raymond Evans, many ex-servicemen "carried the war home in combat-ravaged minds and battle-hardened bodies to inflict it as a private hell upon their wives and children."[10]

In Britain, anxieties about impending social and political upheaval were heightened by the fear that traumatized veterans would concentrate in cities with high levels of unemployment after the war. Melded with

swelling imperial sentiment and a sense of responsibility toward demobi-
lized soldiers, these concerns underpinned enthusiasm for the idea, as a
later report (published in 1920) had it, of *Land Settlement for Ex-Service
Men in the Overseas Dominions.*[11] The prolific popular novelist and sometime colonial administrator and adventurer Henry Rider Haggard played
an influential role in these developments. With the backing of the Royal
Colonial Institute in London and as a member of the Royal Commission
on the Natural Resources, Trade and Legislation of Certain Portions of
His Majesty's Dominions, he travelled widely through the settler colonies,
to stress both the crucial need for imperial vitality and the particular attrib-
utes of British ex-servicemen. They were, he assured his listeners, "the finest
settlers in the world – men who have been thoroughly disciplined, who
know what stress and danger mean, and who know how to face opposition
of every kind."[12] With similar Imperial confidence, Christopher Turnor,
author of the 1920 report, *Land Settlement,* went so far as to outline appropriate mechanisms for placing British soldiers on colonial farms: for
strategic reasons, metropolitan authorities should orchestrate the flow of
ex-servicemen and their families to the dominions; there they should be
accommodated in group settlements comprised of at least two hundred
farms and assured of freehold tenure, ample credit, expert advice, and the
provision of necessary infrastructure.

   In each of the British Dominions, and in the United States (which sent
4.7 million troops to combat and suffered 120,000 casualties), public ex-
pectations and official policy largely coincided in the conviction that land
should be made available to those who returned from the war, but in the
dominions local efforts to implement this commitment rarely mirrored
metropolitan designs. Colonials and their representatives were cautious
about granting the gift of land, their readiest currency, to British soldiers
and sailors before accommodating their own ex-servicemen. And relatively few members of the British forces showed much interest in taking
up the limited opportunities available to them in the colonies. In Aus-
tralasia, politicians and patriots had encouraged men to enlist by promising them farms upon their return. As early as 1915, New Zealand prime
minister W.F. Massey was envisaging "colonies of ... returned soldiers,
planted, as the ancient Romans did, in different parts of their great Empire
after their victories," and later that year legislation was passed providing
for land grants on favourable terms and generous financial assistance
for soldier settlers.[13] Across the Tasman Sea, South Australia quickly followed the New Zealand lead, and other state governments soon emulated
these early adapters. Soldier settlement seemed to promise many things:

repatriation, patriotic compensation and economic self-sufficiency for individuals, and the opportunity to develop and "open up the country" for the benefit of all. By 1916, the Commonwealth government had agreed to provide financial assistance for land acquisition and infrastructure development to facilitate the settlement of discharged soldiers by state authorities.

Noone knew what this commitment might mean, but one reasonably contemporary estimate suggested that if no more than one in every four eligible Australians took up land, and it cost £2,000 each to place them on farms, expenditures would reach £150 million.[14] In the end, numbers were smaller (by about half), and costs were considerably lower, amounting to less than a third of the total envisaged. In New Zealand, land settlement was judged "the best known, the most expensive, and the least successful" of all forms of rehabilitation offered returned servicemen after the war. By March 1924, the government had loaned £22 million to 22,000 ex-servicemen.[15] In both of the Australasian dominions, the commitment to settle soldiers on the land had followed earlier efforts to "burst up the great estates" and promote more intensive patterns of land use. These closer settlement movements, which rested on deeply entrenched agrarian visions of the yeoman farmer (and his household) as constituents of the ideal society, had been buttressed, if not necessarily guaranteed success, by the application of science to agriculture and the growing conviction, early in the twentieth century, that natural limits to intensification could be overcome.[16]

Generally, the Australian and New Zealand soldier settlement schemes have been seen as dismal failures. Concerns were expressed early, by a Royal Commission of Inquiry in the state of Victoria in 1925, which clung to hope even as it recognized shortcomings in the soldier settlement program: "The course lies across an imperfectly charted sea, through many reefs and shoals, and shifting sands called prices. The ship was hastily equipped but it is well-manned, and we believe will ultimately be brought safely to port." A harsher verdict was pronounced by an Australian inquiry four years later, which lamented that 30 percent of soldier settlers assigned land had left their properties. Some have disputed the broad condemnation, noting that persistence rates varied enormously. Even the 1929 inquiry noted that they ranged from 40 percent in Tasmania to slightly more than 80 percent in Victoria, and assessments of outcomes at the local scale provide examples of both heartening successes and dispiriting failures.[17]

On balance, however, it is clear that many soldiers and their families struggled to win a decent living from the fields assigned them. Large numbers of those placed on the land lacked experience in farm management. Postwar inflation and high demand raised the costs of stock and equipment for those developing farms immediately after 1918. Few had sufficient capital. The financial advances provided them were generally inadequate and came with stringent repayment schedules. Individual farms were often smaller than necessary for successful operations in the areas in which they were located, as extensive pastoral estates were divided into separate blocks that averaged less than two hundred acres each in many settlements. Some settlement locations were simply misjudged, leaving soldier settlers on undrained swampland, or setting them up for dairying in wheat-and-sheep country. On top of all of this, agricultural produce prices were highly, and unexpectedly, volatile in the 1920s. "For far too many" Australian soldiers, concludes a recent detailed examination of soldier settlement schemes in Queensland, "the struggle against mud, sand and shells was merely transformed into a battle against the natural environment, abject poverty and governmental neglect."[18]

Contemporary estimates suggested that as many as 750,000 American soldiers would want to take up land at the end of the war. A precedent for large-scale allocations of public land to former soldiers had been established after the Civil War, but half a century later, the public domain was far less extensive. Plans therefore focused on bringing unused, or "waste," lands into productivity. The National Soldier Settlement Bill of 1919 envisaged a $100 million appropriation to provide farms for war veterans. Each project developed under this scheme was to make farms available through the Department of the Interior by clearing, draining, irrigating, or fertilizing land, and each was to include at least a hundred households; plans also called for settlers to live in communities from which they would work the surrounding land. All costs were to be charged to the projects and recouped from land sales, although short-term loans were to be offered for the acquisition of stock and equipment. "Nothing was to be given to the veterans other than an opportunity for immediate employment, credit, and a chance to acquire a farm unit."[19] Still, the bill encountered opposition on several fronts. Some considered it discriminatory for extending assistance only to those soldiers who wanted farms; others took issue with its cost and argued that there was no need to bring new land into competition with existing farms. Modifications and other initiatives were proposed to address the concerns of critics, including revisions to, and amplifications of, the 1902 Reclamation Act by extending its provisions beyond the seventeen western states to which it originally applied and making more money available for reclamation works.[20]

In the end, Congress failed to enact soldier settlement legislation per se. Although thirteen states had approved measures to place ex-servicemen on farms, seven had made their implementation dependent upon federal cooperation and financial assistance. Thus, only California, Oregon, Washington, South Dakota, Minnesota, and Arizona made practical efforts to place war veterans on farms. The details of their schemes varied, but all fell short of their objectives. Those in Minnesota, Washington, and California (which framed the most ambitious scheme in the country) were perhaps least successful. Generally, all of these initiatives foundered because the costs of making land available (and thus the price of farms) exceeded the earning capacity of the properties, which was due to low market prices and, said one later assessment, "poor supervision and lack of settler responsibility."[21]

Canada, which sent 650,000 of its citizens to the Great War and lost over ten percent of them, began to face the challenge of dealing with returned soldiers as early as 1915, when the Military Hospital Commission met with provincial representatives, who agreed to establish committees to deal with the needs of discharged servicemen. Within a year, the British Columbia Returned Soldiers' Aid Commission was recommending the settlement of "all returned soldiers" in cooperative communities located in areas selected by an appointed Board of Commissioners. With approval of the Land Settlement and Development Act in 1917, the province created its own Land Settlement Board in the Department of Agriculture to promote agricultural development and to serve as an instrument for the establishment of "Settlement Areas" for returned soldiers, their widows, and other bona fide settlers on undeveloped agricultural lands. As so often in the Canadian federation, however, it soon became apparent that it was "not possible for any one province to arrive at a solution that would be adopted by all of them."[22] None of the other provinces moved as decisively as British Columbia on this front. Federal-provincial cooperation was necessary for the development of a practical policy. The federal government convened a Parliamentary Committee on Returned Soldiers early in 1917 and six months later, in September, "An Act to Assist Returned Soldiers in Settling Upon the Land and to Increase Agricultural Production" established the Soldier Settlement Board to assist returned servicemen onto the land.

With vast acreages of unsettled territory and extensive areas throughout the west in the hands of the federal government, the Canadian response to the challenge of soldier settlement was quite different from those of the Australasian colonies and the United States. Given the extent of good, uncultivated land near existing settlements and markets, the government early decided to avoid "the settlement of soldiers as pioneers in remote locations or under isolated conditions, removed from markets, in virgin forest areas, or on lands not cultivable without reclamation or other development."[23] Federal lands along railroad routes were reserved for veterans, and in the prairie provinces, eligible ex-servicemen were allowed a 160-acre land grant, to which they could add a similar area under the provisions of the Homestead Act. Basically, the government invited eligible applicants to apply for loans to a maximum of $7,500 for the purchase of land, stock, and equipment and for the execution of "permanent improvements" to their properties. Applicants had to satisfy officials as to their fitness and moral character, and provide information about their assets and abilities.

The press of applications soon exceeded the capacity of the Board of Commissioners to cope with them. Loans could be processed quite expeditiously but establishing men on free Dominion lands proved more difficult. Amendments to the Soldier Settlement Act (effective in 1919) committed the federal government to providing funds for the provinces to purchase or expropriate private and uncultivated land within designated districts for the settlement of soldiers. Anticipating these changes, BC premier John Oliver moved late in 1918 to introduce the provincial Act to Provide Lands for the Use and Benefit of Returned Soldiers (known as the Soldiers' Land Act). Through its provisions, the Lieutenant-Governor in Council (effectively the governing party in the legislature) was allowed to acquire land for soldier settlement with monies from the consolidated revenue fund, and it thus held considerable power "to control land development and the settlement of returned soldiers and bona fide settlers" in British Columbia.[24] Quickly, the province's Land Settlement Board established fourteen settlement areas, one in the Kootenays near Fernie and the others ranging across the central interior, from Smithers south to Rose Lake near Kamloops, but few veterans were attracted to these locations. Disappointed, the premier turned to encourage community settlements. The idea of cooperative land settlement was in the air but the federal government was dubious about both the financial feasibility and the eligibility of such ventures for assistance under the Soldier Settlement Act. Undaunted, Premier Oliver instructed the Land Settlement Board to purchase unoccupied forest and logged-off lands for designation as "Development Areas," where soldiers would work together for modest wages to clear the land before purchasing fractions of it for their own farms.

Three years after the war ended, the federal Soldier Settlement Board had received some 60,000 applications for assistance and deemed approximately two-thirds of them eligible; by the end of March 1921, aid had been extended to over 25,000 soldier settlers across the country. Almost 80 percent of them held loans, amounting in total to $80 million, and the others had taken up free Dominion land without loan assistance.[25] Those found to be lacking adequate farming experience were required to find employment with a "good farmer" until they had gained sufficient knowledge and experience to convince local field supervisors that they were likely to succeed on the land. Until 1921 allowances were provided and, in some parts of the country, special training centres were operated to aid those starting out. In addition, field supervisors visited and advised all those assisted by the board, and a "Home Service Branch" provided help and advice on home economics and farming subjects to soldier settlers' wives.

Contemporary reports were often enthusiastic about these efforts. On 2 September 1920, the Regina *Morning Leader* carried an article by C.W. Cavers of the Soldier Settlement Board touting the progress of soldier settlement in Saskatchewan, which offered "a very excellent field for this great experiment." The disposal of Indian and forest reserves as well as land formerly assigned to the Hudson's Bay Company and "many acres of idle lands formerly owned by private individuals" had provided "a decided fillip" to expansion in the "great West" and increased the country's resources. Over four thousand loans (valued at over $16 million) had already been approved and close to 3,250 members of the Canadian Overseas Militia Force were settled on their new farms. Although some of the soldier settlers failed because of what Cavers described as "ill health," death, "domestic infelicity," or the disappointing quality of the land they were assigned, he had no doubt that in the course of time, thousands "who would have been compelled to seek employment" in already overcrowded cities, would become "producers in the truest sense because of the extremely favorable terms of the Soldier Settlement Act."

A year later, the Soldier Settlement Board was equally positive about its activities in British Columbia, despite the fact that its efforts were spread across three wide – and very different – districts and it was therefore impossible to offer a single narrative of achievement. In its report, the board paid no specific attention to the jurisdictional complexities created by the BC government's Development Areas scheme, and simply reported on the numbers of soldier settlers in the different parts of the province. There were 939 in the Vernon district, scattered across an area that encompassed 50,000 square miles and included the mountainous Kootenays as well as the dry Okanagan. The Victoria district was responsible for just over 500 men, most of them on the Gulf Islands, and in the Duncan and

Comox areas. The Vancouver district extended northwards to the Bulkley and Nechako valleys and eastward to the Cariboo, but fully 650 of the 1,400 soldiers in receipt of loans in this vast area were concentrated in the lower Fraser Valley, in Surrey, Langley, Matsqui, and Chilliwack. A large number were also settled in Richmond. Difficulties were legion: many struggled with the enormous trees on their properties; in the interior, farmers battled drought; land in some parts of the lower Fraser was flooded, and in others it was waterlogged during the planting season; commodity prices were high, beef prices were depressed, and the weather was bad. But the "Home Branch" was active, offering advice to farmers' wives, on everything from making bread to pickling fish, and providing pre-natal instruction. It was "impossible to speak too highly" of the set- tlers' "optimism and determination." Hardship had been bucked "by pluck and resourcefulness." Only later would scholars recount the failure of soldier settlements in the province.[26]

In retrospect, it is clear that strong similarities reverberate through the stories told about soldier settlements across the British Empire (and to a lesser degree in the United States). In the immediate aftermath of the war, politicians and others echoed the conviction of Arthur Meighen, the Canadian minister of the interior, that the "primary and great principle" behind their efforts to encourage soldiers in the development of farm fields was "to secure settlements of ... idle lands, and to make settlers of those who have proven themselves the backbone and stay of the nation in its trouble." To greater or lesser degree, each was convinced that there was no better way to "fortify ... [the] country against the waves of unrest and discontent that now assail us, as all the rest of the world, than by making the greatest possible proportion of the soldiers of our country settlers upon the land."[27]

Such commitments rested upon deep-seated beliefs about the place of agriculture in society. Long and complex genealogies shaped these points of view, and they were emphasized differently as they were threaded through debates about soldier settlement in different places at different times. In general, however, they incorporated three associated and over- lapping visions of agriculture: an arcadian notion that emphasized the moral virtues and personal benefits of rural life and often entailed a romantic critique of modernity; an agrarian discourse that saw agriculture as the real source of all wealth and the yeoman farmer as the embodiment of freedom and independence; and an emerging "Country Life" movement that sought to reform and improve rural conditions through scientific research and implementation of progressive policies in the countryside.[28]

Together, these impulses swathed the postwar development of soldiers' fields in hope.

Time and experience cast these initiatives in a different light, however. Many of those who had been encouraged to take up land struggled to make ends meet. Indignant that those who had fought for freedom had become prisoners of difficult circumstances, contemporary commentators tended to emphasize failures above successes and their accounts led many later historians to portray soldier settlements as examples of good intentions gone awry. Misguided decisions, careless choices, unforeseen market conditions, personal failings, and many other factors were held responsible, in varying degrees, for particular outcomes but, generally, the enormous investments made in settling ex-servicemen upon the land have been condemned for their failure to produce acceptable returns.

Creating a Modern Countryside is written against this canvas of globe-encompassing efforts to establish soldiers on fields (and farms) of their own. At first (and too-fleeting) glance, it might be regarded simply as a useful contribution to the now-considerable array of studies dealing with this broad topic, one that offers new detail about hitherto under-studied soldier settlement schemes on the Pacific fringe of Canada. But this would seriously underrate the value of the contribution that James Murton makes in the pages that follow. By focusing his attention on two of the BC government's most concerted efforts to establish soldier settlements, at Merville on Vancouver Island and at Camp Lister in the Kootenay mountains of southeastern British Columbia, as well as on the Southern Okanagan Irrigation Project, which began as a soldier settlement, and considering them alongside contemporary and cognate efforts to drain Sumas Lake, encourage agricultural settlement in the Cariboo region, and irrigate the dry Okanagan Valley, Murton throws new light on both the development of British Columbia between the wars and on the soldier settlement schemes of this period more generally.

The freshness of Murton's story derives from the somewhat unusual bifocal view that he brings to his work. Recognizing, as he puts it in the first line of his book, that nature haunts the great projects of the state but that historians interested in the processes of state formation have generally relegated the environment to the margins of their accounts, he seeks to re-centre his discussion of the interwar years on the reciprocal, and inescapable, links between changes in the state and changes in the land. Here he draws inspiration from two lines of historical inquiry (and their associated literatures) that remain, at least in Canada, largely and unfortunately discrete. One of these focuses on the various ways in which governments have promoted and facilitated processes of territorial occupation, (re)settlement, and the extension of authority over land and people. This line of inquiry has long and deep roots but its antecedents run variously from ideas associated with Michel Foucault through Philip Corrigan and Derek Sayer's *The Great Arch: English State Formation as Cultural Revolution*, published in 1985, and James Scott's *Seeing Like a State* to Ian McKay's influential article, published in the *Canadian Historical Review* in 2000, which argues that the development of Canada is best seen as a "project of rule" by which the "politico-economic logic" of liberalism was imposed on a vast territory and implanted in the hearts and minds of its inhabitants.[29] Murton extends and refines this latter point by focusing on the moment when the classic laissez-faire liberalism of the nineteenth century (intent on establishing equality of opportunity for individuals) gave way to a more interventionist "new liberalism" early in the twentieth century. Central to this political/ideological shift (which was also seen in Britain and in the United States, where it was incorporated into the broad agenda of the Progressive Movement) was a new conception of the state that encouraged action to ensure "the general welfare of its citizens." This, maintains Murton, led the British Columbia government into soldier and other settlement projects that were exercises in both social and environmental reform.

The second source of inspiration for Murton's bifocal vision lies in environmental history. Several practitioners in this field have examined relations between the state and the environment through a variety of lenses, ranging from official endeavours to preserve wilderness through consideration of the politics of development to government-led efforts at conservation. In this context, Murton draws particularly on the ideas of two American scholars, taking from Richard White a central idea of *The Organic Machine* that efforts to transform the Columbia River were predicated on a desire to make it "part of a larger unity ... composed of nature and machine, for the betterment of humanity," and from Donald Worster the observation that the modern capitalist state was driven by "an ideology of instrumental reason" that "saw no value in ... nature that was not doing work directly useful to humans" (see pages 4 and 5 herein).[30] Central to both of these positions – and thus to Murton's assessment of the interwar efforts to create a new countryside in British Columbia – was the conviction that the state could bring technology and nature together productively, to benefit both humans and the environment. In this perspective, the impulse to place returned soldiers on the land was less a reflection of rural romanticism – a retreat from the travails of modernity – than a well-intentioned attempt to frame an alternative form of modernity, a way of life that offered those who embraced it both access to nature and the advantages associated with modern science and technology. On this account, the soldiers and others encouraged onto the land by the British Columbia government after 1918 were participants in a noble – if ultimately unsuccessful – attempt to transcend the dichotomy between humans and the environment, nature and the machine.

In this, participants in the interwar initiative to develop the British Columbia countryside stand in sharp contrast to most of those who later occupied the lands – no longer cultivated – in the Development Areas and in other isolated parts of the province: members of the 1960s and '70s "counter-culture," whose "back-to-the-land" movement rested on the belief that "the machine" (often construed to include all facets of high modernist society) had no proper place in the garden of nature. By drawing this contrast and reminding readers of the differences that set these two instances of enthusiasm for rural life apart, Murton lifts his study from its preoccupation with a couple of decades of British Columbia history to make the first of several larger points upon which this book invites reflection: History may seem to repeat itself, but it does so only to the superficial observer. Getting "down into the dirt" (to use Murton's metaphorical phrase) of the past, to explore its details and intricate patterns, its puzzles and contradictions, reveals both its complexity and the importance of context and contingency in shaping events. More than this, it should be clear, after reading Murton's book, that historians' views of the past – reflected in the questions they ask and the answers they deem important enough to emphasize – are cumulative and conditional. *Creating a Countryside in British Columbia* rests (in some fair degree, as all historical works do) on the inquiries of others and renders the past relevant, at least in part, as a refraction of current concerns and debates.

Second, this book contributes to our understanding of early twentieth-century Canada in two important ways: by demonstrating that, in British Columbia at least, soldier settlement initiatives were assimilated into larger programs of organized land settlement and helped impart a sense of urgency and moral conviction to existing agendas; and by indicating that British Columbia stood somewhat apart from other regions of the country in its efforts to place returned soldiers in communal settlements in Development Areas, which were chosen because they were relatively isolated and unimproved. Third, Murton invites those interested in the relations between nature and human societies to ponder his book's foundational assertion that "understanding environmental change requires moving beyond the consideration of ideas explicitly about nature to more general logics – such as liberalism – that implicitly encourage a particular form of engagement with nature" (page 6 herein). This is an important summons, not least because it encourages a more historical perspective on the role of the state in relation to the environment than that articulated by several recent theorists of this relationship, at the same time as it cautions against narrow, instrumental interpretations of human-environment interactions. And, finally but no less importantly, this work is, in its way, a tribute to soldiers and other settlers who sought and struggled to develop productive fields in often unpropitious circumstances in a postwar world that they helped to bring into being but that was never entirely of their own devising.

Acknowledgments

OVER THE COURSE OF THIS PROJECT, I have generated a long list of debts to friends, colleagues, mentors, and family. I will attempt to acknowledge all here. I apologize in advance to anyone inadvertently left out.

In Kingston and at Queen's University: my friend Ann Perry, fellow member of the Queen's Own Guinea Pigs John Varty, Jenn Marotta, Chris Pockett, Mike Dawson, Ross Cameron, Amanda Crocker, Ryan Edwardson, Amy Bell, Krista Kesselring, Todd MacCallum, Jennifer Alexopoulis, Sarah Hendriks, Trevor Killins, Matt Smith, Tim Smith, Gord Dueck, Martina Hardwick, Natasha Aleksiuk, Al Doseger, Shari Doseger, Bob Pearson, Joyce Pearson, Cam MacEachern (who saved me much typing time by coming up with the abbreviation "B2L"), Alan MacEachern, Jenne MacLean, Jared Siebert, Kathy Siebert, Laura Macdonald, and of course Ingrid Gagnon. Much thanks also goes to Geneva House and the Next Church.

My love and thanks also go to my family – Dave and Andrea, my parents Heather and Gary Murton, Stacey, Geoff, Joel, and Jeremy, and Mom and Annette – who provided inspiration, support, and encouragement, not to mention food and shelter. Stacey helpfully translated balance sheets, and my mother assisted with the final drafts. Mom and Annette graciously welcomed me into their family and demonstrated unwavering enthusiasm for my work. I have also been fortunate to know the sprawling Ludema clan, in particular Ken and Jo, Karen, Rod, Evonne, Angie, Jackie, Rachel, and Hannah.

Ian McKay was an inspirational (and tireless) supervisor, colleague, and friend. Jane Errington, Jamey Carson, and Elsbeth Heaman offered timely support and advice. Colin Duncan introduced me to environmental history and was an enthusiastic (and unpaid) second supervisor. My thanks to Ian, Colin, and Jamey, as well as Tim Smith and Brian Osborne, for taking my work seriously enough to offer tough, searching questions.

I also acknowledge George Bradak and Rachel Chan at UBC's Special Collections Division. Wendy and Kathryn at the Courtenay and District Museum and Archives were friendly and supportive in the middle of their construction zone. Katy, Jennifer, David, Michael, Ann, Karen, Janet, Carl, Jackie, Myron, and Bill at the BC Archives made me feel like part of the family.

Financial support was provided by the Donald S. Rickerd Foundation, the Dorothy Warne Chambers Memorial Fellowship, and the Association for Canadian Studies. Major support came from Queen's University and the Ontario Graduate Scholarship program. My postdoctoral life was funded by the Social Sciences and Humanities Research Council of Canada, and the book manuscript benefited enormously from my time as a SSHRC postdoctoral fellow among the generous and intellectually stimulating scholars of the UBC Geography Department.

At UBC, conversations with Geoff Mann, Joel Wainwright, Cole Harris, John Thistle, Bob McDonald, Mike Bovis, Sally Hermanson, David Brownstein, and Arn Keeling, among others, were very helpful. Matthew Evenden offered valuable comments on the introduction, and both he and Kirsty have been good friends. The students in my Simon Fraser University History 436 seminar on the history of BC helped me to see this work in a wider context. Special thanks go to Graeme Wynn, a model postdoctoral supervisor who spent much time and took seriously all my research goals.

Thanks to my colleagues at Nipissing University, who have been great friends, and who have shown support and enthusiasm for my work. Jennifer Young quickly and efficiently compiled the table in the Appendix. My thanks as well to the anonymous press readers, who provided important, searching critiques. Randy Schmidt, Darcy Cullen, and the rest of the editing and production people at UBC Press were efficient, supportive, and creative, and overall a pleasure to work with. Thank you to Brandon Bierle and Eric Leinberger for the maps.

Dave Regeczi cheerfully endured drafts of various sorts, provided beer and other gifts, put up with numerous vaguely contemplated plans to visit him in Europe, and has been a great friend.

My deepest thanks go to Catherine Murton Stoehr, who believed in me when I could not, offered endless advice and support, and, above all, showed me that I could do it.

A Note on Terminology
and Units of Measure

Following the lead of Cole Harris' *The Resettlement of British Columbia*, I have used the term "resettlement" in place of "settlement" when referring to plans to populate British Columbia with Euro-Canadian migrants. This serves to remind the reader that the lands that now make up British Columbia were already populated when Europeans arrived, and that white settlement therefore required the removal of Native peoples. When referring to specific settlement plans or programs, when summarizing the thoughts or positions of contemporaries, or where modification would have resulted in grammatical horror, I have left the term "settlement" in place.

I have used the terms "white" and "Euro-Canadian" more or less interchangeably to refer to these settlers. As inaccurate and unlovely (respectively) as these terms are, I know of no adequate substitutes.

The terms "Dominion" and "Dominion government," used occasionally, mean the same as "Canada" and the "Canadian government." They refer to Canada's original official name, the Dominion of Canada, and were in common use in the period covered by this book.

I have preserved imperial units of measure throughout. Though metric units are standard in Canada and in scientific work today, converting historical, imperial figures introduced too many issues of accuracy and meaning. In particular, estimated figures ("four to six feet in diameter," for example) became either falsely precise (1.2 to 1.8 meters) or inaccurate (1 to 2 metres).

Creating a
Modern Countryside

Introduction

ATURE HAUNTS THE GREAT PROJECTS OF THE STATE. One hundred and sixty years ago, the British imperial state began to remake the homes of the Coast Salish, the Nlaka'pamux, and their neighbours into places safe for capitalism, modernity, and white settlers. Colonizers had to balance the systems of property, law, and social values they wanted to impose and the existing realities of the northwest coast of North America. In the process, societies were displaced, geographies remade, and ecologies re-arranged: A new state emerged. Yet the state's engagement with the environment has generally been peripheral to historians' studies. Like a bothersome child acknowledged only infrequently, the environment does not receive much attention in their accounts. I would like to invite the environment to speak at length. I wish to examine the role it played in the formation of the state, and to consider why and in which ways the state intervened to shape the environment. I will argue that soils, rivers, trees, plants, and fire played key roles in the state-formation process, while the changing form of the state authorized historically contingent forms of intervention in the environment. In other words, changes in the state and changes in the land were inextricably linked. The "bothersome child" must be taken into account when we consider the influences that shaped the resettlement of British Columbia.[1]

This discussion demands that we get outside and into the dirt. Imagine for a moment that it is May 1924, and we are standing in a muddy field that was, until a short time ago, Sumas Lake. The mud is thick with dead fish, bewildered ducks circle overhead looking for water. In the distance

we can see what is left of the lake: an expanse of shallow water equal in size
to fifteen hundred acres, steadily shrinking as powerful engines pump the
lakewater into the nearby Fraser River. A project of the British Columbia
government's Land Settlement Board (LSB) is near to successful completion: The lake has almost been reclaimed.

Around this time, the LSB issued a pamphlet designed to sell the new
farmland emerging from the waters. Figure 1 (see p. 53), a reproduction of
the pamphlet's cover, depicts what the LSB thought the land should look
like. The illustrator envisions a patchwork of fields receding into the distance, shrubbery between the fields suggestive of hedges. Tidy houses dot
the scene. The entire landscape is framed by the peaks of the Coast Mountains, which pierce the clouds that shroud the Fraser Valley. The result: a
lovely (if somewhat incongruous) amalgam of BC and England – the
rugged west and the pastoral old country – an imagined geography un-
complicated by reality.

What is also clear, however, is that this is a modern, not an ancient,
countryside. The pamphlet title acknowledges – or perhaps boasts – that
these are "reclaimed" lands, a benefit of industry. These lands were to be
the gift of the British Columbia state, which issued the pamphlet. A later
pamphle made the modern industrial origins of this landscape even
clearer, mixing images of lush, reclaimed land with photographs of the giant
pumps that reclaimed the land and of the provincial legislative buildings.

In the late 1910s and early 1920s, the BC state engaged in a brief
but intense effort to manufacture a new, modern countryside for British
Columbia. This effort, in a place of rivers and mountains not easily given
to farming, would have long-felt consequences. The reclamation of Sumas
Lake was only one element of the project. Though the project was initiated in response to the need to provide for "returned soldiers" – the veterans of the First World War – it quickly expanded. This book is a study
of this process of state engagement with the environment via the imagin-
ing and constructing of new agricultural landscapes. Various aspects of this
project will be considered here – such as the draining of Sumas Lake, the
creation of "soldier settlement" communities at Merville on Vancouver
Island and Camp Lister in the West Kootenays, the encouragement of
agricultural settlement in the Cariboo region, and the irrigation of the
southern Okanagan Valley – along with the discourses that animated and
justified them.

The anxious encouragement of agricultural resettlement (and its fal-
tering progress) is a theme as old as European colonization on the Pacific
coast.[2] What was new in the postwar projects was the idea of modernizing

the countryside and the direct involvement of the state in planning and carrying out resettlement (and thus in large-scale environmental engineering). Both of these factors can be tied to the reworking in the interwar period years of what historians have called the Canadian liberal order. In his increasingly influential call for a re-imagining of Canadian history around this concept, Ian McKay argues that the development of Canada can profitably be thought of as a "project of rule," implanting the "politico-economic logic" of liberalism both "across a large territory" and in the hearts and minds of people.[3] Throughout the nineteenth century in Canada, liberal reformers challenged political and economic orders that emphasized such elements as an established social order, the inherent right of particular men to rule, and endowed rights to land.[4] These reformers called on the state to guarantee an individualistic social order and a laissez-faire economic order, a "formal, rule-bound arena in which competition could occur without unfair advantage or interference."[5] These social and economic changes drove, and were supported by, changes in the land itself; in McKay's words, "social ideology" was "set down on the land and hence made part of everyday ... experience."[6] The cover of the LSB pamphlet, for example, shows a liberal landscape, appropriate to an individualistic social order.[7] Such a liberal landscape of individual properties, bounded by imaginary lines made real by law and patrolled by individual property owners, became a powerful tool of the colonial state as it removed First Nations people from their land.[8]

This sort of classical liberal order, focused squarely on providing equal opportunities for individuals (or concerned with "negative rights," or "freedom from," according to some scholars) was challenged in the later nineteenth and early twentieth centuries. "New liberals," whose ideas became influential in British Columbia in the 1910s, took as their central tenet that the rights of the liberal individual "could no longer be the foundation of politics and social life." Instead, society needed to be "safeguarded through a greatly expanded and much more activist state responsible for the general welfare of its citizens."[9]

It will be argued here that this shift in the liberal project of rule led the BC state into its interwar engagement with the province's environment. The post–Great War resettlement project was an exercise in both social and environmental reform. Soldiers and other settlers would benefit from living in a modern countryside: a rural (and so more healthy and moral) alternative to urban life. But as most arable, accessible land in the province was already being farmed by 1919, further land resettlement meant that the BC government needed to engage in environmental engineering projects on a scale not yet attempted in the service of agriculture in the province. This was something that a newly expanded, more activist state was willing and felt able to do.

Yet though state experts were often able to transform the land, they could never do so wholly according to plan. Transformations were rarely smooth or predictable. Financial and environmental problems, such as the devastation wrought by a forest fire that swept through the soldier settlement of Merville in 1922, plagued the projects. The inability of state experts to apprehend ecological and social complexity was the primary factor in the failures of the program. These failures contributed, as well, to a later, important shift in the project of rule, away from the idea that agricultural settlement was central to the social and economic development of the province.

Accounting for this shift is one of the major purposes of this book. In doing so, the book also considers the importance of the environment to the development of the liberal order in Canada. It is clear that the environment – and not simply space or territory – was a factor in the liberal project of rule. I also seek here to extend the work of Richard White. In *The Organic Machine*, White argues that it is work that connects humans to nature most fully, and that prior to the post–Second World War era of high modernism, many people believed this to be true. They talked of the damming of Washington State's Columbia River (for irrigation and electricity) in order to make it part of a unified whole comprising nature and machine. As part of such an "organic machine," nature would actually be *improved* as it reached a higher state of development. These ideas played a role in British Columbia in the 1910s and 1920s, growing out of the new liberal state's conception of its duty to manage nature for the development of agriculture. In this book, I explore and critique the resulting relationship between the state and nature.[10]

The book also engages in a more general discussion of the relationship between state and environment. A significant body of research in environmental history deals with government and the state. This work falls into a few general categories. First, a number of historians have examined how interest groups (such as tourism promoters, sportsmen, or a select few interested in wilderness preservation) encouraged the state to implement conservation policies and to designate parks in the early to mid-twentieth century. Second, a related literature has considered the development of the twentieth-century alliance between science and the state, and how this alliance has both fostered preservation and facilitated the development and more efficient extraction of resources.[11] Another literature sees the state's relationship with the environment as embedded in the development of modernity. Tina Loo, among others, has argued that the interest of Canadian governments in conservation (in the interwar period) and in large-scale environmental engineering (in the postwar period) should be understood as deriving from modernity's simultaneous embrace of urban bourgeois malaise and scientific and technological triumphalism.[12] Others have shown how the reform movements of the interwar period, which worked so hard to bring the state on board, demonstrated environmental interests as well in their reform of such practices as forestry and agriculture.[13] Finally, Canada's economic reliance on the export of lightly processed commodities (such as fur and timber) has encouraged the creation of an interventionist state by requiring non-market institutions to set the conditions for stable accumulation.[14]

In most of this work, however, the state is less the central object of analysis than it is a body forced into action by various interests, individuals, and/or outside forces. There has been little attempt by historians to theorize, and work through the implications of, the state's interest in the environment. One major exception is the work of Donald Worster. In *Rivers of Empire*, Worster argues that, in the development of the American West, capital has been allied with a "modern capitalist state." The state's purpose is the promotion and protection of conditions necessary for unlimited accumulation of private wealth. (This summary reduces Worster's argument to its essence, however, blanching out his interweaving of such factors as idealizations of the family farm, conservation, and federal and regional politics while he reflects on effects of the west's aridity and the technological and ecological requirements of irrigation.) The result of this approach, suggests Worster, has been the development of a particularly massive and oppressive state apparatus (its central element the federal Bureau of Reclamation), entirely allied with capital. Drawing on Max Horkheimer, Worster argues further that understanding this development requires understanding the ideological matrix of the state. An ideology of instrumental reason shaped the actions of the federal state, which saw no value in a nature that was not doing work directly useful to humans. Thus, for Worster, the modern capitalist state is driven to dominate nature in order to ensure a steady conversion of resources to capital.[15]

Worster is surely correct in his argument that the modern state has set itself the task of facilitating capitalist accumulation. But his argument edges towards the conclusion that capitalist interests and the interests of the state are identical – a conclusion that is by no means obvious. As political scientists and theorists have argued, the state, due to the tasks assigned it and to its control of its own power bases, retains at least a certain degree of autonomy even in advanced capitalist societies. For instance, assuring the long-term health of the capitalist economy might lead the state to oppose short-term interests of capital by imposing such measures as the conservation of natural resources.[16] Others have argued that the state has its own needs and interests. In his consideration of the failure of high modernist state-sponsored social reform projects, James C. Scott suggests that a key factor is the state's ability (or inability) to know and understand the complexities of its social and environmental domain. Unable to manage (or even gather) the volume of data necessary for full knowledge, the state instead has sought historically to make its subjects and terrain "legible" through a process of simplification, abstraction, and standardization. Thus did early modern states encourage the creation of standardized surnames. Given developments in science and technology, the modern state was able to deploy more powerful tools. For example, when Soviet state planners organized a total social and environmental transformation in their creation of collective farms, they blanched out details of local knowledge and relationships, as well as historical and ecological idiosyncrasies. Yet such "on-the-ground" knowledge and face-to-face relationships were key to getting the work done. As showpieces of central planning, the Soviet collective-farm program was contemptuous of local knowledge. This contempt hobbled their critical knowledge of soils, weather, and local work cultures.[17]

Scott's critique of the logic of state planning is powerful and persuasive. Yet state attempts to organize society and environment may derive less from a general "logic" than from historically specific formations. For all the inherent needs and emphases of states, capitalist society and the capitalist state remain historical phenomena, the result of ideologies fought for and debated over time. In late-nineteenth-century Canada, the politico-economic logic of liberalism described a kind of society, a type of economic order, and a particular sort of state with a particular type of instrumentalist relationship to the natural world (as I have suggested above and will discuss more fully below). By the interwar years, this liberal order had shifted into a new liberalism. Thus, understanding the BC state's engagement with the environment in the interwar years means understanding the way in which the actions of the state (as a partially autonomous actor) were shaped by the politico-economic logic of new liberalism. This raises the final major point (and contribution of) this book: to show that understanding environmental change requires moving beyond the consideration of ideas explicitly about nature to more general logics – such as liberalism – that implicitly encourage a particular form of engagement with nature.[18]

The remainder of this introduction examines the development of liberalism in Canada and the United States and the progress of colonialism and land resettlement in British Columbia, in order to lay the groundwork for the chapters that follow.

When one approaches British Columbia from the air, the province appears first as a sea of mountains. On the flight from Calgary to Vancouver, snow-capped, craggy peaks dominate the view, and it is often possible to reach your destination with no more sign of human occupation than the occasional clearcut forest. The landscape can appear ominous, forbidding, and inaccessible – a "vertical landscape" hostile to human habitation and movement.[19] These mountains permeate popular understanding of the province of British Columbia. When I was a child, the country was enthralled by *The National Dream*, the Canadian Broadcasting Corporation and Pierre Berton's dramatic history of the Canadian Pacific Railway (CPR). One of the main characters in the history is CPR General Manager William Cornelius Van Horne. Van Horne is an ambitious autocrat, responsible for pushing an army of employees to work at a record pace of construction; he is also known for ploughing over anything and anyone in his path. In one episode, however, as the railway reaches Calgary, even Van Horne is forced to pause. His dinner companion comments on his brooding manner. Van Horne admits that his attention is on the financial troubles of the railway. But even more distracting is the forbidding landscape "out there." "Those mountains," he explains, "they're in my way."[20]

The description "sea of mountains" has a basic truth to it. Aside from the prairie lands of the Peace River region in the northeastern corner of the province, BC occupies the western mountain cordillera of North America. There are mountains elsewhere in North America, but in the western cordillera they are higher and younger, particularly the Rocky Mountains, which define the eastern border of the province. Moving west from the Rockies to the coast, a series of mountain ranges runs roughly northwest/southeast. These mountains and the coastline sandwich an extensive interior plateau, geologically the oldest part of the province. These geological features are the basis for a series of ecologically and culturally distinct regions (see Map 1). The mild and wet climate (and corresponding lush vegetation) of the coast is what Canadians tend to associate with the entire province. But inland, the climate is drier and more severe, though

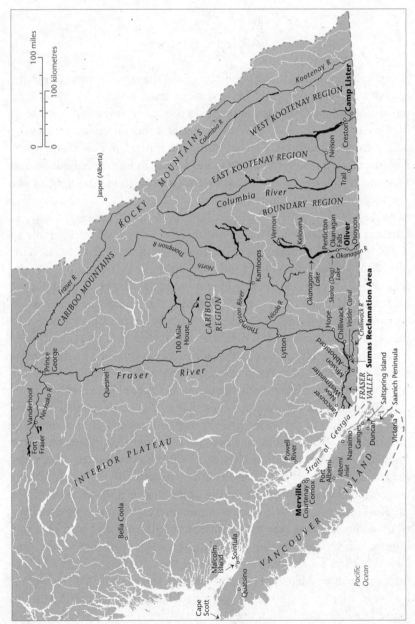

MAP I Southern British Columbia, c. 1925. Shown here are the locations mentioned in the text (major sites in bold). The straight line where the Chilliwack River connects with the Fraser River is the Vedder Canal (Chapter 4).

conditions vary from region to region. The southern Okanagan Valley, between the Monashee and Coast Mountains, is a near desert; the northern interior plateau is much colder.[21]

Overcoming the obstacles to movement inherent in the geography of British Columbia and linking together the various regions – in particular connecting what British Columbians refer to as the "coast" (Vancouver Island and the lower Fraser River floodplain) to the "interior" (everything else) – was central to the colonial resettlement project. But the British were not the first to move across this landscape. The lives of First Nations' peoples were tied in complex ways to the exploitation of resources and often depended on movement between winter villages and various summer gathering sites. Where colonial society differed was in its aim to make the resources of British Columbia available to a world market. Both the popular and the academic histories of BC are replete with stories of the struggle to link the interior regions to the coastal ports (and thus the larger world). There are stories of the heroic construction of railways through the Rocky and Selkirk Mountains, of the paddleboats that connected interior towns like Nelson to the Columbia River and the Pacific, and of the task of carving out through the wilderness a network of trade and travel routes such as the Cariboo Wagon Road.[22] The earliest system of resource extraction – the fur trade – made only a minimal impact on the existing environment and on First Nations societies, and required no formal state to run it. In contrast, European settlement, which would transform the region, was from the start associated with an explicit project of state rule. In 1849, the Hudson's Bay Company (HBC) was given control over Vancouver Island in exchange for encouraging European settlement. Two years later, HBC Chief Factor James Douglas was made Governor of Vancouver Island. In 1858, Douglas faced a wave of (in his opinion) unruly American gold seekers along the Fraser River, and summarily extended his authority to cover the mainland as well. The Crown soon confirmed his action, creating the colony of British Columbia, with Douglas as Governor. From his base in the Vancouver Island capital of Victoria, Douglas moved quickly to secure this nascent project of British rule. He linked regions by commissioning the building of wagon roads, created a political system and a legal system, and moved to secure rights over the land where settlers would live and resources could be exploited. This last objective, of course, involved taking the land from the First Nations societies already living on it, a process accomplished primarily through the arbitrary creation of reserve lands.[23]

On Vancouver Island, Douglas and the HBC's effective control of the state apparatus did not go uncontested. As Tina Loo has shown, liberal-minded settlers protested that the HBC was a business enterprise with its own interests and its own closed-off social structure; giving it the reins of power shut out anyone who was not associated with the company and created unfair competition. Believers in a laissez-faire economic system, these settlers demanded that the company's monopoly over the fur trade be brought to an end, and that individuals be allowed to participate fully in the colony's economy. They looked to the law to establish a properly liberal economy and society, based on standardization of individual rights, a more general security of contract, and uniform enforcement of laws and standards.[24]

Such uniformity was more theoretical than real, however. For one, liberals understood "the individual" through discourses of class, gender, and ethnicity. Only a property-owning British male was a full liberal individual, fully free to exercise such social rights as voting. Further, the attempt to impose a system of liberal governance in colonial British Columbia exposed the way that space, place, and the social patterns of capitalist resource extraction complicated the picture. The European population was small (Native peoples made up the majority of the population until 1891) and spread out in the colony's various regions. Nevertheless, once HBC influence waned in the 1860s, liberals such as Victoria newspaperman and politician Amor de Cosmos sought to impose a grid of liberal power on this variegated landscape, treating all liberal individuals and all places, theoretically at least, as interchangeable parts of an atomistic political and social order. In practice, place could not so easily be abstracted in this way. Judge Matthew Baillie Begbie found this out in the Cariboo: communities of miners were unwilling to accept his decisions, based on formal law, over the rulings of their own local magistrates and juries.[25] Legislators and the elite of the coastal cities were unwilling, however, to give free reign to the customs of the itinerant single men who made up the workforce for the province's resource industries. The work of Christopher Clarkson and of Adele Perry highlight the elite concern that social stability would suffer from these men's lack of a fixed address, their drinking, their frequently all-male households, and their marriage to Native women. The response of the elite was a series of laws and programs – such as family-friendly inheritance and land laws, reform missions to the interior, and the mass importation of white women from Britain as wives for the single white men.[26] The family would be used to stabilize liberal society.

These concerns go far towards explaining the BC state's pre-1940 obsession with encouraging agricultural settlements. But concerns unique to British Columbia do not explain the obsession totally. For one, the BC state was hardly alone in encouraging agricultural settlement in this period.[27] Further, colonization and back-to-the-land schemes elsewhere in this period similarly used agricultural settlement for the purposes of social reform. In the mid-nineteenth century, Quebec's elites responded to industrial capitalism by encouraging settlement to the north and southeast of the old seigneurial lands of the St. Lawrence Valley. Around the same time, the government of Ontario and its colonial predecessor tried to extend settlement beyond the good lands of southwestern Ontario by building colonization roads north into the marginal lands of the Muskokas and northern Ontario.[28] In both cases, colonization was motivated, at least in part, by a firm belief that a rural life, in which the family worked together at home, bolstered family and traditional values and so provided the base of a stable society.[29] In English Canada, colonization was fuelled by Anglo-American rural ideals that associated agricultural development with "material and moral" progress, social control, republican virtue, and a "middle- and upper-middle-class English view of nature rooted in the Romantic poets, John Ruskin, the picturesque landscape, and a broad reaction against urban, industrial life."[30] In a newly resettled place, particularly in BC, the agricultural landscape had a powerful symbolic meaning, inscribing Englishness into the very hills, emphasizing European possession of the land, and enabling settlers to imagine themselves as recreating a version of England in a new place.[31] Thus, agriculture was a key tool of settler colonialism, a way of replacing Native peoples with stable Euro-Canadian rural communities and the re-made landscapes appropriate to such communities.[32]

Farming also redeveloped complex ecosystems, creating simpler systems comprising plants introduced by the settlers, and the pests and weeds that inevitably accompanied them. The relationship between human activity and animal activity changed, as coyotes, wolves, bears, and cougars became nuisances to be hunted down and destroyed in great numbers. Further, farming tied the valleys and river flats of the province to a global capitalist economy. In these remote places, agriculture determined the manner in which, and the purposes for which, ecosystems were controlled. On farms oriented towards export production, species were cultivated first and foremost according to the demands of the market.[33] But we should not exaggerate the completeness of these ties between the land and the global market. The creation of a liberal capitalist agriculture was a complex and contradictory process. Well into the twentieth century, agriculture across the country continued to incorporate significant subsistence agriculture and household production within a larger structure of capitalist resource exploitation.[34] In BC in particular, isolation, marginal soil, and short growing seasons made profitable, full-time agriculture impossible in many places. In other areas, as Ruth Sandwell has demonstrated for Saltspring Island (in Georgia Straight near Vancouver Island), people simply did not care to work full-time producing farm products for the market.[35] Instead, men worked for wages (in the forest, commonly), while women and children kept gardens or chickens and gathered other foods, such as shellfish.

The family often remained at the centre of agricultural production in this period, throughout Canada. Even commercial farms relied on the (unpaid) labour of the whole family. Harriet Friedmann has argued that prairie wheat farms were technologically sophisticated, commercial wheat producers that relied on the nuclear family for labour in the fields.[36] As Sandwell has pointed out, family labour and household production, separated from the cash nexus, thus remained significant a-liberal elements within the liberal order. Paradoxically, however, they were also key supports of that order, "integrated into modern, liberal, and capitalist formations," providing the workforce for the capitalist market in wheat and supporting a labouring class for the forest industry.[37] The liberal order, as McKay has argued, did not sweep everything before it; instead it included ongoing efforts to incorporate the a-liberal into the liberal project.[38]

New Liberalism

By the twentieth century, such efforts had produced a changed liberalism. Liberalism as a discourse – or, in McKay's words, as "something more akin to a secular religion or a totalizing philosophy than to ... [a] set of political ideas" – had little capacity for recognizing and dealing with the effects of space and ecology.[39] As McKay insists, liberalism "begins when one accords a prior ontological and epistemological status to 'the individual' – the human being who is the 'proprietor' of him- or herself, and whose freedom should be limited only by voluntary obligations to others or to God, and by the rules necessary to obtain the equal freedom of other individuals." The individual, for contemporary neo-liberals like former British prime minister Margaret Thatcher, exists prior to (and more concretely than) such abstractions as "society," "the state," or "nature."[40] Thus, classical liberalism effectively abstracts nature out of the picture (such abstraction was actually a key goal of early liberals, as Karl Polanyi made clear sixty years ago[41]). Liberalism encourages the development of an instrumentalist

view of nature, in which the natural world is judged solely on its usefulness to human ends.[42]

By the end of the nineteenth century, such classical liberalism was
under attack from various directions. Classical liberalism, so appropriate
to a nineteenth-century economic world of relatively open markets and
individual entrepreneurs, had less purchase under Edwardian conditions
of large industrial conglomerates and restricted imperial markets. The Victorian social order was also under attack, from working people demanding a place in society and from reformers concerned about the problems
of the poor and the conditions of industrial cities. Various theorists – such
as John Hobson and Leonard Hobhouse in Britain, and Robert McIver,
John Dewey, and Herbert Croly in the US – worked to reshape liberalism
to take these factors into account. Their work drew on an older, more
philosophical revisioning of society dating back to the 1870s – what James
Kloppenberg has referred to as the philosophy of the *via media*, the attempt
by such thinkers as Thomas Hill Green, William James, John Dewey, and
Henry Sidgwick to bridge the gap between idealism and empiricism and
create an epistemology rooted in experience and pragmatism.[43] These
philosophers argued that self and society were not in opposition to each
other, that individuals and their environments constituted a whole. This
understanding led to their conviction that ethical truth could be determined only through experience, and the individual could find his or her
own truth only through engaging with society. Self-realization, Sidgwick
argued, "requires the progressive growth of character through ethical action
motivated by a desire to advance the common good *and* carefully calculated to advance social goals effectively."[44]

The later thinkers took these ideas and developed them into a critique
of liberalism, "based on a conception of the individual as a social being."[45]
This philosophy – referred to as New Liberalism in Britain, incorporated
within the more general rubric of Progressivism in the US – placed new
emphasis on the individual's relationship to society, but also on the individual's relationship to the state and the environment. The state, new liberals believed, needed to re-conceive its role, and move beyond the mere
delineation and defence of the individual's rights to focus on the protection of entire societies and communities. Individual rights should be
expanded to include the right to "equal participation in and fulfillment
from the spectrum of social, political, and economic life." The success of
a society would be measured by a "broad assessment of social well-being,
opportunity, and satisfaction for all men and women," not merely by

adding up total income in the manner of a Victorian liberal or a contemporary neo-conservative.[46]

New liberal ideas interacted in complex ways with the various reform movements that attempted to remake society in the late nineteenth and early twentieth centuries. In Britain, new liberals merged with social democrats in a progressive alliance at the turn of the century, and new liberal ideas were influential in the British labour tradition.[47] In the US, such ideas were part of the larger discourse of progressive reform, fuelling the arguments of the reformers concerned with "social consciousness," "social duty," and the "common good," but having less direct influence on the better-known muckrakers, trust-busters, evangelical social reformers, prohibitionists, and promoters of technocratic government.[48] In Canada, Barry Ferguson argues, historians have largely ignored the influence of the new liberals and their critique of society. Instead, they have focused on evangelical reformers and social-democratic intellectuals, or have argued that reform was a largely technical process of implementing Keynesian demand-management techniques.[49]

Ferguson suggests, however, that new liberal ideas were well developed in Canada, particularly in the work of the four figures at the centre of his book: Adam Shortt, O.D. Skelton, W.C. Clark, and W.A. Mackintosh. In the late nineteenth and early twentieth centuries, these men drew extensively on Anglo-American new liberal thought in developing their analyses of Canadian political economy. From faculty positions at Queen's University in Kingston, Ontario, all four moved into the Canadian civil service. A new liberal belief that society must be understood in its material and social environment led Shortt and Skelton to argue that the geography and resources of North America gave Canada interests separate from those of Britain. They opposed close imperial ties on this account.[50] This understanding of the ties between the social and material environments shaped the new liberals' belief in the natural environmental bases of economic activity. This belief in turn led them to emphasize the centrality of agriculture to economic growth and national well-being. Adam Shortt argued that a renewed agriculture was the key to ensuring the postwar stability of the Canadian economy and a smooth transition from war-time conditions. Later, W.A. Mackintosh emphasized the importance of "staples," such as wheat, in shaping the development of Canada, as well as the influence of natural transportation routes. Ultimately, Ferguson concludes, Shortt believed that "only by coming to grips with the environmental forces that shaped their material life could women and men begin to choose policies and aims which were in their interest." Similarly, Mackintosh argued that the future development of the Canadian economy needed to be based on a proper recognition of the possibilities and limits of the environment.[51]

Michel Girard, who examines the same era in his study of the Canadian Commission of Conservation, also presents an account of state experts concerned with the relationship between economic activity and environmental realities. In 1909, the federal government set up the Canadian Commission of Conservation in order to examine the impact of economic activity on earth, waters, soil, forests, animals, and human health. Up to its dissolution in 1921, Girard argues, the commission attempted nothing less than a comprehensive understanding of all these factors and their relationships with each other, with the intent to create policies that would enable a sustainable system of development based on principles of conservation. The mechanisms of change would be the education of the public and the government, and the creation of industrial activities and production techniques that would do minimal damage to the environment.[52] Commission Chair Clifford Sifton, for example, encouraged research into appropriate crop strains for the colonization of the arid Palliser's Triangle region of the Canadian prairies, and insisted on the importance of preserving the forests in the Rocky Mountains around the headwaters of the great prairie rivers. For progressives like Sifton, Girard points out, the world could be conceived as "une série de systèmes (économique, social, politique, démographique et écologique)."[53]

For Shortt, Mackintosh, and the Commission of Conservation, nature was certainly important to human history. But we need to pay close attention to how they understood the relationship between the two. For Mackintosh, for instance, the constraints of the environment needed to be understood so that they could be properly overcome, and technology and the leadership of the state needed to be marshalled in this effort.[54] Further, what progressive experts said about understanding environmental conditions did not necessarily translate into the sort of complex local knowledge that is clearly necessary – from our vantage point today – for environmentally sustainable development. Environmental historian Neil Forkey demonstrates this point in a study of development and conservation in the Trent River watershed in Ontario. By the early twentieth century, logging had left behind a treeless landscape, largely stripped of soil as a result of destructive forest fires that had ripped through forest litter left behind by the loggers. Forester Bernhard E. Fernow of the Commission of Conservation, however, proved to be less interested in learning about local conditions than in simply imposing German forest management techniques in the interests of shaping the countryside "along ordered and definable

lines."[55] New liberals' belief in the ability of scientific experts to understand and manage nature and society gave them the confidence that they
could create a better model of the sort of systems they believed composed
the world. Yet though new liberals, and progressives more generally, wanted
to understand the environment, their approach suggests that they still
wanted to order and control it, and that their knowledge might not have
extended much beyond general theories.

The BC government's attempt to manage the province's rural environment began with the challenge posed by the return of the veterans of the
First World War. In Chapter 1, I begin the story with these men. In doing
so, I follow on from the work of historical geographer Paul Koroscil, who
recounts the story of "Soldiers, Settlement and Development in British
Columbia" in *BC Studies*.[56] Koroscil argues that the soldier settlements
were victims of a series of flawed decisions. Sites were selected without
proper scientific assessment, while the decision to leave all power over the
settlements in the hands of the government meant that the real needs of
settlers were too often ignored.[57] I largely agree with Koroscil's conclusions, but I find that he leaves a number of key questions unanswered.
Why did the state get involved in setting up community land settlements
in the first place? Why did politicians and bureaucrats make the decisions
they did about how to carry out these projects? Given that creating farmland requires significant ecological change and implies an idea of how or
what nature should be – it should be farmland rather than, say, forest –
what role did the environment play in the story of land resettlement in
interwar BC?

The answers to these questions, I contend, lie in the new liberal nature
of the interwar state and the relationships of this state with the natural
environment of British Columbia. This book explores the new liberal
state's attempt to use state expertise on the natural world to re-work the
natural environment into new forms, as the basis for an alternative, rural
– yet modern – society. It takes seriously McKay's call to understand the
formation of a liberal order in Canada and interrogates the role of the
environment in this new order. By following a set of linked projects from
planning to implementation to aftermath, the book also explores the shortcomings and limitations of new liberal environmental reform. In BC, at
least, the literature on liberalism and the attempt to build a modern province
has yet to be linked with the emergent framework of ecological analysis.
Cole Harris and David Demeritt go some way towards doing this in their
essay on agriculture and rural life in BC, but as the essay considers the entire
history of agriculture in the province, it can only sketch in the outlines.[58]

In the years following the Great War, the British Columbia government was anxious to develop the social, economic, and natural environment for the betterment of the province. The resulting (and inevitably complex) relationships between social and natural environments have been little explored, certainly not for an environment as difficult to shape into a modern countryside as British Columbia.

The book is divided into three sections. Part I explores the way in which soldier settlement sparked the creation of a state-directed land settlement program during and immediately after the Great War. This section argues that these events must be understood within the context of evolving rural ideals, the development of scientific agriculture in BC, and new liberal ideas about the role of the state. In Chapter 1, I consider the relationship between the state and the development of agriculture in BC. Chapter 2 examines more closely the ideology of resettlement, and illustrates how postwar resettlement was conceived as the creation of a "modern countryside."

Part 2 considers the interaction between culture and politics and the environment. Three chapters examine the four most ambitious efforts to build an alternative, rural modernity; in doing so, they consider the various methods in use on the Pacific coast at this time to turn wilderness into farmland. At Merville (Chapter 3), the government's Land Settlement Board tried to build a community of independent farmers and, in the process, to rehabilitate soldiers to become productive citizens. Chapter 4 reveals the limits of the liberal view of nature through an examination of the draining of Sumas Lake. The new liberal ideal of nature-human interaction was explored most fully through attempts to build irrigated farms, at the Camp Lister soldier settlement in the West Kootenay region, but especially through the South Okanagan Irrigation Project. Chapter 5 examines and evaluates these projects.

In the end, the difficulties of reforming nature in BC in the 1920s killed the effort to establish agriculture and to build a modern countryside (Chapter 6). Later, The Great Depression would generate many calls for the poor and unemployed to go back to the land. But the BC state found itself unable to ignore the failures of rural settlement in the 1920s, even as shifts in liberal thought and political practice led the government to doubt that the rural sector was critical to progress in BC.

Part 1

A Modern Countryside

I

Liberalism and the Land

I N DECEMBER 1918, THE *S.S. EMPRESS OF ASIA* was in Liverpool, undergoing a refit. Built in 1913, the ship had briefly been one of the Canadian Pacific Railway's "lady ships," grand luxury liners that connected
the CPR's rail head in Vancouver with Asia. With the onset of the war, the
Asia had been seized by the government and made over into an armed
merchant cruiser; now it was to be transformed once more, into a troop
transport. In January, it steamed out of Liverpool harbour with a comple-
ment of Canadian servicemen aboard: 130 officers, 1,255 men, 6 nurses,
and a few senior officers. Its destination, via the Panama Canal, was Vancouver; before reaching Vancouver, it would dock in the provincial capital and the province's second largest city, Victoria.

In the many idle hours on the long crossing, conversation among the
men turned to the future. A number of them decided that they wanted to
stick together after getting home, and the best way to do this seemed to
be by creating a community land settlement. Onboard, as it turned out,
were some people who would become major players in the attempt by the
BC government's Land Settlement Board to settle soldiers on the land. Lt.
Col. W.S. Latta, formerly of the 29th Battalion, would eventually become
the board's director. Col. Fred Lister, commanding officer of the 102nd
Northern BC Regiment, would take charge of the soldier settlement of
Camp Lister, near Creston in the West Kootenays. A.F. Walker would
recruit men for Camp Lister's sibling settlement of Merville, near Courtenay on Vancouver Island, and would be placed in charge of development
work in the early days of the community.

The *Asia*'s progress home was tracked by an eager press in the BC capital, and the ship arrived in Victoria's Inner Harbour to a hero's welcome of banners, streamers, and brass bands on the dockside. As they approached the city, the men wired Premier John Oliver and requested that he meet the ship and hear out their ideas for getting onto the land. Oliver, ever the friend of the returned soldier, agreed, and onlookers were treated to the dramatic sight of the premier himself, in the midst of the festivities, going aboard and meeting with the men on the deck of the liner.

Soon after, Oliver's government paid for A.F. Walker and another *Asia* man, W.H. Kirchner, to attend a Dominion-Provincial conference in Ottawa on the subject of soldier settlement. When it became clear that no support would come from Ottawa for community land settlement, the provincial Land Settlement Board began acquiring and developing lands on its own, including the land that would become Merville.[1]

And so the dreams of the troops aboard the *Empress of Asia* became reality. Their story would become widely known, and the men became symbols of soldier settlement in BC.[2] Several elements of the tale contributed to its popularity. One was the ongoing involvement of Latta, Lister, Walker, and Kirchner. Another was the dramatic meeting with Premier Oliver.[3] The last was surely the image the returning soldiers impressed into the popular imagination: a company of battle-weary but hopeful men gathered on the decks of the magnificent liner, their eyes turned towards home and the future.

The determination of British Columbia's politicians and the public to help the *Asia* men and those like them was the push behind soldier settlement. Soldier settlement itself helped to establish a wider movement towards the creation of a modern countryside. Yet the idea of a modern countryside was not rooted in the return of the soldiers. The discourse pre-dated the war (as we will see in the next chapter). State involvement in the resettling of BC with Euro-Canadians also pre-dated the war. This chapter examines the history of the BC state and its involvement with resettling the land. I argue that the postwar project of building a modern countryside became possible when the return of the soldiers (and the problem of providing for them) coincided with the election of a government that embraced new ideas of liberalism, calling for state involvement and large-scale planning in dealing with the problems of modern polities. The BC state sought actively to refashion key elements of the socio-political structure of the province. Creating a new, modern countryside – an alternative rural modernity – was a central part of this remaking. The government drew on and extended its record of active encouragement of land resettlement in BC, reflecting its new, more radical approach.

The chapter starts with a short history of Euro-Canadian resettlement in BC before the war. It then considers how problems of agriculture and land resettlement led to plans for scientific reform of these activities in the province. These plans emerged just before the war, and were articulated fully in the Royal Commission on Agriculture of 1914. A third section examines how the Liberal government of John Oliver, as part of a larger reworking of the BC state under the tenets of new liberalism, attempted to put these plans into effect and deal with the problem of returning soldiers.

AGRICULTURE AND COLONIALISM

European settlers, not surprisingly, brought their own agricultural practices with them to British Columbia. Farming fields sprang up around the scattered Hudson's Bay Company (HBC) fur trading posts. Fort Langley (1827) and Fort Victoria (1843) soon became bases for food supplies, while the dry grasslands around Kamloops were used to graze cattle. In the 1850s and 1860s, farm lands spread out in the areas surrounding both Victoria and the newer settlement of New Westminster, the capital of what was then a separate mainland colony. Following on settlement and industrial development, farming also took place in the Okanagan Valley. Cattle ranching was begun by the priests of Okanagan Mission, and was encouraged by a growing population, attracted by gold-mining activities in the area. When the mines proved unsuccessful, ranchers found new markets within the mining communities of the neighbouring Kootenay valley, and later in the coastal cities. In 1892, the Okanagan's twenty thousand cattle far outnumbered the valley's four hundred white settlers.[4]

This picture is useful in highlighting the centrality of agriculture to European resettlement communities, and illustrates the importance of agriculture to urban and industrial growth. The seeming naturalness of this process, however, hides the extent to which the new agro-ecosystems ensured a relationship between the settlers and their environment that was very different from that between the Native peoples of the area and their environment.[5] Generalizations about varied Native groups in British Columbia are misleading and in many ways false. Aboriginal peoples in what is now BC comprised ten cultural-linguistic groups that spoke a number of diverse languages and had distinct cultures within customary social systems. Further, the Native peoples living to the east of the Coast Mountains were quite different from the group of nations along the coast. The coastal nations drew on a richer natural-resource base and had developed more complex and stratified cultures.[6] Nevertheless, we can note generally that most Native subsistence systems were seasonal. Winters were spent in permanent winter villages, and the primary subsistence activities were hunting and trapping. In the warmer months, tribes relocated to customary sites for fishing and gathering plants such as roots, berries, and seaweed.[7] Some cultivation also took place. The Haida people grew tobacco on the Queen Charlotte Islands, and the peoples of the dry interior uplands encouraged the growth of particular roots and berries through regular burning of the grasslands. The Lekwammen (Songhees) tribe, of the area that is now Greater Victoria, maintained fields of *wapato* (Indian potato) and camas bulbs. The text of the Douglas treaties, by which these people transferred their lands to the British, noted that the Songhees agreed to give up their "village sites and Enclosed fields."[8]

Such cultivation practices were qualitatively different, however, from the European system of enclosed fields of monocultures (or the practice of planting only one type of plant in a given area). Over time, European agriculture and ranching altered the ecosystems of significant areas of the province in such a way that they could no longer be used for Native subsistence activities. In addition to such ecological changes, the European settlers introduced the more formal, legal process of dispossession: Native people were assigned to small reserves, and their former lands were given to newcomers. Inadvertent changes added to the impact of deliberate changes, as weeds and plant diseases spread beyond the fields. The Okanagan and Similkameen Valleys became orcharding areas, and the semi-arid interior plateau was given over to ranching. Market gardening grew up around cities, in particular in the Fraser Valley west of Vancouver and, on a smaller scale, on the Saanich peninsula north of Victoria.[9]

Though the practice of colonial dispossession spread unevenly across the province, by the end of the nineteenth century, most Native peoples were effectively marginalized in the new society that had taken over the lands that had been their home. And yet, as John Lutz and others have shown, Native people had been a part of the building of this new, Euro-Canadian society. Starting in the late eighteenth century, fur trading (with the HBC) quickly became a major part of Native economies. After 1850, Native people made up the majority of the workforce for European enterprises, and were doing most of the actual farming in the province. In the 1870s, they could be found farming in the southern interior, and in the 1880s, they were doing much of the labour-intensive work in the hop fields of the southern coast.[10] Native labour benefited the Native people and their Euro-Canadian employers. The harvesting industries of the early settlement period – farming, fishing, canning, and logging – did not require much labour in the winter. This suited the Native people, who were accustomed to leaving their villages in the summer in their seasonal quest for food and supplies. Throughout the nineteenth century, the money made by Native people was most often used within the context of their own cultural systems. In particular, these new sources of wealth encouraged the custom of the potlatch, which centred on the redistribution of wealth through lavish gift giving. The potlatch was the major institution by which chiefs cemented their power. The new wealth obtained from wage work for European settlers allowed more people than ever before to hold potlatches and so secure their position within the hierarchical societies of coastal BC.[11]

Nevertheless, this satisfactory arrangement did not last. After the arrival of the Canadian Pacific Railway (CPR) in the mid-1880s, the growth of new industrial enterprises – such as sawmills, railways, and steamboats – required a more regular workforce. The CPR also ensured the rapid growth of the non-Native population. Sometime between the 1881 and 1891 censuses, Native people became a minority in the province, their population declining as the white population grew. The need for Native labour declined correspondingly. The federal government banned the potlatch, ostensibly because it was deemed detrimental to the cultivation of the "proper" traits of thriftiness and accumulation. The circumstances that had made Native peoples a valuable component of the provincial workforce had changed, and the economic significance of Native peoples declined – though they remained important to seasonal, labour-intensive economies such as fishing, canning, and agriculture.[12]

The marginalization of Native people within the new society was not an accident, of course, and neither was the role of agriculture in this process. From its beginnings, agriculture in BC was used explicitly for purposes of social engineering. The British colonial office, following political economist Edward Gibbon Wakefield's ideas on settlement, believed that the purpose of agriculture should be to foster appropriate Victorian values in the new colony. To this end, the Puget's Sound Agricultural Company, a subsidiary of the HBC, attempted to carry out a Wakefieldian system of land settlement, setting the minimum land holding on its Vancouver Island farms at twenty acres, and arbitrarily setting the price of land at the steep rate of £1 per acre. Every land purchaser was required to arrange for the immigration from Europe of five single men or three married couples. Under the supervision of a gentleman bailiff employed by the Puget's Sound company, each of these labourers would be paid £17 per year, plus room and board, and would be given twenty acres of land at the end of five years' service.

The intention of this project was to create a new landed class, along with a group of smallholders. But the labourers had a distressing tendency to bolt, heading to California to try gold panning, or to Oregon, where free grants of 640 acres were available. Meanwhile, the bailiffs were keeping up their "supervisory" role and living the life of English country gentlemen. Captain Edward Edwards Langford built a country manor at Colwood farm (across the harbour from Victoria), entertained lavishly, and charged it all to the Puget's Sound Agricultural Company. In 1853, his socials, picnics, and riding parties cost "eight times his actual salary: '£137 for Flour; £80.9.3 for Salt Pork; 1606 lbs of Sugar; 257 lbs of Tea; 70 Gallons of Brandy, Rum & Whiskey, and Wine; and £474.12.1 Cash.'"[13]

Fantasies of recreating an English country class structure soon came to an end. The new colonial elite, however, remained concerned with fostering proper social values through agriculture. Traditionalists in particular worried about the effects of individualism and industrial activity on the stability of Euro–British Columbian society. Liberals such as Victoria newspaperman and politician Amor de Cosmos had to deal with conservative "nation builders" worried that unchecked individualism, much of it associated with male resource workers, threatened the social order.[14] Everyone agreed that a stable, land-based society was a good thing; the compromise was limited state intervention. Property and inheritance laws were designed to provide stability for the family by limiting a husband's freedom to sell family property and to acquire debt on it. A husband could not sell his land if his wife was living in the colony, and on his death, the property passed automatically to his spouse. If individual, labouring men were destined to exist in a world of unstable wage work, then women and the family would be the stable and independent basis of the social order. By encouraging the creation of small-scale family farms and protecting the inheritance rights of wives, the state would bolster the family and ameliorate the effects of proletarianization.[15]

The reformed property and inheritance laws were added to a land policy that, as a whole, was dedicated to the creation of stable family farms. Land laws were designed to do three things: encourage resettlement, limit speculation in land, and bring in revenue for the government. They were based on the concept of "beneficial use": land had to be used in such a way that it would contribute to the creation of rural society and rural economy. Those purchasing land had to "improve" it, through land clearing and the creation of fences and farm structures, before they could purchase more land. Leaseholders had to show that they were fulfilling the terms of their lease – that, for example, they were actually grazing livestock on land acquired for this purpose. Land acquired by pre-emption was subject to similar restrictions.[16] Pre-emptors were required to maintain residency on the land for a certain period of time and to improve the land to a state-set value per acre. Once these conditions were met, the province would issue a certificate that allowed the pre-emptor to purchase the land.[17]

With these laws, the transformation of arable sections of British Columbia from Native lands to European-style agricultural lands proceeded. This conversion increased in pace with the building of transportation facilities in the 1880s (the CPR being the most significant but by no means the only example of this phenomenon). Farming became more commercial and began to expand rapidly. Farmers formed agricultural associations, such as the British Columbia Fruit Growers' Association (1889), in order to help improve marketing and farming methods.

Agriculture and Ideology

Liberal, relatively hands-off policies were the basis of the BC state's resettlement strategy up to the years immediately preceding the Great War. By 1914, when the Royal Commission on Agriculture signalled the start of a new approach, general consensus was that its results were mixed. Liberal land laws were designed to cultivate an agrarian ideal of individually owned farms providing secure employment to a (male) farmer and his family. In agrarian ideology, such farmers were the foundation of a country's wealth, while their independence guaranteed the country's freedom and democracy.[18] But results on the ground were always more complex and more contradictory than liberal agrarians hoped. Speculators held land off the market, hoping for an increase in value. The introduction of irrigated agriculture also brought land companies into the mix. Some settlers refused to accept the state's ideal of neat farms growing specialized crops for market, while others rejected the liberal idea of land resettlement entirely and opted instead for collective schemes. The Royal Commission's new liberal prescriptions – for state-directed action in support of the individual farmer, and for measures to help the farmer better participate in the capitalist market – were representative of the more general way in which new liberalism tried to correct the imbalances of laissez-faire liberal land policies.

The model liberal agrarian region was the lower Fraser Valley. Here, settlers from southern Ontario and the United States, well versed in the agrarian ideas of those regions, created a new, grid-like landscape of fields and fences. This landscape was not created easily, however.[19] The rivers, floodplains, and grasslands of the lower Fraser Valley, from Georgia Strait to the Fraser Canyon, had long been a rich source of food for Native peoples from across the larger region. In the summer, Clallam speakers came from Puget Sound to the tip of Point Roberts and, along with Straits-language speakers from the Saanich peninsula and the Gulf and San Juan Islands, used reef nets to catch salmon. The Squamish came from Howe Sound to gather shellfish, fish, and birds in English Bay. The Musqueam, a Halkomelem-speaking people who wintered on the north shore of the Fraser River across from Lulu Island, had fishing and gathering sites in the Gulf Islands. The Nanaimo people, also Halkomelem speakers, gathered at their plank-house fishing camp – where the Pitt River met the Fraser – to fish for oolichan and sturgeon. In early August, most of these people moved upriver to the foot of the Fraser Canyon to gather salmon. At the end of the season, they gathered *wapato* from the marshes along the edge of the Fraser before gathering for a celebration at the mouth of the Pitt River.[20]

Transforming this Native landscape into a Euro-Canadian rural landscape required work. Though Native peoples had relied on marshes and floodplains for *wapato* and a variety of other edible plants, and as places to gather fish and hunt birds, these swampy areas did not suit European agricultural plants.[21] Laborious ditching and diking were necessary, along with clearing and ploughing the land. One settler, Harry Burr of Ladner, employed Chinese labourers for 189 days in order to set up his farm.[22] Despite the hard work and commitment needed, by the early twentieth century, the Fraser Valley had come a long way towards achieving agrarian success. From the late 1890s, valley farmers increasingly turned to dairying; in the early twentieth century, dairy farming became the dominant form of farming in the area. Fraser Valley dairying was capital-intensive and market-oriented, and as a result, dairying came to be seen as "men's work," and was no longer part of the farm wife's duties. Dairy farms were still family-owned and -operated, but they depended on new technologies (such as air-tight silos for storing feed), new strains of dairy cattle, and government expertise and inspection. The major market was Vancouver, which, after 1910, was linked with Chilliwack by the BC Electric Company's interurban railway.[23]

Even in the Fraser Valley, making the agrarian model work was frequently a struggle. Producing a commodity for market meant dealing with competition, both local and non-local. Marketing cooperatives, most notably the Fraser Valley Milk Producers' Association (1913), tried to stabilize prices by controlling production, processing, and delivery. Like all cooperatives, however, the association was threatened by independent farmers who could undercut prices. Throughout the interwar period, the association struggled to bring stability to the industry. Elsewhere, liberal agrarian land laws were even less effective at creating a landscape of capitalist commodity production. According to historian R.W. Sandwell, Saltspring Island settlers manipulated the pre-emption system to serve their own interests, clearing enough land to support only a home and some subsistence agriculture. In fact, the majority of settlers never tried to become commercial farmers. Instead, they survived on the food they could grow, on hunting and gathering, and on small sales of agricultural produce. They also took on wage work in the fishing and logging industries, and temporary work with the provincial government.[24] These patterns must have been common on the thousands of semi-subsistent family farms scattered across the often agriculturally marginal areas of the province.[25] The land laws did lead to the establishment of successful farms and, in places like Saltspring Island, they could be manipulated to produce homes and a basic subsistance. But the many empty lands – either abandoned by settlers or kept off the market by landowners more interested in speculation than farming – were a testament to the limits of the legislation.

Agricultural resettlement in the dry lands of the interior plateau was informed by a different discourse. In the interior, resettlement farms focused on fruit production and were dependent on irrigation. Attempts to develop a fruit industry were made in several areas, including the West Kootenays and the lands around Kamloops. But it was only in the Okanagan that fruit production flourished. Here, too, the ultimate goal of most settlers was independence on a small family farm. But environmental conditions and contemporary discourse undermined some of the independence and egalitarianism of settlements fostered by agrarian ideals. Firstly, the need for irrigation meant that arid regions could not be developed by individual settlers. Instead, land companies took charge. In the Okanagan, companies dammed rivers to create water storage basins in the hills overlooking Okanagan Lake, and then also tapped the rivers closer to the lakeside hilltops and benchlands where the farms were located.[26] They transported water in new, man-made systems, through flumes (large pipes) or, more frequently, through earth and concrete ditches, providing the farms with a steady supply of water. The companies then subdivided the land and sold the lots to aspiring farmers. Settlers were thus at the mercy of the irrigation works and those who operated them; the system also linked the fate of the farms with that of their neighbours.

Secondly, the land companies' advertising and subsequent settlement were informed by the discourse of arcadianism, which stressed the beauties of nature, the authenticity of country life, and the personal growth and enrichment attainable through daily contact with the natural world – for those refined enough to appreciate it. Land companies promoted fruit growing as a gentlemanly profession – an art – associated with "refinement, culture and distinction."[27] *British Columbia Magazine* and the *Fruit Magazine* both featured images of plump, healthy, glowing fruit, hanging off the branch in great bunches.[28] The promise of an arcadian existence in a warm climate appealed particularly to members of the urban British middle classes, for whom this sort of country life would otherwise be out of reach. Nearly twenty-five thousand middle- and upper-class Britons emigrated to BC between 1891 and 1921. In places such as Kelowna and Summerland, fruit farmers set up clubs and played cricket and football, organized polo matches, established private schools and Anglican churches, conducted fox hunts, and attended the productions of the Kelowna Musical and Dramatic Society.[29]

This arcadian vision was popular until just after the First World War. But it had begun to lose its glossy sheen even before the war: there were difficulties constructing the society and the natural environment needed to support settlers' English country lifestyle. Fruit growing was labour-intensive and not possible to do alone, particularly if one aimed to live a gentlemanly life. Hired labour, however, was expensive and difficult to come by. Desperate for workers during the war, fruit farmers endorsed the idea of women working in the fields, even though this undermined their arcadian ideal. But they remained vehemently opposed to hiring Asian labour. Even success created problems. By 1911, the expansion of the fruit-growing business in the Okanagan flooded the market and drove down prices. This problem was exacerbated by a parallel increase in fruit production in Washington State.[30] Farmers attempted to establish cooperatives in order to control prices. Until the 1930s, however, similar to the events of the Fraser Valley, organizations such as the Okanagan Fruit Union (1908) foundered due to their inability to take in all the farmers in the area.[31]

Environmental problems added to the economic problems. In the Kootenays, which were touted as a fruit utopia into the 1920s, most of the orcharding failed. The harvest was only slightly later in the year than in the Okanagan, but late enough that frost destroyed many crops. As well, the absence of a large, central valley meant that farms were scattered, which inhibited the creation of marketing cooperatives. Near Kamloops, temperature extremes ended the experiment in commercial fruit farming.

Frosts killed off all but the hardiest strains of fruit. Farms were promoted and sold on the basis of the area's average temperature, but temperature extremes were the critical factor. Low temperatures destroyed crops and prevented young trees from maturing.[32]

In the Okanagan, the presence of Okanagan Lake moderated extremes of temperature. But even here, the industry faced problems. By the eve of the Great War, the wooden irrigation works built by the land companies had begun to fail. Farmers had trouble even maintaining these systems; they could ill afford to replace them. The pre-war economic weaknesses of the industry and the costs associated with the irrigation works led to the collapse of the land companies after the First World War. The land companies were replaced by a system of irrigation districts: provincially organized, grower-controlled, local bodies that maintained and operated the irrigation systems. The districts, as well as new and more effective marketing and packing cooperatives, stabilized the Okanagan fruit industry in the 1920s.[33]

Liberal land resettlement was also challenged by some British Columbians who rejected liberalism in favour of small, community-based settlements. Such "intentional communities," like those with agrarian and arcadian ideals, held the beliefs that a person should be able to make a living from farming alone and that living close to nature would lead to a better society and a better world. They rejected, however, the possessive individualism and competition of liberal society in favour of collective approaches to work and property and an emphasis on the community rather than the individual. These communities also tended to be united by a common ethnicity.

Aside from these broad similarities, the various settlements were shaped by diverse motives and beliefs. Consider the most famous of these groups, the Doukhobors. This Russian Protestant sect believed that salvation was achieved through participation in the "community of the saved." Rejecting all authority but that of God, the Doukhobors lived apart from their neighbours in the West Kootenay and Boundary regions, working communally and inhabiting large, multi-family homes. Their success as farmers, however, raised the resentment of their neighbours.[34]

While the Doukhobors were motivated primarily by a particular religious vision, the Norwegian colony at Bella Coola had more varied and less spiritual motivations. The colony aimed to provide familiar surroundings and a second chance for Norwegian farmers whose operations had failed in Minnesota. The Norwegian communities also strived to achieve something different from – and higher than – liberal society. Their constitution placed the abstention from alcohol above all other rules. The colonists chose property by lot and pooled resources to buy staples. But their efforts were hampered by poor forest soils, and the settlers turned quickly to logging and fishing.[35] They were more successful, however, than the group of Danes that settled near Cape Scott on the northern tip of Vancouver Island. Inspired by the vision of Danish-American fisherman Rasmus Hansen, who had visited the area and fallen in love with an enclosed lagoon "filled with halibut, ducks and geese," the Danes struggled from 1897 to 1909 before finally abandoning the settlement.[36]

The Finnish settlement of Sointula ("the place of harmony"), on Malcolm Island off the northeast coast of Vancouver Island, was conceptually more coherent, and its members more ambitious than settlers at Bella Coola and Cape Scott. Sointula was founded by mine workers anxious to escape the Dunsmuir mines at Nanaimo and Wellington. They called in utopian socialist Matti Kurikka to lead their proposed settlement. Under Kurikka, Sointula became a heady brew of spiritualism, socialism, and Finnish nationalism. Kurikka drew on theosophy, a form of spiritualism that stressed unity among people and between people and nature, and the ideas of Saint-Simon, Robert Owen, and Tolstoy. He named the chartered colonization company that was to run Sointula the Kalevan Kansa Colonization Company, in honour of the Finnish hero Kaleva.

Sointula began as a highly optimistic colony of coal miners as well as "shoemakers, doctors, poets, theosophists, anarchists, and philosophers."[37] Meals were taken communally, and everyone received the same wage (though those with difficult jobs worked fewer hours). In 1903, the 238 residents engaged in plays, dancing, orchestral concerts, and intellectual discussion groups. But the settlement was built on an unstable economic base. Colonists struggled to do the farming, fishing, and logging necessary to support the colony, and the colony's finances suffered. Kurikka's ideas also began to strain the unity of colony members. His advocacy of free love and his desire to raise all children in a community nursery rather than with their families were controversial. The community began to split into two camps – one that supported Kurikka and one that followed A.B. Makela, a much more orthodox socialist whom Kurikka had invited from Finland to help him run the colony.

The colony's demise was assured when Kurikka secured a contract to build bridges in North Vancouver, a contract for which he made a bid that was far too low. The colony lost even more money, and Kurikka and half the colonists left, soon to attempt to found an all-male utopian settlement in the Fraser Valley. Makela tried to carry on, but a case of embezzlement threatened the colony's finances further, and creditors confiscated the colony's lumber to pay off bad debts. On 27 May 1905, the Kalevan Kansa Colonization Company went bankrupt and was dissolved. But as at Bella Coola, the town itself survived. Former colonists purchased land from the receivers and continued to live on Malcolm Island. Makela, after a brief and disappointing return to Finland, took back his job as lighthouse keeper on Malcolm Island, where he lived until his death in 1932. He held to his socialist principles as late as 1928, and was carried to his grave behind a hammer and sickle flag.[38]

All three colonies rejected liberal society in favour of, variously, communalism, cooperation, religion, or socialism. They looked for alternative ways of living, often expressed spatially by the location of their settlements off the beaten track. The Doukhobors succeeded, but most other colonies failed. They were hampered by poor land and the unwillingness of settlers to subscribe to a shared community vision, and their geographical isolation hindered participation in the larger capitalist economy. Like more mainstream settlements, these colonies found it difficult to make a living out of farming alone.

In the years following the Great War, the soldier settlements would share the dedication to community and cooperation that served as the foundation for the settlements at Bella Coola, Cape Scott, and Sointula. The soldier settlements particularly, and the postwar settlements more generally, were part of a larger movement to solve social problems by going "back to the land." At the same time, as we will see more fully in succeeding chapters, the postwar settlements embodied a different strategy from that of the earlier settlements – one designed to make the countryside part of the liberal capitalist world.

The post–Great War soldier settlements grew out of the perceived limitations of liberal land resettlement; they served as counterpoints to the more radical settlements at Sointula and elsewhere. More directly, they were designed to overcome the failures of the most recent soldier settlement project, the attempted settlement of Boer War veterans on farmland in the early years of the century. In 1908, the Canadian government's Volunteer Bounty Act offered 320 acres of Dominion lands to Boer War veterans. This initiative proved to be a disaster – 95 percent of the 1.25 million acres handed out in Saskatchewan, for example, was acquired by speculators.[39] The earlier experience of the BC government should have given Canada some warning. In BC, the province's 1901 South African War Land Grant Act allowed veterans, their family, or others designated by them to pre-empt 160 acres of Crown land. Only about half of this land actually went to veterans. In all, 117,000 acres were granted to 854 people.

Of those, 407 were ex-soldiers, who acquired 63,000 acres. The remaining 54,000 acres went to people who bought the land scrips that had been issued to soldiers.[40] Countering speculators and ensuring that the land remained in the hands of the veterans would prove to be difficult challenges for the soldier settlement planners.

Land speculation was a problem for land settlement planners generally, not just those who planned soldier settlements. The tendency of speculators to hang on to land in the hopes of selling at a higher price at a future date was generally believed to be a major hindrance to the development of agriculture in the province, as well as a major factor in the prevailing pattern of scattered, isolated farms. Speculation and scattered settlement were two of the more visible failures of the laissez-faire land resettlement policies; the BC Royal Commission on Agriculture was determined to fix them. In its 1914 report, the commission advocated that the old policies of liberal land resettlement be replaced with a new, progressive approach. It recommended an intensive, scientific, and highly organized effort to settle British Columbia's unoccupied areas. In agricultural districts, the commission noted, much good land remained unsettled. This land should be planted with crops appropriate to conditions, and then farmed intensively. For this scheme to work, the province needed a much larger rural population and a denser settlement plan, that is, smaller lots. To accomplish this, the old policy – that anyone might pre-empt blocks of up to 320 acres of staked-out land – had to be changed. This policy had led to "sparse, widely scattered settlements, with a consequent expense for roads, bridges, schools, etc. ... the settler and his family lack educational and social opportunities, co-operation is difficult or impossible, and consequently marketing is impossible."[41]

The commissioners argued that the major impediments to the development of agriculture were the competition of cities for land, which drove up prices; the lack of cooperation among farmers; and – a key point – the lack of capital for land clearing and improvement. These problems were to be dealt with by the state. A major recommendation of the commission was the establishment of the Agricultural Credit Commission to issue low-cost development loans to farmers. It also suggested that a central body should organize agricultural associations and that schools should improve the teaching of rural subject matter. "With a large population in close settlements," the commission noted, "the development of rural life, with all its advantages, would thus be made possible."[42]

The commission's emphasis on problem solving through scientific research, government commissions, and education (both through schools and through agricultural associations) was typical of progressive-era reform efforts. Its recommendations set the tone of future developments, though its lack of concern about the poor condition of the province's irrigated farms would prove to be an oversight. The Agricultural Credit Commission was established in 1915, and went on to become the Land Settlement Board (LSB), which organized soldier settlements and associated projects. The LSB's major initial concerns were to encourage the establishment of a larger rural population on small farms, to facilitate the creation of marketing and other co-ops, and to counter speculators by ensuring that the land be developed or conveyed to someone who would develop it. Like the Royal Commission, the LSB saw the possibilities that science and effective organization held for development of rural life, particularly in the untested lands of BC. Neither the board nor the commission doubted the old rural ideals. They presumed agriculture's role as the foundation of the provincial economy and its moral and aesthetic superiority over city life, as well as the beauty and the recreational possibilities in the rugged wilderness of British Columbia. What the commission slighted, however, were the environmental problems associated with creating a countryside through land clearing, reclamation, and irrigation. These activities would become major preoccupations of the LSB, and (as the previous experience of the irrigation companies might have hinted at) would prove to result in immensely complex, immensely contradictory, and immensely expensive processes.

THE WAR AND THE NEW LIBERALS

The commission's call for the state to assume a greater leadership role in BC's agricultural development was not wholly drowned out by the sounds of the war that began the same year the commission delivered its report. Along with the 1915 establishment of the Agricultural Credit Commission, the province created a separate Ministry of Agriculture (a key recommendation of the commission) the next year. As well, amendments and updates were made to legislation concerning the formation of agricultural associations and the creation of diking and irrigation works.

In fact, it quickly became clear that the war would boost rural settlement. The Returned Soldiers' Aid Commission, created in 1915 in order to oversee the province's efforts to deal with returned soldiers, assumed that land settlement would be a major part of its program. In the following year, the Conservative government passed legislative acts that allowed soldiers to pre-empt land and then acquire title to it for free. Major legislation on the issue, however, would not be created until the election of the Liberals under Harlan Brewster in 1916.

Brewster, a former bookkeeper who had become rich in the salmon-canning business, entered politics in 1907. By 1913, he had climbed his way up to the position of party leader, a challenging post after the disastrous election of 1912, when the Liberals lost all their seats in the legislature to Richard McBride's Conservatives. Brewster aimed to rebuild the party by promising to bring the age of reform to British Columbia. The Conservatives had been in power since 1903 and were starting to wear out their welcome. William Bowser, who replaced McBride as Premier in 1915, paled in comparison to his popular predecessor. Brewster took aim at what he called Tory fraud and corruption. His platform was based on the need for new land and agricultural policies and for social reforms. He called for land for settlers and help for farmers (fruit farmers in particular), and for prohibition and female suffrage.[43]

In the election of 1916, the Liberals crushed the government, winning thirty-seven seats to the Tories' nine. Brewster soon showed himself to be a good judge of political character, appointing to his cabinet four future premiers, including John Oliver as Minister of Agriculture and Railways and Thomas Dufferin "Duff" Pattullo as Minister of Lands. He also delivered on his promise as a social reformer, bringing in prohibition and granting female suffrage.

Brewster saw only about a year and a half as premier, dying in office in March of 1918 from pneumonia contracted while he was returning from a meeting with the prime minister in Ottawa. In that short time, he set the government on a new liberal path that would be followed cautiously by his successor, the more old-fashioned John Oliver. Two of Brewster's first acts as premier were to announce an end to the Victorian patronage system and to bring in new liberal intellectual Adam Shortt to remake the civil service.[44] The government then embarked on an ambitious program of reforms designed to insert the state into the regulation and control of society and economy.

The reforms covered a variety of areas. The desire to manage and stimulate the economy led to the creation of a Department of Industry and to the development of a series of measures aimed at workers. These measures included establishing a Workmen's Compensation Board and a Department of Labour, and introducing legislation to regulate hours of work (the institution of the eight-hour day); guaranteeing regular payment of wages in certain industries (the Semi-Monthly Payment of Wages Act); and setting a minimum wage. Other legislation was more social than economic in character. Pensions for mothers without husbands were instituted at the end of this period of Liberal power in 1927, as were old age pensions.[45]

These new, liberal-style reforms also extended to measures to manage the environment. In 1917, following a suggestion made by new Minister of Lands Duff Pattullo, the Liberals created the LSB under the Department of Agriculture.[46] The LSB replaced the previous government's Agricultural Credit Commission, which issued development loans to farmers, and was charged with taking active measures to settle and develop agricultural areas of the province. In recognition of the importance of land settlement to the problem of returned soldiers, the LSB's enabling legislation dictated that the board would offer a $500 rebate on land purchased by a British Columbia returned soldier or his widow. The board was an autonomous body that reported to the minister of agriculture, then John Oliver. Oliver's publicly stated aims for the board were primarily economic. Too much money was being spent on importing food from outside the province, he pointed out: $25 million in 1914 alone. Increased agricultural production in BC would mean that the resources of the province could go instead towards developing British Columbia. Oliver also put great stress on the idea that the board, and by extension the farmers whom the board would help, must be financially self-sufficient. "The aim of the government," stated Oliver, "is not only to increase agricultural production, but to increase it economically. The question must always be borne in mind is the cost justified by the result possible to achieve [?]"[47]

At the same time, Oliver was a known believer in rural virtues and their potential value to pampered city folk. He once laid out his gendered picture of rural virtue by commenting that "too many people right here in Vancouver are wearing broadcloth who should be in overalls. Too many women in fine dresses should be in plain gingham."[48] Oliver had been born in Derbyshire, England, and had farmed in Delta (in the Fraser Valley); he liked to declare that he was just a simple dirt farmer. Once, in a debate over the government's use of Orders-in-Council, the Leader of the Opposition sneered that Oliver knew "all about feeding pigs" but nothing about the law. Rather than shying away from the suggestion that he was a rural simpleton, Oliver deftly spun the insult on its head. Orders-in-Council, he explained, were for adding detail to legislation: On a threshing machine, "if I were to screw the boxings too tight and snug, I would have a hot box and the machine would not go at all. Or if I did not allow sufficient end-play, the machine would bind. It is the same with the machinery of legislation; if you fill a Statute with too much detail, you come to the place where it is absolutely unworkable."[49]

The board itself consisted of staff from the former Agricultural Credit Commission, five directors responsible for settlement activities in different parts of the province, and a chairman. The Liberals chose Maxwell Smith as chair. Another great believer in rural virtue, Smith was much more susceptible to flights of rhetorical fancy than the often-blunt Oliver.[50] Smith was the picture of the gentlemanly westerner, according to one enthusiastic journalist. Wearing a slouch hat, "his hair ... a trifle long behind," with "a flowing and graceful contour of a mustache," Smith had "the prominent nose and chin, the optimistic eye, the breezy manner, and the lengthy slimness ... typical of the son of the Golden West" – qualities that we see now, lamented the reporter, "too infrequently."[51]

Smith also had other solid qualifications for the job. He grew up on a farm in Ontario and had worked as Dominion government fruit inspector for seven years. His other activities were not so agricultural. He had worked at "commercial pursuits" in the American West and in publishing in Toronto, and had lived in Vancouver. As the former editor of the *Fruit Magazine*, Smith had promoted aggressively the virtues of rural life. "The editor ... believes," he stated in a 1911 editorial, "that agriculture is the basic science upon which rests the superstructure of all our national wealth; that the abnormal growth of cities ... is rapidly producing a condition which threatens to undermine and endanger our national stability." Farm life, he said, "must be made more attractive and the pernicious fallacy, that it is less respectable and profitable than that of the city, relegated to the oblivion from which it never should have been conjured."[52]

For Smith, the LSB was the means to bringing into being a new countryside. Though it would continue to loan money, the LSB's most important function would be establishing an organized system of land settlement and development, the "sane and commonsense administration of a practical land development policy." Following his minister but also in line with his insistence that agriculture must be shown to be profitable, Smith stressed that the LSB would be run "on sound business principles." Development work would be designed to be "sufficiently revenue-producing to re-imburse the Government for the expenditure, while at the same time facilitating settlement under reasonably advantageous conditions."[53] It would remain to be seen whether or not this optimistic formula could be made to work.

Along the lines of other progressive-era reform institutions, the LSB began the process of creating its land settlement plan by gathering data. Smith's directors fanned out across the province, submitting reports from the more northerly regions of the province, near Prince George; Vancouver Island and the coast; the Fraser Valley; the East and West Kootenays;

and the Okanagan Valley, Kamloops, and surrounding areas. They reported on soil conditions, existing growth, and climate; current agricultural production and markets; topography and potential and existing transportation routes; and the layout of the farms. The director for Vancouver Island and the coast investigated the Bella Coola and Sointula areas for further settlement possibilities, but rejected both locations. Director D.D. Munro recommended that the board concentrate its efforts in the north on the Bulkley and Nechako Valleys – what promoters would call "New BC" – and it was here that the first two Land Settlement Areas would be established. The directors in charge of the Fraser Valley and the Okanagan enthused about the possibilities of the Sumas region and the southern Okanagan Valley, both of which would become sites of major development projects.[54] The directors were also sometimes explicit that their goal was to encourage Euro-Canadian settlement. In his report from the region near Lytton, Lillooet, and Ashcroft (to the west of the Fraser Canyon), Munro reported that the Chinese were buying up the best lands and employing indentured servants from China and Native women as field workers. This, felt Munro, was dragging down the moral character of the area, undercutting one of the prime attractions of rural development. If nothing were done about it, he warned, "many of our most fertile districts [would] be ... entirely out of the control of the white man."[55]

By 1919, these investigations were over, the LSB having established itself and its development programs. To support the chair and five directors, the board had a staff of eighteen, including six people working in five branch offices outside Victoria. The board's development work was divided into four major schemes. The Land Settlement Areas scheme affected the largest area of land. This program was aimed primarily at lands owned and being kept off the market by speculators. When the LSB decided to designate a particular portion of land as a Land Settlement Area, the owner was faced with three options: he could develop the lands to the standards set by the board; he could pay a tax that increased the longer he held onto the land; or he could sell the land to the board at its appraised value.[56] By 1919, the board had acquired more than eighteen thousand acres in five Land Settlement Areas in New BC, and had allotted ten thousand acres to sixty-eight settlers, most of whom were returned soldiers. A second major LSB program was the continuation of the work of the Agricultural Credit Commission, making loans to established farmers in order to help them retire debts, purchase livestock and equipment, erect buildings, and improve their land. The LSB also encouraged the creation of cattle clubs, in which farmers in far-flung settlements could pool their resources to purchase and ship cattle.

Two other programs were more ambitious. As we will see in Chapter 4, the LSB had taken over the work of the Sumas Dyking commissioners and had begun the work of draining Sumas Lake, "reclaiming" the land for farming. Finally, the Land Development Area program made use of unemployed returned soldiers to clear logged-off lands and prepare them for production. The soldiers were also to be employed to build schools, roads, and homes. In return, the soldiers would receive first rights to the land they had developed. The soldier settlements at Merville and Camp Lister (Development Areas 1 and 2, respectively, were developed under this program. By November 1919, 350 returned soldiers had been employed by the board and were working in four development areas.[57]

As the war came to a close, the LSB emerged as a primary actor in the management of soldier settlement, and the major player in the attempt to refashion British Columbia into a modern countryside. Yet the most significant figure in the new liberal management of the province's environment was probably Minister of Lands Duff Pattullo, who had originally conceived of the idea of the Land Settlement Board.[58] Pattullo was born into an old Liberal family. He was a great believer in the traditional virtues of liberalism and in the idea that liberalism had to change in order to embrace modern circumstances. From 1916 to 1941, he served successively as Minister of Lands, Leader of the Opposition, and Premier. He was the most notable figure in BC politics during this period.

Pattullo came to British Columbia from his hometown of Woodstock, Ontario, where his father had been a newspaperman and a prominent local Liberal.[59] George Pattullo defended the interests of George Brown's Reform (or Liberal) Party in the pages of the Woodstock *Sentinel*, participated in organizing the party on a province-wide basis in the late 1870s, and attended countless political meetings in support of Liberal candidates. Oliver Mowat often stayed at the Pattullo home while visiting his riding in the area. On one particularly memorable visit, Mowat brought along an entourage of the most prominent Liberals of nineteenth-century Canada, including Honoré Mercier, Edward Blake, Richard Cartwright, W.S. Fielding, and David Mills. The senior Pattullo had a portrait of Wilfrid Laurier in the living room, and was associated with both Laurier and the family of William Lyon Mackenzie King.

Duff Pattullo thus grew up among theorists and exponents of liberalism, and saw firsthand the realities of campaigning and backroom politics. These influences would be clear when he entered the family business of politics. But as a young man, Pattullo's priority was to get off the family farm and seek adventure in the wider world. His restlessness led him into hard times in New York City and London in 1894. London was his low point: after crossing the Atlantic on a cattle boat, he spent ten grim days living on the docks. After his time on the Thames, New York seemed like heaven. Soon he returned to Woodstock, penniless, but with the satisfaction of having survived. Yet the restlessness had not disappeared. In 1897, Major James Walsh was dispatched by the Canadian government to establish a government in the Yukon Territory in order to control the Klondike Gold Rush. George Pattullo called in an old favour and got Duff a place in the expedition.

Pattullo would never again live in Ontario. From Dawson City, Pattullo went to Prince Rupert, BC, where his reputation grew, even as his real estate deals plunged him further into debt. His entry into politics in 1915 was as much due to his need to find a way out of debt as to his political principles. Dawson City and Prince Rupert instilled in Pattullo a love of the north and its small resource towns, a passion for British Columbia's wilderness, and faith in the province's resources. In his campaign, he employed the knowledge of politics he had gained growing up in the Pattullo family home. He was well liked, endowed with a natural kindness and an interest in people. He was also dashing and paid close attention to his always impeccable attire: he took two white flannel suits with him when he left Woodstock for the Yukon. This dapper, intelligent, and popular figure from the under-represented region of New BC (which many saw as the future of the province) was a natural choice for the role of cabinet minister.

Pattullo was determined to create an efficient Lands Department to replace what he saw as the mess left behind by the previous government. His primary goal was getting settlers on the land – a goal that differed little from that of previous ministers. But the distinction of Pattullo's approach was that he aimed to manage the entire process rather than simply bringing settler and land together. Like reformist liberals generally, Pattullo believed that government had a legitimate role in the economy in those areas where private enterprise could not do what was required.[60] In 1918, he began work on the system of irrigation districts that would rescue the Okanagan's irrigated agriculture from the failures of the land companies. Pattullo arranged to have the government buy up the deteriorating irrigation works. He then passed legislation allowing for the creation of local irrigation districts to run the works, and set up the Water Conservation Fund to lend these districts operating capital. The loans were to be repaid as the economy improved. When companies pointed out that their investors might lose money, Pattullo replied that he was more concerned with the welfare of the farmers.

For Pattullo, the irrigation districts were obvious sites for government management.[61] Without their creation, he declared, the major Okanagan cities of Kelowna and Vernon "would have suffered grave disaster .... I hope I may not appear egotistical when I say that I look with much gratification upon what I did for the Okanagan and Similkameen Valley."[62] Here Pattullo showed himself to be a new liberal. The irrigation districts and the government's reform agenda generally were part of an "attempt to meet the complicated problems that have arisen in a highly industrialized world with the machinery provided by our democratic political institutions." The turn of the century had brought "a different conception of the role of the state," making state management of economy, society, and environment necessary.[63]

Pattullo's vision, however, focused on management for the benefit of the liberal individual. For all his new ideas, like most other practicing new liberals, Pattullo never demonstrated a belief in reshaping society in the manner called for by the philosophers of new liberalism. James Kloppenberg argues that the reforms of the new liberals depended on the remaking of the individual into a social being. The individual was to be thought of as deriving his or her existence from his or her interaction with society.[64] This is a step beyond merely seeing the state as a body for ensuring individual prosperity in a complex world, and it is a step that Pattullo never took. Further, as John Oliver's insistence on the LSB's ultimate self-sustainability shows, others were farther from taking this step than was Pattullo. The Liberals' policies, then, aimed at engineering social and environmental change while leaving the liberal individual largely unchanged. It would remain to be seen how this compromise philosophy would work in practice.

SETTLING THE SOLDIERS

If the progressive orientation of the Liberal government owed its character primarily to Brewster and Pattullo, the government's concern with soldier settlement came from John Oliver. It was Oliver who had stood on the deck of the *Empress of Asia*, bargaining with hopeful young men. He knew that the desire of those men to farm was not unusual. The Land Settlement Board's 1918 survey of 728 men in military hospitals found 291 who wanted to farm, 239 of whom claimed experience farming (though only 36 of the men interviewed had $500 to invest).[65] His beliefs in the superiority of rural life and the common man contributed to his willingness to grant the soldiers' wishes, though as premier he was also motivated by other concerns. He believed that soldier settlers would serve to bolster agricultural production. The returned men could be put to work with modern land-clearing equipment, and could then farm the newly cleared land themselves. Further, finding the men work to do would help to frustrate the plans of "a certain element" determined "to organize for revolutionary purposes."[66] Soldier settlement, in other words, would shore up liberal society and help head off the possibility of radical alternatives.

With the war drawing to a close in the fall of 1918, Oliver was determined to nail down the procedure for dealing with the settlement of the returned men. In September, he wrote to the prime minister, Robert Borden, requesting that he convene a meeting with the provincial premiers. Borden agreed. In November, Oliver and Pattullo, along with former *Asia* men and LSB employees A.F. Walker and W.H. Kirchner, travelled to Ottawa. All returned satisfied, at least at first. Walker and Kirchner were left with the impression that the Dominion might help with their community settlement plans, and Oliver with the understanding that the federal government planned to assume control over soldier land settlement through its Soldier Settlement Board (SSB). As well, the Dominion agreed to take overall responsibility for the re-establishment of returned men, including the provision of vocational training. The provinces' main duties would be to make suitable lands available to the SSB, to set up a system of labour bureaus to help soldiers find work, and in general to cooperate with federal government efforts.[67] British Columbia had already taken care of the first of these commitments. In April of 1918, half a year before he traveled to Ottawa, Oliver had passed the Soldiers' Land Act, which gave the Department of Lands the power to reserve parcels of Crown land for the use of soldier settlers. Throughout the remainder of that year, the Department of Lands' new office of British Columbia Soldier Settlement set aside various undeveloped lands around the province, amounting to about sixty-five thousand acres.[68]

As time wore on, however, it became clear that the federal government intended to run matters on its own terms. The result was not always satisfactory to Oliver. The Canadian government proved to be unenthusiastic about the preparation of land for settlement. Though the Canadian Minister of Immigration and Colonization had promised to expand the Soldier Settlement Board "so as to enable it to deal with every phase of soldier settlement work," in its final form established in February 1919, the SSB was essentially just a bank.[69] It offered twenty-year loans for soldiers to buy and improve land. Loans were also available for those soldiers who secured grants of 160 acres of Dominion-owned land. In June, Oliver complained of the effects to Arthur Meighen, then minister of the Interior. "In this Province conditions are entirely different to those of the other provinces," he explained. The Soldier Settlement Board had "the effect, very largely of change of ownership of unimproved lands but is not adding very materially to the settlement of unimproved land with the Province." Success was being threatened by the SSB's lack of interest in "clearing" and "reclamation." "If the full measure of success is to be obtained in this Province from soldier settlement," Oliver argued, "it will be necessary to settle a large number of these men on lands which are not at present improved."[70]

By "the full measure of success," Oliver meant not just the creation of soldier farmers but also the social and economic benefits that Oliver saw as flowing from a revival and modernization of the province's old liberal land resettlement plans. Meighen and the federal government saw soldier settlement as a way of making returned soldiers self-sufficient and so independent of federally funded pensions. Such a welfare scheme was not enough for Oliver, who saw soldier settlement as the leading edge of a larger, state-directed expansion of British Columbia's agricultural sector and rural population. Yet Ottawa had little interest in the management of environment and society, such as the land clearing and reclamation that Oliver insisted was necessary. As for the BC government's new liberal plans for a community land settlement, the federal Conservatives were opposed, suggesting that the idea – already presented to the BC legislature several months before Oliver's letter to Meighen – contained "communistic" features.[71]

Ultimately, though, federal opposition meant little. When Oliver wrote to Meighen, the Department of Lands had already begun to move beyond merely reserving Crown lands. The department's office of BC Soldier Settlement had begun to enquire about purchasing the holdings of the Southern Okanagan Land Company, previously investigated by the Land Settlement Board, with the intention of installing irrigation works. The Soldier Settlement Office acquired these lands at the end of the year. It now had two major duties. First, it conveyed reserved lands to the Soldier Settlement Board for distribution to returned men. More significantly, like the LSB, it now prepared to engage in the active management of environment and society, developing the urban and rural life of the southern Okanagan Valley through its South Okanagan Irrigation Project (see Chapter 5). Meanwhile, the LSB had already purchased, tested, and surveyed the land for the Merville settlement. When Oliver wrote his appeal to Meighen, there was little question that the BC government intended to proceed with a state-directed program of land settlement. Unfortunately, it did not look as if the returned soldiers would bring with them much in the way of federal funds. Nevertheless, the opportunity to solve both the immediate problems of the returned men and the longer-term problems of liberal land resettlement was too good for the provincial government to pass up.

CONCLUSION

Soldier settlement was only part of a larger program of organized land settlement in BC, but it lent an air of urgency to the entire project. It was necessary for the government to deal with the *Asia* men and other returned soldiers, and to do so fairly. Like the crowd on the dock in Victoria, the whole province was watching. This urgency helped to propel (and to sanction) large and ambitious projects. One long-contemplated undertaking, the "reclamation" of the lands lying under Sumas Lake, could not be carried out until this era of new liberalism and soldier settlement had begun, as we will see in Chapter 4. Thus, the soldier settlers were at the heart of the BC government's program of postwar land settlement, even where they were not the actual settlers.

By the end of 1919, BC's political leaders were receiving some indications of the scope of the returned soldier problem. The Returned Soldiers' Aid Commission had granted relief payments amounting to, on average, $47 per person to 950 returned soldiers who had no money and whom no other organization was willing to help. On a more positive note, 1,269 men had been given their monthly gratuity payments in a lump-sum form, allowing them to start businesses or to buy furniture. In December, however, confidential reports received by Simon Fraser Tolmie (then BC's senior MP) from the Royal North West Mounted Police spoke alarmingly of unsettled conditions in Victoria. The police force's comptroller told Tolmie of a "very serious condition ... practically no employment ... four thousand five hundred un-employed in the city." The police also warned Tolmie that veterans' groups were associating with "labour." Coming only six months after the end of the Winnipeg General Strike, where veterans had solidly supported the strikers, this must have been worrying news indeed. In early December, the Mayor of Victoria wrote to the premier, warning him: "Unemployment situation very critical. Work required at once, or trouble likely to occur. High cost of living making situation worse. Wooden shipbuilding only thing that will relieve situation." Matters had not, apparently, improved by the next year, when Oliver wrote to Arthur Meighen: "Conditions of unemployment of returned men very acute here." Oliver asked him to rush his reply.[72]

The police reports sent to Tolmie betray the RCMP's by-now well-documented concern with "radical" organizations, but it is not clear how accurate a picture they paint of conditions in Victoria. What is clear is that senior politicians were concerned with the state of at least one of BC's major cities in 1919. Such reports could only have strengthened their belief in the need to establish permanent homes for ex-soldiers in the healthier, more moral environment of the country. Luckily for the politicians, by the end of 1919, such programs were in place.

In an immediate sense, these plans rested on the recommendations of the pre-war Royal Commission on Agriculture. The commission had called for a scientific, state-directed, centrally organized effort to develop agricultural lands left untouched by the previous laissez-faire land policies. That the BC government could contemplate enacting comprehensive plans to create a new countryside through development and settlement plans was a result of new liberal ideas advocating the positive action of the state in creating the social, economic, and environmental conditions for the prosperity of the liberal individual.

At the same time, the history of agriculture in BC was bound up with long-standing ideals of country life, whereas the recommendations of the Royal Commission reflected the shape of countryside ideals in the modern world. The plans of the LSB and the Department of Lands, as well, rested on plans for soldier settlement drawn up by other bodies, in particular the government's Returned Soldiers' Aid Commission. As we will see in the next chapter, the return of the soldiers provided the opportunity for the government of BC to make the wider ideals of a modern countryside – an alternative modernity – into reality.

2

Soldiers, Science, and an
Alternative Modernity

GROWING UP IN THE AGRICULTURAL COUNTRY of southwestern Ontario, Fred Clement surely had no idea that he would one day find himself contemplating the possibility of farming in British Columbia. Clement was born in 1884 to a farming family in Virgil, Ontario, near Niagara-on-the-Lake, and grew up working on his family's one hundred acres. He later remembered that his family was happy but "very poor." In 1905, deciding that the family farm could not support everyone in the family, Fred went to Model School and became a teacher.[1] Though his perspective may have been coloured by his adult career as a professional horticulturalist and dean of agriculture at the University of British Columbia (UBC), Clement would remember that his desire to farm – especially to solve the problems of farming – would never let him rest. He pondered the use of fertilizers. He delved into the reasons for differences in crop quality in various parts of a field. He studied economics and marketing in order to explain why he could never get satisfactory prices for his farm products.

Finally, in 1907, Clement entered Ontario Agricultural College in Guelph. A list of his various jobs upon graduation reads as a survey of work in scientific agriculture in central Canada: agricultural representative for Elgin County; director of the Horticultural Experiment Station at Vineland, Ontario; and lecturer at Macdonald Agricultural College, Montreal. He was profiled by journalist Peter McArthur, who wrote regular columns on farming and country life for the *Farmer's Advocate* and the *Toronto Globe*. In his short, personal memoir, Clement presents himself as something of

47

a folksy sort; in McArthur's picture, however (in relation to McArthur's self-portrait as the doltish but enthusiastic city boy let loose on the farm), Clement is the very symbol of scientific know-how. He was "Mr. F.M. Clement, B.S.A., representative of the Ontario Department of Agriculture," bearer of scientific knowledge and proper techniques. In one story, McArthur described how he lit a fire of green wood, rags, and oil in the middle of his orchard, so that the smoke would warm the trees and protect them from frost. "When Mr. Clement finally came," he griped, "I couldn't wait to get his horses unhitched until I had told him what I had done, and what do you think? He just roared and laughed! Now I don't think that's fair. Scientific farmers have no business laughing at the rest of us. It is their business to do fussy things and let us laugh at them." At the same time, McArthur lovingly related how Clement's pruning of a tree was like art, the scientific farmer working with "life" the way a painter works with paint.[2]

Shortly after his visit to McArthur's farm, Clement left for BC, taking with him his youth and experience in the Ontario farm country, his scientific training, and the sense that this training qualified one to work with nature. In BC, he would become a faculty member at the new Provincial University (now the University of British Columbia), established in the years before, during, and after the First World War. University President Frank Wesbrook wished to make the university useful to the developing province; as part of this agenda, he put an emphasis on developing a good Faculty of Agriculture.[3] Research was to be aimed at increasing production, improving conditions in rural areas, and making agriculture into "a profession comparable in all respects to other professions."[4] As his first appointment, Wesbrook hired Leonard S. Klinck as dean of agriculture. Klinck was a native Ontarian and a graduate of Ontario Agricultural College; he was teaching at Macdonald College when he was hired by UBC.[5] On the advice of Klinck, Wesbrook hired Clement as professor of horticulture and head of the department, and another Macdonald College lecturer, P.A. Boving, as professor of agronomy. Wesbrook impressed upon them "the need for placing emphasis on Science and on serving the industry and the people of the province."[6] But when Clement and Boving arrived at the campus, they found few facilities for carrying out these instructions. The campus was little more than a few shacks and some land cleared for experiments. "Moreover," Clement recalled, "looking at the mountains which seemed to dominate the landscape, we could not help wondering just what industry we were to serve. Paul [Boving] voiced our mutual doubts when he asked: 'Where is the land?'"[7]

One answer to Boving's question was that the land had to be created. This was true physically, as we will see in Part 2. But it was also true on a metaphorical level: the land would be created from the knowledge, skills, and vision of people like Clement, Boving, and Klinck, and the politicians and farmers who brought to the project their own countryside ideals and skills. This chapter examines the idea of the alternative, rural modernity that these people hoped to create. While their vision rested on an older rural idealism, these men hoped to apply science and technology to rural life in order to create something new, a modern life lived close to nature. With the return of the veterans of the Great War, they got a chance to put their ideas into effect, refining their vision into a practical plan for bringing about a modern countryside.

THE COUNTRYSIDE IDEAL

The idea for an alternative modernity rested on older versions of what we might call, following geographer Michael Bunce, the countryside ideal. This term encapsulates the conviction, common at the time, that a strong rural sector was a necessary base to any economy and, in offering a better way of life, also the basis for a good society. Life outside the city was understood to be slower, more natural, and more in line with human rhythms. The idea of the country held connotations of virtue and wholesomeness. It was beautiful and peaceful, calming and relaxing. At the same time, farming represented simple values, hard work, and hardy individuals, along with a sense of community. Finally, the farmer's work was, as Peter McArthur wrote in the years before the Great War, a "partnership with nature."[8]

This list of images and values, however, gives little sense of the historical contingency of country ideals. The countryside ideal has its roots in the Romantic reaction to the rationalized, grid-like, spatial order that parliamentary enclosure imposed on the English landscape. The Romantic poets, Wordsworth in particular, developed an innovative understanding of nature as an autonomous entity, existing according to its own rules. For Wordsworth, nature exemplified more than just an ordering: it was a "principle of creation," something infused with the very spirit of creation itself.[9] This understanding has both complicated and existed alongside the triumph of rationality and its instrumental view of nature. It has been part of the continuance of spiritual and animistic ideas in Western culture.[10]

Thus, even as Britain celebrated its orderly Victorian culture and its success as the workshop of the world, the countryside was celebrated as the very heart of England. "Oh, to be in England," wrote Robert Browning in the mid-nineteenth century, "Now that April's there."[11] Others stressed the harmony within traditional rural manners and class structures, and the harmony between English rural folk and the land. In the interwar period, journalists such as H.V. Morton, memoirists such as W.H. Hudson, and authors such as Rudyard Kipling and Ford Madox Ford painted vivid pictures of lush country and peaceful, orderly villages wherein everyone knew their place and was content. This was an arcadian vision of the beauty and harmony of an ordered landscape, of England as a green and pleasant land.

In much of North America, arcadianism was never as strong as it was in England. Though it was important in the representation of the fruit lands of California, the Pacific Northwest, and British Columbia, the tradition of agrarianism was dominant. In post-Revolutionary America, Thomas Jefferson's Republican party understood agriculture to be the central, indispensable industry, the bedrock of a democratic economy and society. It was a rational vision of a decentralized republic of independent yeoman farmers. The farmer was the best citizen because farms were self-sufficient; the farmer was beholden to no one. Agrarianism also stressed the naturalness of farm life and its resulting goodness and morality.[12] The basic elements of this vision have proven to be extraordinarily resilient. Though the Republican idea that only the farmer could be the proper democratic citizen quickly weakened, the more general sense that farmers make the most solid citizens remained strong. In the nineteenth century, evangelical Christians saw the farmer as the natural repository of simple Christian virtues. Under the Jacksonian Democrats, the family farm was seen as the proper basis of commerce. With the frontier thesis, Frederick Jackson Turner postulated that the family farm was the basis of America and American values. All these ideas were developed and supported by novels and articles on agrarian virtue and the benefits of small-town life. Such articles ran in *Lady's Book* and *Harper's*. Sarah Hale published a steady stream of writing in *Ladies' Magazine,* and wrote the novel *Northwood,* a best-seller about a young man who returns to a better life in a small town. Hale also established the holiday of Thanksgiving – possibly the most important holiday on the American calendar – thus ensuring the presence of a form of agrarian values in American homes to this day.[13]

Agrarianism never quite penetrated political discourse and national identity in Canada to the same extent that it did in the United States. The ideal of an agricultural frontier of small farmers was never so plausible given the limits to agricultural land in much of the country, the abundance of forest lands, and the legacy of hierarchical settlements such as the Wakefieldian scheme attempted on Vancouver Island.[14] In providing a framework for understanding and in underscoring the importance of the farmer to society and economy, however, agrarianism was of great importance in Canada. "A well-devised system of small holdings will do more to develop the agricultural prospects of British Columbia than any other one thing," declared a pamphlet from the province's Bureau of Provincial Information.[15] Just before the First World War, the *Fruit Magazine* preached that farmers were "the most important class of producers in the country, who cannot even make a living without adding valuable and permanent wealth to the state." What BC needed was "a numerous, stalwart and prosperous rural population, which is the one essential necessary to help the needy, heal the sick, feed the hungry, clothe the naked and open the eyes of those who are blind to the best interests of the people of this great Province."[16]

THE PANORAMA OF MOUNTAINS

British Columbians thus drew on common, venerable traditions of countryside idealism in creating the discourse of the new countryside. They made these traditions their own by combining them with appeals to the beauty of British Columbia's mountains, forests, and rivers, and the pleasantness of living in their midst. In doing so, British Columbians also modernized the countryside ideal, marrying it with the more recent wilderness ideal that appeared in the late nineteenth century.[17]

Anyone familiar with British Columbia will be unsurprised to hear that those working on the early-twentieth-century version of the countryside ideal made much of the delights of the province's mild climate and the joys of its mountains and wilderness recreations. Climate was touted as a major draw. The less moderate climate of BC's interior and the north, where much of the postwar settlement would take place, got little mention in promotional literature. "The climate and soil of British Columbia," opined the BC government's Bureau of Provincial Information in 1903, "added to its many natural attractions as a place of residence."[18] Promoters also drew on contemporary racial theories that linked the success of European "races" to climate, suggesting that not only would BC be a congenial home for European settlers, but also that its weather would breed success.[19] BC's climate had "all the features which are to be met with in European countries lying within the temperate zone, the cradle of the greatest nations of the world." As a result, it was "well adapted to the development of the human race under the most favourable conditions."[20] Opportunity cries out, the *Fruit Magazine* declared, for "newcomers of thoroughbred breed ... to come to some one of our beautiful valleys and build homes of peace and plenty under the smile of British Columbia's sunshine."[21] Potential settlers agreed. Like W.G. Capelle, who told the Land Settlement Board that all he was looking for was "an independent living in a little better climate than we have in Manitoba," a great many of the letters from farmers interested in relocating to BC in the postwar years mentioned climate as an attraction.[22]

Equally important was the appeal of the wilderness. BC's farms came to be seen as a marriage between rural life and an easily accessible outdoor playground; the farms were set in a verdant green countryside framed by towering, snow-capped mountains (see Figure 1). Provincial government information booklets portrayed rural BC as a sportsman's paradise. In the booklet *New BC,* the Bureau of Provincial Information detailed the game available to Nechako valley residents, including salmon, trout, sturgeon, whitefish, deer, rabbit, and bear ("caught by the Indians with snares set in the same manner as a rabbit snare"). There were also "beaver, otter, fisher, lynx, marten, wolverine, fox and muskrat, ducks, and geese,"[23] which served as other sources of food. The promotional *Man-to-Man Magazine* spoke of the chances for fishing, while a CPR promotional booklet agreed that, for "the man of limited means in the early days of his home making," the abundance of game was invaluable.[24]

Hunting, fishing, and farming all took place amidst the beauty of BC's mountain-crowned farmland, the "panorama of mountains ... impress[ing] its charm and grandeur upon the least observant; awe-inspiring peaks, whose snow-clad crags pierce the clouds, alternate with more friendly and softer heights, at the foot of whose sombre tree-clad slopes nestle comfortable homes and fruitful well-tended orchards, which add to the scenery an air of homeliness and progress that is a pleasant contrast to the more severe spectacle of precipice and wilderness."[25] This is farming in the clouds, in an abundant land of "mountains stored with precious and economic minerals, watered by lakes and streams of crystalline purity, and clothed with a wealth of vegetation which demonstrates the universal fertility."[26]

CITY AND COUNTRY

The idea of wilderness farms was a particular example of a wider cultural phenomenon: the widespread concern with the growth of the city and its perceived social problems, and a belief that contact with nature, in the form of either wilderness or countryside, was necessary to restore the health and morality of the people. These ideas were a response to genuinely massive social change. Between 1891 and 1911, the populations of Montreal and Toronto doubled, while the populations of Winnipeg and Vancouver quintupled. In 1911, 45 percent of Canadians lived in cities, up from 38 percent ten years earlier. The urban population had increased by

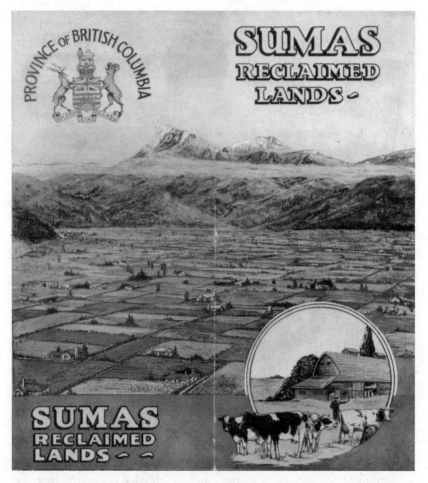

1   The cover of a pamphlet to promote land sales at Sumas. The artist captures the modern countryside ideal in its British Columbian variant. Small, tidy farms are separated by English-style hedges, the whole scene framed by soaring mountains. The modern is present in the reminder that these are reclaimed lands, and perhaps in what appears to be a pipeline or a canal cutting across the background.

62 percent, the rural population by only 17 percent.[27] Many understood these changes within a cultural framework that set the country and the city on opposing sides of an unbridgeable dualism. The city was opposite the Romantic and transcendentalist invention of nature and the country. In the most extreme forms of this rhetoric, the city was home to vice, corruption, crime, and poverty. Vancouver poet D.C. Ireland wrote:

> I am tired of the shifting City,
> And the ceaseless cry of the streets
>
> Sing me a song of the free life
> When a man is a man again
> When the joy of life calls madly
> And the pain is a lesser pain.[28]

The city had lost the solid virtue of real, meaningful work, complained Archibald Lampman:

> In chambers of gold elysian,
> The cymbals clash and clang,
> But the days are gone like a vision
> When the people wrought and sang.[29]

The Presbyterian Church's Board of Moral and Social Reform and Evangelism studied "the problem of the city" and worried about the descent of Canada's urban areas into a form of hell. Embracing the idea of the superiority of the countryside, the board encouraged an improvement of the conditions of farm life and a return to the land.[30] In *Rural Life in Canada* (1913), Rev. John MacDougall deplored the decline of rural communities and argued that the solution lay in bringing the benefits of the city to the country. He quoted approvingly from Horace Plunkett, who noted that towns in the US had better production technology, better organization of businesses, and better recreation and entertainment facilities than did rural areas. Thus MacDougall counselled the creation of farmers' cooperatives and the extension of telephone service and modern, healthy forms of recreation to the country. He also advocated that the church encourage and support schools in the teaching of new agricultural techniques to improve the farm.[31] To audiences in Halifax and at Knox College in Toronto, MacDougall explained that the church should not teach the growing of better cabbages. But it should "teach men ... that it is their duty to grow better cabbages ... it is for the church to deal with the moral prerequisites of better husbandry, and hold out the better resultant life as an incentive."[32]

In British Columbia, Rev. R.G. MacBeth would have agreed. In his 1920 pamphlet promoting land settlement in BC, he contrasted the "pure and virile blood" of the country with the "anaemia" of the city. The city brought about an "unnatural precocity" in children, and subjected adults to "constant unrest": "it is difficult to maintain home and family life in the city owing to many distractions and the disturbance caused by employ-ment of varying kinds," but the "farm home is the centre of the farm work."[33] Stronger families, then, were one of the major benefits of encour-aging rural life. At the same time, MacBeth's antimodern image of an organic unity between home and work is clear: "farm work" was under-stood to mean the work of the fields, and "the farmer" was understood to be a man. In discussions about farm-production improvement, it was the male farmer, not his wife (whose supporting labour was nevertheless assumed), who was the centre of attention. One striking example of this is the work of Peter McArthur, who rarely – if ever – mentions the family that his farming was to support.[34]

The general desire for strong, rural families sometimes, however, focused attention on the role of women. MacDougall noted with concern that women outnumbered men in rural counties all across Canada; he mar-shalled a barrage of statistics to prove his point.[35] As well, MacDougall was concerned about the imbalance in the spread of new technologies in rural areas. The acquisition of "labor-saving devices" for the home could often lag behind that of those for the field. He used the example of water sup-ply. The vast majority of farms depended on wells; women were required to carry water by hand from the well to the house. His solution was house-hold science courses. Once women were aware of what they could achieve with better equipment, said MacDougall, they would advance as quickly as the men.[36]

MacBeth, whose booklet was intended to promote BC agriculture (not point out its problems), praised the effects of modern technology: "There are medical men within reach of settlement everywhere. Good roads abound through this Province, motor cars annihilate distance and the rural telephone is reaching out into remote parts." As well, the problem of land clearing that had hampered settlement in the thick coastal forests could now be done "with far less exertion on account of the softer wood and the modern methods," the latter including steam donkeys and blast-ing powder.[37] MacBeth was impressed by the progress made by the Merville soldier settlers who, he said, had in only two months cleared large areas and even planted gardens.[38]

Peter McArthur, more a journalist than a poet, and more a preacher than a promoter, was somewhat more equivocal. He felt the city was "no longer the place for a man of wholesome ambition."[39] Yet he could see that the city was being used as a symbol for a larger system that threatened both city and country – a system that McArthur referred to as "the machine and organization." Scientific agriculture, he worried, might defeat itself by devoting too much attention to the goal of greater production. "What is the use of reducing the cow to a butter-fat machine," he asked, "the hen to an egg machine, and so on, if the men who look after them are reduced to work machines?"[40]

SCIENCE AND THE NEW COUNTRYSIDE

But though McArthur worried about the way that scientific agriculture was being done, he would surely have agreed with the Revs. MacDougall and MacBeth that modernization of the countryside (in large part through the use of scientific agriculture) was the solution to its problems. Those who thought this way were often referred to as "Country Life" reformers, after the Country Life Commission appointed by President Theodore Roosevelt in 1907. Many historians have argued that such reformers were less interested in celebrating rural life than in "making the countryside more like the city."[41] But to argue this is to accept the equation of city and modernity against which these rural reformers fought. Reform along scientific lines was not thought of as a concession, a necessary evil to prop up the rural economy. Science would improve the countryside by allowing for a better understanding of (and so a closer partnership with) nature – the very thing that made the country unique and superior to the city in the first place. To Peter McArthur, scientific farmer Fred Clement was an artist, one who "gets his effects by working in accord with Nature." He was also a symbol of a great hope for the future, "the type of clean-cut, intelligent young fellow ... that you would have found a few years ago preparing ... for law or medicine ... Are the farmers of the future to be of this type? I can hardly believe it, and yet it should be true."[42] These reformers wanted a new countryside, an alternative, rural modernity, where new knowledge and new technologies could be married to traditional gender roles and traditional values.

James W. Robertson, expert in dairying and one-time president of Macdonald Agricultural College, regularly extolled the virtues of rural life, proclaiming to an audience in St. John's, Newfoundland, that "the farmer toils all day long, from sunrise to sunset, and seeks his well earned repose with a well tired body, yet he is glad that his life is a daily co-operation with Nature herself. Life is good to him; he can do so much good; he is a power in the land for health, happiness and stability. That is *agriculture*."[43] Science promised the knowledge necessary to make this vision a reality. It would create a "new spirit of the farm." "Formerly the farmer tilled his soil and planted his seed," explained author Agnes Laut, "and if it grew, it grew; and if it didn't, it didn't." Now science could examine the seed, the way it was planted, and the characteristics of the land it was planted in. By examining the soil, agricultural scientists could tell if "nature had planned for corn" to be grown there. Claimed Laut, "Science has taught the farmer the trick of obeying nature's law instead of breaking himself trying to break the laws."[44] Robertson described the idea in grander terms, sounding at points like a contemporary environmentalist when he remarked that the Canadian landscape was "a superb heritage. We did not make it, buy it or achieve it ... We entered upon the unearned ownership of an inheritance, the greatest any people ever possessed ... One likes to look upon it in the green garments of summer and also when covered by the sparkling white of winter's cloak, to gaze on the everlasting hills, the sweet valleys, the running streams and the vast plains." He hoped to "visit the homes of the people who live here and see whether they match this land. If they do not, is not the fault that of our education? Is anything better worth our while than to help the people to match this matchless heritage?"[45] Thus, one of the great promises of modern reform was that it would bring people closer to nature, rooting them in the land and in their communities through a deeper understanding of nature, derived from science. In doing so, reform would boost production, making it not only possible but profitable to live in nature, on a farm.

Unlike some progressive reformers, Robertson and agricultural scientists in general did not believe that the experts needed to be in charge of the carrying on of scientific agriculture. They believed that, given proper instructions, farmers could carry out the necessary reforms themselves.[46] They stressed the importance of primary, secondary, and post-secondary education; research; and adult instruction. Reformers such as Maxwell Smith, editor of BC's *Fruit Magazine* before the war (and chair of the LSB after the war), consistently criticized the public school system for not teaching enough about agriculture and nature.[47] As a result, "the masses of our youth are, by their training, directed to the congested cities and only a few find their way to the country"[48] (see Figure 2). While public schools were to provide basic instruction and motivation to stay on the farm, more advanced knowledge was necessary to aid in the proper selection of crops and the evaluation of soil and site type. Here the university was central, providing basic research; a pool of experts; and, at UBC, degree courses in agronomy and agricultural science, as well as "short courses" on particular subjects aimed at working farmers.

Scientific agriculture was particularly attractive in a province where many, such as newly arrived agronomy professor Paul Boving, could see only a sea of mountains, and where much of the arable land had been farmed for only a short time, if at all. And so BC's provincial university, just starting up in the pre-war years and still housed in temporary accommodations, placed great emphasis on developing a Faculty of Agriculture,

THE MASSES OF OUR YOUTH ARE, BY THEIR TRAINING, DIRECTED TO THE CONGESTED CITIES AND ONLY
A FEW FIND THEIR WAY TO THE COUNTRY.

2   This cartoon, from the promotional *Fruit Magazine*, shows a great faith in the power of education to shape society, while it critiques the school system for not teaching scientific agriculture. The list of curricula is: "Arithmetic, Geography, Geometry, History, Algebra, Latin, Literature, Greek, Physics, French, Chemistry, Bookkeeping, Typewriting, Shorthand, and all practical subjects. Also elementary agriculture (where thought expedient) and nature study, botany, etc."

as indicated above. Even in the temporary confines of the Fairview campus, well away from the fields at the new Point Grey campus, UBC offered credit courses on the scientific basis of agriculture, with classes on the evolution of farm technology and farm organizations. "Irrigation and drainage" projects were presented as "highways of progress," while the examination of the rural-life problem featured readings from Rev. John MacDougall. Dean Klinck also gave public talks on this subject.[49]

Probably more noticeable in the day-to-day lives of farmers, however, was the instruction and inspection activities of the Department of Agriculture. The department had established a wide range of agricultural programs by the eve of the First World War. It employed a team of local representatives and inspectors to examine crops and look for infestations, diseases, and inferior crop strains. The department also organized promotional exhibitions abroad and crop competitions designed to encourage the use of good seed and proper techniques. It sponsored farmers' institutes and women's institutes and gave short courses in the farmers' institutes on proper methods of dairying and orcharding, among other topics. In 1910, the department set up a packing school, giving instruction on the packing of fruit. Keen to promote cooperation, especially in marketing, it passed enabling legislation for the creation of the British Columbia Fruit-Growers' Association, as well as stock-breeders' and "dairymen's" associations. The department also leaned on the efforts of others. Official reports note the experiments in dry farming being conducted by the Department of Lands in the Nicola Valley and the Cariboo, and the central Dominion Experimental Farm located in Agassiz in the Fraser Valley.[50]

There are indications, even in official reports, that the process of modernization did not always go smoothly. Ministry of Agriculture reports speak obliquely but tellingly of the work of inspectors being carried out "with a fearless hand," and of their use of scientific knowledge for "inducing the co-operation of the growers with what at times appeared to be drastic measures by official Inspectors."[51] Still, by 1913, the province had put in place an extensive system designed to increase production and improve rural life by giving producers access to the new knowledge of scientific agriculture.

SOLDIER SETTLEMENT AND THE NEW COUNTRYSIDE

In the years before the First World War, boosters, agricultural scientists, the Department of Agriculture, and the Provincial University developed a

vision of what agriculture in BC could and should be. Drawing on traditional agrarian virtues, the contemporary wilderness ethic, and the discourse of scientific agriculture, they envisioned a countryside inhabited by
individual, independent farmers and their families, united by cooperation
and community, and living in a spectacular setting of soaring mountains,
plentiful game, and easily available recreation. Rural communities would
have the latest in modern conveniences, and be linked to the wider world
through telephones and good roads. Farms would be run according to the
latest research in scientific agriculture, and farm homes would be equipped
with modern comforts. The family would be the centre of society, farmers and their wives performing their expected roles. This modern countryside would offer an alternative to the version of modernity found in
overcrowded, unhealthy cities. Up until 1914, the central technique for
realizing this modernity was education, in the form of public-school teaching, university degree courses, university-managed outreach courses, and
media propaganda. But the crisis of the returned soldiers after the Great
War presented an opportunity to go beyond this. As many soldiers as
desired this rural lifestyle would be sent back to the land, where they
would be remade into solid citizens, serving as the vanguard for the creation of an alternative, rural modernity.

In British Columbia, planning for the problem of returned soldiers
started in 1915. Government officials were worried about the effect of releas-
ing large groups of rootless young men into what they expected (rightly,
as it turned out) would be a depressed postwar economy. It was felt that
soldiers needed to be de-militarized, reeducated to function as well-
behaved, liberal individuals responsible to no one but themselves.[52] They
also needed to be employed. Canada's urban mayors envisioned gangs of
restless ex-soldiers causing trouble on street corners.[53] Authorities in BC
felt particular pressure to solve this problem, as it was assumed that the
province's mild climate would draw more than the province's share of
returned soldiers to the province. Given that BC's much-celebrated climate actually existed only on the coast near Vancouver and on Vancouver
Island (which were also the most heavily populated areas of the province),
it was clear that the problem would be primarily an urban one.

Getting these men out of the city and "back to the land" would be
good both for them and for society as a whole, and seemed to be the obvious solution. Given all the advantages of modern agricultural science and
technology, the soldiers could hardly fail as farmers. Proponents of the plan,
using the rhetoric of progressive social reformers, argued also that soldier
settlement would function as therapy and social regeneration. Immersion

in a more natural life would cure soldiers of traits such as martial tendencies and deference to command, which threatened to undermine liberal individuality back in Canada. Finally, soldier settlement was embraced because it was a long-standing practice (see Figure 3).

The Canadian tradition of distributing land to soldiers could be traced back to New France. French soldier settlements and British settlements along the St. John and St. Lawrence Rivers in the wake of the American Revolution were founded primarily for strategic reasons. Settled groups of ex-soldiers served as a deterrent, and could become a fighting force if deterrence failed. Following the War of 1812 and the abating of the American threat, soldier settlement continued as a convenient way of developing new countryside. Soldiers were offered land on the prairies after both Riel Rebellions in 1870 and 1885. While the presence of troops offered security from possible American and Métis or Native threats, the soldiers' contribution to Canadian security was more important as part of the overall plan to resettle the prairies with Euro-Canadians and develop the grasslands into commercial farms.[54]

By the late nineteenth century, soldier settlement was a normal part of the practice of resettlement more generally. This history was the impetus behind the settlement of Boer War veterans. Though the Boer War initiative was an utter failure, most of the land going to speculators instead of soldiers, the Canadian people had seen the tradition of soldier settlement in practice just a few years before the Great War. Canadians were also inspired by the examples of their neighbours and allies. Though the US Congress rejected the soldier settlement plans of the Secretary of the Interior, Australia, New Zealand, and Britain sent returned soldiers to the countryside after the Great War, and the California State Land Settlement Board created the soldier settlement communities of Durham and Delhi.[55]

In 1915, the prime minister and provincial premiers met in Ottawa to discuss the issue of returned soldiers. The provinces agreed to create commissions to study the problem of employing and "rehabilitating" ex-soldiers; in November, the BC government formed the Returned Soldiers' Aid Commission (RSAC). The RSAC was a collection of civilian volunteer experts overseen by the Provincial Secretary. Prominent charities such as Vancouver's Canadian Club and the District Trades and Labour Councils of both Vancouver and Victoria sent representatives. The commission indicated its concern about urban problems by including two representatives from Vancouver and Victoria and one each from New Westminster and Nanaimo. Two advisory committees were also appointed, one charged with devising plans for technical training of returned men and one with making

HELP THE WORK OF
RECONSTRUCTION

"AFTER THE STORM"

BUY WAR SAVINGS STAMPS

3   BC Archives offers little information about this image, but we can infer much from internal evidence: Your money, invested in war savings stamps, will help put together a good postwar society. The returned soldier discards his uniform, gun, and helmet, turns his back on the factory, and prepares for work on the land. Both he and the land, presumably, will be reconstructed. Perhaps there is even an implied comparison between the devastation wrought on Europe and the good work the soldier will do on the land at home.

plans for agricultural training and land settlement. The second committee was composed of some of the academic and bureaucratic leaders in the development and promotion of an alternative modernity: L.S. Klinck, dean of agriculture at UBC, as well as the government's Deputy Minister of Agriculture and its Director of Elementary Agricultural Education.[56]

As the war progressed, the spectre of the soldiers' return emphasized the fear of city life and the corresponding veneration of country life that had already existed in Canadian intellectual, artistic, and bureaucratic circles before the war. "Whatever is going to be done should be settled before the men become helpless and disgruntled drifters," one correspondent told the premier.[57] "A serious state of congestion and unemployment in the larger Canadian towns" was possible, warned another.[58] Even worse: unless Canada prepared to absorb Canadian and British soldiers clamoring for farms, "our population will fall back to poverty, high infantile mortality will continue, and possibly an industrial revolution will threaten to involve the whole Empire in a cataclysm."[59]

The relative numbers of people living in the city was hurting "national vitality." Going back to the land was the solution. Here the soldier could be rehabilitated, and lead a general movement of city people to the country, where they would find "permanency and ultimate prosperity."[60] The Canadian National Reconstruction Groups, a think-tank out of Montreal, deplored the trend towards the city and suggested the sort of program of scientific improvement of agriculture and country life favoured by BC's promoters of an alternative modernity.[61] The war, it argued, afforded the opportunity for building something new, moving beyond the rigidities of custom and the simplicity of High Victorian liberalism. It was tearing down "the old relationships between the classes; the old ideas of security and fixity of tenure, privileges, occupations, and customs; the old system of 'laissez-faire' and individualism." For the working class, the world had changed. Soldiers and munitions workers were now considering their new power and importance in society, "and yet their utter impotence unless they closely co-operate and combine. They have seen a great outpouring of seemingly endless national wealth for the purposes of Destruction, and will not, on the return of peace, be denied a greatly increased expenditure for the purposes of security, comfort, and health."[62]

The Reconstruction Groups, with its scepticism about individualism developed outside of the nation and the social order, and with its emphasis on cooperation and increased expenditure, advocated the reformation of society along new liberal lines. It saw the war as the opportunity to build a new society, including a more modern – and so more vibrant – countryside.

At the same time, physically and mentally damaged soldiers had to be rehabilitated and eased back into society. Here the federal government took the lead, first through its Military Hospitals Commission (MHC) and then through the MHC's successor agency, the Department of Soldiers' Civil Re-establishment (founded in 1918). The MHC saw possibilities for rehabilitation and retraining through agriculture. Its ideal returned soldier, the handicapped "Private Pat," declared that "The country life's the life for me, with a cow and a hen and a honey bee – and a few other things."[63] A March 1917 report of the Commission on Vocational Training in BC noted that most of the disabled men were being trained for clerical positions. Others were being trained in engineering[64] and woodworking. But at the Esquimalt Convalescent Home near Victoria, returned men practised gardening and poultry raising. Beekeeping was to be introduced in the summer, and "an effort is also made to keep the latest literature on Agriculture at hand and available for returned men, who have found both encouragement and inspiration from the regular visits of the specialists attached to the Agricultural Department (Provincial)."[65] As well, thirty-five men were waiting to participate in a community land settlement plan.

BC's Director of Elementary Agricultural Education agreed that farming could rehabilitate the disabled. He suggested in a 1915 report that physically disabled veterans could work at "lighter forms" of farming, for example, "gardening, fruit-growing or poultry-raising." The permanently disabled could be kept in a soldiers' home, where they would be kept active doing gardening and horticulture, poultry raising and beekeeping – good outdoor work, "varied and healthful." The director enthusiastically told the story of "the best amateur gardener in Canada today," who "for one whole summer operated without assistance a one-acre fruit and flower garden, although unable to walk or even stand while working."[66] A Great War Veterans' Association report was so confident of the capacity of the land to provide for returned men that it recommended that "a man ... physically unable to carry on in full" would be placed "immediately on the land whether he is experienced or not because his pension would give him a small income; in other words he will not want, he can go and experiment."[67] Finally, an anonymous writer proposed to BC's RSAC that agriculture was the obvious solution to the problem of "taking care of and finding employment for a large number of Returned Soldiers, who are in various stages of physical condition, from total disability to a questionable physical condition for ordinary employment."[68]

Country life was understood to be inherently healthy and thus good for returning the convalescent to full health and productivity. A report on sanitaria for tuberculosis, in the possession of an official at the government's Tranquille Sanitarium near Kamloops, suggested that once the patient was partially recovered, he should spend time on the Sanitarium Industrial Farm Colony for "a process of hardening and re-education to work." It added that "the Colony is part of the Sanitarium life and treatment and the term 'after-care' should not be used in this connection."[69] An annual report from the British "Village Centres Council for Curative Treatment and Training of Disabled Men" stressed that the men will work "in the open air." The council's plan was to "enable men with their families to occupy cottages and homes and 'a bit of land' on fair terms during the curative period," so that ultimately they "may be able to return to their former homes and previous occupations, or earn a new livelihood in agriculture, horticulture, and other healthy rural trades or callings."[70] Clearing land would provide "a healthy and congenial employment" for veterans.[71]

The therapeutic powers of nature could also be useful in dealing with the problem of the healthy returned soldier and his unfortunately militarized mentality. In this sense, soldier settlement was an extension of the therapeutic orientation of other aspects of soldier rehabilitation. It was therapy for the physically fit soldier, a way of re-integrating him into normal civilian life. Further, soldier settlement was a way of integrating the soldier into a new form of modern life, a rural life that preserved the old virtues while drawing on new tools of expertise and planning. It also acknowledged the new idea that the state should be expected to provide a living for its citizens.

As part of its effort to make itself useful to the province, the University of British Columbia and its Faculty of Agriculture took a central role in the re-education of returned soldiers. For the academic year 1918-19, Dean Klinck developed a three-month short course, offered three times during the year, in the basics of scientific farming. Instruction was broken down into five units: agronomy (soil, drainage, and crops); animal husbandry; horticulture; the management of poultry; and carpentry, blacksmithing, math, and bookkeeping. The courses were avowedly practical, combining instruction in the laboratory and in the field with practical clearing and tilling of land and harvesting of crops.[72] Klinck designed these courses to help those city men with an interest in and aptitude for farming but without the necessary experience and knowledge. The men, he felt, were deserving of whatever help could be given them. By extending ideas of conservation to human as well as natural resources, he believed that British Columbians would be "wise if we avail ourselves to the utmost of what the returned soldiers bring us."[73]

There is nothing to indicate that Klinck's desire to help the soldiers was less than genuine, and the only help he requested was that accommodations and board for the men be provided by the federal government. Nevertheless, his faculty derived great benefit from its service to soldier settlers. By 1925, in addition to having its own building and an extensive system of fields, the faculty could boast of a series of buildings for research and teaching on dairy farming, as well as buildings devoted to horticulture, beef, horses, sheep, and pigs, many of these built by the federal Department of Soldiers' Civil Re-establishment.[74]

While the university provided instruction, the task of developing the actual plans for sending soldiers back to the land fell to the Returned Soldiers' Aid Commission. From its first report in 1916, the RSAC had seen rural settlement as a key part of its program to "rehabilitate" returned soldiers. As part of this report, the three-man committee charged with investigating agricultural training and community settlement outlined a plan that would be largely put into action in the development of Merville.[75] Surrounding this plan, however, was a series of other land settlement proposals. Examination of these and the committee's final plan shows us two things: first, the concentration on community or "colony" settlements, a policy that would be readily embraced by the provincial government but rejected by the federal; and second, the way the commission extended the ideas of scientific agriculture into scientific land settlement, a complete system for establishing new, modern, rural communities.

The various proposals in the files of the RSAC concentrated on five key issues. These were the problem of land clearing; the question of location with respect to markets, transportation facilities, and cities; the type of land and layout of the settlement; the type of farming that should be carried out; and the problem of costs. Proposals came from bureaucrats such as the Deputy Minister of Agriculture and the Director of Elementary Agricultural Education and interested bodies such as the Victoria Board of Trade (all three of these being members of the RSAC). Proposals were made also by members of the public. What is remarkable about these submissions is their ambitious level of detail.

The issue that received the least attention in the proposals was land clearing, which would turn out to be the thorniest problem. Most agreed that a work-gang scheme was needed. Some recommended that the men remain under military discipline; others, including future premier Simon Fraser Tolmie, suggested that enemy internees be used for the initial work.[76] Several proposals wrestled with the problem of how to make commercial farms viable without locating the farms too close to the city. RSAC planners wanted to keep the soldiers away from city influences; at the same time, many proposed small five- to ten- to twenty-acre farms. Farms of this size were most suited for small-scale mixed farming, where easy access to markets that could purchase garden produce would be critical.[77]

Planners were most interested in the issue of what they often called the "central station," a centrally located area for community services. The central station concept was a representation in space of the key ideas of cooperation and access to sociability and modern services by which planners hoped to overcome the traditional rural problems of isolation and backwardness. Some suggested somewhat radical designs, such as a large farm that would house up to five hundred men not yet ready to take on their own farms. Most suggested what was, essentially, a town centre: the location of the church, school, hospital, and stores for the whole settlement. But this centre would also support communal facilities – a cooperative creamery for processing milk products, communally owned heavy machinery, community-owned farms to raise and supply breeding stock and chicks, and an experimental farm that would supply knowledge. The central station might also support industrial enterprises that could furnish necessary inputs – tile manufacturing, brick making, sawmilling, and flour milling.

Cooperation, as the Director of Elementary Agricultural Education was careful to say, was not conceived to mean "a radical equalization of profits which tends to break down the great saving principle of individual responsibility and reward for individual effort." Cooperation, as embodied in the central station, was the pooling of resources and the opportunity for community life – or, as one plan put it, "social surroundings, organisations, practical advice and co-operative systems."[78] The central station would do away with the isolation and loneliness of rural life, help deal with the increasing complexity and expense of agricultural equipment and practice, and alleviate the difficulty of securing supplies and marketing agricultural products in a world of ever larger and more distant markets.

Finally, most plans called for small holdings dedicated to market gardening or sheep and poultry raising.[79] Most also took a stab at estimating costs, many assuming that a significant portion of the cost would be absorbed by the government.[80] The final set of recommendations made to the government by the RSAC planners, however, largely rejected the idea of outright government spending on soldier settlement. Like the Land Settlement Board, RSAC planners embraced instead a policy of loans and cost recovery. The plan called for a central townsite, containing mills, stores, and a demonstration farm. Experts would be available to advise the settlers. Each settler was to get twenty-five acres, of which ten would be pre-cleared. Loans would be available to pay for the stocking of farms, such loans to be used under the supervision of the government. The purpose of the plan, according to the commission, was to "express our appreciation ... to those men who have fought and suffered in defence of our National Liberties," by allowing them to "go on the land and become self-supporting under the most favourable conditions." Contrary to the view of many of the RSAC reports, however, the commission recommended that the government could hope to recover about 70 percent of the cost of land clearing, charging each farm a portion of the total cost, and about 65 percent of the total cost of developing the settlement.[81] The experience at Merville and Camp Lister, where this plan would be applied almost in its entirety, would prove these cost-recovery estimates to have been overly optimistic.

The RSAC plans constituted a form of scientific land settlement, an expansion of the procedures of scientific agriculture into a total system of state-directed community building – plans for bringing a new, modern countryside into being by the judicious application of expert knowledge and state direction. Further, the plans were an indication that the belief in creating an alternative rural modernity existed outside the circle of agriculture professors, boosters, and bureaucrats. They were also popular with Victoria businessmen, interested laypeople, veterans' groups, and, as we saw in Chapter 1, influential politicians such as Premier John Oliver and Minister of Lands Duff Pattullo.

For all these people, the soldier settlements were about something more than a way to address the immediate problem of soldier unemployment. They were about something beyond the soldiers themselves. The Director of Elementary Agricultural Education thought that the return of the soldiers might start a movement towards the country that "shall command the admiration of people everywhere," and lead to increased agricultural production and "permanency and prosperity within our own borders." "The present crisis," he declared, "seems to me to offer unprecedented opportunities for the organization of several model rural communities which would stand out as standards of excellence for many years to come and which would point the way to the successful development of rural life in Canada."[82] In 1922, W.H. Kirchner – former *Asia* man, Land Settlement Board employee, and defender of the idea of community land settlement at the 1918 soldier settlement conference in Ottawa – noted that Merville and Camp Lister were "the modern, scientific form of land settlement." They were, he claimed, "far more than a spasmodic attempt to settle a few hundred men on the land; they are, in fact, the advanced guard of an entirely new economic era for the Dominion of Canada and are calculated to raise the whole status of rural life for centuries to come."[83] Perhaps soldiers were not the only ones who could be rehabilitated. Perhaps everyone could be – even Canada itself.

Soldier settlement, then, was a plan for bringing about an alternative modernity, a comprehensive plan ultimately aimed, at least for the most enthusiastic, at the transformation of society. But as James C. Scott has argued, such plans have limitations that their supporters – in this case, the interwar supporters of the alternative modernity – cannot see.[84] Supporters of the alternative modernity, like progressive reformers more generally, were confident that scientific knowledge and new technologies would allow them to successfully manage the transformation of society and environment. In putting their plans into effect, however, they discovered that their scheme was not as comprehensive as it might have seemed. As we will see in Part 2, their plans did not take into account the sort of environmental and social nuances inherent in establishing successful farms, which depend on balancing a complex and locally varied array of human and ecological factors.

In June 1918, Clement James Freeman of Victoria wrote to Premier Oliver, asking for a personal recommendation to accompany his application to the Canadian government's Soldier Settlement Board. "I am a resident of Victoria," he explained, "and enlisted in the old original 50th Gordon Highlanders Aug 1914, and left Canada for England with the First Canadian Contingent of the same year, having served three years and eight months overseas, of which two years and one month were spent in France." Now, "having to provide for a wife and family, I wish to settle on the land, and in this way to earn my living, and make a permanent home on a farm." Oliver was sympathetic. He sent the letter on, trusting that a letter arriving from the Premier's office would attract the notice that Freeman hoped for. "To the extent ... possible," he assured Freeman, "I am glad to aid you in every way."[85] Oliver's response was unsurprising. Of all the people in his government, he above all had made the plight of the returned soldier a priority. In his determination to reward the sacrifice of the men of the Canadian Corps, he reflected a much wider sentiment in British Columbian and Canadian society, one that by 1919 had led to the founding of new rural communities, and the creation of a new countryside. With this, a new character – the environment – enters the story. Its role in interwar settlement will be the subject of Part 2.

Part 2

Where Apples Grow Best

3

Stump Farms

SOLDIER SETTLEMENT
AT MERVILLE

LORENCE LILY CLARK[1] was a young war bride just three months out
of England when she arrived with her husband, George, at the soldier settlement at Merville, in the Comox Valley on Vancouver Island.
Forty years later, still living in Merville, she recalled her experiences for the
local newspaper. "I came to Merville on August 6th, 1919, a bright, beautiful day," she remembered, "the warm air was full of the sweet scent of
newly sawn pine, and the last of the summer's blackberries. Newly created
shacks were all over the place; and I had never seen so many huge stumps
before." She remembered playing piano for the Prince of Wales' visit to
Merville, six months after her arrival, first accompanying the settlement
children in "O Canada" and "God Save the King," and later at the community dance, "my very first dance, as my parents strictly objected to
dancing, and during my single days I had only been allowed to go to one
dance, sponsored by the local Football Club, to look on but not to dance."
Her written memories ring with good humour and delight in the antics of
the settlers. She recounts how, while the Prince was being shown around
the settlement, a few settlers secretly smashed a window in the back of the
new schoolhouse and climbed in to retrieve the Prince's gift – a silver key
that had mistakenly been locked inside.[2]

Lily Clark arrived in the summer with the wives of the married settlers,
after the men had had a chance to clear some land and put up some temporary shelters. George Clark had arrived earlier in the summer with the
initial group of returned soldiers, as had another settler, Frank Little. Little was born in England in 1874 and came to Canada in 1895. He lived and

worked in Winnipeg and the Yukon before finally meeting his wife Hanna
in Vancouver. Frank and Hanna lived in Atlin, Spruce Creek, Vancouver,
and Atletz, BC, taking up farming as their occupation upon their move to
Vancouver, and taking with them from place to place their growing family – eight children (five daughters and three sons) by the time they arrived
at Merville. In 1917, Frank enlisted and was sent overseas. Arriving in
Merville two years later, he at first worked in the central camp set up by
the Land Settlement Board (LSB) for the men to live in while building the
Merville town centre. He looked after cattle and horses and worked in the
cookhouse and bunkhouse. Soon, though, he got what he had come for –
a farm. By June, clearing operations were still ongoing and the farms
would not be occupied until the next spring, but LSB officials decided
that it was time to distribute the first farms. The original forty families
drew lots, and the Littles were awarded three lots making up 63.6 acres in
the Merville subdivision, near the town centre (see Map 2, page 81).

Henry Curry became the 150th settler when he arrived in August of
1919. Perhaps due to his later arrival, his bachelor status, or the luck of the
draw, he landed a less plum spot for his farm – an 89.5-acre lot in the
remote Kitty Coleman district. This placed him in the same general area
as the Clarks, though Lily did not move out to the farm until two years
after arriving in Merville.[3] When she did, she regretted the change. Life in
the Merville town centre meant dances and box socials, neighbours
dressed up as Santa Claus distributing oranges and candy to the children,
and the birth of her first daughter. The farm meant life on forty-four acres
in a distant corner of the settlement area, a lonely, isolated existence compared to the warm community life of the town centre. Yet, remembered
Clark, "the beach in those days was beautiful indeed. Many wild flowers
bloomed there then which have almost entirely disappeared in later years.
Then the wild larkspur was almost waist high, and the yellow dill bloomed
beside masses of delicate little pink flowers and bright blue lobelia." And
after a few years, the socials began again, though with, perhaps, a new
edge. On one occasion, "to our great amusement Mr. Curry sang – quite
impromptu – 'Half of Kitty Coleman is mine, lassie, and I've a little shack,
lassie, and you can have the blooming lot, if you'll only pay the taxes on
it, lassie!'"[4]

For the most part, though, Clark's memories emphasize the hopes of
the settlers and the goodness of what existed at Merville. The great forest
fire that swept through the settlement in 1922 was for her a "deep, searing
tragedy," but also showed the hardiness of settlers who refused to give up
on their land.[5] For her, the settlement was an opportunity to live an adult,

independent life. Opportunities like this drove people to Merville, though perhaps something of Clark's good humour was required to keep them there. In the isolation of her farm, Clark was nevertheless able to take refuge in the beauty of the nature around her. At the same time, her memories show us some of the ways settlers shaped the environment around them, perhaps not even realizing they did so. Clark recalls the size of the larkspur and of the fields of flowers, and laments the loss of the ladyslipper and the bluebird. Yet it seems likely that these species disappeared due to environmental changes wrought by the Merville settlers. And while she concentrates on the undeniable courage and determination of the settlers in the wake of the fire, such large blazes were common where forests, settlers, and industry came together.

Merville was the most idealistic of the projects to create an alternative modernity, based as it was on cooperative work and the deliberate formation of a community structure. Merville and its sister settlement Camp Lister drew most directly on the scientific land settlement plans of the Returned Soldiers' Aid Commission (RSAC). But the creation of a rural modernity depended on more than just community; it depended on the creation of an appropriate countryside. In the end, the planners and settlers of Merville could not create the countryside they wanted. Scientific land settlement failed to allow for the sort of adjustments to local social and environmental conditions critical to the establishment of a new rural area. It could not adequately take into account such factors as weather, the difficulties of land clearing, and the way in which settlement and logging together created a fire-prone landscape. True to the initial plans of the RSAC and the LSB, the government insisted that the settlement be largely self-sustaining, yet settlers possessed little ready capital. Off-farm work in the area was scarce and for women almost non-existent. The increasing need to resort to such work meant that only families had a real chance of making it – single male farmers faced a virtually impossible task. The combination of these factors made the establishment of farms at Merville a difficult proposition.

ASSESSING THE LAND

The Land Settlement Board's province-wide hunt for arable land had left it enthusiastic about the possibilities of Vancouver Island, and especially the Comox Valley. On the east coast of the island, facing the British Columbia mainland across Georgia Strait, the Comox Valley sits under the mountainous shadow of the Vancouver Island Mountains, which run down the centre of Vancouver Island and define its geography of settlement. Then, as now, most settlement was concentrated on the eastern and southern coasts and in the odd interior valley. The climate is mild by Canadian standards, moderated by the warm, damp westerly winds that blow in off the Pacific. These same winds drop prodigious amounts of rainfall on the entire island, in particular on the west and northern coasts. The east coast, though still wet by the standards of interior dwellers, is much drier. The Clayoquot area, for instance, on the west coast at the outlet of Alberni Inlet, received 114.49 inches of rainfall in 1913. Port Alberni, farther inland, received 63.44 inches, and Hornby Island, just south of Comox on the east coast, received only 45.18 inches.[6]

The largely treeless lowlands surrounding the mouth of the Tsolum River were the heart of settlement in the Comox Valley (see Map 2). Here, regular flooding had produced a plain of rich alluvial soil, which the Comox and Pentlatch First Nations maintained through burning. But the Comox and Pentlatch lost control of these lands early on. Sometime before 1864, colonial officials laid out a reserve of 155 acres. When the Joint Indian Reserve Commission arrived in 1876, it found instead a Native settlement on 250 acres of gravel and heavy forest. The original reserve lands lay next door, but these lands had been pre-empted by a white settler. The commissioners cancelled this illegal pre-emption and enlarged the reserve by a hundred acres; it was unable to do more as all the rest of the land in the area was already owned by white settlers. Such rich farmland had gone quickly, and the reserve commissioners were unwilling to violate property rights. Surrounding lands were less promising, at least for agriculture. Heavy rainfall and a pre-contact fire cycle that saw major forest fires only every 150 to 350 years had produced dense, towering forests of western red cedar, hemlock, and, in particular, the mighty Douglas fir. This was a landscape of huge trees, thick underbrush, and periodic swamps, and the soil was less fertile, consisting of marine deposits and glacial moraine.[7]

Thus, logging became the major activity in the area. Early logging took place along the seacoast and the rivers, making use of these waterways to move logs to market. Logging the inland forests required the use of large-scale, steam-powered logging equipment in order to yard and transport the logs. In 1910, such industrial logging arrived in the Comox Valley with the formation of the Canadian Western Lumber Company. Capitalized at $15,500,000, it was one of the biggest enterprises in BC and the province's largest logging company. Canadian Western combined the assets of the Fraser River Lumber Company – fifty-two thousand acres of Comox Valley land, a purchase that had driven the company into bankruptcy – with the access to Canadian and British capital available to William Mackenzie and Donald Mann of the Great Northern transcontinental railway. Through its subsidiary, the Comox Logging and Railway Company (CLR), Canadian Western began to log its new Comox Valley lands.[8]

Rural boosters commonly argued that the best strategy for logged-off land was to turn it into farmland. This logic likely led the LSB's inspectors to the Comox Valley eight years later.[9] They were impressed by what they saw. There was agricultural potential everywhere; they predicted crops of vegetables and small fruits, livestock and fodder, grains, berries, root crops, sheep, and hogs.[10] In late 1918, with the war over and the prospect of returned soldiers looming, the board became interested in fifteen thousand acres of logged-off land between three and nine miles north of the town of Courtenay. What had been thick forest was now a landscape defined by its encounter with the Comox Logging Railway: rolling hills covered with charred stumps, logs, and some undergrowth (though in some areas the forest still stood). One aspect of the land differed from what the planners at the RSAC had in mind. While their colony settlement plans spoke of central stations accessible to all, the land that would become Merville was in a number of sections crisscrossed by creeks and already existing roads and divided by the remaining forest. But the LSB's local director, in charge of the reconnaissance of land on Vancouver Island and the coast, was generally pleased with the area. Having spent two days inspecting the land and quizzing area residents for local information, he concluded that, at five dollars per acre, "considering location, climatic conditions, and nature of the country, it is worth at least this amount."[11]

At this point, some of the science seems to have been left out of scientific land settlement. It appears that no soil survey was taken of the entire area before its purchase. Instead, the LSB relied on a report prepared by UBC agronomist Paul Boving that considered part of what eventually became Merville. Boving's survey covered between four thousand and five thousand acres to the east of the eventual Merville town centre – likely what became the Kitty Coleman district – about one-third of the eventual fifteen thousand acres of settlement area.[12] Of this land, Boving concluded that about one-third was "high, dry and very light soil"; one-third was soil that was still quite light but had better humus (decomposed organic matter critical as plant food); while the remainder was "really good agricultural land, although of somewhat light nature." The very light soil, he declared, was lacking in plant food and in the capacity to hold moisture. "It is a question," he reported, "if this part of the area would lend itself to successful crop production ... it would scarcely be fair to expect the average settler to make a living on this land," although "it might be possible to improve it."[13] The next-best category of land was at a lower elevation than the very light soil, and needed draining of stagnant water and probably the addition of fertilizers. Boving was cautiously positive about this. The last category of land contained all the elements lacking from the other types, though Boving did mention that nitrogen, a key nutrient, "might not be immediately available to the plants." This land, as well, "is generally covered by timber, or at least heavy stumps," but it "would be well adapted for agricultural purposes, provided clearing can be done at a reasonable price."[14]

In February 1919, the chairman of the LSB wrote to Agriculture Minister E.D. Barrow, recommending (on the basis of Boving's partial report and the surveys conducted by LSB directors and by the Ministry of Forests' Commissioner of Grazing) that the government move quickly on purchasing the lands, in order to leave sufficient time for surveying and subdivision. He further recommended that returned soldiers be employed to clear it. This would provide them with work and, if they wanted it, with land to settle on. At the very least, a speedy purchase would see the land developed and available for sale.[15] In the spring, the LSB dispatched government surveyor R.P. Bishop to survey their new purchase, now officially the LSB's Development Area No. 1.[16]

Bishop was generally pleased with the layout of the area. True, his liberal sense of rational planning was offended by the jumble of odd-sized lots arranged at strange angles to each other, due to the disturbance of previous surveys by logging and fire. Also, because the three grades of soil identified by Boving were scattered throughout the area, it would be difficult to ensure that all farms had sufficient good land. But he found the area to be already well serviced with roads, some of which could be developed into major thoroughfares. The Island Highway ran right through the area, as did the Comox Logging Railway. The Esquimalt & Nanaimo (E & N) rail line, connecting the Comox Valley with Victoria, ended at Courtenay, just south of the settlement. However, as the railway's right-of-way ran right through the area, the LSB was optimistic that Merville would soon be located right on the E & N's mainline. There were Canadian government wharves at the southeastern part of the settlement area, at the town of Comox and at Little River. Moving crops to market would not be a problem. Also, Courtenay was already a "highly progressive" rural area, possessing a creamery and a condensed milk factory. "For the purpose of settling quickly a large number of returned men," wrote Bishop, "I consider that it would be hard to find a better piece of ground."[17]

This report was written in May 1919. Bishop stayed in the area until the next year, completing the subdivision of the remaining lands. By the fall he was sounding a more pessimistic note: "The great bulk of this [land]," he reported, is "more or less waste ground. There are, however, a few scattered pieces of better land which might serve as the nucleus for sheep farms." Other parts of the land were even less promising. In some areas, Bishop was unsure as to whether grass would grow, and he commented of some spots that he was not sure if they could pay back the costs of even a very rough clearing.[18] Bishop's description of another area gives a feeling for the type of land he was encountering. To the south of the lot was "a side hill sloping gently to the North. The soil is a little better than the general average of the country but not quite up to the quality on the ten farms which have just been completed." To the east was "about 20 acres of pretty good bottom land ... with rather dense brush. About 40 acres of muskeg [was] on the North and about sixty or seventy acres of swamp land of which latter about 40 & 50 acres might be called first class. The balance of the swampy land gets more and more peaty till it verges on the muskeg type." The good swamp land would, of course, still require draining.[19] Surveying still more land in the far northeast corner of the area, Bishop found it necessary to plot farms of up to 120 acres in order to compensate for the poor soil scattered irregularly across the landscape.[20]

At the same time, Professor Boving gave the LSB more details – none of them encouraging – as to the possibilities of the soil at Merville. The soil, stated Boving, lacked enough humus to retain sufficient moisture. In this sense, it was like soil he knew near Vancouver, land which did not produce crops well in the first few years of cultivation. He recommended that the Merville ground be prepared by growing crops of rye, clover, and vetches, and suggested that the application of phosphoric acid fertilizer was necessary. In Vancouver, he noted, "we do not count on putting in any crop, with reasonable prospect of success, without adding some phosphoric acid to the soil in one form or another."[21]

Overall, then, the land at Merville had some advantages: it was mostly cleared of forest (though not of stumps); it had a pre-established and relatively extensive road network; and it was close to the communities of Courtenay and Comox, which could act as markets while also supplying transportation links southward to Victoria and across Georgia Strait to Vancouver. On the negative side, the land was of doubtful quality, and the extent of really good land was clearly limited and not evenly or regularly distributed throughout the area. Composed of four largely separated areas, it could not be the kind of concentrated settlement envisioned by the planners of the RSAC.

Still, it must have seemed to those in charge that there was enough good land to offer a possibility of success, and they may not have seen the bad land and the tough clearing as drawbacks. Challenges were to be expected in the countryside. Challenges were what formed rural character and tied a man to the place he had won over from nature. They were what rehabilitated restless, morally suspect, rootless soldiers, and turned them into solid citizens. The land also had the advantage of being affordable to the government. We might see these lands as at best a mixed bag, with no significant amount of exceptional land and some reasonably good land in need of years of development. Looking through the prism of the ideals of a modern countryside, however, the individuals involved in Merville saw primarily the possibilities.

Establishing Merville

The first parties of returned men arrived to start the development of Merville in April 1919. Of the four areas that were to make up Merville, the most developed was the "Camp Centre" or "Headquarters" area (see Map 2). The centre of operations for the Comox Logging Company since 1911, Headquarters was a company town with administrative offices, a roundhouse and railway maintenance shop, along with freestanding homes for married men, stores, a post office, a hotel, a ball diamond, and a tennis court.[22] The land around the town had already been subdivided. Other areas were rougher. The Tsolum and Kitty Coleman areas were named for the rivers that ran through them. The Tsolum area was towards the western side of the settlement and included the lands around the upper Tsolum River and its tributary Dove Creek, upstream of the rich bottomlands. Kitty Coleman Creek ran into the Strait of Georgia near the northeastern edge of the development area. Merville was simultaneously the name of the development as a whole, the name of the small town developed by the LSB along the Island Highway roughly in the centre of the settlement, and the name of the area formed by the farms clustered around the town.

The LSB placed Lieutenant A.F. Walker, formerly of the *Asia,* in charge of land clearing operations.[23] Under the board's development system, work was to be done by teams of men under LSB supervision. The men were paid $4 per day, minus $0.40 for each meal at the cookhouse. The board would prepare a portion of the land for cultivation and build a house and fencing on each lot as well other necessary infrastructure, the

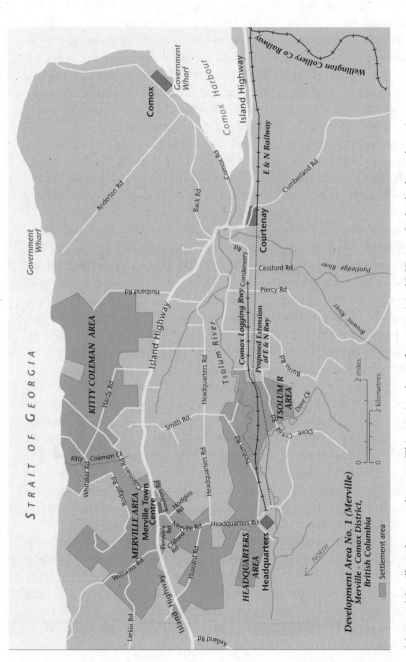

MAP 2 Merville and surrounding area. This map is redrawn from an original LSB map. It clearly shows the various transport connections available to the Merville settlers. But note as well how far parts of the settlement area are from the Merville Town Centre. The most developed farms were clustered around the town centre.

Within the map:

STRAIT OF GEORGIA

Government Wharf

Government Wharf

Comox

Comox Harbour

Island Highway

Wellington Colliery Co Railway

Anderton Rd

Back Rd

Comox Rd

Courtenay

E & N Railway

Cumberland Rd

Cessford Rd

Piercy Rd

Puntledge River

Browns River

Condensery Rd

Comox Logging Rwy

Proposed Extension of E & N Rwy

Husband Rd

Island Highway

KITTY COLEMAN AREA

Hardy Rd

Tsolum River

Headquarters Rd

Smith Rd

Headquarters Rd

Tsolum Rd

Burns Rd

TSOLUM R AREA

Dove Ck

Dove Creek Rd

Kitty   Coleman Ck

Whitaker Rd

Rodger Rd

Coleman Rd

MERVILLE AREA

Merville Town Centre

Boulton Rd

Hodgins Rd

Fenwick Rd

Clifford Rd

Merville Rd

Howard Rd

Williams Rd

Larkin Rd

Island Highway

Kelland Rd

Headquarters Rd

HEADQUARTERS AREA

Headquarters

NORTH

Development Area No. 1 (Merville)
Merville - Comox District,
British Columbia

Settlement area

0   2 miles
0   2 kilometres

costs of which would be paid back by the settlers over a period of time. A camp was started seven miles up the Island Highway from Courtenay (named "Nelem's Camp," after the then chair of the LSB). Soon after it was established, it became known as Merville, named after the site of a head-quarters of the Canadian Corps in France. In May, bunkhouses, a cook-house, an office building, stables, and a general store were put up at the townsite. By June, one hundred men were there and, in July, the married men began to put up shacks to house their wives and families. By July, fifty families had begun living in the shacks, which had anywhere from one to four rooms and were clustered around the site's central buildings.[24]

The presence of these families and their superior accommodations – superior to bunkhouses, anyway – speaks to the importance of the family to the settlement efforts at Merville. When the draw for initial land allot-ments (for the first forty settlers) was held, preference was given to mar-ried men. But this is not to say that the LSB recognized the importance of women's and children's work to successful farming. To the Land Settle-ment Board, the "settler" was always male and, as we will see, his capabil-ities were assumed to be the critical factor in the success or failure of the farm.[25] Women and children were important not for farming but for pur-poses of social engineering. As Christopher Clarkson and Adele Perry have shown, the BC government's support for rural settlement in the nineteenth century was rooted in an attempt to stabilize the society of single men encouraged by resource industries to settle in BC.[26] Merville was an updated version of this nineteenth-century idea.

Surveyor R.P. Bishop, still in the area in early 1920, outlined Merville's role in the establishment of a new, stable, community-based social order. He predicted that Merville would be the nexus of logging, land clearing, and agricultural activities. In Merville, men could live in a settled, stable, Anglo-Saxon environment, close to their wives and children. They would be available to man the forest industry and to push forward development through further land clearing; in return, money from local development would stay in the area. Merville would be the centre of an integrated sys-tem of industrial, agricultural, and community development.[27]

First, though, the land needed to be cleared. This was a multi-step process. First came slashing and piling – in other words, cutting down bushes and collecting branches and other debris that had been left lying on the ground. Next, the stumps needed to be removed. Then, grubbing and piling involved collecting larger materials into stacks. After this, the land had to broken and ploughed, and, in a number of cases, drained.

Slashing and piling was relatively simple, if back-breaking. The stumps were a larger problem. They were packed with blasting powder and cracked to the point where they could be pulled out of the ground. Blasts had to be contained enough so as not to harm the people in the vicinity, and the powder had to be placed carefully in the stump so as to successfully crack it. Yet since each stump was different, success or failure depended on the skill and knowledge of the person setting the powder. In other words, because of ecological complexity, this was a task that defied central control and planning.[28]

Once the stump was cracked, a block and tackle was attached to it, and it was ready for the grubbing and piling stage. Grubbing and piling was done with a steam donkey, essentially an immobile steam engine driving a large pulley, used in logging to yard or "donkey" logs into piles.[29] Here, a cable was run from the donkey's pulley through another pulley on a semi-vertical pole (a "gin pole") to the tackle on the stump. The donkey engine then yanked the stump out of the ground and dragged it to a large pile of wooden debris. A similar process was used to pile up leftover logs. When this was accomplished, tractors were used to break and plough the land in preparation for planting. The LSB did not carry out these operations on the entire area, however. Instead, crews worked along the edges of main roads, clearing the front ten to fifteen acres of every farm.[30] This was still a major operation. The crews started with a single donkey engine in June, received two more in July, and a fourth in August. By this point, there were two hundred men clearing in the area.[31]

This attempt to reconstruct the landscape exposed a variety of environmental complexities. One problem was the uneven distribution of good land. Clearing only those lands along the roadways could (and did) leave good land still covered with stumps while exposing stony ground.[32] A more serious factor was the sheer size of the stumps. The loggers worked with handsaws. In order to avoid the wide base of very large trees, they cut notches at a point farther up the trunk and inserted long planks or springboards to stand on.[33] The frequent result was that stumps were not only four to six feet in diameter, but they could tower over a person's head (see Figures 4 and 5).

Such giant stumps were difficult to remove completely. The huge blasts required to dislodge them sometimes severed the trunk, leaving the roots underground. As the stumps were dragged away, their branches could snap off and be buried, or the weight of the stump might bury smaller logs and stumps. All this leftover material had to be ploughed out of the ground. Blasting and dragging also damaged the soil that the settlers were dependent on. Blasting threw up sub-soil that covered the topsoil necessary for growing crops. Dragging churned up the ground and also covered the topsoil.

The great weight of the steam donkeys caused further complications. The largest and most powerful machines in the area, steam donkeys had to be made to move themselves: loggers wrapped the steam donkey's cable around a convenient tree and fixed it back onto the skids the donkey rested on. Cranking the cable then moved the engine. In order to avoid having to go through this tedious process too often, crews left the donkey where it was as much as possible and made huge piles of stumps and branches, sometimes gathering five acres of material in one spot. Getting rid of these piles was not easy. Before they could be burned, they had to dry out, which could take all summer in the wet coastal climate. Burning had to take place on dry days with little wind, as the piles of dry wood produced great bonfires. The clumps of dirt left on the roots of the stumps smouldered for weeks and left behind a "mass of half-burned logs, stumps ... and baked earth covering upwards of an acre," all of which had to be removed.[34]

Land clearing did not lend itself well to precision planning and management. Each stump differed from every other, and no standard technique

4   "High Stumps Campbell's Ranch near Courtenay." A photograph taken by the BC Forest Service in the area of Merville in 1926, intended to show the amount of waste in contemporary wood-harvesting methods. We see something different: the challenge faced by the settlers trying to clear the land (though these stumps were likely higher than most, as the title of the photograph suggests).

could be used to blast, drag, and burn them all. Complications such as long-term smouldering and damage to the soil were difficult to predict and avoid. Such complexities drove up the costs of the land-clearing process. A report estimated that work in the summer and fall of 1919 cost an average of $210 per acre. As winter moved in, the LSB, afraid of the unemployment level in the cities,[35] decided to continue work. Some men were given the task of cutting fence posts and building fences. For those still clearing land, the heavy winter rains made working conditions difficult. It was wet and cold, and the ground was nearly impossible to work with. Over the winter, the costs of land clearing increased to more than $300 per acre. Yet progress had been made: by December, four hundred acres of land had been cleared of debris, and the stumps had been blasted. On a further 373 acres, debris had been gathered, though stumps remained in place. Forty-eight acres of ground had been broken.[36]

The overall development of Merville was also proceeding. LSB work teams had constructed twenty-eight homes by December 1919, and six were under construction (see Figure 6). Each farm got a well. Fencing was put up on all the farms in the Merville and Headquarters subdivisions and around areas that had been burnt down and rough cleared as pasture lands

5   A photograph in the same series as Figure 4. Showing an unknown location on Vancouver Island, the image gives a further sense of the challenge facing the settlers. Note the man leaning against the stump in the mid-foreground. A springboard notch is cut into the lone stump in the immediate foreground, and in other stumps.

in the Tsolum subdivision. The men also did some preparatory road work, blasting out the roadbeds and doing some rough grading. In September, they cleared land for, and constructed, a school; by the next month, the school served seventy-three students. In the same month, the federal government awarded Merville a post office, symbolically affirming the town's status as a genuine settlement. Before the end of the year, the final necessary stitch in the community tapestry was sewn: using equipment donated by the LSB, the settlers moved a small Anglican Church building three miles down the highway to the new town.[37]

The most spectacular event of this period, however, occurred in October. If the establishment of the post office confirmed that the town existed, then the visit of Edward, Prince of Wales, seemed to confirm the legitimacy and importance of the project. No moment of the visit demonstrated this more clearly than when the Prince drove into town on a hot and dusty day and was greeted by a "21-stump salute."[38] In this gesture

6   This photograph was taken by J.W. Clark, who put on promotional, illustrated lectures celebrating agricultural and hydro-electric development in British Columbia (see Chapter 5). The photograph is likely intended to promote the success of the LSB in creating permanent homes for settlers. The image itself supports this analysis – the home is solid-looking and modern, and finished with decorative vines, flower and shrubbery beds, and striped awnings.

were brought together all the goals and plans represented by the town – the hopes for a future of loyal, moral, rural settlers, ensured by the judicious application of the tools of modernity.

Prince Edward was greeted by a group of returned soldiers and their wives and families. He was asked to open the new school, using a ceremonial silver key presented to him by Mrs. Jones, the Sunday school teacher. She greeted the prince in Welsh, wearing a black satin dress and the medals awarded to her son, killed in action with the Flying Corps over Belgium. After talking with Mrs. Jones, the prince toured the site, inspected the operation of a donkey engine, and "graciously expressed himself as being greatly interested and highly pleased with the whole operation of development, it being the first of its kind he had ever seen." Then, expressing his wish to return at one point in the future, the prince took his leave.[39]

THE END OF DEVELOPMENT

As the spring of 1920 approached, the people of Merville had reason for optimism. Farms had been laid out, land had been cleared and seeded, homes had been built, and the small community was beginning to grow. The settlers had managed to pull through the winter. But by the spring of 1920, the BC government had decided that developing the area was a bigger and more expensive proposition than it had anticipated.[40]

At the end of May, the development program (in which work was performed by teams of waged workers under LSB control) was abandoned. Potential settlers were no longer to be employed to clear the land. Those who wanted farms would receive a land allotment and be free to work their own land. One report, probably written in 1927, gives what would become the board's standard justification for its actions. The report noted a number of problems: first was the "impossibility of making the land ready for crop at a cost within the limit of its value for agricultural purposes."[41] The board had underestimated the difficulty of transforming eastern Vancouver Island into a proper countryside. Second, the board noted that the rising cost of living in the immediate postwar era had led to increased costs of material and equipment and steadily growing demands for increased wages. The board also noted, with some justification, that much of the work of preparing the farms had already been done, and that the settlers were anxious to get out on the land.[42] Yet as is made clear in an internal March 1920 memo from the LSB to the Minister of Agriculture, cost was the primary concern. Though the price per acre for development work was considerably lower than the price charged by private contractors, it was still higher than what the land could be sold for. A number of years later, the LSB would find itself unable to sell semi-developed farmlands in the settled rural area of the Fraser Valley at $200 per acre.[43] Yet at Merville, the board was unable to even clear stumps for less than $210 per acre. Costs were proving to be considerably higher than the price that the federal Soldier Settlement Board (which the LSB counted on as a major customer) was willing to pay.[44]

Development work was discontinued in May as this month generally saw a lower unemployment rate than did other months. Settlers were sent off to work on their own property. Temporary shacks from the Merville town centre were rushed out to allotments where houses had not yet been built. The board promised to hire only settlers – by which they meant male settlers – at $4.40 per day for any future board work, to arrange work on the roads with the Public Works Department for whomever they could, and to offer "encouragement and assistance" to anyone who wanted to work in other industries. The cookhouse was closed down, and steam donkeys and other land clearing equipment were sold off. Items useful for agriculture (such as the temporary shacks from the previous summer, beds, and agricultural implements) as well as horses were sold to settlers.[45]

From the point of view of policy and ideology, however, there was as much continuity as change in the shift away from the development system. The shift was consistent with the LSB policy that developments must ultimately be self-sufficient. This goal had led the board to abandon the plan developed by the RSAC, ceding direct control of the land-preparation process. But the larger idea of the modern countryside had not been forgotten. The RSAC plans had aimed to encourage cooperation and community through the building of a town centre, which was now up and running. Further, the LSB retained essential elements of state control and expert oversight, doing so through a new system of reduced farm prices and "progress loans."

In preparation for this new system all lots in the settlement were assessed by an appraiser, accompanied by representatives from among settlers. The board drew up agreements of sale specifying that settlers were to "reside permanently on their farm, clearing, cultivating, and farming same in a good and husbandlike manner," thus satisfying the BC government's goal to settle the land with thrifty, virtuous farmers.[46] In exchange, settlers were offered up to twenty-five years to pay off the land. Interest, at 7 percent, would not accrue until October 1921, and no payments were due until

October 1922. Further, the board offered every landowner progress loans, with development work on the land as security. The value of any proposed improvements would be estimated by the board, and then money would be advanced to the farmer up to a certain percentage of the estimated value. Finally, the board also offered loans for the purchase of cattle. By the end of the year, settlers had purchased from the board twenty cows and six teams of horses with harnesses and wagons, and had also privately bought thirty-two cows, nine horses, eighty-one pigs, and "several hundred" chickens.[47]

This new system was still to be managed by LSB experts on the ground. K.G. Halley was appointed the new supervisor for the area. Halley was instructed to help "each settler to develop his farm by his own initiative and energy."[48] But he would also oversee all loans issued, considering the farmer's plans for the development of his property before approving the funds. He would also oversee and direct the improvement work that farmers undertook on their own land.[49] Halley clearly felt it was his duty to keep an eye on things and run the show. Concerned with keeping everyone busy, he told all settlers whose land still needed clearing to begin work. In July, he or his assistant planned to visit each farmer and decide which improvements would be carried out and what amount the board would give the settler once the work had been completed. Halley's plans were met with some hostility, which he addressed by finding work for settlers (particularly work on the roads), and by "scattering" settlers to their isolated farms.[50] In this, Halley was clearly acting to forestall problems noted back in February, when the board had commented on the issue of committee organization among the settlers. The board insisted that "all organization action by the settlers must stop short at the point where there is the danger of any committee control of expenditures or working plans."[51] Such matters could not be allowed to fall into the hands of those who might try to undermine liberal individualism and expert control.

Nothing could hide entirely the problems that resulted from the practice of placing settlers on remote lands still partially covered in stumps. The heavy equipment needed to clear out the stumps was gone. Halley recommended that the land be rough cleared of brush and logs and planted immediately, in the hopes that eventually the settlers would have enough money to clear out the stumps themselves. The image of cows grazing next to the remnants of once giant trees in the "stump farms" of Merville would become a familiar one among settlers and critics. One joke that circulated among the settlers told of a farmer who had asked for cattle with narrow horns, so that they could wander between the stumps more easily.

Moving into forest and logged-off lands also required some adjustments to accommodate older uses of the land. Favourite local hunting spots were now playgrounds for settlers' children. The farms in these areas had inadequate fencing and the houses, nestled under trees or behind towering stumps, were not clearly visible from a distance. The board was powerless to stop people hunting on unfenced land, however, and could only recommend placing warning signs in visible spots.[52] Children playing in an area where forestry, farming, recreation, and sometimes subsistence hunting were conducted alongside one another would just have to be careful. Halley was also concerned that the combination of the remnants from clearing operations and settlement over a wide area would pose a fire hazard. He recommended that one of the settlers be appointed fire warden, for "[w]hen the weather becomes hot, the stump piles and dried brush of this district will become a serious fire menace." The summer of 1920 saw a number of wood-waste fires.[53]

WINTER

Over the next two years, the system of progress loans was found to be lacking, plagued by insufficient capital and too much debt. Harvests were bad, which meant there was little capital to be obtained through the sale of agricultural products. Work was hard to come by. For many Merville farmers, going further into debt to the LSB was the only way they could obtain the cash they needed to purchase food and supplies and, ironically, to pay off their ever-mounting debts to the board.

In July 1920, Hanna Little, a representative of the Merville Branch of the Ladies Auxiliary of the Great War Veterans' Association, reported that there was "little or no money at all here." "Now we all know you must (especially with children) have a certain amount of cash," she said, for "grocery, milk and meat bills, as well as [to] buy clothing for (from 5 to 8 children) large families such as some have up here."[54] The harvest of 1920 did not help the situation. The potatoes were watery, and the hay was bad.[55] By November, four of the original settlers had abandoned the area; 126 remained. Development continued, fuelled by LSB loans. Barns and houses were built, the school continued to thrive, and a number of the men found work on the roads. Meanwhile, Halley hoped to improve community spirit by flooring the former cookhouse for dancing, and by helping the settlers obtain an electrical power system and a film operator for the projector and films donated by the YMCA.[56]

But by December, the limits of the new scheme were becoming apparent. Work slowed and sometimes stopped in bad weather. Rain washed out roads, and heavy winds blew the roof off an LSB shed and the Little family's barn. Eleven men collected paycheques for doing a little work on the roads, and fifteen others were out of work after being laid off by the Comox Logging Railway. Meanwhile, in the absence of good maps and survey markers, Halley and his crews were having trouble locating land that had already been worked on.[57] Poor road conditions were pushing up the costs of building materials. The rain hardly stopped the entire month, and lowland areas were flooded. Settlers could not "make a living with the few cows they possess," Halley explained, but "there is no work in the district, and to provide more cattle at the present time will not assist in any way because of the price of hay."[58] In desperation, Halley began loaning some settlers enough money to provide them with a small income. But it was clear that already some settlers' debts were too heavy to bear.[59]

January was little better. The settlers were not happy, Halley reported. In February, as winter eased, conditions improved slightly. The roads were still in bad shape, but work on clearing land and planting gardens had resumed. But Halley warned that a number of the settlers had already been loaned more money than the value of their farms warranted.[60]

In April, the board decided to deal with the problem of mounting indebtedness by cutting off the progress loan system. No further advances would be made, though money would still be available for selected projects and for the purchase of livestock. The original purpose of the loans had been to enable settlers to improve their land and build up a small amount of equity so that they could make a living for themselves; but this had not happened.[61] Halley, on the ground at Merville, was left to deal with the consequences of this failure. The discontinuation of the loan program cut the settlers off from their only reliable source of capital. Halley chastised the board for its decision: "However reasonable one's stand may be," Halley wrote, "it is very difficult to convince men with a family [of the reasonableness of the board's decision] when they can get no work and are faced with actual hunger, and this will be the case with a great many in this area, good men as well as others. There are very few men indeed in the area who have any money."[62]

In May, at the request of the Merville Community Association (the settlers' representatives), William Latta came to Merville to investigate conditions personally. Latta was the former commander of the 29th Battalion, an *Asia* man, and now a member of the LSB. He found that, of the families living there, sixty-five were "practically self-supporting," though fifty-six of these had outside work and only farmed in their "spare time." Other families were so in debt to the board or had such unpromising farms that he concluded the board could not give them any more money at all. Other settlers could not support themselves on their farms but showed promise and would be helped.[63] In July, Latta travelled to Merville again, this time to serve on a three-person committee charged with investigating conditions at the settlement.[64]

Latta's reports demonstrate the extent to which farm operations depended on household labour, and the extent to which the LSB seemed unaware of this. Of the sixty-five settlers whom he found to be almost self-supporting, all but nine "engaged in outside occupations ... and only do a little on their own farms in their spare time." Those settlers who were not at all self-supporting were almost all single men.[65] Presumably, only those able to rely on women's work were able to make a go of it. This is not surprising, since women's household production (of food in particular – through kitchen gardening, and tending to cows, poultry, and pigs) was critical to daily survival on most farms.[66] At Merville, as later inspectors discovered, women and children often ran the entire farm in the absence of the husband.[67] Yet the LSB worried little about the work of the farm wife, saving its money and advice for matters of clearing and planting cash crops. Certainly Latta and the board did not entirely ignore families. But the man was considered to be the linchpin of success, and his work was the work in need of modernizing. This attitude left single men in a difficult spot. Latta seemed unaware or unconcerned that single men would have little chance of becoming self-supporting, since most of the time, no one was working on his farm.

Throughout the summer, the settlers continued to build the infrastructure necessary for the community to function. Barns, chicken houses, sheds, and homes received settlers' attention, as did land clearing, fencing, and other improvements.[68] The fall harvest was more successful than the previous year's had been. Although the settlers lacked manure for fertilizer and were unable to cultivate their land properly, they were able to turn out a healthy garden crop, particularly of potatoes. A lack of humus in the soil (which UBC's Professor Boving had identified as a problem in 1919) hampered the growth of oats and field crops. But the clover crop was successful; as a result, it was able to sustain the 31 horses and 131 head of cattle now living in the settlement. As October approached, however, "the chief concern of Board officials and of settlers themselves" was (according to Latta's investigation) "how to live through the coming winter."[69] Many of the settlers had milk and vegetables but no cash for clothes, shoes, flour, or sugar. And their debts to the board were now coming due.

The settlers most deeply in debt were those with the most adequately supplied farms. They owed more money because the LSB had done more work on their farms during the initial development stage (and the LSB charged a percentage of the costs of this work to each farm). Further, as they had few large-scale improvements to make over the winter of 1920, these families had not been eligible for progress loans, which were secured on the value of future improvements.[70] In order to tide them over the winter, Halley had given them unsecured loans. Thus, farmers on developed lands typically owed more, and also carried a debt load that was detached from the value of their farms. These families, among whom the Littles were included, had debts that averaged $3,100. Married settlers on previously unimproved land, like the Clarks, tended to owe about half this amount. Single settlers, like Henry Curry, might owe half again that debt, or $700. A year later, having paid nothing towards their debts, the Littles owed $3,780.89, and the Clarks owed $1,578.99. Curry owed $1,370.90.[71]

A brief look at the financial dealings of Curry and the Littles in the fall of 1921 gives a sense of the bind in which the settlers found themselves. It also reveals some of the implications of the board's gendered definition of "farmer." In September, the board wrote to Curry, advising him that he would owe $136.15, including $24 of interest, on October 2. Curry had worked for the local sawmill over the summer, but the mill had not yet paid him, and he had no cash. Even when he received the cash from the mill, however, it went directly into paying local debts (for such things as board). He had nothing to offer the LSB. The board offered him a grace period of six months, in the meantime charging him only the $24 in interest. Desperate for cash, Curry took a job with the Comox Logging Railway, which paid him $2.60 per day, minus $1.25 per day to the company for board. He promised to repay the LSB with whatever was left over. As his wages did not cover his debts to the board, and as he had no one to work the farm, Curry was caught in a vicious cycle. Looking for a way out, he suggested that Halley sell his team of horses and keep the $100 deposit Curry had originally put down for them. Halley agreed, assuring the board that Curry was a good man, and proceeded to sell off part of Curry's farm.[72]

Meanwhile, Little began in September to sell calves, pigs, and chickens, and to issue invoices to the LSB, presumably to help pay down his debt. Little had high hopes, but like all the settlers, he was skating close to the edge and was short of cash. "I have been depending on drawing some money on the progressive loan to bring my place to where I could make enough to live on," he explained, and "I have had to put $100 into hay to carry me over the winter and as my cows do not freshen until ... February so I'll not have a cream cheque until the first of April." Of the $14 that the board had arbitrarily seized and applied to his debt, he would be "much obliged if you could forward same as it is these things I have to depend on for a living."[73]

Such problems continued to plague the settlers. In all of Merville that fall, only one farmer had paid all his debts and owned his land. Maxwell Smith's hopes that the LSB could produce financially self-sufficient settlements now seemed unrealistic. Four men were no longer living on their land, having been given permission to seek work elsewhere, while three other settlers were unaccounted for. In total, only 115 landholders (not including their families) remained in the area, down from 126 the year before.[74]

The winter gave no respite. January 1922 was bitterly cold. Road work was discontinued. At the end of the month, Halley wrote to Victoria in a mixture of anger and panic. The ground was frozen two feet down, and there was no work in the area. The settlers were destitute. The store was unwilling to run further credit for ten of the settlers and was planning to cut off the credit of others. Too much hay was being used to keep the livestock alive in the cold weather. "I will be quite unable to cope," Halley warned: "So far as I can see several settlers at an early date will actually be facing starvation. If you can procure no funds for assistance I cannot foresee how some of these people will be able to live."[75] But the board continued to put its hopes into making settlers self-sufficient. In early February, the board sent Halley a memo discussing various payment plans by which it could help with the cost of seed, cows, horses, and miscellaneous items. An exasperated Halley replied that it was "a difficult matter for me to make suggestions knowing that ... the great majority [of settlers] have no cash at all."[76]

Debt continued to dog the settlers. One wrote to the board in January and explained that he would not be able to pay what he owed as his entire income for the previous year did not amount to the total of the debt. He had earned almost nothing from his farm, and since November had been needed at home to attend to his eldest son, who had been ill.[77] Little offered the LSB $9 towards the interest on his loan, but told them that he would not be able to pay anything on the principal. In the spring of 1922, however, he borrowed more money for livestock, a team of horses, and a wagon.[78] Meanwhile, Halley had managed to reduce Curry's debt by $227, by selling off his horse and wagon.[79]

By the spring of 1922, then, the board that had been the major supplier of capital in the area was becoming the major absorber of capital. It moved from providing financial support to Merville to collecting farmers' money by helping them to sell off the equipment necessary to their work. Self-sufficiency – that is, living off the product and proceeds of one's own farm – had always been one of the selling points of soldier settlement. Yet bad soil, poorly-prepared land, a scarcity of time (particularly for single men) to work on farming, and the inevitable difficulties of cultivating new land resulted in poor harvests. The settlers could not support themselves in this way. More serious in a capitalist economy was the settlers' desperate lack of cash, due to the paucity of both local work and marketable agricultural products. The only source of capital for the settlers was the LSB, which meant debt for both the settlers and the government.

A Refusal to Mourn

By 1922, the board was growing tired of the situation, even as the settlers' committee, the Merville Community Association began to propose alternative solutions to the basic problems of land clearing and debt. In February, the settlers proposed another land-clearing scheme, whereby the board would loan them money and they would work cooperatively on each others' farms.[80] In April, they looked for relief from their debts by having them rolled into the long-term payments they were due to make on their land, and by the elimination of the partial cash payments required to acquire livestock and farm implements. The board rejected both proposals.[81]

The summer of 1922 was unusually hot, and crops suffered. Strawberries did well, though, and some settlers made some cash by selling cream and eggs to the creamery in the neighbouring town of Comox.[82] As the summer wore on, a series of forest fires broke out and burned steadily in the Comox Valley. In itself, this was hardly surprising: fires were a common occurrence in logged forests, the result of errant sparks from steam engines and the rich fuel source provided by the wood waste left behind by logging operations.

On 1 July the settlers gathered at Williams' Beach in the Kitty Coleman area for a Dominion Day picnic. They brought roasts and salads, breads, buns, cakes and pies, fruit, and lemonade. During dinner, a Ministry of Forests employee dropped by and recruited several men to help fight a forest fire that had broken out nearby on the lands of the International Timber Company. This particular fire was brought under control, but the woods north of town continued to burn. By 6 July, everywhere was parched and dusty. Around noon, a fierce wind came from the north, fanning the fires and driving them south. Hundreds of firefighters fought to contain the blaze, but burning bark and moss blew over their heads and ignited the forest behind them. By the afternoon, black smoke blotted out the sun, and bits of bark and leaves rained down on Merville.[83]

At six o'clock in the evening, a sudden wind changed the direction of the fire and drove it straight towards town. Lily Clark was three miles away from the townsite on her farm at Kitty Coleman. She remembered that "one moment the sky was radiantly, spotlessly blue, and the next there came a huge brown cloud from the northwest, in shape like a tremendous rose, the spreading petals of which were edged with glittering fire. It filled the whole sky in a few minutes, and the smell was terrible."[84] The fire swept south between the Island Highway and Headquarters Road, towards the Merville subdivision, burning down any farms in its path (see Figure 7). Then it moved into the town itself.

When he arrived back at his house in the town, LSB employee Geoffrey Capes found that Halley was off fighting the fire and that Halley's wife and children were taking refuge at his house. "I told everybody to get what they could and come out," he later wrote in his diary; "meanwhile I got my car out." Mrs. Halley, Nell Capes, and the children saved

7 "Burned Out Forest near Merville after a Fire Has Passed Through." This photo of the Merville fire highlights its destructiveness. Note the standing trees still left in the background, illustrating the seemingly random nature of the burning.

the Halley's dog, Shrapnell, a cat and two kittens, and Cape's terrier, Roughie. And, "in the hurry Nell brought out an old hairbrush worth nothing; the children each had a Kewpie doll. Nell also had the foresight to bring a bottle of whiskey; also my overcoat; and that was all any of us saved."[85] Capes drove out of town through thick smoke and high winds. He dropped his family and the Halleys in a field and told them to wait for him or, if he did not return, to head for Kitty Coleman. Then he returned to his house. Fighting through blinding smoke, he managed to save a packet of bonds, and then noticed the shopkeeper's truck parked outside the store. He left town again, found a volunteer to help rescue the truck, and returned once again to the smoke-choked settlement. When he finally returned to the field where he had left his family and the Halleys, he could hardly see through the smoke. He shouted and heard nothing. But Nell and Mrs. Halley, hearing the shout and thinking he was telling them to leave, took the animals and the children and started on the two-mile walk towards Kitty Coleman. Capes, meanwhile, searched Courtenay frantically before discovering (an hour or so later) what had become of them.

Much of the original centre of the settlement – the community hall, the LSB buildings, Halley's house, and Capes' house – burned to the ground. Then the wind shifted to the west, and the fire burned past the back of the general store as the shopkeeper rushed in to try to save his building. He and two friends threw buckets of well water on the sparks until the Courtenay fire brigade arrived. Private citizens from Courtenay drove cars up the Island Highway, picking up settlers who stumbled out of the fire and taking them down the road to safety.

Frank Little stayed behind on his farm northwest of the town, trying to save his house and animals. When his barn went up in flames at seven o'clock in the evening, Mrs. Little took the younger children to a neighbour's house, while Frank and his sons Dave and Wayne stayed behind to fight the fire. Wayne soon followed his mother, but Dave stayed with his father. Two hours later, Little and Dave smelled hair burning on cows in the field; Dave set off to chop down the fence and let them escape. When he did not return, Little decided that he must have continued on to a neighbour's house. In fact, Dave had been trapped by the blaze as he tried to get to Merville. A few yards from the Merville store he was overcome by the smoke and fainted. Dave was later found by firefighters, lying on the ground twenty feet from the edge of the burn. He was covered in burns and his lungs were destroyed; the men tried to carry him to hospital in Courtenay, but he died on the way there.[86]

Dave's death would be the only fatality. In the evening, the wind died down, the blaze slowed, and firefighters were able to build a firebreak. As night descended, the fire was brought under some semblance of control. Volunteers from Courtenay continued to gather up the remnants of the Merville community. Capes reached Halley on the phone and discovered that Halley had picked up their families on Kitty Coleman Road. They drove the women and children to a friend's house, gassed up their cars, and returned to town. They found that the fire had burned right up to the back of Shaw's store, but had spared the store along with the garage, the tea rooms, the school, the teacher's house, and the church. But the wood-shed directly behind the store had disappeared, and the blacksmith's shop, in the same block as the store and the other buildings, was completely destroyed. Capes and Halley found a crowd of people around the store and offered to drive them to Kitty Coleman, but most preferred to stay and take their chances. Capes evacuated a few people and then returned to the town, where he found the storekeeper serving soft drinks, tea, and food from his stores.

When Capes returned, he found Frank Little. "He was a wreck," he recalled, "his clothes torn, his face black. He was very cut up about Dave ... [he] staggered about like a drunken man and I helped him into the car, and drove him to Ault's place, where Mrs. Little and one of his girls were." To add to the turmoil, Wayne Little was also missing; Capes promised to find out what had happened to him. Later, he was able to phone the Lit-tles and reassure them that Wayne had survived. He had turned in the opposite direction from his brother, towards Headquarters, and was picked up on the road.[87]

Capes and others spent the next several days evacuating settlers at risk from a revival of the flames. Lily Clark reluctantly let Capes drive her and her two babies to Courtenay, where they spent four days waiting out the fires. Even after they returned, "the air every morning was so robbed of oxygen that it was painful to breathe." Clark "could not see our barn from the house (which is not fifty yards away) until about ten o'clock, by which time the sun had lifted the dreadful pall."[88] Not all the settlers were so lucky, as Clark well knew. In addition to the losses in the town, eighteen families and seven single men lost their homes, and five other settlers lost their barns. All the Land Settlement Board buildings, including the orig-inal structures at the townsite of Merville, were destroyed.[89] The farms of Henry Curry and the Clarks escaped unscathed. But the Littles, aside from losing Dave, also lost their barn, an outbuilding, fencing, a wagon, ten dairy cows, and personal belongings (see Figure 8).[90]

8   "Ruins of Residence after Forest Fire at Merville, BC"

In order to help settlers deal with these losses, the Merville and District Relief Committee was quickly formed. The committee was made up of prominent residents of Courtenay and Merville. The basement of the Presbyterian Church in Courtenay became a clothing distribution depot, and the Agricultural Hall became the central relief station. Volunteers served meals and put up tents as temporary accommodations for the refugees. By 20 July seventy to eighty people were eating at the hall, and twelve families were living in the tents.

The government also sent assistance. Premier Oliver, walking into a meeting of the relief committee the day after the fire, announced that his government would pay for temporary housing and reasonable relief costs, and would help settlers rebuild their homes and farms. More immediately important, a truck loaded with blankets and clothes arrived from Victoria. Having begun to meet their material needs, Mervillites and their supporters began to address the emotional and spiritual needs of the community as they gathered on Sunday to attend the funeral of Dave Little. The Anglican bishop of Columbia, who led the service, counselled courage and promised Mervillites "the support of the whole province in their brave fight against such repeated blows of fortune."[91]

The Merville fire was a disaster on a major scale. Over the course of two days, it burned 24,600 acres of forest, logged-off, and settled land; destroyed $163,155 worth of timber, railway equipment, buildings, and other property; and, of course, took one human life.[92] But it should not be called a natural disaster, the result of "blows of fortune." This would hide the extent to which the conditions for this disaster were set up by human use of the land in the Comox Valley. In fact, the fire has much to tell us about the sort of human–environment relationship brought about by this attempt to build an alternative modernity. On one hand, the strenuous efforts to re-establish the settlers demonstrates the power of the alternative modernity ideal. Belief in country living sent the families back to the land, armed with the best available scientific understanding of how to deal with the burned-out territory. On the other hand, the causes of the fire themselves indicate some of the limits of the ideal.

Oliver's government demonstrated quickly its commitment to the re-establishment of Merville by sending LSB district representative Col. Latta to the site, along with another senior bureaucrat charged with assessing the damage and coordinating relief efforts.[93] In doing so, these men carried out in part just the sort of disaster relief expected of the state. But the immediate commitment to resettling the soldiers suggests the power of the countryside ideal. What could not be allowed to be destroyed, according to the local paper, was "the thousand and one little things that man and his mate laboriously build up through the years and call 'home,' that Anglo-Saxon word that has no equivalent in other languages." The paper warned that "it's a man's job, this going back to the ashes and a settler should think deeply before he decides that his vocation is indeed the land. But as far as we can ascertain most of them never had any other thought but to go back. Merville is now their home. To such men the state must be generous for they are the backbone of any nation." Despite Merville's difficulties, the editor still saw the town as key to the building of a prosperous province.[94] That settlers were understood to be male and assumed to be breadwinners was important to this image. Men, particularly men responsible for others, could not be expected to back down from a fight with nature.

Convinced of the worth of their project and determined not to let circumstances defeat them, the settlers prepared to rebuild Merville. Concerned that provincial government funds would be limited, they publicly requested that the relief camp be shut down as a cost-saving measure. In its place, they suggested that the government compensate Courtenay families for putting up Mervillites, and begin rebuilding houses at Merville as quickly as possible. Meanwhile, various entertainers from the area staged a concert at the Agricultural Hall in order to lift the spirits of the homeless.[95]

On 3 August, it was announced that the relief camp would be shut down and most of the settlers would return to the land.[96] The weather was still hot and dry, though the threat of fires had receded. It had been a long summer. The local paper was poetic: "For three months 'the gentle dew of heaven' had been absent from this our earth." No less than $20,000 had been spent paying firefighters in the Comox area alone, and there was a "smoke pall in the air and any breeze we may have [was] laden with the hot breath of burning timber."[97] There was some talk that the fire had destroyed the soil at Merville – a claim hotly contested by the LSB, which explained that, instead, it had probably helped. The fire had left a bed of ashes in which grass seed should grow well, and "quickly and thoroughly cleared land that would have been brought into such a condition only by the expenditure of a great deal of time and labor. On the whole, Captain Halley believes the fire has been an excellent thing for the Merville district and its settlers."[98]

The board decided to take advantage of the clearing job the fire had done for them by seeding the entire area with a mixture of grasses, free of charge to settlers.[99] In some severely burned areas, the fire had left large amounts of salt on the surface; the reseeding of these areas had to wait until heavy rains washed the salt deeper into the soil. For the most part, though, the fire presented the settlers with a golden opportunity to win the war with "undesirable" plant life. Seeded grasses would grow before other plants; livestock grazing would ensure their victory. The board was more selective in assisting individual settlers. "We do not wish settlers to go back onto places where there is no reasonable prospect of their making good," the Premier declared shortly after the fire, "nor do we desire those who have shown their unfitness in the past."[100] In general, the board pledged to rebuild settlers' homes, offering settlers a credit equal to the amount spent building the homes in the first place. Settlers were expected to do the rebuilding, although all arrangements for "plans, specifications, supplies, material, employment of labour, etc."[101] still had to be approved by Halley. The board was willing to replace stock, implements, and plants for which they were owed money, and it promised to rebuild all burnt fencing. Some settlers, however, were offered an amount only just equal to the board's equity in their home; others were offered assistance in finding new work. Presumably, the latter were the settlers whom the board felt showed the least promise as future farmers.

By the end of the summer of 1922, conditions had been set for a return to normalcy. Yet the spectre raised by the fire did not go away, for this had been no ordinary burn. The Merville fire was a magnitude of "which even the oldest settlers have had no previous experience." One official commented that in his twenty years of experience with forest fires, he had "never seen anything of a similar nature."[102] The fire had attacked seemingly at random, reducing some areas to ash while leaving immediately adjacent areas untouched. The fire had ignited other spot fires, as hot, dry winds carried burning brands ahead of the main blaze. The Merville fire was, in fact, an especially intense type of blaze, the sort of "firestorm" that can occur where forest, logging operations, and new settlements meet.[103] And it did not go away easily. Southeast winds fanned the blaze into renewed life one week after the fire at Merville. After burning down a mill in the neighbouring town of Bevan and causing the residents to evacuate, the fire died out only when the winds did. Government investigators had no real explanation for this, suggesting vaguely that "there must have been something in the nature of a local cyclonic disturbance."[104]

A subsequent coroner's investigation and a civil case, both arising from Dave Little's death, considered a wider range of factors. In the process, they questioned whether the fire could be considered an Act of God or if it was, in fact, the result of human agency. The inquest concluded that the fire had begun as an amalgam of various fires, with a variety of origins –

some were slash fires burning out of control, one had started on a local ranch, others had been lit by sparks from logging locomotives. Some of the blazes originated on lands controlled by the Comox Logging Railway, others by the rival International Timber Company. Some had been lit originally as far back as the spring, but had smouldered and flared up since then.[105] This complex picture made determining who started the fire very difficult, if not impossible.

In his judgment on the civil case, though, the Honourable Mr. Justice D.A. McDonald declared that the immediate source of the fire was irrelevant, and he rejected as well the Comox Logging Railway's argument that forest fires were inevitable and that unusually high winds and dry conditions were responsible for the blaze. Instead, Justice McDonald focused on the deadly combination of sparks and fuel that the Comox Logging Railway's operations had fostered. The company's operations, covering about ten thousand acres immediately north of the Merville settlement, regularly left behind unmarketable logs, stumps, trees, and bracken on logged-off lands. Its rail lines were laid through narrow openings in the woods wide enough for only the tracks. Over the years, the company had allowed wood waste from clearing operations, and from the railway's timber-loading process, to pile up next to the tracks. The company's locomotives had no spark arrestors until May of 1922 and, according to witnesses, sparks from Comox Logging Railway steam engines had started one of the original critical fires in April – before the arrestors were installed. Another fire was ignited in June by sparks escaping from a faulty spark arrestor. The winds of 6 July swept the various fires in the area into each other, igniting ten million board feet of debris lying on the Comox Logging Railway lands north of the settlement. McDonald ruled that the company was negligent in producing a dangerous fire-prone environment.[106]

The presence of settlers in this dangerous environment only made matters worse. The dried timber used to build the houses, barns, and fences of the Merville settlers served as ready fuel for the hungry fire. Farms immediately south of timber stands suffered particularly badly. As well, settlers did not have the ability to adequately protect themselves. According to the Comox Logging Railway, settlers had not cleared the snags from near their homes,[107] and had not created proper fire breaks, allowing wood waste to gather around their homes. A number of the settlers did not have wells, and very few had pumps. The need to construct firebreaks speaks to the difficulties of settling in a working forest. But more important was the desperate situation of the many settlers who simply did not have the time to clear their lots properly or the money to buy pumps. A number of settlers, in fact, were not available to protect their homes because they had been working on the roads and – ironically – firefighting.[108]

The Merville fire occurred when three critical developments converged: logging provided fuel for the fires, the railways provided the initial spark, and the Merville settlement placed additional fuel and people in the blaze's path.[109] The ideal of the modern countryside had been predicated on the ability of scientists and planners to manage the relationship between settlers and the environment. The Merville fire suggested that the ability of scientists and planners to do so was limited. They had aimed to establish independent capitalist farmers in an idealized countryside, but they had achieved instead something else: an unstable, fire-prone landscape. Now, not only did the modern countryside face a chronic shortage of capital and the economic and environmental difficulties posed by poor soil and land clearing, but the fire at Merville suggested additional environmental constraints: the problem of managing nature, and of predicting and dealing with the consequences of environmental change.

DECLENSION

The great fire marked a turning point in the history of Merville: never strong, the settlement now proved unable to recover. Through the rest of the 1920s, financial and environmental pressures forced many of the settlers to abandon their farms. Not surprisingly, given the losses in crops and infrastructure due to the fire, the following winter was again hard. Late in 1922, the Merville and District Relief Committee distributed cheques, bales of clothing, blankets, and additional money for Christmas, including $235 to the Little family.[110] By the end of January 1923, most of the settlement was in debt to the local storekeeper, to a total of $4,000.[111]

The rest of the decade saw continual reassessments of land prices and debt repayment conditions, as the government attempted to recover some of the costs associated with Merville and the settlers attempted to establish their farms and gain legal title to their lands. The events of 1923 set the pattern. Banding together with the Courtenay Board of Trade, the settlers charged the government with failing in its moral duty to them. They had been told that the land would be sold at cost, that they would receive ten cleared acres and ten more acres rough cleared, a house, and a barn. Instead, the development program had been abandoned, and the settlers were saddled with overpriced land. They asked that the land be re-appraised and sold, subject to thirty-year mortgages. Though resentful at what it saw to be the settlers' lack of gratitude, the government agreed to the suggestion that a three-member re-appraisal board be appointed: one member would be chosen by the settlers, one by the government, and one by both.[112] As a result of this board's report, the government agreed to reduce the settlers' overall debt by a total of $100,000.[113]

Frank Little got through the next winter by working for the board, while still receiving payments from his progress loan.[114] In March, a fire burned down the Merville garage, which was to have been part of the modern highway and auto system connecting Merville with its surroundings.[115] As spring came in 1923, the landscape of the Comox Valley once again demonstrated its instability. An April fire burned out nine families in the Kitty Coleman area. Another fire, fanned by strong winds and a lack of rain, burned out a large section of woods and eventually two lots in the Merville area.

Under financial pressure and possibly beginning to realize that the settlement of Merville was not to be, the LSB showed nothing like the support it demonstrated after the larger fire of 1922. It refused to re-seed any of the burned areas, and in May, it laid off Halley and Capes, the only LSB employees still in the area. The board had become to Merville what it would be to all the lands it controlled throughout BC from the end of the 1920s to the 1970s: a landlord, and little more.[116]

In January 1924, the LSB declared that it had lost $314,293.84 on Merville, though it did note that more than one hundred farms had been established: "Where four years ago there was not a furrow turned or a single human inhabitant," there were now "families ... established on the land in homes of their own."[117] In the opinion of the board, Little was doing well, while Curry spent most of his time working outside the farm.[118] George and Lily Clark were struggling but succeeding on their lot by Kitty Coleman beach. George cleared and planted by hand. "The soil was very poor and full of rocks," their daughter recalled, "but they managed to raise vegetables, fruit, chickens and put in an orchard." Still, George was forced to work in the lumber community of Powell River, across Georgia Strait on the BC mainland. Lily was left with two babies and no telephone, electricity, or running water.[119]

In the summer, the board formally foreclosed on some settlers who had already abandoned their farms.[120] In the Merville town centre, the former tea rooms had shut down, and the leaseholder, Ann Simpson, could find no one to rent them. There were still 104 settlers in the area, though not all were the original settlers.[121] In May, Justice McDonald awarded damages in the case of the Merville fire to forty-seven settler families. The Littles, who were already well insured, received just $150 in damages, but were awarded a $2,500 personal injury award for the death of their son.[122]

By April of 1925, there were sixty-eight lots for sale in the Merville area, ranging from unimproved land to those with a house, barn, clearing, fencing, and a well.[123] Though the Littles were doing well, like Curry, they had made no payments by early 1926 towards the purchase of their land.[124] That year, Frank and Wayne Little began working for the Comox Logging Railway.[125] By 1929, there were still sixty of the original settlers left at Merville, though only twenty-four of these had managed to make the payment required by their new, reduced mortgages of 1928.[126] By 1944, fifty of the original settlers were still in the area, including Curry and the Clarks (who had purchased their lots) and the Littles (who had an agreement to purchase). Altogether, 119 farms were occupied.[127]

In 1936, Hanna Little died; the next year, Frank re-married. He lived until 1962, dying at the age of eighty-seven. Meanwhile, George Clark had fallen from a roof while working part-time as a carpenter; injuries from this accident, in conjunction with his injuries from the war, left Clark semi-disabled. Lily made money teaching music and playing for dances, and she also formed an orchestra and played music at the church until 1949, when she had a stroke. The Clarks stayed in Merville until 1962, when they sold their home on the beach at Kitty Coleman and moved to a home for the aged in Courtenay.[128]

Merville continued, and even experienced something of a revival in the 1960s as a back-to-the-land community. Today, the area contains a number of farms, hemmed in by forest. In the end, the experience of the soldier settlers became a lesson in perseverance and survival. Writing in 1959, Lily Clark wanted mainly "to show the lighter side of our lives ... to point out the gallant determination of the settlers and their wives to cling to their hard won acres ... I honestly respect and revere [them] as the very 'salt of the earth.' I suggest it would be a good thing to keep a record of the old timers, so that their memory may be kept green, long beyond this, their fortieth year of residence in Merville."[129]

Any place that can produce such warmth and generosity cannot be labelled a mistake or a failure. As the LSB would sometimes point out, Merville worked in the sense that it established farms and homes. Yet none of the larger goals associated with the settlement were met. Rather than leading the way to a new form of settlement in planned rural communities, Merville cast doubt on the ideas of its creators. Rather than providing a stable home and a good living for men who had served their country bravely, and for the families of these men, the project abandoned them all to a difficult life with little monetary reward. It did not turn out to provide a new, more modern version of the old dream of a rural anchor to liberal capitalism in BC.

Merville had been an experiment to establish an alternative modernity, a rural version of modern life. At the heart of this alternative modernity was the cultural image of an idyllic countryside inhabited by independent farmers, made more livable by modern technology, and more productive (and so more profitable) by modern techniques of scientific agriculture. This alternative modernity would be created through scientific land settlement. The failure of Merville must be understood in terms of the various components of this cultural, economic, and environmental vision. Culturally, the project attempted to impose an idea of the countryside that was (for all the rhapsodizing about green fields nestled in the mountains) rooted in old ideals of the English countryside. While it worked for the eastern parts of North America, this view of nature was difficult to impose on the thick coastal, forested environment typical of coastal BC. One solution to this problem was the managing of environmental change in a scientific way. Yet the techniques of scientific land settlement did not account for the various environmental factors that would influence the settlement process. The size and shape of stumps caused complications. Surveying and clearing operations could not adequately manage for the variety of soils in the Merville area. The surveyor gave some settlers very large farms; those organizing land clearing sometimes had to leave good soil covered by stumps. Variations in weather were not adequately considered. The environment proved to react unpredictably to the settlers' attempts to reshape it, the great fire being only the most spectacular example of this.

Environmental difficulties simply added to what would still have been significant economic problems. Simply, the settlement was designed to deal with unemployed ex-soldiers. The soldiers had little in the way of capital – a necessary requirement of starting a farm. Successful agriculture demands that the farmer get to know various soil differences and microclimates of the area, a process that takes time. This is particularly true of a farm on marginal soil covered with massive stumps. At the same time, there was relatively little work to be found outside the farm. If the government had been willing to support its new liberal ideas with the appropriate funding, this problem may have been overcome (as it was in the South Okanagan – see Chapter 5). But as Oliver's and Smith's comments suggested at the founding of the LSB, the government had never intended to take on the funding of large projects. The LSB's projects were to be self-supporting; the government expected to be reimbursed for any expenditures made on behalf of the settlers. Anything else would have destroyed the classical liberal individualism that still lay at the heart of the government's version of new liberalism and the alternative modernity. Such a liberal vision proved inadequate for the making of a new countryside at Merville.

4

Creating Order at Sumas

L ATE IN 1919, A HIGH-POWERED GROUP of politicians and bureaucrats, consisting of Premier John Oliver, Minister of Agriculture E.D. Barrow, and William Latta of the Land Settlement Board (LSB), travelled outside Vancouver and into the agricultural area of the Fraser Valley. At the little town of Huntingdon, near Chilliwack, Oliver and the others met with a group of local landowners. On the agenda was Sumas Lake, or, to be more specific, the LSB's plans to do away with it. With the approval of the landowners and the agreement of mainstream opinion in the province, the LSB would drain Sumas Lake.

Draining the lake was an old idea. Plans were first proposed in the 1870s. For those who favoured an orderly, settled countryside, Sumas Lake was an ongoing problem. For one thing, it was hardly orderly. Subject to the seasonal flooding of several rivers, it was unusually variable. Over the course of a year, it might be anywhere from nine to thirty-six feet deep; maps could agree only on its general outline. In 1894, what is still the largest flood on record on the Fraser River caused the lake to double in area, covering both of the local Indian reserves in water.[1] The lake was also simply a barrier to resettlement. Nestled between Sumas Mountain on the north and Vedder Mountain and the US border on the south, it was skirted by roads and contained, most of the time, by a series of dikes over which a railway track ran. In a province with little flat, clear, and arable land, Sumas Lake occupied a large chunk of potentially prime farmland not sixty miles from Vancouver (see Maps 1 and 3).

The LSB planned to "reclaim" the lands under the lakewater for farming and also to impose order on the lake and this part of the Fraser River. John Oliver's purpose in visiting the area, however, was not to trumpet the good news to the owners: he had come in order to deliver a warning. He wanted to dissociate his government from any responsibility for the project's ultimate cost. Though the government was to put up the funds for the scheme, project costs were to be covered by the current landowners in the area and by the sale of the reclaimed lands. The secretary at the Huntingdon meeting recorded Oliver as stating that "the general impression was that the Government were backing the scheme; he was here to right the people's minds re this point and denied any such implication; stating plainly in the following language 'The Provincial Government is taking no responsibility whatever for this scheme; understand that clearly.'"[2] The Sumas Reclamation Project, to be run by the LSB, would be financed under the same cost-recovery arrangements Oliver had set out for the LSB at its founding. These arrangements reflected the ideal of the liberal individual, which remained at the heart of the government's version of new liberalism and of Oliver's own agrarian beliefs.[3]

Oliver later claimed that he issued a more elaborate warning than what the minutes of the Huntingdon meeting recorded. "I pointed out ... [to them] the absolute unreliability of engineers' estimates," he claimed; "I pointed out to them the past experience of diking indebtedness in the Fraser Valley. I went further than that, and I pointed out to them that as a result of the war, costs of labor, cost of material, had increased enormously."[4] If Oliver really did say all this, then he showed great prescience, for the Sumas project quickly became an enormous financial disaster and an ongoing source of controversy. Though Sumas Lake was drained and new farmland was created out of the former lakebed, the project failed to create security for the farmers on the edges of the lake. It failed as well to create the landscape of small, idyllic farms pictured in LSB promotional material, or to diversify the province's food supply by turning these lands to the production of grains. The goal of the project was to bring order to this area of the Fraser Valley, as part of the creation of a countryside appropriate to the vision of an alternative modernity: a well-ordered, privately-owned, productive, rural form of nature. These were goals of the state on which the local landowners agreed, for despite Oliver's warnings, the landowners did eventually agree to finance the project. Further, the landowners held on to the idea that the project represented progress, even after it became clear that it had helped them little, if at all. But while it is tempting to point to the Sumas Lake project as another failure of a state attempt to improve the human condition, we must look beyond the state to contradictions in the ideal of a modern countryside – an ideal that united the Liberals and the landowners.

DISORDER

By 1919, the draining of Sumas Lake and the protection of the surrounding lands from flooding was a long-hoped-for project. It acquired the political will and adequate funding only when the return of the soldiers coincided with the new, postwar commitment of the Liberal government to active management of land settlement. This was not a soldier settlement project. The Land Settlement Board had always indicated it did more than just soldier settlements, and Sumas reflected this. But it was because of the soldiers that the LSB was able to bring to a boil an idea that had been simmering since the nineteenth century.

The agreement of the white male settler-farmers that mostly made up the local landowners was also crucial. In focusing on this group, though, we should not forget that the landowners were not the only inhabitants of the Sumas region, just the ones with the closest relationship to the levers of political power. Other stories about the lake could be, were, and are told, as has been vividly demonstrated by Laura Cameron's multi-narrative of Sumas Lake's history, *Openings: A Meditation on History, Method and Sumas Lake*. And even the experience and understanding of the lake by white male settler-farmers was quite different from that of state planners and engineers. For, while planners and engineers assumed the superiority, if not the naturalness, of an orderly nature, everyone in the Sumas area had learned to live with the fundamentally disorderly creature that was Sumas Lake.

The strongest factor in Sumas Lake's disorder was its connection to the Fraser River. The great river fed it tidal effects from the Pacific Ocean, and its regular floods swelled the lake as well. The head of the Fraser is in the Rocky Mountains near Jasper and the continental divide, on the eastern edge of British Columbia. Initially flowing northwest, it turns south near Prince George, crossing the rolling, arid expanse of the interior plateau before it meets the mountains. At Lytton, the Thompson River (itself the result of the joining of the Thompson and the North Thompson at Kamloops) flows into the Fraser, and the resulting very large river cuts the spectacular Fraser Canyon through the mountains to Hope. Here the river turns west into the alluvial floodplain of the lower Fraser Valley. Near Vancouver, it splits into two large arms and flows around the Vancouver suburb of Richmond and into Georgia Strait. Along the way to the coast, the Fraser picks up soil and debris, and the river is brown and muddy-looking as it traverses the Lower Mainland.

This description of the modern-day Fraser, however, hides as much as it reveals. It enables us to entertain a view of nature as timeless, the Fraser River as unchanging. But nature has a history, as any number of environmental historians have reminded us. The history of Sumas Lake confirms this argument. Every summer, the Fraser rises and (often) threatens to flood parts of the lower valley. But the distant sources of the Fraser, the river's large tributary (the Thompson), and weather complications in the mountain ranges of BC make these floods unpredictable. Flood waters are the result of melting in the Rocky Mountains and the Cariboo Range, through which the Fraser flows. Snow melt can also increase water flow at the head of the Thompson River. The critical element is hot weather in the interior of the province, which produces a large snow melt. Should cold weather in the late winter in the mountains, leading to a large snow pack, be followed by hot weather in May, the conditions for floods on the lower Fraser are set. The timing of the peak flood on the Thompson is also critical. Generally the Thompson's floodwaters pass through the lower Fraser before the flood from the Fraser's own headwaters, as the Thompson is farther south (thus the snow melts earlier) and closer to the Fraser Valley. Occasionally, however, the high waters of these two rivers coincide, as happened in 1894 and again in 1948. The result is a large flood in the Fraser Valley and the river delta south of Vancouver city.[5] The 1894 flood rose to twenty-five feet, nine inches on the high water gauge at Mission, causing millions of dollars of damage to homes and businesses, and prompting the government to begin diking works.[6]

So the Fraser was not constant and unchanging. It changed level and character over the course of a year, and from year to year. Its tendency to flood at irregular levels and unpredictable times, and its tendency to meander across its floodplain and occasionally cut new channels for itself, was a wholly natural part of the way the river worked. Such was true of other rivers in the area as well. In 1890, the Vedder River, which up until this point had flowed into the Fraser River to the east of Sumas Lake, cut a new channel for itself. It turned west into the lowlands near the Fraser and flowed into Sumas Lake on its southwestern side. Engineers planning the demise of the lake now had to contend with a much larger body of water.[7]

The changing conditions of the Chilliwack River, from which the Vedder flowed, also complicated the behaviour of Sumas Lake. The Sumas River was comparatively regular. It drained mostly flat land, its levels rising due only to rain, and thus did what was expected of it: it swelled in the winter. Under hot summer conditions, when the Fraser was likely to flood, the Sumas dried up. The Chilliwack was another matter, and flooding on this river presented a different problem. Compared to the source of the Fraser, the source of the Chilliwack was in a mountainous area lower in elevation, further south by four hundred miles, and affected by temperate winds from the Pacific. Although melting snow did produce some flood waters in the spring, the real problem came in the late fall or early winter when a combination of rainfall and new snowfall melted by warm winds raised river levels. Aside from flooding, the rainfall had two other problematic effects. The rains could also raise the Fraser, while at the same time causing the Chilliwack to choke with debris such as gravel, sand, silt, and even trees. While not a problem for Sumas Lake, this debris was an obvious concern for anyone hoping to build a dike.[8]

Fed by floods and pulled about by tides, Sumas Lake was intermittently shallow and small, large and deep, and everything in between. Parts of it were swampy and its edges were ill defined. Yet it was never the marshy wasteland that development boosters said it was. When the lakewaters receded, fields of blue grass sprang up in the silty soil. The grasslands of Sumas Prairie attracted osprey, bald eagles, flycatchers, and great blue herons, while the waters themselves were home to migratory salmon, round-fish, and sturgeon. At the time white settlers arrived, hazelnut trees and wild strawberries also grew in the area. English naturalist John Keast Lord, visiting the area as part of the International Boundary Commission in the late 1850s, described a "pretty" and "picturesque" site. Barbara Beldam, granddaughter of an early white settler, claimed that the area must have appeared to her grandfather as "the proverbial Garden of Eden."[9]

Those living in and around the lake accommodated the lake's variability. For example, the lake's floods figured into the teachings of the Stó:lō people. One story told of how a group of people survived a severe flood by tying their canoes to Sumas Mountain. Gradually the waters receded, and when this happened *Xexa:ls* (the transformers) visited those who had survived the flood and taught them "the right way to live, work and pray."[10] People of the Sumas First Nation caught sturgeon using a weir on Sumas River, gathered *wapato* (wild potato) on the prairie lands around the lake's edge, and killed ducks for food. The people of the Sumas First Nation were also accustomed to the clouds of mosquitoes that arrived in the summer: they built a village on stilts in the middle of the lake, where the mosquitoes did not go. Later, First Nations farmers grazed cattle on the borderlands, as did the white settlers who began to arrive in the 1860s.

Because the lands adjacent to the lake were flooded regularly, they did not pass into private hands, and so could function as a commons. Local people also fished and hunted in and around the lake and used it for boating, swimming, and skating. Flooding could be taken in stride – Laura Cameron quotes one early white settler, Mrs. Fadden, describing the great flood of 1894: "the water was 'spreading over garden, over orchard, quite high. Fine day.'" Mrs. Fadden also recalled how "wild roses used to bloom just at the top of the water. And there was the very lovely perfume that came from them as the water came up to them."[11]

For a time, local people were allowed to continue with this negotiated and subtle interaction with Sumas Prairie. This relationship, however, always existed within a set of larger structures that defined the relationship between this place and these people, and the wider world that encompassed them. The presence of white settlers was a sign of this changing relationship, the result of colonialism and a set of land laws and ideologies designed to facilitate and justify the settlers' presence. This was a world in which white settlers were at home and the Stó:lō were not. Though we can see that white farmers and Native people often used the lake and its surrounding lands in similar ways – grazing their cattle on its grasses, hunting for deer and birds, fishing and vacationing – their differing relationship with the Canadian and British Columbian states meant that the Stó:lō's access to the land would diminish as that of their white neighbours increased.

In 1858, as miners moved up the Fraser in search of gold, Gov. James Douglas had reserves of between 400 and 9,600 acres laid out for the Stó:lō in the Fraser Valley. As far as the colonial government was concerned, these lands were all that the Stó:lō now controlled out of all the lands they had once lived in. Yet even this land was too much according to the governments that followed Douglas. The Fraser Valley contained simply too much good farmland for it to be left in the control of Native people. In 1867, Chief Commissioner of Lands and Works Joseph Trutch had the Stó:lō reserves reduced in area by 92 percent, leaving only three small reserves in the vicinity of Sumas Lake: the Upper Sumas, Aylechootlook, and Sumas Cemetery Reserves.[12] As well, Native peoples were excluded from pre-empting property in BC. Despite various efforts to revise them, Trutch's reserves largely remain in place today.

With the land now cleared for white settlement, the 1870s saw the first of many schemes to control the fitful nature of the Fraser and the other, lesser rivers in the area, and to do away with the lake entirely. The first act of the provincial legislature to regulate diking at Sumas was passed in 1878. This act also allowed for reclamation work in neighbouring Chilliwack and Matsqui. Gilbert Malcolm Sproat of the Joint Indian Reserve Commission, formed to settle the question of Native reserves in BC, protested on behalf of the Matsqui Band. Noting that local First Nations people had not been consulted, Sproat pointedly stated that they "must have winter and summer grazing land ... reasonable area and their fishing places ... Is this unreasonable for a law abiding people whose land title is inextinguished?"[13] Sproat's protest was cut short; the provincial government assured the Dominion that Native people would benefit from reclamation, as it would improve the value of their land.[14] This argument would become a standard justification for seizing First Nations land and, later, for justifying the expense of reclamation works. It was a largely meaningless argument, however – one that did not consider how the land had been and would be used. Though whites as well as Natives would lose their use of the prairie commons for grazing and the lake for hunting and swimming, the white farmers were in a far better position to take advantage of any benefits that reclamation might bring. As Sproat saw, the Stó:lō, confined to small reserves and existing on the political, social, and cultural margins of white society, would suffer more than benefit from reclamation.

ORDER

The 1878 act was amended four times, then superseded by other acts in the 1890s. A government-sponsored scheme in 1894 saw further plans drawn up, tenders issued, and bids accepted, only to have the work cancelled due to lack of funds.[15] The twentieth century saw three serious attempts to drain the lake, not including the LSB's, all of which ultimately failed due to unwillingness or inability to commit the necessary funds. In 1905 the Sumas Development Company of Seattle proposed redirecting the Vedder River back into its old channel. However, this would have created a violent current needing large dikes to contain it. Local owners, afraid of a breach in the dikes, protested. A new plan that would have diverted the river into a different channel met their approval, but financing failed.

The most hopeful of the three schemes came along three years later, when the BC Electric Company became interested in the Sumas problem. BC Electric was the province's largest corporation at the time, running the streetcar and interurban system in Vancouver and providing much of the electricity for the Lower Mainland. It had a corporate interest in being rid of Sumas Lake, in that the waters almost entirely cut off the route for the corporation's planned extension of its interurban lines to Chilliwack. In the end, though, the corporation's London head office decided to abandon the attempt, in favour of an interurban line that sat on top of a dike snaking around the southern shore of the lake (see Map 3). In 1914 the L.M. Rice Company, also of Seattle, went so far as to register plans and prepare a table of the assessments to be levied on local owners. However the Canadian government held title to the lands under Sumas Lake, as part of the "Railway Belt" lands conveyed to the Dominion to pay for the Canadian Pacific Railway. They refused to grant title to the lands until the works were completed, but the Rice Company's financing depended on having clear title before starting work.[16]

Throughout these developments, local landowners maintained formal support for the various schemes. In 1893, legislation had created a board known as the Sumas Dyking Commissioners. This board, which reported to the landowners, officially oversaw all diking schemes. Thus, the landowners were formally in charge of all diking plans. This situation was further complicated by the passage of the Land Settlement and Development Act (by which the Land Settlement Board was created). A section of this act authorized the LSB to act as diking commissioners. In 1917, Minister of Lands Duff Pattullo suggested to E.D. Barrow, Minister of Agriculture, that the LSB could take over as Sumas Dyking Commissioners if local landowners were to petition the board to do so.[17] It is not clear what subsequent role the government might have played in mobilizing the landowners, and clearly some landowners were more excited about the project than others. The LSB questioned landowners who had not signed the petition; one of them, Joseph Schmidt, stated his opinion that those leading the charge for reclamation were "educated men and talk like a streak and put things in a light to further their purposes." He was also concerned about how the project would be paid for and whether the government would assume financial responsibility. Even Schmidt, though, thought the diking project would be an improvement to the area. "I myself have more lowland than highland and if the dyke is a success I have a good share in it," he explained, "but I am doing well as things are and will not venture too much to be harassed and embarrassed with extraordinary taxes."[18]

Schmidt believed there would be little opposition to the diking plan. Sure enough, an October petition requested that the diking commissioners sever their contact with L.M. Rice and company, and that the LSB take over. Thus in February 1918, the LSB officially accepted the role of Sumas Dyking Commissioners, which put it in charge of the reclamation of the Sumas lands.[19] By taking on the role of diking commissioners, technically a separate body from the LSB, the board ensured it could not be held

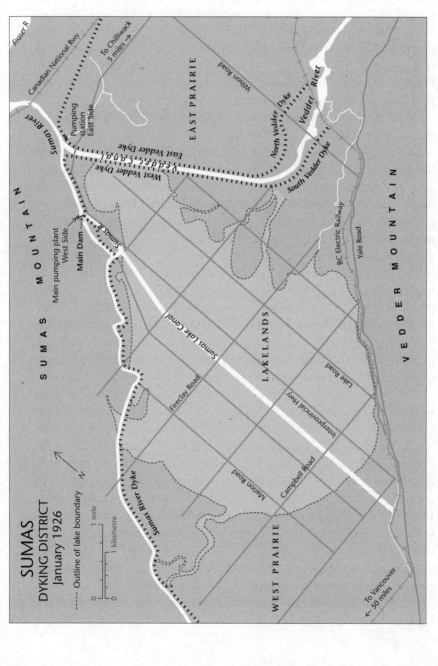

MAP 3   Sumas dyking district. Dashed lines show the outline of the former lake. Note the Fraser River in the top right corner.

legally responsible for the cost of the reclamation project. Meanwhile, Barrow kept up landowner interest in the scheme by organizing a conference to discuss the mosquito problem. The conference was held in September, following an especially bad mosquito season. Barrow declared that it would be "criminal neglect" to not deal with the problem now, and marshaled Dominion Entomologist Gordon Hewitt and Hewitt's chief assistant in BC to give expert testimony in support of lake drainage as the only truly effective solution. The previous year, points out Laura Cameron, Hewitt's assistant had suggested biological control measures as well, but now was fully in support of drainage.[20]

The new diking commissioners immediately hired engineers to review and revise the plans drawn up for earlier attempts. The final plan was very similar to the one that had been proposed by BC Electric. Key was the diversion of the Vedder River into the Fraser (see Map 3). The Vedder, with its disturbing ability to change its own course (and thus alter nature itself), was the most disorderly component of the Sumas Lake area. The river would be intercepted at the point where it cut through the embankment on which sat the BC Electric line. From the embankment, two dikes would be built, one on each side of the river. These would curve northwards and become the East and West Vedder Dykes, diverting the Vedder into the Sumas River near to where the Sumas joined the Fraser. At this point, the East Vedder Dyke was to connect with a dike running along the southern edge of the Fraser. The West Vedder Dyke connected to the Sumas River High Level Dyke, which in turn connected with the main dam in the Sumas River. The dam was designed to keep the flood waters of the Fraser from backing up the Sumas River and flowing into the lake.

The Vedder dikes had to be designed to contain a stream flow of up to twenty-seven thousand cubic feet per second. Further, as the newly diverted Vedder now ran into the Sumas River and thus into the Fraser, the dikes had to be made large enough to withstand flood water backing up the Vedder Canal. Finally, as the canal ran through low ground for most of its length, the dikes had to be larger than any other dikes on the project. The canal was to be three hundred feet wide and fifteen to twenty feet deep, fifty-eight feet thick, with one-hundred-foot-wide protective earth walls (or berms) inside each dike. It was to carry up to sixty thousand cubic feet of water per second.[21]

Designed to contain a flood as big as that of 1894, these dikes constituted the major protection works. The other half of the project was drainage. The entire Sumas Reclamation Scheme was designed to create farm lands by draining Sumas Lake and to drain surrounding lands previously subject to inundation. The lands affected were divided into three areas: the lakelands and the east and west prairie sections. The east prairie constituted of five thousand acres of land between the East Vedder Dyke and the town of Chilliwack, and the west prairie section was fifteen thousand acres of land to the west of the lake. Reclaimed, the lake would yield ten thousand acres of land. The east section was to be drained via a network of ditches; water would flow into the Fraser when water levels were low and be pumped out when the Fraser was in flood.[22] The lakelands were to be kept dry with ditches that would drain into the Sumas Lake canal, built across the middle of the old lake bed. These waters, coming from land that was always below the level of the river, had to be pumped into the Fraser via a major system of pumps constructed near the main dam. The west prairie section also drained into the Sumas Lake canal, as well as into another canal, but constituted a separate system that could be allowed to drain out by gravity for about nine months of the year.

The east and west prairie sections were mostly lands already owned and cultivated. The landowners in these areas would be the immediate beneficiaries of the protection works. They would gain relief from the yearly floods, which threatened crops planted on lowlands or rendered such lands good only for pasture. This fact, and the fact that the landowners had asked the government to carry out the work, fuelled Oliver's argument that these landowners should pay all the costs not covered by sales of the reclaimed lands. Though the government had a long interest in the reclamation of the Sumas area, it had always assumed that its role would be largely hands-off. The government's role, through the office of the Sumas Dyking Commissioners, would consist of organizing work that would be carried out by private concerns. When the LSB assumed the role of diking commissioners, it inherited this idea.

That the LSB was now taking on work previously assumed to be beyond the government's purview demonstrates the changing role of the state in the new liberal era. It also shows us clearly how the Oliver government perceived this new role and its limits. On the one hand, its enthusiasm for the project demonstrates the government's view that the work was always intended to be of benefit to the entire province. If Oliver did not think this were so, he would hardly have included a special provision in the Land Settlement and Development Act allowing the LSB to take on such work.[23] In fact, Oliver assumed in 1917 that this work would be one of the first priorities of the new board.[24] Powerful people agreed. In August, the Vancouver Board of Trade sent Oliver a letter containing a petition from a farmers' convention, arguing that it was imperative that the province produce more food for itself and that, therefore, the government should decide immediately on the reclamation of the Sumas lands. The convention also wrote a letter to LSB Chairman Maxwell Smith, claiming that farmers had been urging the reclamation for three years.[25] The newspaper *Vancouver Daily World* declared that the project was of special interest to Vancouver and more generally would "greatly enrich [the] province."[26]

Thus, Oliver's claim that the government was merely acting on the wishes of the area landowners was dubious. That he made the point so emphatically to the owners and to anyone else who would listen – stating to the press that "the government guarantees nothing ... The property will have to carry the scheme" – suggests that he knew this.[27] Yet making the landowners financially responsible for the work made perfect sense according to the government's version of new liberalism, in which state development projects were ultimately aimed at the prosperity of the classical liberal individual. That so few challenged this argument suggests that BC's citizens were not far from Oliver in their understanding of the relationships between the individual, the society, and the state. It also likely demonstrates a belief in the idea that science and nature working together would lead to abundant production on the reclaimed lakelands. Everything now depended on three things: the capacity of project engineers to smoothly rework the river into a more ordered form, the ability of agricultural scientists to develop the lakelands, and the capability of the land to sustain abundant agricultural production. Should any of these conditions not be met, some feared that costs could exceed the $1,800,000 budget that the owners approved in March 1920.[28]

BUILDING THE WORKS

The contract to build the diking works was granted to the Marsh-Bourne Construction Company in April of 1920. Planners were confident that they could understand, and therefore expeditiously reorder, the environment at Sumas. Initial work quickly suggested, however, that they may have misjudged the situation. Problems arose from the combination of the annual flood cycle, the shaky financial condition of the company, and the technical constraints of the dredging equipment. The flood, which usually arrives in May, almost immediately halted construction. When work began again in September, it was clear that Marsh-Bourne did not have the financial resources to do the job. It supplied only one dredge for work on the dikes, and when the company tried to get another, it was seized in Vancouver due to Marsh-Bourne's inability to make payments on it. The Land Settlement Board was forced to step in, buy the dredge, and rent it to Marsh-Bourne. One more dredge and additional money and expertise became available through a new partnership between Marsh-Bourne and a firm from Tacoma, Washington. But most of the new equipment arrived only shortly before May of 1921, when the Fraser once again flooded the area and brought work to halt.[29] Thus by June of 1921, little work on the Vedder Canal – the key to the system – had been completed.

What was revealed by the summer of 1921 was a troubling gap between state planning for the Sumas area and local complexities. First, Marsh-Bourne and the LSB had stumbled on (there is little evidence that they anticipated) a central environmental constraint in the work. Simply put, work on the project could not be done gradually. The structures had to be substantial enough by May to withstand the arrival of the flood waters. A sufficient number of machines had to be working at once in order to complete work in the seven months of guaranteed low water. Further, due to the timing of the Fraser floods, the work had to be carried out in winter. The need for speed meant that the older, cheaper, more common steam-powered dredges were not adequate, as their great weight made them slow to move about. The most modern and expensive equipment was needed – generally electric-powered dredges, which also required running electric power lines to the site (see Figure 9).

Second, despite Oliver's insistence that the property owners were ultimately responsible for the project, the LSB reacted with disdain to the landowners' increasing concerns about the progress of the work and the possibility of mounting costs. To property owners' requests for financial information and progress reports, LSB Director Davies declared that he found it "impossible to treat these communications as being anything but the inquiry of certain rate payers within the Sumas District." He then suggested that their inquiries sullied the good name of the minister of agriculture, who had their best interests at heart.[30] Despite the landowners' financial liability, they were to leave the experts in charge.

The owners safely ignored the LSB, now in direct control of the work since Marsh-Bourne had declared bankruptcy in June, and tried to close the gap between planning and environmental constraints by adding another dredge. However the rivers, almost as if they objected to the efforts to control them, stubbornly refused to cooperate. In October a storm caused a flash flood on the Vedder that wiped out partially completed dikes and bulkheads on the canal, severely damaged the East and West Vedder Dykes, and spread lumber and pilings across Sumas Lake and prairie.

9 Dike construction, most likely the Vedder Canal, on the Sumas project, ca. 1922.

Then winter began to pound the project. In November a ten-day ice storm halted construction, and in December storms, floods, and a hard frost caused further damage to existing structures. A log jam in the river forced the current into the East Vedder Dyke, causing severe damage. The construction camp was left in a foot-and-a-half of water, water was a foot deep over the BC Electric tracks, and eight hundred feet of track were wiped out. Supplies to the work camp, which came in by river, were cut off when the rivers froze.[31]

In an attempt to make up for these delays, the board put two more dredges on the project in early 1922. But the spring flood arrived before they were able to protect the west prairie section and the lake area through the completion of the Sumas River Dam. The engineers hoped that a temporary earth dam might do the trick. As the flood approached, the dredges were still working on the dikes, and engineers were not able to move the dredge "Tobin" to work on the dam until just before the water hit. In the end, despite much time and effort, the dam collapsed under the waters of the Fraser. The east prairie section fared better. In April, the Vedder Canal was completed, sealing off the east prairie from the lake, while the Fraser dike was finished in time to protect the prairie from the annual flood. With the completion of the pumping plant, consisting of two sixty horsepower pumps inside a concrete bunker, the east prairie protection and drainage system was officially complete. Costs continued to mount, however, as it became clear that several dikes would have to be built either higher or longer than originally planned.[32]

The next year saw the completion of the reclamation works with the building of the Sumas River Dam, and mounting costs due to poor planning and the constraints of the flood cycle. Construction on the dam began with no final plan and no cost estimate. The engineer finally settled on a concrete and earth structure. Four sluices would drain water from the west prairie area and the lake when the Fraser was low. When the river was in flood, the sluices could be closed and water could be pumped into the river. By June, when the water rose, the structure was ready, though extra funds had been spent on an additional shift of workers in order to make this deadline. As the level of the Fraser climbed to ninety-two feet at the measuring point, it became clear that the structures were holding. The system worked. The only task now was to drain Sumas Lake.[33]

The lake still had a short time to live. The pumping was put off until winter, when low water would make the job easier. Meanwhile, the project's chief engineer offered his assessment of the work. "To the average layman," he declared, "it is hardly conceivable that Sumas Prairie, after all

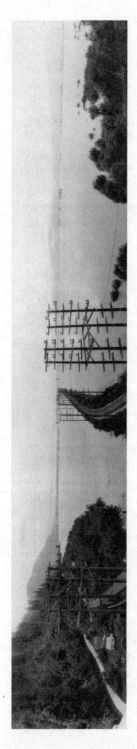

10 Looking west from Vedder Mountain, this photograph shows Sumas Lake in full flood, overflowing the dikes on which ran the BC Electric Railway tracks. BC Archives indicates this photo was taken in the 1930s, but other sources give 1916, a much more plausible date, given that the lake clearly exists in this shot.

11 A 1924 photograph shows the recently reclaimed lands in a sweeping vista. This view appears to look north from the BC Electric substation on Yale Road, roughly the same spot in which Figure 10 looked west.

the years of discussion, is at last reclaimed from the Fraser floods." But it was true. Now, "the natural elements are being controlled to the lasting benefit of mankind," and "there seems to be very little doubt regarding the ultimate draining of Sumas Lake and the productivity of the submerged lands."[34] About the draining of the lake, at least, he was right. By May of 1924, only fifteen hundred acres of lakelands were still under water, and only to a depth of less than one foot. Though stories circulated afterwards of sturgeon left behind in marshy areas, and of ducks that still tried to land on the former waters, by 26 June 1924, the lake was gone (see Figures 10 and 11).[35] Ordering the Fraser and the lake to the satisfaction of LSB planners, however, had required greater effort and greater costs than originally anticipated. The process of turning the drained lands into productive farms would be similarly problematic. And watching all this, their hands protectively over their wallets, were the landowners.

THE VALUE OF THE LAND

The productivity of the lakelands remained an open question. The province now owned the lands outright. Upon the completion of the work, the Dominion government had sold the 12,200 acres of railway belt land lying under the lakewaters to the province for $1.[36] Now, like the larger biophysical environment around it, the ecosystem of the lakelands needed to be re-ordered. But if the building of the reclamation works raised doubts about the ability of the engineers to order and control the capricious nature of the Fraser River, then the development of the lakelands called into question the abilities of agricultural scientists to produce productive land economically. It also called into question everyone's faith in the value of the soil of the lakelands. The initial soil report indicated that the land contained good concentrations of important minerals but was short on nitrogen. It was also somewhat sandy and prone to erosion and drifting. To solve both its lack of nitrogen and its physical problems, the land needed more humus (soil rich in organic matter), which could be obtained by planting the land with legumes and leafy crops.[37]

The board, however, had already decided to plant a small cash crop of oats in order to demonstrate the value of the lands (see Figure 12).[38] In July, the board began subdividing the cropped lands into fifty-two lots of approximately forty acres apiece.[39] It soon appeared that the board may have rushed matters. The crops could not be planted until the soil had dried out, and the resulting lateness of the planting and the nitrogen deficiency of the soil meant that the crop did poorly.[40] The lakelands proved to need a complex drainage system, and the heart of the drainage system, the Sumas Lake Canal, would not be completed until November. The LSB proceeded to build ditches around every farm, sometimes on three sides of the lot.[41]

A few months after the lake was drained, a larger and more intractable problem arose: a forest of willows grew up in the damp lakebed, seemingly overnight. The trees spread faster than LSB employees could cut them down, choking out the timothy and clover grasses that had been planted in order to improve the soil. By March of 1925, twenty-five hundred acres of the former lake bed were covered in the trees, taking over two thousand acres of the three thousand of timothy. The board attempted to strike back by ploughing under two thousand acres of trees.[42]

By the end of 1925, the board had spent $86,742.63 on the development of the lakelands – "on general work, ditching, buildings, bridges, dredge work, fencing lake, horses, [and] implements."[43] By early 1926, the land was ready to sell, though the LSB calculated that it would need to charge $200 per acre in order to cover costs. The board hoped to rid itself

12   A display of the first crop of grains produced by the Land Settlement Board. Note the progression from raw plant to more processed foods.

of the willow-infested land by leasing it, offering to pay partial taxes and supply clover seed in return for the lessee's agreement to plough down and destroy the trees.[44]

The board's sales pitch placed the project firmly within the ideal of an alternative modernity. The land was portrayed as the gift of modern engineering techniques, the outcome of a seamless unity of nature and the machine. Advertisements stressed the fertility of the soil, the mild climate, the area's proximity to the city, its "modern conveniences" in the home and on the farm, and, "last but not least, a beautiful setting of mountain, river and pastoral scenery" (see Figure 13). The heavy machinery of reclamation was the means by which this ideal nature was brought into being. Advertising pamphlets were full of photos of heavy equipment, whether the dredges building the Vedder Canal or the great electric motors of the pumping plants. Next to these were line drawings of genial, beaming farm wives, holding chickens under their arms and petting goats. Photos showed cherries, chickens, and a record Holstein. In one image illustrating the unity of farm life and modern conveniences, fields of grain ripple in the wind in front of a Model-T, obscuring everything but the car's roof.[45]

The Sumas Reclaimed Lands offered "40 acres! a healthy life! a comfortable living!" The pamphlets promised "health, happiness and good living!" Growing villages and "hospitable people" could be found nearby. All this was the result of the intelligent manipulation of the environmental legacy using modern techniques: "Nature provided Southern British Columbia with the alluvial delta of the great Fraser River and reclamation by man added to the fertile valley lands."[46] Nature had prepared this place for the Sumas project. Here would be built an economically productive, healthy and virtuous community, a modern settlement in the midst of the mountains, rivers, and plains built by nature.

This idyllic scene, however, was not to be – at least not right away. Though the LSB issued a lavish advertising pamphlet in 1927, the area's new administrator, Bruce Dixon, decided that the land needed more work: the drainage system had to be completed, the willows continued to be a problem, and the soil continued to show a "marked deficiency in nitrogen content." Dixon put up barns, planted demonstration crops, and tried to address the nitrogen problem by growing clover. But a crop of thirteen hundred acres of grains failed completely. Dixon's one sale – 637 acres to the Canadian Hop Company in 1926 and 1927 – would lead to large-scale agricultural production, not to the sort of individual family farms pictured in advertising material.[47] Nor would it help diversify the province's agricultural base, specifically with the grain crops the LSB hoped for.

13   A promotional pamphlet designed to sell lands at Sumas folds out to reveal this panorama, which glories in both the technical achievement of the project and the lush agricultural landscape that reclamation has produced. It also trades on BC's mild weather, which was always thought to be an attraction for settlers.

Hops were an established crop in the Fraser Valley, dependent on available Native pickers. Hop farming would, then, employ Stó:lō workers on land that had once been theirs.

In 1928, a new Conservative government replaced the Liberals and moved to get rid of the remaining lands at Sumas and to settle some of the scheme's debts. The 8,700 remaining unsold acres (of 10,000 acres reclaimed) were contracted out to a real estate firm to sell at the reduced price of $125 per acre, with the promise that the LSB would build a house for each settler at a cost of up to $2,500. In comparison to what the LSB had hoped to get for these lands, this was akin to a fire sale, and the lots were snapped up. What is more, many of the lots sold were the sort of small farms that the board had hoped to sell (though more than 2,500 acres were sold to two buyers). The Sumas project was now settled.[48]

A later accounting showed seven thousand acres sold at around $100 per acre.[49] Though $100 was a respectable price, it was considerably lower than the price needed to break even on the construction costs. The LSB's balance sheet on the project in 1932 showed sales of the lakelands amounting to $1,134,580.54, although $908,143.68 of this was still outstanding. This was about 60 percent of the initial cost estimate that the owners of land in the area had voted on in 1920. By 1932, though, the cost of extra expenditures on building the works and developing the lakelands had pushed the total outlay on the project to almost $6 million. Taking into account the value of unsold land and other unrealized assets, the project was saddled with a deficit of just over $3.5 million. This money would have to be made up by taxing the landowners of the east and west prairie regions.[50] It was these landowners who would pay for the difficulties of ordering Sumas Prairie.

THE LIBERALS AND THE LANDOWNERS

By 1930, the Conservative government had faced up to the fact that it would have to pay a substantial portion of the costs of the project. Throughout the 1920s, the Liberals had consistently refused to consider this notion. During construction, they refused the landowners' requests for information on the progress and costs of the work. After the lake was drained, evidence proved that the project had suffered from a crippling lack of planning, and that planners' confidence that the lakelands would quickly become productive farms was unwarranted. Critics suggested that the Marsh-Bourne company had got the contract through its Liberal connections, and had never been properly capitalized.[51] Nevertheless, Oliver's government never wavered from its insistence that the owners must ultimately pay the bill. The lakelands, donated to the province by the federal government, would be the province's only contribution to the costs of the project.

The owners got word of the increase in costs in 1923, and the next year their fears were confirmed when the assessments of their property arrived. By 1925, with the lakelands yet to go on the market, the landowners notified the government that they could not hope to pay off their debts and continue farming. The landowners' plight quickly became controversial – so much so that, in order to calm both the press and the opposition, the government convened a special sitting of the legislature's agriculture committee to consider the assessments. The hearings ran for four days in December 1925; Premier Oliver and Minister of Agriculture E.D. Barrow represented the government, while longtime opposition critic J.W. Jones and lawyer Henry Blackman spoke for the landowners. Many landowners also appeared as witnesses. All offered their views on the worth of the scheme and on who should pay for it.[52]

There was little argument over whether the reclamation project was a good or bad thing. Both sides embraced the idea that technology could improve nature, and both valued an ideal of the independent farmer making a comfortable living. All generally agreed that the project was a success, a great improvement. In practical terms, though, this success meant little to the landowners, who could not both pay for the project and make a profit. Ignoring this argument, the government rested on its defence that the owners had agreed to pay, and that the dikes had brought marvelous improvements to the area. The government was well versed in this latter argument, having previously used it to justify building the Vedder Canal through the Aylechootlook band's reserve (without first asking the band's permission).[53]

The hearings opened with Premier John Oliver, who lost no time in declaring that the government had merely acted on behalf of the owners. In its role as Sumas Dyking Commissioners, the board was merely the agent of the owners. The owners, Oliver claimed, should have taken into account the unreliability of engineers' estimates and the fact that previous diking schemes had run over budget. The government, he argued, could not be held responsible for a scheme initiated and controlled by the owners, no matter how little control they might have wielded in practice. "There is no connection between the Government and the Land Settlement Board as Dyking Commissioners," he explained bluntly.[54] This declaration might have come as a surprise to readers of the previous year's promotional pamphlet, which featured a quote from Barrow declaring that "the Sumas Reclamation Project has been carried out entirely by the Government of British Columbia."[55]

The government's other argument was that the project had improved the prospects for farming in the region. With proper attention to modern, scientific techniques, farmers could do very well. Barrow told the owners that all they had to do was grow the proper crops. He cited the example of his own farm in the area, where he had made a healthy return growing crops of grasses (timothy, clover, and hay). Yet Blackman, the owners' lawyer, disagreed. Barrow's story of agricultural success, he stated, ran counter to the experience of almost every other farmer he had met: "we take it from the standpoint, not from the man who has a comfortable income, that can do anything he likes in the way of farming, but from the standpoint of a man who has to work for his living and go on the land and property, pay the purchase price of it in addition to the taxation."[56] The landowners demanded an assessment for diking costs of no more than $5 per acre. The results reported in a study by a landowner named Mr. McCallister justified their request. McCallister used scientific agriculture against the government. His farm had been the subject of a study by Professor Hare of UBC's Department of Animal Husbandry. The study had compared farm yields with costs of production. Drawing on his knowledge of local prices and on Hare's data and Hare's methods for calculating costs, McCallister concluded that it cost him $20.65 to farm one acre, which amounted to $4.25 in profit per acre. Yet the LSB had estimated his annual assessment would be $9.44 per acre.[57]

Witnesses were challenged insistently by the government as to whether the project had not in fact cleared the way for growing more profitable crops. The plan backfired, however. Witnesses' answers demonstrated primarily that the project had offered little benefit to the landowners at all. First, testimony revealed how, previous to the diking project, farmers had found ways to work around the flooding. A Mr. Samson explained that he and others had "run cattle over the prairie [lowland] part of it and we farmed the higher lands on our place with grain." Cattle could be placed on the land in mid-March or early April until some time in June, taken off for about six weeks as the land flooded, and then put back on the land in mid-July or August. Samson testified that he could not ultimately make a profit on the land when it was worked this way (though, as he rented it out, presumably someone else could).[58] Still, his testimony illustrated how farmers could work around the floods. For the farmers who used the un-owned borderlands of the lake as common pasture land, the dike was actually a setback.[59] Further, many farmers insisted that dairying was the most profitable form of farming in the Fraser Valley. McCallister claimed that "the old bossy cow is the most profitable operation there is in British Columbia today ... there is no other business in the farming line that will produce as much return, in my estimation, as the dairy cow." "You don't admit," challenged the government's Mr. Souter, "that the improvement of the land would enable you to grow more profitable crops than keeping dairy cows?" "I don't admit that," McCallister responded.[60]

Farmers complained of their lack of success with sugar beets, potatoes, and clover. Grains, such as oats and barley, could be cultivated, but it was difficult to make money from them. The grain buyers "just pay you pretty near what they can squeeze out of you. I have only sold one car of grain this year, and the rest is in a granary, and ... I cannot sell it to anybody."[61] Although no one at the proceedings mentioned it, the most likely reason for the Sumas farmers' inability to sell grain at reasonable prices was competition from the prairies, which were just coming into full production at this time. Like the small farmers in Washington State studied by historian Richard White, Sumas farmers could not hope to compete with the prairie grain factories and the publicly funded railways designed to deliver their harvests nationwide.[62] By contrast, milk was perishable enough that it was still supplied to consumers by local sources, and the large market of Vancouver was just a short trip away by rail or road.[63]

The owners' central problem was that the dikes had not improved their lands to an extent commensurate with their elevated taxes. Reclamation had made it harder, not easier, for them to make a living. And yet in some ways, the project remained a success in their eyes. At one point, the owners' representative, Mr. Blackman, asked farmer Angus McIver, "We are not complaining at this particular juncture about the completion of the work, which after all is a great benefit to that district?" "Yes," McIver replied, "and there is no question but it is an outstanding benefit to the country at large." McIver did point to one concrete benefit, namely, that the diking had relieved the mosquito problem in the area.[64] Dairy farmer John Conover, asked if there was any water on his land, commented, "Gosh, no. Now the scheme is a success, there is no doubt about that."[65]

Though the dikes had not helped these and other farmers make a better living, they could nevertheless judge the scheme to be a success because it had done what they wanted it to do: it created a properly ordered and civilized countryside. Conover had wanted the flood waters off his land and the mosquitoes gone, as "we did not want to live forever in a place that was not fit to live in." Though he had not particularly needed the dike, he was "public-spirited enough to vote for it so that the community would come under it, so that we could live and not live like Indians." Another farmer's objection to the taxes was that the income he was left with was "not a sufficient amount for a farmer to raise his family on and be respectable ... If we are going to put a batch of Chinamen down there in that area, maybe they can make it go but we cannot."[66] From this point of view, to the extent that the high taxes worked against the creation of a properly white countryside, they defeated the purpose of the diking.

In the end, the government reduced the assessments to $5.50 per acre, approximately what the owners had asked for. But this did not mean that they were now willing to pay any of the costs. The total amount that each landowner owed the government remained the same, and interest charges would continue to accrue. As well, any future moneys spent by the LSB, acting as Sumas Dyking Commissioners, would eventually come out of the pockets of the landowners.[67] Obviously, such a plan had the potential to generate massive debt, and by 1928, the size of these debts forced the government to reduce the total amounts owing. Landowners' debts for the cost of construction were cut by as much as one-third, and the terms of payment were lengthened.[68]

By no means did the changes of 1928 bring this tepid drama to a close. The government continued to make concessions that failed to prevent the further accumulation of debt (such debt leading in turn to more concessions). In 1946, yet another commission reconfigured the payments. Full payment was now expected by 1981.[69]

The 1946 commission also revealed more clearly some unexpected environmental legacies of the project. Some farmers noted that the soil was drier than it had ever been, so dry that they had to irrigate. Another farmer stated that the scheme had not been worth the cost for the local landowners. It had dried out the soil and taken away the free pasture lands on the former lakebed. In the end, he declared, "the cost was too great for the land to stand." The major beneficiary, as symbolized by the Trans-Canada Highway cutting through the old lakebed, was not the local landowners but the province as a whole.[70]

The Liberal government's failure to recognize this fact, which was clear from the start, speaks of the limits of the new liberal vision of managing nature and society for the betterment of the individual. The owners of the east and west prairies were not the only beneficiaries of the Sumas project. Yet in order to justify the project within a new liberal framework, which still placed the liberal individual at the centre, Oliver and others had to find a group of individuals closely associated with the project's benefits and costs. The Oliver government was never willing to put out the funds necessary to pay for a project that was, in reality, larger than the neighbouring landowners. Both the government and the local landowners agreed that the Sumas project was worthwhile in its ability to create the conditions for a modern countryside. But the creation of these conditions could not, in this case, be paid for by the landowners.

CONCLUSION

In its ambition to order the Sumas Lake area, the Sumas Reclamation Project was far larger than anyone in 1920 realized. Though engineers and agricultural scientists assumed that nature should be ordered, the lake and its rivers were at their most natural in a disordered state. Surging, unpredictable floodwaters choked with debris, changes in the river channels, and a lake that grew and shrank through the year were not signs of a problem.

So when the engineers tried to contain the Fraser between consistent banks and keep its annual flood from spreading out across Sumas prairie, they were not working with natural processes; instead, they were trying to change them into new forms. They did not make allowances for the sudden floods that washed out dikes or for the bad weather that halted work. No one seemed to take into account the implications of the Fraser flood. First, the spring flood meant that most work had to take place in winter. More seriously, the flood cycle put a box around their efforts. The need to have works finished in time to withstand the year's floods meant that a large and expensive amount of equipment and labour had to be employed in order to finish dikes or dams in the seven-month window that the floods allowed. Finally, the assumption that the lakelands would immediately become superior farmland proved unduly optimistic. Instead of selling the lands and paying off construction costs, the LSB found itself spending money in battles against the weed-like growth of willows, in building up the soil by growing cover crops, and in constructing barns, houses, and fences in order to make the land more saleable.

The high costs were also attributable to other factors. The Marsh-Bourne construction company was guilty of sheer incompetence, and bad planning abounded. The project also fell victim to the inevitable difficulties of estimating the cost of complex engineering works. But essentially, the inflated costs of the construction phase of the project were the result of an attempt to work against nature rather than within it.

Attempts to pay these costs showed the limits of the new liberal vision of the relationship between the state and the individual. While John Oliver's government was willing to take on social and natural engineering, it did not want to pay for it. Ultimately, however, the landowners could not handle this financial burden. As in the joke about the liberal who tries to save someone from drowning (by throwing a ladder halfway out, and expecting the drowning person to do the rest), Oliver and Barrow stressed the wonderful benefits of the scheme without considering whether or not it actually helped the farmers pay for the dikes. In the end, the lakelands were not as good as had been claimed, and they were sold for less than anticipated. Owners were left to pay off capital costs. Scientific agriculture was expected by Barrow and others to work with scientific land reclamation to produce a superior agricultural crop such as grains. But it could not overcome the physical geography and the state-funded infrastructure that made wheat farming precarious and dairy farming profitable in the Fraser Valley. Thus, already a dominant industry in the area, dairying remained the most profitable way to use the land. Another established crop, hops, continued to be important as well.

Ultimately, though, the state and many of the landowners supported the idea of building an alternative modernity, and agreed that countryside was a superior form of nature and that it could be achieved in British Columbia through the application of expert state management. The landowners agreed with state representatives that the reclamation represented progress, despite their own negative experiences. Thus, it is important not to overplay the conflict of interest between state visions and local experience. The draining of Sumas Lake replaced the local accommodation of the lake in favour of a state-sponsored vision of progress, as Laura Cameron argues and as James Scott might point out.[71] But the support of the owners shows that this was not a case of the state versus the local residents, but of the way that ideals can penetrate local experience and motivate a particular type of development.

On Sumas Prairie, the lake refuses to disappear entirely. A major freshet on the Fraser River flooded the area in 1948, and it was inundated again in 1990. Memories of the lake persist as well, though now, of course, mainly in recorded form. The efforts to order the fitful nature of Sumas Prairie continue.

5

Achieving the Modern Countryside

ALL THAT EX-PRIVATE COCKAYNE WANTED from the Land Settlement Board was a chance to settle on the land. But in early 1918, frustrated by his continued residence outside the country, he appealed instead to the powerful Minister of Lands. In Duff Pattullo, he found a willing supporter. Pattullo was not one to sit idly by, even when a matter lay outside the bounds of his official authority (as did the Ministry of Agriculture's Land Settlement Board). He had proven this with his letter to the Minister of Agriculture two years before, when he proposed the original idea for the LSB. Upon receiving Cockayne's letter, Pattullo promptly dispatched a withering letter to LSB Chair Maxwell Smith, taking him to task for the way that he had failed the ex-private. It was not enough to point a man towards the information available from the Ministry of Lands, Pattullo said; instead, "the minute the Board locates any one who desires to go on the land, they should follow it up just as assiduously as though they were selling the man a piece of land belonging to themselves." They should pursue the request like real estate agents closing a deal. "You will recall," Pattullo noted sarcastically, "that I insisted that the Board should be called a 'Land Settlement' Board, for the purpose of designating just what the Board is supposed to be, namely, a Board that will induce land settlement."[1]

Smith was apparently not cowed. He replied one full week later, with a leisurely examination of the purpose of the board and how it worked. For Smith, the board's priority was to set the conditions under which the settlement of farmers "of limited means" could take place. He aimed at plans that would "disturb the pessimistic growlers who always cluster, like flies, on the great revolving wheels of the chariot of progress." But for the present, when these plans had not yet been put into effect, the board could not help ex-Private Cockayne and his like.[2]

Smith's objections were reasonable within the context of how the LSB worked. Even seven months after this exchange, the board was not ready to offer up lands for actual settlement. Its activities had been confined to detailed examinations of potential settlement lands, assumption of control of some diking districts, and planning for development projects.[3] For Pattullo, who prized quick action even at the expense of mistakes, these projects must have seemed timid.[4] The differences between the two men went beyond personality, however. As we saw in Chapter 1, the commitment of Smith and the board generally to the new liberal concept of government as the creator of the conditions for individual wealth only went so far. If for Pattullo this meant the active pursuit of the welfare of individuals by the government, then for the board, which took a more classically liberal approach, this meant merely establishing the conditions conducive to such welfare.

The South Okanagan Irrigation Project had the same roots as the LSB's land development projects at Merville and, as we will see below, at Merville's companion settlement at Camp Lister. It was a project of the Department of Lands' office of BC Soldier Settlement. Like the LSB, this office drew on the plans of the Returned Soldiers' Aid Commission. The South Okanagan project, too, began as a plan to settle returned soldiers on individual farms, and to employ them in the work of developing those farms. It, too, envisioned the creation of a new town and a new surrounding countryside. It, too, depended on reshaping the environment into an idealized, irrigated landscape that brought together humans and nature.

The difference between the project in the South Okanagan and the settlements at Merville and Camp Lister was Duff Pattullo. Pattullo's sense that modern society required a new role for the state allowed him to consider the possibility that the government might absorb some of the costs of the project; his political power allowed him to make it happen. His belief that the state could take positive action resulted in the project becoming more of a total plan than the LSB ever managed to put in place. The South Okanagan project eschewed whatever local involvement the LSB had still allowed in favour of control by experts employed by the state. State experts were in charge of virtually every aspect of the project, and these experts were able to use their access to funds to overcome the environmental complexities that had defeated the LSB. More ambitious than the Sumas Reclamation Project, more successful in its transformation of nature than Merville, the South Okanagan Irrigation Project illustrates what it took to bring the idea of an alternative modernity to fruition, and enables us to evaluate the alternative modernity more fully as a way of bringing together humans and nature.

IRRIGATION AND THE LAND

The idea of using the technology of water control to create idealized rural communities was not unique to British Columbia. Giant dams like the Columbia River's Grand Coulee, in the US Pacific Northwest, were intended to generate electricity that would become a cheap and plentiful source of power for a great network of small family farms.[5] This vision also propelled the work of the US government's Bureau of Reclamation in California, in particular its Central Valley Project and its work in the Imperial Valley. In June 1902, the federal Newlands Act limited irrigated farms to 160 acres, with the intention that they would be taken up by a series of family farmers. Such farms were to be self-financing, the Bureau of Reclamation so creating the perfect liberal agrarian society. But this is not what happened. According to Donald Worster, the Bureau of Reclamation fell in love with gigantic technological mega-projects that could be understood and controlled only by trained technical experts. The bureau's ultimate aim was to refashion nature to be more rational and ordered, to prevent the waste of water that was being put to no useful human purpose. One result of these large projects was land so expensive that only large-scale agribusiness could afford to work it profitably. The vision of small farmers was replaced by a reality of huge farms run strictly for profit and worked by gangs of itinerant labourers. Power quickly fell to two groups – the technocrats who ran the irrigation works, represented at the local level by the irrigation districts or water users' communities, and the capitalists who owned the farms.[6]

For Worster, deeply moral and driven by a great love of the natural world, this is a cautionary tale about the results of excessive ambition and pride and a lack of sensitivity to the natural world. Worster's great enemies are the water engineers, who were sure of their ability to reform nature into something better. Oppressive agribusiness emerged when the engineers' love of massive engineering works joined with capitalism and an instrumental view of nature.[7] He draws (critically) on Wittfogel's "hydraulic society" thesis, in which Wittfogel argues that societies that have relied on dams and irrigation works have always tended towards despotism, as those with control over the water became the most powerful people in the state. Worster argues that the American West has become a modern hydraulic society. The vision of liberal agrarians on small farms was unworkable in the modern US West and was quickly overshadowed by the desire of engineers to design and build great projects.[8]

Others have called into question Worster's argument that damming turned the West's rivers into something little better than canals. Both Richard White and Mark Fiege look closely at the continuing power of natural processes to shape and limit human action, even in the face of modern industrial engineering. Focusing on the Columbia River, White argues that development has transformed the river, but not irrevocably. Dams must regulate a natural flow that they are powerless to stop entirely. Droughts and floods continue to affect the system, and the salmon run has had to be accommodated, though this has been done by transporting salmon upriver on barges. The Columbia has become not a machine but something else, an "organic machine," a mixture of the human and the natural. Neither a celebration of the triumph of human reason nor a lament for the loss of nature captures what has truly happened.[9]

Mark Fiege's study of the irrigated landscapes of Idaho likewise finds evidence for the continuing power of natural processes to shape the efforts of irrigators. Fiege charts how plants and animals invaded irrigation ditches, how such ditches had to follow natural contour lines (even dry streambeds), and how the application of water to land changed groundwater levels and, at times, created springs. Like White, who argues that the dreams of creating what I have called an "alternative modernity" must be taken seriously, Fiege also argues that the efforts of irrigation engineers and their supporters were not all about control. To the myths of industrial control and the improvement of nature, irrigators added the garden myth, bringing together the factory and the garden in a "mythic, metaphorical landscape that might be called the industrial Eden." Overall, Fiege argues, irrigators created not a transformed environment but a "hybrid landscape" that contained both human elements and the elements of nature.[10]

BUILDING LISTER

Ultimately, Worster goes too far in suggesting that the ideals of an alternative modernity were mostly a way for the state to justify the creation of large-scale capitalist accumulation. Certainly such an argument cannot explain a project like Camp Lister, where the belief in the liberal, small-scale farmer was held to a fault. The LSB's goal at Camp Lister was not so much to put nature to work at all costs as it was to create a particular countryside. Here, small farms preceded irrigation works, and eventually hampered their development.

The differences between the LSB's and the Ministry of Lands' efforts in land development are most clear when we examine their concurrent experiments in fruit farming and irrigation. As at Merville, Camp Lister was to be developed by employing returned men to clear the land and build farmhouses, fences, and barns. At Lister, though, the goal was fruit farms, each one between twenty and forty acres in size, to be built on a seven-mile-long, five-thousand-acre area of benchland above the Goat River, three-and-a-half miles south of Creston.

Purchased from the Canyon City Lumber Company in 1919, much of the land was logged-off and burned. Small poplar, birch, and brush had established themselves. Unlogged areas were covered mostly with fir, balsam, tamarack, and yellow pine, but also with cedar.[11] Though the board claimed that the area was quite level, differences in elevation could be significant. In some areas, mountain slopes made up much of the land. One area of about 160 acres featured 25 acres of bottom land in one corner, another small area of 3 acres of bottom land separated from it, and a small area of benchland 150 feet up from the valley floor. The remaining 110 acres or so were mostly treed mountain slope.[12] When irrigation was attempted, the differences in elevation between the various farms would prove to be a major difficulty.

The settlement was named Camp Lister after Col. Fred Lister, assigned by the LSB to head up the project. Lister was a good Liberal Party man, who had also been on the *Empress of Asia,* where a group of soldiers had hatched an idea for a community settlement.[13] As at Merville, work began under the "development system," where gangs of potential settlers worked under a Land Settlement Board supervisor. The smaller trees and sparser growth of the forests meant that clearing here was easier than it had been at Merville. But seventy men still spent two years packing stumps with powder, blasting them out of the ground, and hauling away the remains with a steam donkey and heavy tractor. The effects of this disturbance on the local ecosystem were apparent. In the summer of 1920, a cloud of dust hung over the settlement, churned up by clearing, ploughing, and road traffic. "If a dog crossed the road," one settler remembered, "a small cloud of dust followed it and when the November rains came the settlers thought they were once again in Flanders' trenches. Cars, trucks, horses, and women folks often got bogged down when they had to make use of the roads, and what a relief when the frost came and froze the mud until the spring thaw."[14]

The difference between wrestling with the coastal forest and struggling with the smaller trees at Lister was also apparent in the results. By February of 1922, ninety lots covering approximately two thousand acres had been developed to the extent of the original plan – that is, five acres had been cleared on each lot, a house had been built, and the lot had been fenced in.[15] Thus, when the LSB brought the development system to a close, they were more justified in doing so than they were at Merville. Still, escalating costs played a large part in its decision. Settlers were dispatched to their individual farms, to make their living from farming and outside work.[16]

Development work continued, though now under a system of individual contracts.[17] The costs of improvements were added to the purchase price of individual lots. In the spring of 1921, the LSB purchased 10,500 fruit trees, mostly Wealthy, Macintosh, and Delicious apples. Twenty-eight lots were planted, and the board set up a nursery for settlers who wanted to purchase trees, on credit, in subsequent years.[18] Wells were drilled for drinking water on the farms that needed them.[19] By mid-1922, fifty-nine farms of between 200 and 250 trees each (on average) were established in the area.[20] The board's plan now was for the settlers to wait out the five to seven years necessary for their trees to mature and begin bearing fruit. In the meantime, the board suggested that they plant small fruits, potatoes, peppers, and cantaloupes.[21]

Life at Lister was hard, though not without its satisfactions. At the start of development, single men lived in bunkhouses. Married couples, in keeping with the assumption that rural settlement would reinforce the nuclear family, lived in one-room shacks. The shacks were built of unseasoned wood, though, and were drafty. Later, the shacks were transferred out to farms to become homes for single men. For couples, the board built homes from three standard plans, using shiplap, boards, and shingles.[22]

The adjustment could be particularly difficult for British-born wives of Canadian soldiers, or for those brought up in the city. One of the early settlers was Canadian poet Earle Birney, then thirteen, who settled in Lister with his family. One of Birney's enduring memories of the place was how hard his family worked. According to biographer Elspeth Cameron, the family "picked strawberries and raspberries from dawn to dusk, sorted and packaged them, drew water when there was any, cared for livestock, drove produce daily to the Erickson railway station, weeded, fended off predators and garden pests with guns, traps and poison, mended and repaired an endless series of items and devised irrigation systems to survive the dry spells."[23] Others got by keeping bees, chickens, and cows, feeding live-stock on cut grass and working for nearby fruit growers.[24] Settler John Bird found work as postmaster, and in 1923 he took over the former LSB general store and began work for the board as caretaker of abandoned homes.[25] As the abandoned homes suggested, some settlers were doing poorly. Harvests suffered from lack of water.[26] Some, still mentally and physically wounded by the war, simply found such a hard and insecure existence to be too overwhelming.[27]

Birney, however, delighted in the wildlife just outside his door. He and other settlement children went swimming and hiking on Goat Mountain and organized parties and picnics. The settlers held Christmas parties with singalongs, and others must have gone off hunting and fishing the way Birney and his father did.[28] But life was too difficult and too cash-poor in Lister for Birney. After only a few years, Birney left Lister to work in a bank, first in the regional centre of Creston and, soon after, two hundred miles away in Vernon.[29] In Lister, settlers were unable to keep up with their payments to the LSB. Suffering from bad harvests, annoyed that the cost of food and lodging in the development work camps had been added to the purchase price of their lots, and possibly wary of the experience of their fellow settlers at Merville, settlers refused to sign their agreements for purchase.[30] Some settlers made interest payments on their debts, while others abandoned their lots.[31]

The climate in the area was a central problem and the LSB's W.S. Latta acknowledged as much (though he referred instead to the "weather"). While he complained of the settlers' "lack of enterprise," he also noted that "there is no doubt that a certain amount of pessimism on ... [their part] ... is justified on account of the dryness of the past few seasons." Only six farms were capable of producing crops without irrigation.[32]

Yet in fact, this situation should not have come as much of a surprise to the LSB, which had already been told that irrigation was at least desirable and likely necessary for successful agriculture in the area. The Creston Board of Trade informed the board in 1920 that, in dry years, irrigation was "almost essential, especially for small fruits and vegetables."[33] This opinion was seconded by the government's local water rights engineer, W.J.E. Biker, who was of the opinion that irrigation was "essential" for twenty-acre farms in the area. Biker believed that small fruits and garden produce (the sort of crop that two years later the board would suggest settlers grow while they waited for their trees to mature) would fail without irrigation.[34]

The LSB, then, was aware of the need for irrigation. It did not admit so publicly, ignoring the issue in advertising material and assuring corre-spondents that irrigation was unnecessary.[35] But in 1920, they secured the right to divert water from two local creeks, and over the course of the decade, defended their rights to this water.[36] In 1922, the board decided that, due to "unsettled conditions" at Camp Lister – perhaps the problem with getting people to sign purchase agreements – it would not commis-sion a study of an irrigation system at this time.[37] In 1923, though, District Engineer Biker sent a study to the comptroller of water rights, one that reveals much about the problems with water at Lister.

Biker started by noting that the scheme would be expensive, and even so would need to exclude some lots that were situated at so great an ele-vation as to make the cost truly prohibitive. Covering 475 acres, his plan required eight separate irrigation zones, which would deliver water in suc-cession. His estimated cost, based "on data supplied by the Land Settle-ment Board which they state are 'susceptible to errors,'" was $70,900, or $155 per acre, placing the scheme well beyond the means of the average cash-poor soldier settler.[38]

The major problem was that the settlement had not been laid out with irrigation in mind. The lots were scattered and lay "at very different ele-vations. The area required to be irrigated lies partly in a hollow and partly on the near side of the surrounding hills, and partly on the far side of the hills furthest from the only source of water supply." Biker's map of the area, of which Map 4 is a representation, shows that the source of the problem was the LSB's attempts at egalitarianism and independence, which led to their policy of clearing a few acres from every settler's lot. These few acres were cleared, as at Merville, along the main roads; the result was that farms were strung out along these roads, and the area as a whole contained a large amount of undeveloped land. To address this problem, Biker sug-gested irrigating a larger area, 510 acres, concentrating on lowland near the community townsite. Using the same dam system, but requiring less pip-ing, and involving three irrigation zones instead of eight, this scheme would cost substantially less: $28,640, or $56 per acre.[39]

The LSB never went ahead with this plan. One concern was likely that, though cheaper, the plan was still expensive. By 1923, it must have been clear that settlers could not be asked to pay for it. Yet the LSB was bound to undertake only those projects that would be self-sustaining. Also, set-tlers were already on their farms. The board's reluctance may also have had to do with the fact that the scheme threatened the ideal that had sent the returned men to the country in the first place. As in the much larger

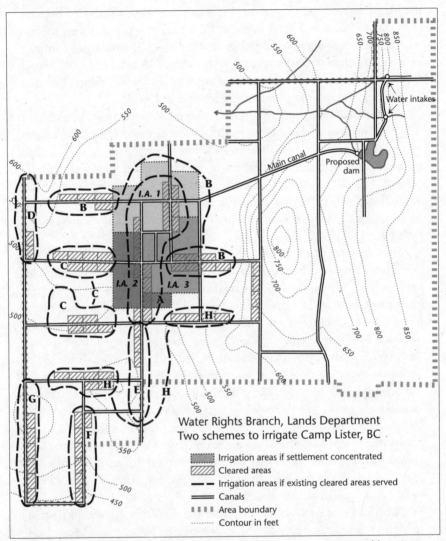

Water Rights Branch, Lands Department
Two schemes to irrigate Camp Lister, BC

Irrigation areas if settlement concentrated
Cleared areas
Irrigation areas if existing cleared areas served
Canals
Area boundary
Contour in feet

MAP 4   Two schemes to irrigate Camp Lister, BC. This map combines two blueprints drawn up by Water Engineer Biker, one for each of his irrigation plans. It illustrates the way in which the layout of cleared areas complicated attempts to irrigate the Lister settlement. The shaded areas indicate the three irrigation areas that Biker proposed to build if settlement could be concentrated in one area. The dashed lines show the larger number of irrigation areas that would have to be built to accommodate already cleared and settled areas.

projects in California (discussed by Donald Worster), such a scheme would have turned independent farmers into employees. The plan fulfilled neither the land settlement boosters' landscape ideal, nor their vision of rural communities for returned soldiers. It would not have built the community of liberal, individual, self-supporting farmers that the LSB had envisioned.

By 1929, only thirty-one lots remained settled; only seven of these were deeded to their owners. Ninety-three lots lay vacant. The Birneys had abandoned their farm and returned to Banff by 1922. Others stayed on. John Bird was postmaster for twenty-seven years and served as the church warden for thirty-five. Col. Fred Lister, fired as a result of the dispute between the settlers and the board over the signing of leases, eventually returned to the area and purchased land. In 1929, the new Conservative government revived the town by setting up the Lister Waterworks District, running a pipe from a nearby stream to settlers' homes. New settlers arrived, brought in by a colonization company from Germany. Hilton Young, who wrote his memories of Lister some thirty years later, remembered with bitterness that the Germans received a government-financed water supply, while the Canadian soldiers had not.[40]

WATERING THE DESERT

The LSB's reluctance to irrigate the small-scale Lister contrasted with the ambitions of the South Okanagan Irrigation Project. From the start, the Okanagan project proposed to supply water to an entire arid river valley, to reform a large chunk of the "dry belt." The dry belt was the contemporary label for a semi-arid region in the interior of the province, including the Okanagan and the uplands of the interior plateau. The area is an extension of the arid regions of northern interior Mexico and the northwestern US, and features the most extreme climate in BC, with hot summers and cold winters. Grasslands dominated here; where these grasslands continue today, plant communities feature bunchgrasses and shrubs such as sagebrush and antelope-brush. Scorpions, black widow spiders, and rattlesnakes live in the grasses, along with mule deer, white-tailed jack rabbits, mice, and spotted bats.[41] The Okanagan project aimed to irrigate a twenty-five-mile-long, one-to-two-mile-wide stretch of this country, along the Okanagan River (see Map 5).

In the early 1920s, Ministry of Lands officials knew little about the climate of this area. Most of their knowledge was derived from extrapolations from data gathered at Penticton (only about twenty-five miles north

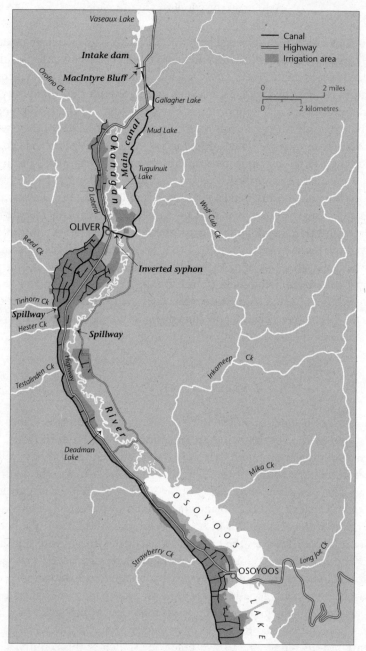

MAP 5   The South Okanagan Irrigation Project. This map is not dated but appears to show the canal system at a more developed state than at the time of the completion of the main canal. Notice "D Lateral," which services areas on the high ground, south of the intake dam and west of Okanagan River, which the main canal avoids.

but, owing to its location between Okanagan and Skaha Lakes, climatically quite different). They projected an average winter temperature of 34°F to 36°F (1°C to 2°C) and an average summer temperature of between 66°F and 71°F (19°C and 22°C). Records for rainfall were available, and indicated that there would be about ten inches per year, but these records were based on only a few years of measurements.[42]

Up until the time the Ministry of Lands grew interested in the southern portion of the Okanagan Valley, the land had been used for grazing cattle. Yet the land held the possibility of successful agriculture, if only a reliable water supply could be ensured. The soils in the region were formed by the retreat of the glaciers of the Fraser Glaciation, ten thousand years ago. The retreating glaciers blocked the Okanagan Valley, resulting in a glacial lake that deposited silts and clays onto what was then the lake bottom. These formed the basis for the benchlands that now rise from the shores of Okanagan Lake and the Okanagan River. These benchlands were where much of the agriculture of the region took place. Post-glacial processes completed the work of forming the southern Okanagan Valley. Outflow waters cut into the lake deposits, forming the Okanagan River. The good agricultural soil of the area was the result of aeolian (wind) erosion. Over time, wind picked up soil from bare areas such as steep slopes and floodplains, and deposited sand and silt particles nearby. The result was fine soil, up to three feet in depth, making agriculture possible on land that would otherwise be very rocky.[43]

The land that would make up the South Okanagan project had been owned since 1905 by the Southern Okanagan Land Company. The company was formed in 1904 by W.T. and L.W. Shatford, who raised $500,000 in order to buy out Thomas Ellis, the "Okanagan Cattle King." Ellis began buying up land in the southern valley in 1865, eventually acquiring thirty thousand acres, stretching from the American border as far north as Naramata. The Shatford brothers purchased the most southerly twenty-eight thousand acres of Ellis' empire, along with 3,200 head of cattle and 100 horses, for $400,000. They hoped to emulate the land companies in the more northerly parts of the valley by subdividing the area, installing irrigation works, and selling the land as orchard lots.[44] In the meantime, they went into the cattle business.

To facilitate their irrigation scheme, the Shatfords commissioned at least three studies of the area by engineers. F.H. Latimer, who would later run the government's project, submitted a study of soil conditions, while a more extensive study of the engineering works and possible crops was carried out by American Elwood Mead.[45] Latimer found that, in general, the agricultural lands consisted of wet bottomland, some of it treed, and drier grasslands on elevated benchlands. The most useful section of bottomland was at the northern part of the area. It had rich, black, sandy, loam soil, but only about one hundred cottonwood-covered acres were dry enough to be good agricultural land. The remaining bottomland, which bordered the river for the length of the area, was quite wet and covered in willows, alders, black birch, and poplar brush. Most of the agricultural land was on the benchlands. These were bounded and divided by unusable land – either steep slopes or alluvial deposits of rock and gravel formed by outwash from Tin Horn and Hester Creeks.[46]

Mead reported that the soil was fertile, made up of fine clays and course gravels, three-quarters of it being sandy loam. More importantly, it was irrigable. It did not "bake or crust" when water was applied to it. Half the surface was made up of long, gentle slopes, which could be irrigated easily. The remaining area of more severe and less predictable slopes would require more extensive irrigation works. As an irrigation area, the South Okanagan had the advantage of a steady supply of water from the Okanagan River, and of rail connections with markets in the remainder of the country, particularly Calgary and Winnipeg. Mead predicted that grapes, peaches, apples, pears, and small fruits would grow well, and pointed out that tomatoes and cantaloupes, which could not be grown farther north due to the cold, did well in the southern valley. The length and narrowness of the area was a problem, however, raising the cost per acre of irrigation. Mead closed with suggestions as to the route of the main canal, details of the main dam that would divert water into the canal, and cost estimates.[47]

Based on these reports, the company estimated that 14,700 acres could be irrigated for $934,128.[48] Such expenditure proved to be beyond the company's means, and when the government came calling, the Shatford brothers were only too happy to sell.[49] Pattullo and his officials had originally considered the development of various sites in the interior plateau, west and south of Kamloops. In the summer of 1918, though, Pattullo toured the southern Okanagan lands and was impressed by their potential for development into a new Okanagan, to rival existing developments at Vernon, Kelowna, and Penticton.[50] The northern valley had originally been developed by private industry, but the days of private industry in the Okanagan seemed to be gone. The Shatfords had failed to install the necessary irrigation works, and the land companies that had developed the rest of the Okanagan were being replaced, by Patullo, with local water management boards.[51]

In developing the southern Okanagan, the government was able to draw

on the several existing plans commissioned by the Southern Okanagan
Land Company, and Pattullo played up the connection with Elwood Mead,
known for his work on irrigation in California. The area had few white
inhabitants, and was free of the trees that had so complicated the work at
Merville and Camp Lister. The Ministry of Lands could do as it saw fit,
and employ the sort of expertise that would ensure success. The scheme was
to be a modern technocratic project in which the government would have
the chance to demonstrate its ability, through proper planning and by
learning from its past mistakes, to do the job right. It would be "the government's principal effort in modern large-scale agricultural settlement."[52]

In December 1918, the Ministry of Lands acquired from the Southern
Okanagan Land Company the twenty-two thousand acres that were to make
up the South Okanagan Irrigation Project. It announced that it intended
to make "all or a portion of it" available to returned men, and also to employ returned men on the project.[53] The project was to be administered by
the superintendent of British Columbia Soldier Settlement, Major J.W.
Clark. Clark had been appointed in September, and was a logical choice given
his experience. Before the war he had worked as a rancher near Kamloops
and served as superintendent of the nearby prison farm from 1912. He enlisted
for service in the wartime Canadian Army, from which he was later transferred to the post of agricultural officer of the British Third Army.[54]

Clark's position at the head of the project was more a nominal position
than a real one, however. He issued yearly reports on the progress of the
work, and eventually organized and ran the project nursery and its experimental farm. The actual construction of the irrigation works was under
the control of the Ministry of Lands' Water Rights Branch. The Water
Rights Branch was in charge of investigating, granting, and adjudicating
disputes over claims to use the waters of the province, generally for agricultural purposes. Any diversion of water required the prior permission of the
branch, which granted (or rejected) claims to the use of the water on the
basis of the "wise principle" of "beneficial use" (which, according to one
history of the branch held that water should be used "economically and
beneficially").[55]

To head up the project, the government brought in civil engineer and
land surveyor Ernest A. Cleveland, who would later become comptroller
of Water Rights. Cleveland's name is now remembered primarily through
his later work on the design of the Vancouver water supply system, a key
component of which was the Cleveland Dam. When he was appointed
to head up the South Okanagan project, Cleveland was already one of
BC's leading engineers, having worked on a variety of projects, including

surveying regions, railways, and the design of waterworks and diking systems in the Vancouver area municipalities of Point Grey, Richmond, and Burnaby. He also worked on Vancouver's Second Narrows Bridge and investigated irrigation projects in British Columbia, the US, and Mexico.[56]

By 1919, all the plans and personnel to build the canal were in place. The first contract to excavate the main irrigation canal was let in July and construction began shortly after this.[57] "The ditch" was the heart of the project, a gravity-powered, concrete-lined artificial stream, which (by the time of its completion in 1927) snaked across the valley floor and around the dry hills of the southern Okanagan from McIntyre Bluff, just north of the present town of Oliver, to the US border (see Map 5). The main canal drew on the waters held back by the main diversion dam below McIntyre Bluff. Heading south, the canal dove under McIntyre Creek and the main north-south highway running through the Okanagan Valley, arriving at the new Oliver townsite at 3.36 feet above the valley floor (see Figure 14).[58]

From the dam to Oliver, the canal travelled on the east side of the Okanagan River in order to avoid a steep slope on the west side of the river. The irrigable land, however, was to the west. In order to carry the water to the

14   "Main Canal at Oliver near Station 90." All the photographs in this chapter are from the illustrated lectures of J.W. Clark, intended to promote the South Okanagan project. Note how the canal appears both to bisect the landscape and conform to it.

valley bottom and across the river, the canal ran into an inverted syphon, seventy-eight inches in diameter. This massive pipe, constructed of wood and creosote, ran into a steel pipe that carried the water under the town. At the outlet of the steel pipe on the west side of the river, the canal resumed its course south. But its journey was not an entirely simple one. In order to get the water around steep hillsides and over gullies, the canal ran periodically into flumes, metal pipes sitting on wooden cradles. These flumes could be considerable creations in their own right – one, six miles south of Oliver, was three miles long. Flumes were expensive to build, and occasionally subject to washouts as high waters brought rocks and debris down the canal (see Figure 15).

The problem of high waters was serious enough that spillways were used to keep floods from overwhelming the canal. When water levels rose to a certain point, the water began to run through a pipe and into a tank with a quarter-inch hole in the bottom, which allowed some of the water to drain off. Serious floods would fill the tank until the weight of the water opened automatic gates, allowing it to gush out and down the spillways. Spillways were built into existing streambeds, such as at Hester and Tinhorn Creeks.

The last major components of the system were four pumping plants, which supplied water to several areas too high to be fed by gravity from the canal, but of such agricultural potential that they could not be ignored. In fact, these lands were often of superior quality to the more easily-watered lower lands, a fairly common situation in the Okanagan. Water was delivered to individual farms through a series of concrete lateral pipes.[59]

HUMANS AND NATURE IN THE IRRIGATED LANDSCAPE

The design of the South Okanagan project was shaped by recognized problems in existing irrigation systems, and by the perceived environmental constraints and potential of the area. Project engineer Ernest Cleveland's investigation of irrigation projects in BC led him to several conclusions about the environmental context and the history of such works in the province. Cleveland believed that, within its limited agricultural areas, British Columbia had favourable climate and soil conditions, well suited to the dense, intensive cultivation of high-value crops. This was especially true of the interior valleys, though in many of these areas – those with annual precipitation less than sixteen to twenty inches – irrigation was necessary.

15 "Outlet of Flume #21 and Canal (not yet completed)"

The topography of these areas, however, made irrigation difficult. "Perhaps in few places where the art [of irrigation] is practised," he noted, "has nature offered more challenges to man's ingenuity to secure sufficient water for a season's use, store, carry and distribute it, at a cost within commercial limits."[60] BC's interior valleys were narrow, and their meandering rivers expanded into lakes that covered much of the available level land. This left most of the good agricultural land on elevated benches. If this land was to be irrigated without expensive pumping, then the region's large lakes and rivers could not be used as the sources of water. Instead, Okanagan irrigators had to depend on smaller streams. In order to overcome the problem of wide and violent variation in the flow of these streams, irrigation systems had to include storage dams so that water could be reserved and doled out periodically. Reservoirs were common in irrigation and hydro systems. Yet appropriate sites for these dams were comparatively few in the BC interior. Basins or depressions in which water could be stored tended to be located near the headwaters of streams, where there was little upstream water available for storage. The situation was further complicated by the ruggedness of the hillsides and the "generally broken and rolling nature of the irrigable lands."[61]

These difficulties were only inadequately addressed by the various land companies in their pioneering work on BC's irrigation systems. Though aware of the difficulties, most companies downplayed them or proceeded with inaccurate or faulty knowledge. They did not take sufficiently into account the seasonal variation in stream flow, so their storage facilities were often inadequate. Often their knowledge about the available water supply was inadequate, and they did not consider that the demand for water would increase as orchard trees grew larger. They used earth ditches and wooden flumes, disregarding the problem of water loss through seepage into the soil and through leaks in the wooden flumes. There was little consistency in the amount of water delivered to each user (the Water Rights Branch would later set a standard rate of two-and-a-half acre-feet of water per acre of land). The rates charged to each user were often not carefully calculated – a critical point, as once the land was sold, the land companies often left the operations of the work in the hands of "water companies" whose income depended solely on water rates. Usually, these rates were too low to pay for the maintenance and operation of the system.[62]

The South Okanagan project was designed to correct the mistakes of the water companies and to deal more efficiently with environmental constraints. It also made use of the one major environmental advantage of the area – its access to the waters of the Okanagan River. Cleveland noted that, aside from one other project, the South Okanagan was the only irrigation system in the province able to take advantage of the steady supply and the easy storage afforded by tapping a major river. On the other hand, the project could not escape the problem of wet bottom lands and high benchlands; a significant chunk of the project's water had to be pumped up from the main canal. The project engineers expended much effort to secure the most efficient and most powerful pumps. Other aspects of the project would also incorporate the most modern technology available. Though the initial plans had called for an earthen ditch, Cleveland went with concrete. Due to the nature of the soils in the area, he argued, an earthen ditch would have lost too much water through absorption, and would have been subject to washouts. Zinc flumes were used in place of wooden ones, for durability and to avoid leakage. Spillways, lateral canals, and pipes were all of concrete.[63] The whole system was designed, built, and operated by the Ministry of Lands, using the best experts available. Such expertise and modern technology would guarantee the success of the system.

Building an irrigation system, then, required a thorough knowledge of environmental conditions and constraints. It also involved bending to the variability of nature. Adequate storage facilities were necessary to compensate for variations in stream flow. Spillways accommodated sudden variations in water level. Influenced by new trends in ecology, some historians have begun to stress the general unwillingness of twentieth-century North Americans to see change in nature as normal. Nature was to be timeless and unchanging; where it wasn't, nature could be helped to achieve a properly ordered state (as at Sumas).[64] Clearly, though, Cleveland was willing to recognize and deal with nature's inherent propensity to change. In this, he more closely resembled the engineers that Mark Fiege found in Idaho (who dreamed of technology's ability to create a garden) than he did Donald Worster's man of instrumental reason.[65]

Cleveland aimed to re-order the riparian system of the southern Okanagan. The resulting landscape would be improved, he and others were sure. The project would impose the order necessary to "transform a wilderness into a garden," by going under "vagrant stream-bed[s]" and meeting the "varying disposition of the topography" with ditches, pipes, and flumes. Yet this does not mean that Cleveland and others involved in the project aimed to fully rationalize nature, or that they could not or did not value the natural world. Cleveland's report on the project, started in 1923 and added to over the next seventeen years, featured tenders and contracts, engineering diagrams and specifications, detailed cost breakdowns for components, and particulars on electrical-energy usage. The report also included a collection of photographs that began with scenic images of Okanagan and Dog Lakes, and then documented the construction of the main canal, the diversion dam, flumes, orchards, and the project's demonstration farm. Images of placid lakes and rugged rock faces (see Figure 16) were accompanied by images of construction and its impressive results.[66]

Promotional pamphlets for the project likewise emphasized a confluence of nature and the machine. Panoramas of the valley lands were set alongside images of the modern building technology that would be used in the valley's transformation and the rural plenty that would follow – trees heavy with ripe, round fruit; families picking together; hillsides covered with crops; and snaking irrigation flumes before Okanagan Lake and the hills of the opposite bank.[67] As the slogan at the end of one text declared, "Where apples grow best, man lives best."[68]

This message was also delivered in the traveling lantern slide lectures of Major J.W. Clark. In 1921 or 1922, Clark suggested to Pattullo that he present illustrated lectures of fruit-growing and irrigation in the southern Okanagan as a way of advertising the project. Pattullo must have approved because by February, Clark had begun to gather prints and negatives from whomever could supply them – mostly people connected with the project. Clark also solicited photographs of fruit trees from faculty at Ontario

16   "Overhanging Rock at Vaseaux Lake"

Agricultural College, and scenic shots of the Okanagan Valley from J. Murray Gibbon, publicity agent for the Canadian Pacific Railway.[69] Clark also took a large number of photographs himself. From these, he put together what would eventually become an extensive collection of lantern slides.[70] Lantern slides were glass plates about twice the size of modern slides, containing a positive image. In use up to the 1950s, they were widespread where visual information needed to be displayed – university art and architecture departments relied on them, and "magic lantern shows" were popular as a way of presenting exotic foreign scenes to audiences.[71] Canadian government immigration agents also used lantern slides lectures to entice potential immigrants.

The lantern slide format would therefore have imparted an air of learning and progress to Clark's presentations. In Calgary, Winnipeg, Edmonton, and other places in western Canada, in India in front of audiences of retired Indian Army officers, at Kiwanis Club luncheons, and in high schools, Clark used lantern slide images to inform his audiences of the new countryside being created in the South Okanagan.[72] As did the pamphleteers of the LSB and the Ministry of Lands and as did Ernest Cleveland (who drew the photographs in his report from Clark's collection), Clark showed irrigation machinery producing comfortable homes, bountiful orchards, and happy families. Slides showed that developed towns were in the area; images of wilderness lakes and mountains celebrated the untouched nature nearby.[73] The South Okanagan Irrigation Project, Clark and others argued, ultimately made possible a home in nature.[74]

ON THE DIFFICULTIES OF REFORMING NATURE IN BRITISH COLUMBIA

The planners and builders of the South Okanagan project were certain in their belief that the project represented the coming together of humans and nature. This book has argued that the concept of humans and nature coming together was central to the ideal of an alternative modernity, the goal of building in the countryside a better, more natural form of modern life. Studying the South Okanagan project allows us to comment on the ideals of the alternative modernity as a way of reconciling humans and nature. It allows this because it achieved its primary goals, though at a greater financial cost than had been planned. The system was completed in 1927. The canal was lined with four-inch-thick concrete and was capable of carrying water to a depth of 5.2 feet, which meant that the canal

could deliver up to 230 cubic feet of water per second. The concrete ditch
was supplemented at key points by the woodstave syphon that carried the
water across the valley at Oliver, and by twenty-seven zinc flumes that
took over from the main canal where gullies and steep slopes got in the
way. To deal with floods, the project also incorporated seven spillways at
the entrance to the syphon, at Hester and Tinhorn Creeks, at the US border, and in other spots.[75] Four pumping plants delivered water to about
nine hundred acres of benchland located above the main canal.[76]

The first pamphlets came out to advertise the first land sales in March
of 1921. The lots offered were small, most around ten acres; the aim was to
create "fruit and garden lands," and "opportunities for home-seekers." The
lands were offered at lower rates for returned soldiers (and their widows)

17   "Captain Panteous showing size of cants on July 7th; cantoloupe field," 1925.
Photographic proof of the success of the project: kneeling in a field of abundance, Captain
Panteous is the picture of the British gentleman farmer with his pipe and knee socks.

than for ordinary settlers (as they would be well into the 1920s). Soldiers were to get a break on the down payment (10 percent of the purchase price versus 20 percent) and were eligible for the same $500 rebate that the government offered to soldiers who purchased from the Land Settlement Board.[77] But this was the extent to which the Ministry of Lands singled out soldier settlers. Unlike the LSB projects at Merville and Lister, in the Okanagan project, there were no conscious attempts to create community, no drawing lots as a way to distribute land. Though Ministry of Lands planners had consulted the same community land settlement plans as had the LSB, building the irrigation works and making them pay for themselves was their top priority.

From the earliest land sales, Duff Pattullo, Ernest Cleveland, J.W. Clark, and other members of the project devoted their skill and expertise to making the project a success. Pattullo's major contribution was to keep the funds flowing. By February of 1921, the office of BC Soldier Settlement had used up the $1.8 million allotted to it, the vast majority going to the South Okanagan project. In a letter to the Premier, Pattullo asked for another $100,000 to keep the project going until the end of March, by which time, he promised, a selection of land would go on the market. He warned that shutting down the project now would be "very disastrous" and "not thinkable."[78]

When the lands did go on the market (in May), over $80,000 of property was sold. This represented only 342 acres of more than 1,200 acres put up for auction. About 300 acres of this land, at between $250 and $300 per acre, were sold to returned soldiers. Taking advantage of their exclusive right to purchase land on the first day of the auction, the favoured terms of purchase offered them, and their knowledge of the area gained from working on the construction of the irrigation system, returned men snapped up a portion of higher-priced land just south of the Oliver townsite.[79]

Meanwhile, the costs of the project were mounting. By November 1922, over $2.2 million had been spent on construction – more than double the highest estimate in the plans commissioned by the Southern Okanagan Land Company. Cleveland estimated that another $1,100,000 would be necessary. The primary reason for this increase, Cleveland explained, was the necessary improvements made to the system, including the switch to concrete canals and ditches and to zinc flumes. It had also been discovered that the systems designed by F.H. Latimer and Elwood Mead for the Shatford brothers could not deliver enough water to the twelve thousand acres the Ministry of Lands hoped to irrigate. The system as a whole had had to be made larger.[80]

The Shatford brothers had also not anticipated the sort of total program of scientific land settlement that the Ministry of Lands would carry
out in the South Okanagan. The townsite of Oliver, including offices for
the project, was developed. A nursery had been started on site in order to
ease the problem of supplying adequate numbers of fruit trees to the settlers.[81] A demonstration lot, intended to show settlers what they could
grow and the sort of output they could achieve, was started in the summer of 1919. It was planted with garden vegetables, cover crops such as
clover and alfalfa, berries, walnuts, apricots, peaches, nectarines, three types
of plums, four types of grapes, four types of pears, and nine kinds of apples.[82]
As well, three hundred acres of sub-standard land was dubbed the "Development Area" and was irrigated and planted by project personnel.[83] All of
these initiatives added to the overall cost of operations. Finally, high postwar prices, which had been followed by an economic slump after 1920,
also drove up spending.[84]

By 1924, the major components of the system were in place, though
parts of the main canal still needed to be lined with concrete. Distribution
systems to deliver water all the way to the fields were in place for five thousand of the twelve thousand acres to be irrigated.[85] The following year,
however, it became clear that many of the settlers were in trouble. An
audit showed that almost $30,000 was owing for interest on land sales,
and settlers were behind by almost $12,000.[86] Premier Oliver visited the
site and came away unimpressed. Only 1666.78 acres had officially been
sold, and this was an inflated figure, as it included the nursery and the
development area. The soil was a major problem. Made up of various
types of brown, grassland soils, it was thin and sandy, lacking in organic
matter. Often atop an underlay of gravel, it drained too well. The common furrow system of irrigation, in which water was drained into ditches
cut across the field, tended to lead to excessive water use, which leached
the soil of nutrients.[87]

Oliver, noting that land sales had been largely stagnant over the past
two years, concluded that the selling price for the land was too high. Settlers could not pay for improvements to their land along with interest and
water charges and other costs such as school taxes. He recommended that
interest and water charges be demanded promptly, but that payments on
purchase prices be made over a much longer time period. Washing his
hands of the matter, Oliver scolded Pattullo, noting that the area was "a
serious reflection upon both the policy and the administration of the Government," and advising that such "regrettable conditions" should be dealt
with immediately.[88]

Pattullo's response was in keeping with his character. He travelled to the South Okanagan and announced to the settlers that 25 percent would be taken off the purchase price for land already sold. The money would be applied to outstanding interest, principal, and water charges. Settlers would be able to start fresh, Pattullo promised – all outstanding debts would be covered. New purchasers of land need not pay interest for two years, and need pay only half the interest for three years after that and nothing on the principal for ten years. Anyone willing to work, Pattullo declared, could now make good in the South Okanagan.[89]

Showing confidence in the present and future state of the South Okanagan Irrigation Project was something Pattullo had always done and would continue to do. Yet his confidence was based, at least in part, on facts; events would soon provide some support for his positive outlook. By 1925, the area farmers had established a marketing co-op, the Oliver Growers' Co-operative Association, and a cannery at Oliver.[90] Project personnel had been advocating the growing of cantaloupes as an intercrop for several years; in 1925, the advice paid off. In 1924, 1,268 crates of melons had been shipped; the following year saw 18,968 crates. The case was similar for tomatoes, another intercrop. The Oliver Cannery packed nine thousand cases in 1924, and twenty-three thousand in 1925. Some farmers made from $250 to $300 per acre on these two crops.[91] As well, the trees began to bear fruit, producing sixteen tons of apricots.[92]

This is not to say that all was suddenly well. One farmer had his water cut off for eleven days when he ran behind on his payments. In the enforced drought, he lost four hundred crates of cantaloupes and three loads of hay.[93] Irrigators living in areas served by pumps complained about their water charges. They had agreed to pay extra for any amount of water used over the limit of 2.5 acre-feet per acre, the standard duty of water set by the Water Rights Branch.[94] But they made the agreement before they realized how much water the land in the South Okanagan required. Their irrigation water was disappearing, the result of porous soil and high levels of evaporation. Compared to the more temperate northern sections of the valley, the southern Okanagan experienced higher average temperatures, lower relative humidity, and strong, dry winds. This made it difficult to keep water on the land. Many farmers were using from four to five acre-feet per acre. A petition (signed by every landowner except those away for the winter) asked that the farmers receive more water at the normal flat rate.[95] They had to wait for the end of the year and a new Conservative government before they got their wish. As part of a larger revaluation of

Liberal land settlement projects, the Conservatives also reduced the price of river bottom lands, benchlands with particularly bad soil, and unsold lands within the project bounds.[96]

By 1928, the South Okanagan Irrigation Project had converted almost nine thousand acres of grassland for new, human-centred uses. Almost thirty-five hundred acres had been sold or leased for agricultural production.[97] By the mid-1930s, most of the 189 people farming the area before 1929 were still there. Twenty-five hundred people now lived there, producing peaches, pears, apples, apricots, cherries, prunes, tomatoes, cantaloupes, and cucumbers.[98] In the longer term, though, the agricultural future of the region lay in tree-fruit production, particularly apples. More than half the fruit trees in the South Okanagan were apple trees in 1930; the rest were apricots, peaches, pears, and cherries.[99] A semi-arid grassland was on its way to becoming a simplified ecosystem of mostly fruit trees, its growth ordered as much by the market as by ecological conditions.

This ordering of nature had, however, come at a significant financial cost. F.H. Latimer, eventually the project engineer, estimated in 1907 that the system would cost $616,373 to build. In 1919, his estimate was revised to $935,000 to take into account increased costs of material and labour. An audit conducted in 1928, after the completion of the main canal, concluded that by the end of the year $2,991,567.10 would have been spent on construction. This figure did not include the $350,000 spent on purchasing the lands in the first place, an amount that had not been recovered by 1928.[100] The major source of the increased costs, as Cleveland indicated in 1922, was the need to address various environmental complexities that arose as the project progressed.

The re-ordering of the South Okanagan would also never be wholly successful or complete. There was more to the region than farmers and land. Existing practices of humans and other animals were threatened by the project. For example, early plans called for a fish ladder around the main diversion dam, to allow salmon and trout to swim up the river. Before the dam was complete, though, Cleveland was told to scrap the fish ladder. The Provincial Fisheries Department was concerned about black bass entering Okanagan Lake from Washington State; they wanted the dam to block the bass' route up the river. Obligingly, Cleveland agreed, and the dam was built without a fishway.

Dominion Fisheries officials had never felt sure of this plan, however, and after the dam was built, the Penticton Board of Trade announced that they did not like the plan either. Black bass were already in the lake in significant numbers, the board claimed. The lack of a fish ladder only stunted game fishing in the Vaseaux, Skaha, and Okanagan Lakes. The Provincial Fisheries Department asked Cleveland to reconsider his decision about the fish ladder. But while the department based its request on the presence of black bass in the lakes, it seemed to have had little evidence other than the board's declaration that the fish were there. That the department accepted such slim and suspect evidence suggests it may have been less concerned with fish than with the continuation of a popular and profitable recreation activity, and with pleasing the upper-class men who liked to fish. In the end, a ladder was built, though not until seven years after the original controversy. [101]

On the other hand, and to the annoyance of settlers and project employees, some creatures found the irrigation project beneficial. In 1923, a grasshopper (or locust) outbreak caused considerable damage to young fruit trees in the area, killing seven thousand trees in the development area alone. The grasshoppers hatched in the grasses of unworked lots, and then migrated to new orchards, where they found an abundant food source. In late October 1923, an entomologist from the Canadian government warned that a seven-year cycle was likely to hit the South Okanagan lands the following year with an even more destructive population of grasshoppers. The government authorized the expenditure of $3,000 on a poisoning program, under the control of the Dominion entomologist. In the end, the grasshoppers turned out to be less destructive than expected. Yet the grasshopper problem, inevitable given the new food source the settlers were introducing, did not go away. Countermeasures (such as setting out poison bran for grasshoppers to eat) continued to be necessary.[102]

The valley's riparian system, of which the canal was now a part, proved to be an even larger and more intractable problem. In 1927, Richter's Pass Creek broke into the canal, causing sections of the concrete lining to heave, eroding the earth behind the lining, and washing sand and mud into the canal. The same year, a rock fall damaged the concrete on another part of the canal. The following year, a boulder fell on the canal and shattered twelve feet of concrete wall, interrupting service for two days. In addition to these dramatic events, the canal required regular upkeep to control weeds, remove sand and dirt, and repair expansion joints and seal cracks.[103]

A debate in June 1921 pointed towards a future complication. Through the building of the irrigation system, the system's diversion dam, and dams farther up the river, the government's Water Rights Branch had become responsible for managing water flow on the Okanagan River. No one knew quite how to do this, however. Officials argued that water levels in the lake had to be kept low in late winter in order to keep the spring run-off from damaging land surrounding Okanagan Lake and Okanagan River. But their conclusions, based on only a few years of data, could only be tentative.[104] Water rights officials simply did not know enough about the natural systems that they now had to manage.

It soon became apparent that though the dams put the Water Rights Branch in charge of river flow, they did not allow for very precise management. Water levels on the Okanagan River were controlled by river gates in Penticton, upstream from Oliver. Changes made at Penticton, however, were not seen at the canal head until three or four days later. In the meantime, rains may have swollen the various creeks that flowed into Okanagan River below Penticton. The great fear was that a serious flood would destroy the syphon that carried the canal water from one side of the valley to the other at Oliver, which would disable the entire system.

In May of 1948 a series of flash floods on McIntyre creek threatened to do just that.[105] The main canal flowed under the creek just after leaving the main dam, and the floods washed sand and debris into the canal and partially plugged up the main syphon. Project engineers were forced to frantically clear the canal and to dig the creek back into its original bed. In this way, they averted disaster.

A more permanent solution was the Okanagan Flood Control system. Under this plan, the Okanagan River was widened and straightened through a system of channels and dikes. A dam was built at Penticton, at the bottom of Okanagan Lake, in order to control the level of the lake and the amount of water released into the river. Skaha Lake, just downstream of Penticton, acted as a buffer. Farther downstream at Okanagan Falls, "drop structures" reduced stream flow by forcing it over three vertical drops, limiting the problem of erosion in the irrigation system. This measure successfully controlled flood waters, but it did have one troubling side effect: it lowered the water table in the southern Okanagan Valley, threatening Oliver's water supply and forcing the town to build a reservoir.

Meanwhile, the act of irrigation itself was having the opposite effect, and raising the water table. By 1951, years of applying water to the soil of BC and neighbouring Washington State was causing the water table to rise. Growers were asking to leave the irrigation project in favour of drawing water from wells on their own property. The rising level of subsurface water was even creating new, small lakes as the seepage filled in small depressions.[106]

CONCLUSION

The engineers and planners of the South Okanagan Irrigation Project conceived of themselves as working with nature. Their efforts towards this were rewarded with an irrigation system, and thus a transformation of nature, that largely worked. Where the South Okanagan's water rights engineers altered their plans (at great expense) to fit their project to the existing topography and river system, the Land Settlement Board tried to impose its vision of the ideal countryside, without considering the key environmental constraint of water availability. The LSB system, in which the board set up only the framework of development but left the risks and the payment to the settlers, did not manage to transform the Camp Lister area in the way the board had hoped. Transforming nature so fundamentally was a task that could be undertaken only with the full power of modern expertise and planning, and the financial backing of the state. The increased funding and greater expertise associated with the South Okanagan project, along with Pattullo's dedication to positive and forceful action in setting the environmental conditions for social development, were key to the project's success. At the same time, the project discarded the idea of creating community, which the LSB had tried to do at both Lister and Merville.

The planners of the South Okanagan Irrigation Project believed that they were working with nature – an idea that was noble, but flawed. In the end, they achieved a changed nature, a new ecosystem. They did not aim at total transformation or total mastery, nor did they achieve it, as the ongoing environmental complications associated with the project demonstrate. But though they spoke of working with – and not against – nature, ultimately their goal was the imposition of a new, ideal landscape. They could not fully achieve this goal. The environmental effects of their actions were complex and contradictory. But to the extent that they made a hybrid landscape, they did so in spite of the vision of the modern countryside that inspired their efforts.

At the same time, the vision of a modern countryside was a hopeful and important one. It spoke of the possibility of nature and humans coming together. This was an ideal that would not survive the grim years of the Great Depression, a story we turn to in the next, and final, chapter.

PART 3

BACK TO WORK

6

Patullo's New Deal

THE BROWN FAMILY HAD REASON TO DESPAIR of Canadian land resettlement schemes. Disabled war veteran W.P. Brown, his wife, and their eleven children came to Canada in 1927 under the 3,000 Families Scheme, a joint Canadian and British effort to settle imperial citizens on farms in Canada. Given a farm near Edmonton under a loan from the federal Soldier Settlement Board (SSB), the Browns lasted just two years. Their farm failed, "owing to the Land," and, leaving everything behind, they settled in Saanich, outside Victoria. Now with only two of their children working and Mr. Brown on relief, they were in "desperate straits," and hoped for some help from another resettlement program, the Dominion-Provincial Relief Land Settlement Program, popularly known as the "back-to-the-land" scheme. "We would be willing to go anywhere it's possible to grow enough stuff to live on," Mrs. Brown declared. "We should expect to grow at least enough wheat for flour. And food."[1]

The Browns were just one of more than a thousand families writing to the Minister of Lands in 1932 and 1933, looking for help from the back-to-the-land scheme to get onto a farm. All were desperate, though not necessarily as desperate as the Browns. The Great Depression hit Canada hard, and western Canada especially hard. The western Canadian economy was dependent on the sale of wheat, lumber, and minerals abroad, and so was devastated by the collapse in foreign demand. On the prairies, drought combined with unsustainable farming practices to produce a series of disastrous dust storms in the arid Palliser's Triangle region. In these "dust bowls," farms literally almost blew away.[2] The poverty of western resource producers slammed the eastern manufacturers who sold them equipment and the railway companies that shipped their products. Business investment plummeted. Total investment for all the period of 1932 to 1934 was lower than annual investment for any one year from 1927 to 1929.[3] In BC, markets for the province's lumber, minerals, and agricultural products seemed to disappear. Salmon sat unsold in cans. The collapse of agriculture on the prairies deprived Vancouver of its role as middleman in the grain trade, and made the city host to unemployed men who travelled west in search of work.

In need of help, many turned to the land. For the political and economic elite of the province, back-to-the-land was a way of containing the social crisis. For the unemployed, it was a way of getting by. Veteran G.C. Goodison of Kelowna, in the Okanagan Valley, told the Ministry of Lands that he had some garden seed and plants, twenty-four chickens, one ton of manure, and a line on an abandoned farm, the Raith Place, eight acres on the Vernon road just outside of town. Otto Wohlleben of Ashcroft, outside Prince George, had land he could use and a friend who could supply him with seed. "The only thing I require to give me a good start and get off relief," he wrote, "is a team of horses ... I have tried my best to get work of any kind including the Ashcroft Cannery so that I could purchase the team myself, but I cannot get a job of any kind."[4]

In 1937, four years after most of the letters in the Ministry of Lands' Relief Land Settlement files were written, Frank Garner Smith of New Westminster was still on relief and hoping to get onto the land. Like the unemployed W.P. Brown, who had ceded to his wife the task of asking for help, Smith demonstrated the way in which the breadwinner ideal shaped for some the dimensions of the crisis. "I feel my position keenly," he wrote, "being a young married man and having nothing to offer to my family which makes me sad and discouraged. I have worked hard for others and tried hard to get along under all conditions, but to gain any success for my wife, family and self I have failed financially and physically. Now I am reduced to work for my little relief, for which I am very grateful to the Government and also to this city." The best solution, he thought, was "to go on the land, as this life suits our health and we are adapted to this work ... I know I will be very happy with my wife and family on a farm."[5]

Smith's confidence in the happiness of farm life was founded more on faith than on reality. Land resettlement in the 1920s had been about the possibility of creating a new form of modern life. But in the 1930s, it was (as these letters indicate) mostly a policy of despair. From their remote farm northeast of Vancouver, Benjamin Jones and his wife wrote that they were doing well. The geese were honking, the lake still unfrozen even though it was almost December, and there was no snow. They had a cabin, "all finished and we should be very warm and comfortable all winter. There is lots of wood – no need to worry about using too much." There was "lots of meat here – moose and deer are plentiful, and all summer we caught lovely trout in the lake." Clearing was light work, they reported, the land being covered only by birch brush, four feet high. On the negative side, "we grew a few carrots and turnips, but they weren't very successful, as the ground was not worked enough, or manured properly." They had six hens; "they were laying a little when we got them, but have stopped now."[6]

On their farm near Fort Fraser, west of Prince George, the family of Joseph Sherwin was worse off than the Jones family. Though it was only 2 September, their crop of potatoes had frozen in the ground. Oats were coming up poorly, and they did not have enough money for food. "I could cut down my living if I had a gun," Sherwin wrote, "but I have not got one." But "what we need in the worst way is footwear as we are going around in our bare feet ... if you could send up some boots for us it would be a great help ... Our sizes for boots – 7, wide. Ladies 5 E E. Boys 3 and childs 11."[7]

Sherwin's plea for help bounced from the mayor of New Westminster to various provincial government officials. Everyone meant well but at the end of the month Sherwin wrote to the mayor again to say that nothing had been done. Like the Joneses, he had wood, but no heater to use it in. He had land ready to be ploughed, but no plough. He needed a rope with which to operate his well, and nails to finish his barn. His family was getting by on some meat and potatoes given to him by a neighbour. "There is no chance of making a dollar," he said, "as the farmers are all on relief." Local officials informed him that they could do nothing without word from higher up.[8]

The Joneses and especially the Sherwins were most likely extreme cases, with farms in especially remote and unpromising locations. Yet the problems that hounded them – lack of capital, untested and unproductive land, and a depressed agricultural economy that was defeating already-established farmers – would also doom the back-to-the-land program as a whole.

The back-to-the-land program – officially the Dominion Relief Land Settlement Program – was a Canada-wide response to the desperation of the Great Depression. In northern Saskatchewan, it resulted in the formation of whole communities.[9] In BC, the program was mostly small and underfunded, and was never received enthusiastically by the government. For one thing, the legacy of the 1920s dampened the government's enthusiasm. By 1928, when the Conservative Party under Simon Fraser Tolmie took power in BC, many of the settlers had left Merville and, especially, Camp Lister; most of the land at Sumas was still unsold; and the South Okanagan Irrigation project was over-budget. The Tolmie government reacted with limited enthusiasm to the federal government's back-to-the-land plan. Premier-in-waiting Duff Pattullo criticized the Conservatives and called for more commitment to the program. But by the time he gained power in 1933, he had embraced a variant of New Deal liberalism in which development projects were more about pump priming and employment than about reversing the flow from city to country.

The Great Depression led to a brief and fitful revival of the idea of land resettlement. But the hopes embodied in the ideal of an alternative modernity were largely gone, however, replaced by the desperate and ultimately unworkable goal of building subsistence farms as a measure of relief. In a larger sense, the new liberalism within which the goal of a rural modernity made sense was itself brought down by the crisis of the 1930s. By the middle of the decade, the ideal of an alternative modernity was dead, and with it the idea of agricultural expansion as key to the development of the province.[10]

SIMON FRASER TOLMIE, AGRICULTURE, AND THE GREAT DEPRESSION

The Tolmie government came to power determined to deal with the problems of resettlement that remained from the 1920s. Tolmie transferred the LSB to the Ministry of Lands and charged William Gaddes, as "Colonization Commissioner," to coordinate land resettlement in the province. Across central British Columbia, a large number of "bush farms" – farms hacked out of the forest on pre-empted land – were being abandoned. The new direction taken by the government with regard to land resettlement was first suggested in a memo written by the province's director of publicity, Bruce McKelvie. McKelvie proposed that farms be made smaller. This would reduce the tax burden on settlers, and address the problem of isolation by making settlement more concentrated. Cooperative marketing and cooperation in making improvements should also be encouraged, he felt. None of these ideas were novel. But what was new was the director's denunciation of organized land settlements (such as the South Okanagan Irrigation Project) as expensive and unnecessary, and his suggestion that the government encourage experienced farmers to settle the land, rather than "artisans, shop-keepers, bakers and candle-stick makers."[11]

Meanwhile, W.H. Gaddes, appointed Colonization Commissioner two days after Christmas, was concentrating on the LSB and the South Okanagan lands, which he felt were the best available lands for settlement in the province. These lands had already cost the government much to develop, and they represented an ongoing expense. A year into his appointment, Gaddes reported that of the 10,000 acres reclaimed at Sumas, only 1,063 acres had been sold. The Camp Lister settlement at Creston, he reported, was "at a standstill," a situation he hoped to remedy by placing a few families there each year (he had previously indicated his optimism about the area). By lowering the charges on the land, installing domestic water and irrigation systems, and switching from fruits (which were subject to damaging frosts at Camp Lister's altitude) to mixed farming, Gaddes felt the settlement could be successful.[12]

He was less optimistic about Merville, despite the greater number of settlers that remained there. He admitted only that the LSB had done a good job of limiting its obligations to the settlement, thus keeping its costs down. One hundred families still lived there but improved land was being abandoned. Moreover, "the place is not very attractive and although several parties have investigated it, no sales have resulted." His conclusions about the Okanagan project were damning. The land was too expensive, it was not suitable for fruit, and it was often simply of poor quality. He recommended lowering land prices and encouraging dairying and other practices more suited to the marginal soils. Gaddes also looked into the sale of the remainder of the LSB lands and of Crown lands, and investigated the financial affairs of the diking districts and, especially, of the Okanagan irrigation districts.

On the eve of the Great Depression, then, agricultural matters in BC were largely in their normal state. BC land was being settled, but not extensively enough for anyone's satisfaction. Capital-intensive projects were in various states of financial trouble, and the flow of people to the land was matched by a flow of people from the land. As at the start of the decade, resettlement in the most promising agricultural lands outside of the Peace River region – portions of Vancouver Island and the Fraser and Okanagan Valleys – was largely complete, if hardly stable. Available land could be found only in bush farms and in the development areas created by the previous administration. The Depression would exacerbate the problems of the 1920s. But at the same time, somewhat paradoxically, it provided one last chance for those who hoped for some sort of alternative modernity.

Though the start of the Great Depression is popularly pegged to the New York stock market crash of October 1929, it was only when the dark, lean months of 1930 dragged into 1931 that it became clear to everyone that this was no ordinary downturn.[13] Not that 1930 did not supply plenty of foreshadowing: First to be hit was Vancouver, which absorbed those fleeing the province's crisis-ridden resource industries. The stock market crash led to the collapse of the city's building trade, which robbed the province's forest industry of a major customer. Vancouver's port suffered from the decline in grain shipments from the prairies. Already by December 1929, unemployed men were protesting at the City Relief Office, while the city police arrested "communist agitators." In January, unemployment tripled, and the police continued to break up demonstrations. The Tolmie government, concerned with fiscal responsibility like its Conservative counterpart in Ottawa, did little. Though 1930 proved to be an exceptional year for the salmon run (which cycles periodically between meagre and exceptional returns), this abundance led only to ruin: salmon canners packed over two million cases that they were then unable to sell. Markets collapsed in the lumber and mining industries, and the economic conditions only worsened the problems of the troubled Okanagan fruit industry.[14] Per capita income declined by 47 percent between 1928-29 and 1933, the fourth largest decline for the period in the country, following the three other western provinces (per capita income in Saskatchewan dropped 72 percent).[15]

To add to the province's difficulties, unemployed men began to come to British Columbia looking for work. Most commentators assumed that the men were motivated by the prospect of a milder climate, though there was also a tendency on the part of North Americans to think of the west as a land of wealth and opportunity. The unemployed men formed impromptu communities in rural areas and, in larger areas like Kamloops and Vancouver, near the railway tracks. These communities were dubbed "jungles," underscoring the vague threat they seemed to pose to those who preferred an arcadian or agrarian countryside. They were essentially transient communities, where unemployed men could help and support each other. Of the jungle at Kamloops, one man remembered that "six or more men together could get by with a little rustling but one man alone would starve to death ... I remember one time there were twenty-four of us jungled together – we ate good meals."[16] Some unemployed men on the coast of BC moved in the opposite direction, travelling to the desolate prairies in search of work.[17]

By 1931, it was clear to the Tolmie government that it had a crisis on its hands. A worried N.S. Lougheed, the new Minister of Lands, wrote a telegram to Tolmie in May: "Have been making some study [of] unemployment conditions [–] lumber[,] fish and mining industries [are] not improving ...

very little new work opening up (stop) am convinced conditions BC will become acute early winter ... think cities will only be able to take care married men and unless we make plans well in advance take care single men outside cities situation may become very serious. Am advised agitators now quietly organizing."[18] In the fall of 1931, the province drew on federal relief funds to establish the first of the relief camps. Unemployed men were moved out of the cities and into isolated settlements, where (the government hoped) they could be contained and controlled. Over the course of 1930 and 1931, it became apparent that the Tolmie government was largely incapable of handling the crisis, a point underlined by a series of scandals over graft and corruption in the relief system.[19] The government's response took on an air of panic, as Tolmie issued statements deploring the strain his ministers were under and pleading for patience and understanding.[20]

BACK TO THE LAND, AGAIN

As the relief camps indicated, the land was key to the government's attempts to relieve the pressure of unemployment. Lougheed suggested a variety of land-based relief activities: work in federal parks or forest reserves, road building for logging operations, completing the Pacific Great Eastern Railway between Quesnel and Prince George, and putting fifteen hundred men to work at clearing government lands in the Fraser Valley. Some business leaders were in favour of community settlements (such as Merville, presumably), land settlement, and the subsidization of prospectors.[21] Many expressed a faith in back-to-the-land settlement schemes as a solution to the problem. There was more to this faith than merely the belief that the land could be used to absorb the surplus of industrial society, to store the reserve army of labour, as James Struthers has suggested.[22] What emerges from the commentary of the time is that there was a sense that society was disordered, and could be put right by restoring the natural place and order of rural life. If the ideal of an alternative modernity had looked to the future, to an improved form of modern life, then its conservative Depression-era variant looked instead to the past.

This orientation, embraced by the Conservative government, was rejected by Pattullo and the Liberals, although Pattullo, too, no longer spoke in terms of an alternative modernity. New farms should be established, Pattullo argued, but not in order to reform society, and certainly not to return to a past Golden Age. For Pattullo, back-to-the-land was a technical solution to a difficult problem. "Do you know that the best-off man in this country is the farmer?" he told a Vancouver audience in 1931. "It is perfectly true there is no sale at a profit of agricultural products today, but there is this about it – the man who can grow his requirements, the vegetables and fruit and so forth for his own requirements, is in a very happy and fortunate position. I think it is better than stalking the streets of Vancouver looking for the job that he never picks up."[23] Rural settlement, then, was about subsistence.

For Tolmie and Lougheed, however, back-to-the-land was more than subsistence. Tolmie believed that people were naturally drifting back to the land now that the city had lost its attraction. Dealing with the movement should be a central concern of the government. Echoing earlier arguments, Tolmie suggested that the move to rural areas could benefit the province. British Columbia was not yet supplying itself with agricultural products, and the new farmers could meet this need. Further, the purchase of land would contribute to provincial revenues.[24]

At the heart of the problem was a fundamental disjuncture in modern society, as the government outlined in a brief to the Government of Canada. "The Prime Minister and the Members of the Executive Council of British Columbia" suggested that the situation was due to a decline in the need for labour arising from new machinery and a revolution in farming techniques.[25] This decline resulted in a glut of goods on the market. Farmers could only sell at a loss, which meant that they could not afford necessary tools, let alone consumer goods. This led to a further contraction in the economy. Public works relief programs exacerbated the problem, the document argued, perhaps alluding to the soldier settlement programs that Pattullo proudly touted as evidence of the Liberals' far-sighted and courageous response to postwar problems. The money from these programs was likely to be spent unproductively, argued the document, and the government would then be saddled with the cost of construction and upkeep of the new works.

The only solution was subsistence farming. "The day of farming to make money has departed," the document declared: "It is imperative that we should revive the times when the inhabitants of this country ate nothing which they had not raised, and wore nothing which their wives had not spun." This was the only answer to the current crisis' inevitable challenge to the existing social order. It would relieve the capitalist system's tendency towards employment insecurity, and it would provide stability and security to the most humble of society, thereby avoiding the violence that would undoubtedly ensue should these people embrace communism and attempt to take the possessions of others.

The Tolmie government's brief still embraced a belief in the solidity and morality of rural life and the infinite capacity of the countryside to provide. Like the proponents of an alternative modernity, the brief placed the creation of a stable farm family at the centre of the back-to-the-land scheme. In doing this, it affirmed the central importance of the male farmer as citizen and public actor, going so far as to imply that women were not "inhabitants" of the country. But with its dependence on an antimodern imagery of homespun clothes and abundant crops, it was also a counsel of despair. Sixty years after conservative legislators had insisted that BC needed to encourage the establishment of farm families in order to balance and stabilize the creation of a liberal capitalist proletariat, the brief went further, declaring liberalism and modernity to have failed. Though marginal farmers might have been useful as reserve labour, the brief anticipated that they would become instead a permanent class of subsistence farmers.

The sombre tone of the government's brief differed markedly from the enthusiasm of Minister of Lands Lougheed for going back to the land. Lougheed had great faith in the idea, and his comments on rural life in the Depression read as if the great economic crisis barely existed. In June 1931, he suggested that the government could hire unemployed men to clear land in the Fraser Valley for small chicken farms. The stumps could be left in place, and the land could easily be sold at a price that would cover the cost of both the land and the clearing of it.[26] Lougheed's report to the premier on the natural resources of the province described "sapphire-blue lakes bordered with orchards and girt with timber-clad mountain slopes," and confidently envisaged 22 million acres of agricultural lands, the development of which was "a challenge to the pioneer spirit of the Empire."[27] The minister's confidence only grew as the Depression worsened. Back-to-the-land would save the government considerable money over the costs of relief, he stated in late 1932. "The speaker did not concede that British Columbia is not an agricultural province nor that agricultural possibilities are already overdone," the *Province* reported. Four months later, Lougheed's faith was even stronger; he declared that "British Columbia's best days are yet to come" and celebrated the westward trek of unemployed men. The Depression offered an opportunity to change society for the better: "I feel we have learned a very severe lesson. If we can get the idle men out of the cities and back on to the land for their own support, it will not be long before British Columbia emerges to greater and sounder progress than it has ever known before."[28]

Lougheed was supported by various members of the province's elite. Throughout 1932 and into 1933, various back-to-the-land plans arrived in

the premier's office. Fell and Scharfe, the real estate agents who had been
employed by the Tolmie government to sell the Sumas lands, sent in a
complete scheme. Colonization Commissioner Gaddes and Publicity Commissioner Bruce McKelvie offered suggestions about settlement plans. Concerned citizens sent the premier complete, handwritten programs. Some
of these came from outside the province; others came from those who
might personally benefit, such as the marginally employed engineer Edward
Townsend from Vancouver and returned soldiers Joseph Smith and A.M.
Robertson of Victoria. A group called the Yeomen of Britain suggested
large-scale settlement of British farmers in the province, arguing that the
move would certainly provide spin-off work.[29]

One settlement plan came in from G.R. Bates, who had worked for the
Land Settlement Board at Merville. This experience had not shaken his
faith in community land settlement plans. The back-to-the-land program
he suggested incorporated most of the elements of the Merville plan – he
even suggested another progress loan scheme, despite the fact that progress
loans had tended to drive Merville settlers into debt. Bates' approach was
typical: many of the back-to-the-land schemes incorporated key elements
of the community settlement plans of the 1920s. They advocated that
land, implements, and stock be provided for settlers, and that house construction and land clearing be provided or that settlers be recompensed for
their work. In any case, retaining a spirit similar to the liberal individualism of the 1920s settlement plans, most plans proposed that all the costs
of settlement eventually be paid off by the settlers. The new plans generally maintained the focus on cooperation in marketing and purchasing,
and the spatial embodiment of cooperation in the form of a community
centre. All assumed the capacity of the land to provide for settlers' needs,
and the necessity of increasing the rural population; most presumed that
experts were required to guide the process of development.

Some writers were aware of the problems of previous settlements. The
most common solution was to tweak the terms of repayment: for example,
some writers suggested that a system of land taxes replace direct repayment.
Often these solutions formed the most detailed sections of the proposal.
Other writers suggested changes to the size of the land grants; some advocated 160 acres per farm, while others (such as Lougheed) advocated small
farms of only a few acres. Tolmie wrote of Lougheed's plan for small chicken
farms on partially cleared lands to the Canadian Minister of Labour.[30] A
few writers proposed essentially to give the land to private companies, and
allow them to run the scheme. Common to all the schemes, however, was
the new understanding that settlers were not really expected to make a living

off their farms. The plan was for subsistence farming, at least initially. "A man on the land is off the congested labor market for most of the year and has a chance to work for himself and family even if he only manages to exist for the first few years," explained F.C. Brown of the Canadian Western Cordage Company.[31]

It is worth repeating, however, that these plans were not simply calls to sweep the unemployed out of sight. Many of the strategies reflected the general assumption that something was wrong with the current system, and that some kind of fundamental change was required. Back-to-the-land appealed to those who, like returned soldier Joseph Smith, were "opposed to this Red Flag element, and have not lost faith in the Land of their adoption." G.R. Bates thought that an aberrant era was over: "Will we ever again see wages so high that it will be to the financial advantage of the small farmer to throw up his farm and become a wage earner? Personally I doubt it."[32] If industry was threatened, the land remained the source and centre of a strong economy.

Not everyone was convinced. Powerful critics included farmers' groups, a Conservative riding association, and senior bureaucrats. These people pointed to one or both of two significant problems: the cost of the settlement schemes, and the already distressed condition of rural areas. The Maple Grove Conservative Association on isolated Lasqueti Island wrote to the premier, requesting that the government help cash-poor farmers already on the land. Representatives of Fraser Valley farmers complained that back-to-the-land would only depress prices further by encouraging even more overproduction. The proposal to use lands that had reverted to the government (due to unpaid taxes) was a non-starter, "inasmuch as such lands were vacated because they did not pay the taxes charged to them or contribute to the sustenance of those formerly occupying them." Rural municipalities were already in financial trouble, paying for relief and education, and back-to-the-land promised to increase the costs of education. The Fraser Valley branch of the British Columbia School Trustees Association pointed out to the premier that it was costly to provide schools for children who lived outside the settlement centre. And it was these very remote, unoccupied lands that were targeted by back-to-the-land promoters.[33]

Colonization Commissioner Gaddes, meanwhile, remained convinced that all back-to-the-land plans were simply too costly. Asked to comment on one scheme, Gaddes replied that, while he was sure it would work, it would require "large sums of money, and the difficulty is in this and other plans, that there is no source from which the necessary funds can be supplied." Tolmie, dissatisfied, wrote back and testily asked for more details.

Though Gaddes' response politely proposed a stripped-down version of the original scheme, he clearly remained unconvinced. In answer to the common suggestion that back-to-the-land would not cost more than direct relief, Gaddes noted that "the cost of any settlement scheme which aims at putting unemployed on farms and making them self-supporting is about ten times as much as direct relief." To ensure that the premier had not missed the point, he explained further: "that is, direct relief could be maintained for ten years for the cost of a doubtful experiment of land settlement."[34]

Perhaps it was Gaddes' tour through the land settlement projects of the 1920s that had nurtured this negative attitude, or perhaps it was born of his time in the Ministry of Lands, where Deputy Minister H. Cathcart was also a consistent critic of land settlement. Cathcart, too, believed that settlement schemes were too expensive and made little sense given the depressed state of the rural economy. He pointed out that even where no direct assistance was offered to the settler, support in the form of surveying, road building, and utilities might still have to be supplied.

Cathcart argued further that such schemes made little sense given that land was readily available – either almost free through pre-emption or cheap through the purchase of tax-reverted lands or empty lands in one of the LSB's Land Settlement Areas. "It would be rather difficult to suggest more reasonable inducements unless it should be decided to make absolutely free grants to each intending settler," he commented sarcastically: "Possibly the settler might at the same time desire a bonus to induce him to stay upon the land and work it." For Cathcart, the entire history of organized land settlement was a litany of failure:

> In regard to community settlement, reference might be made to several undertakings of this nature in the past, viz. Bella Coola, Norwegian settlement; Cape Scott, and northerly Vancouver Island, Danish colonization; Malcolm Island, Finnish colonization. None of these met with favourable results, with possibly the exception of Bella Coola, and perhaps if the outlay made in this valley since the settlement first took place up to the present time were figured out, it would be felt that this has been rather a costly proposition. Mention might also be made of the soldier settlements at Merville, Camp Lister and South Okanagan. I think it would be fair to assume that had these lands been subdivided and placed on the market without the heavy initial expenditure and subsequent outlay, these settlements might have been just as far advanced and the communities self-supporting.[35]

For the senior bureaucrat in the Ministry of Lands, then, the history of organized settlement demonstrated that organized settlement was costly and unproductive. The market should structure land resettlement, unencumbered by attempts to build communities or provide alternatives to capitalist modernity.

The opposition of Cathcart, Gaddes, other bureaucrats and political appointees, riding associations, and school trustees was not enough to stem entirely the enthusiasm of provincial elites and politicians for the idea of sending the unemployed back to the land, particularly not when other levels of government could be saddled with part of the bill. The one significant, organized back-to-the-land effort was the Dominion Relief Land Settlement Plan. The plan was conceived by the Dominion government, funded jointly by Canada, the provinces, and the municipalities, and administered by a volunteer committee of politicians and interested businesspeople.

In this project of the Canadian government's Department of Labour, families were to be assisted in settling on selected farmlands, where they would be given two years to become "self-supporting." Each level of government would contribute a maximum of $600 towards the costs of establishing a family on the land. This money was to be spent on transportation, equipment and supplies, food and other subsistence needs, and general costs associated with resettlement. Of this money $500 was to be allotted to the settler in the first year, with the remaining $100 to be held for emergencies in the second year, when the family would presumably be on its way to becoming self-supporting. As the plan was run by volunteers, no money was to be spent on administration, and the land would be provided free by the province and the dominion. The plan was to be administered by the province, with the names of settlers being recommended by the municipality.[36]

In May 1932, in response to a telegram from the Canadian government outlining the parameters of the scheme, Minister of Lands Lougheed opened a meeting of the BC Government Relief Land Settlement Committee. The committee included representatives from the federal government's Soldier Settlement Board; Gaddes, the Colonization Commissioner, representing the provincial government; and representatives from the City of Vancouver, the City of New Westminster, the Union of BC Municipalities, the Vancouver Board of Trade, and the Canadian National Railways. W.S. Latta, formerly of the Land Settlement Board, was appointed secretary. Though designated as an advisory in various records, this committee actually ran the scheme, drawing up the contract and application form to be filled out by settlers, and selecting settlers from the names forwarded by the Cities of Vancouver and New Westminster.

The committee requested and received the help of officials from various other departments to carry out the actual work of selecting land, arranging for transport, purchasing and providing supplies to the families, and supervising the settlers for two years. Particularly important in this work were engineers from the public works department and district agriculturalists, experts paid by the Department of Agriculture. Latta was the only official whose paid job was to work on the Dominion Relief Land Settlement Plan.[37] The lands came from a variety of sources. They might be left-over lands from the federal Soldier Settlement Board or the provincial Land Settlement Board, tax-reverted lands, or lands purchased from private owners (if the lands could be acquired at a reasonable cost).[38]

The committee moved quickly, selecting settlers from lists supplied by Vancouver and New Westminster. But in March 1933, the BC government announced that the province could afford to fund only fifty families. The committee's plans to fund sixty-seven families, and to extend the plan to cover the smaller cities of Trail and Burnaby – and their hopes of accommodating some of the one hundred people from unorganized territory (for whom the BC government would have to put up $400 each) – were out of the question. Now, the benefits of the plan would be extended only to the families of Joseph Sherwin, Ole Olson, Tom Platts, and ten others from New Westminster, as well as to the Vancouver families of Benjamin Jones, Christian Simpson, George White, Alain Gagnon, and thirty-four others.[39] Of the more than one thousand people who had written to the Ministry of Lands looking for a farm, these people were the lucky ones.[40] Most correspondents received standard letters of regret.

By July, most of the families had been settled on their farms and, the committee reported, were doing very well: most had good houses, gardens, a cow or goat, and chickens, while some had planted crops. The families were in various places throughout the province. Many were in central BC near Prince George, Quesnel, and Vanderhoof. A few were in the Fraser Valley, and a couple families were placed near Duncan on Vancouver Island. Christian Simpson's family got a farm in the Sumas Dyking District, George White's family was placed in Moose Heights near Quesnel, while Alain Gagnon and his family now lived in Engen in the vicinity of Vanderhoof. Some committee members visited families in the Fraser Valley and "found every one without exception doing very well. The families were contented and greatly pleased with the outlook for the future." As time wore on, however, the picture began to look more troubled. Reports came in that some families had returned to Vancouver. By October, six families had exhausted their $500. The Sherwin family, as we have seen, was short of everything, including food and shoes. By December, a total of four families had left their farms. "The amount of $500 for the first year ...," Latta reported, "[was] totally inadequate." Fourteen families were on relief, and he expected that "the majority, if not all, of the families in the Interior will have to be taken care of by direct relief" at some point in the winter.[41]

In the end, no more settlers were sent out. Each year, a few more families abandoned their farms, though more than half made it to the end of the Depression. By the end of 1934, forty families remained, the majority sustained by special grants of additional money or relief, in addition to the $100 held back for their second year. Thirty-six made it through the next year, with the help of an additional grant of $100 and direct relief for some. Both Latta and relief officers from Vancouver, seeming to disregard earlier talk of subsistence farming, noted that the settlers could not become self-sufficient without a better market for agricultural products. At the end of 1936, the BC government failed to renew its agreement with Canada, and the plan failed. Thirty-three families remained on their farms; the others fell victim to ill health, found better work opportunities elsewhere, or met with other, unspecified circumstances. The $700 that was eventually allotted to each family, Latta reported, was inadequate in nearly every case.[42] Over the next three years, seventeen more families left their farms. The gradual improvement of the economy over this time possibly contributed to this, providing families with other opportunities. On the eve of the Second World War, sixteen families remained on their farms, and of the six that the provincial government considered to be its responsibility, none was close to purchasing the land it had been given.[43]

"The back to the land idea is sound," the newspaper *New Outlook* reported, "because ... [t]he land is 'mother of us all,' and when men are seized with the longing or the necessity to go back to the land it may be more than a mere sentimental whim or a drab economic urge that is troubling them."[44] Though we might wish to strip this idea of its slightly dated language, it contains an essential truth. We get our food from the land, in particular from agriculture. It is likely that the need to be connected with nature in some fashion is a deep human longing. But this does not mean that the land will always provide.

The Relief Land Settlement Plan was based on a vague and desperate sense of the land as saviour, a sense that found expression in the idea that settlers were "going out on a purely subsistence basis," as Gaddes explained.[45] Belief in the feasibility of subsistence farming was rooted in faith rather than fact, however. Subsistence farming could exist in an established agricultural area, given the existence of a social system set up to deal with crop failures and other periodic problems. In the case of the Relief Land Settlement Plan, no such system existed. In the first year in the Quesnel region, poor weather and previously unfarmed soil led to crop failure. The settlers were so poor that they could not fence out game and cattle, which destroyed much of their oat crop, and many could not afford a horse to help clear and plow.[46] In a healthy agricultural economy, the new settlers could have worked off their farms as agricultural labourers or in the woods until their land could pay. This was not possible given the poverty of neighbouring farmers and the isolated location of many of the farms. Subsistence farming was no solution to the Depression; instead, bad economic conditions made the prospect of subsistence farming an even less viable option. As those charged with carrying out the scheme and those concerned with established farming systems realized, settlers would succeed or fail based on their ability to live within the existing framework of capitalist agriculture.

A NEW DEAL

Unemployed people remained interested in the program, though, and the Ministry of Lands continued to turn people away until the end of the decade. The ministry received more than one thousand pages of enquiries in 1934.[47] Despite this interest, the government does not seem to have seriously considered sending out more settlers. In addition to the obvious flaws in the plan, the program was the victim of a change in government. Back in power, the Liberals brought with them a new understanding of the proper relationship between the state and the economy, an understanding that would shift the place of agriculture in provincial development.

On 1 September 1933, the five-year mandate of the Tolmie government ended, and Tolmie reluctantly called an election for 2 November. Tolmie was desperate. His government was thoroughly discredited by its inability to solve the Depression. Pattullo gleefully publicized cases of Conservative inaction and patronage. The government's combination of inaction and gross error gave Pattullo plenty of ammunition. In 1930, Tolmie had replaced his finance minister with J.W. Jones, an MP from the Okanagan and a long-time critic of the Liberals' land settlement policies. Jones preached economy but also called for tax hikes; his first budget brought in a 1 percent surtax for married men on all wages over $25 per week and for all others on wages over $15 per week. For his efforts, he became known as "one percent Jones." But, as Pattullo pointed out, it would take the surtax on the wages of twelve hundred working girls to add up to the expense of the new British Columbia Agent-General in London.[48]

In April, the premier received a visit from a group of businessmen (led by forestry millionaire H.R. MacMillan) who expressed their dissatisfaction with the government's financial management. Tolmie decided to allow a committee of businessmen full access to the government's books, in order to investigate and report on the matter. The recommendations of the resulting commission, known as the Kidd Commission after committee member George Kidd, shocked everyone. The commission called for a drastic cut to provincial spending, including cutting off the University of British Columbia entirely and ending free public school at age fourteen. More seriously, it recommended reforms that amounted to an attack on the parliamentary system. The size of the legislature was to be cut from forty-eight to twenty-eight members, the cabinet reduced to six members, and the Lieutenant-Governor given the right to veto spending bills. The commission also attacked the party system and advocated a coalition government. The general tenor of these recommendations was confirmed, and extended, when the *British Columbia Financial Times* suggested a benevolent dictatorship for the province.[49]

Pattullo was outraged, and Tolmie refused to implement many of the commission's ideas. Yet the report was proof of big business' condemnation of Tolmie's government. In the month prior to the election, Tolmie took up the cause of coalition government, arguing with Pattullo that the time had come to put aside party interests. Pattullo remained unconvinced, and said so, and the Conservative party itself was hardly more enthusiastic. Former Conservative premier William Bowser returned to active politics to lead the Non-Partisans, a supposedly non-party coalition but one not allied with the Liberals. The election thus pitted a divided Conservative party against Pattullo's comprehensive program of "Work and Wages." The other factor was the new Co-operative Commonwealth Federation (CCF), fighting its first election in BC. On 2 November, the voters dealt the Conservative party a blow from which it has never recovered, electing only one of Tolmie's followers and two of Bowser's followers. The Liberals won thirty-four seats, and the new CCF formed the Opposition with seven seats.[50]

The election of Pattullo's Liberals does not wholly explain the lack of enthusiasm for the Relief Plan, however. As we have seen, Pattullo had been calling for renewed back-to-the-land efforts for several years. Yet Pattullo's calls for a back-to-the-land program disappeared almost immediately after the election; in their place were plans for New Deal–style public works projects. Pattullo's papers offer us no direct insight into why this happened. It may have been that Pattullo had lost faith in back-to-the-land schemes some time before and had simply retained the idea in his platform in the belief that it would be popular. This would explain the suddenness of the post-election shift. But more fundamental, certainly, were two other developments: the bureaucracy's clear ongoing distaste for any sort of city-to-country land settlement, and Pattullo's own evolving political philosophy.

The new Minister of Lands, Wells Gray, dissuaded potential settlers by telling them that the new government had not had time to formulate policy on relief settlement. Internal documents paint a less promising picture. Within the ministries of Lands and of Labour, bureaucratic and ultimately ministerial opinion was that not only was there little money available for land settlement plans, but matters were so bad in the countryside that it made no sense to send relief recipients there. Shortly after the election, Pattullo's Minister of Labour suggested that land settlement plans were more expensive than the province could afford and required experienced farmers in order to work. The plans were unsuited to dealing with the unemployed from decimated industries. Back-to-the-land should take a back seat to providing for the four thousand farmers who, unable to sell what they had grown, had applied for relief. The minister suggested a program of public works and building construction.[51] The Administrator of Unemployment Relief had earlier been stiff and blunt with the outgoing Minister of Lands over the question of money for land settlement plans: "I feel it my duty to point out to you that this Department has not been provided with sufficient funds to carry on for more than a limited period," he stated. Then he stepped outside of his authority: "Unless adequate provision is made to take care of expenditures for Direct Relief for the current fiscal year I cannot permit any of the funds presently authorized to be used for other than Direct Relief purposes."[52]

In the place of back-to-the-land, the minister proposed getting the federal government to provide help with two of the traditional reasons for agricultural underdevelopment in BC. These were the problem of land clearing, and the isolation of farms from each other and from markets. Luckily, federal Minister of Labour Norman Rogers agreed, and had recently arranged for the allotment of federal money for the resettlement of farmers.[53] The result of their exchange was the Farmers Re-location and Re-establishment Plan, which provided $1,000 for relocating farmers who needed it on new lands, and $500 for helping established farmers to improve their land.[54] By 1938, plain-speaking Unemployment Administrator

E.W. Griffith was reminding the minister that "the viewpoint of this Department is that we should first devote all of our efforts to the re-establishment or relocation of all settlers now on relief before any new land settlement policy is embarked upon."[55] Back-to-the-land, it would seem, had fallen into the background, a victim of a lack of provincial funding (particularly as the Farmers Relocation scheme was funded primarily by the Dominion). Yet these developments must also be seen in the light of a history of failed attempts to move people from the city to the country. By the mid-1930s, this history had convinced many of the impracticality of such schemes.

If the bureaucracy thought that back-to-the-land was simply too difficult to make work, however, the scheme's demise was also the result of policy shifts on the part of the BC Liberal Party. The Minister of Labour's talk of public works and construction projects indicates this, as does his comment in a letter to Pattullo: "both you and I have in our minds" such ideas.[56] The Liberals had been elected on a reform platform very similar to that of Franklin Roosevelt, whom the premier admired. A new liberal idea like back-to-the-land had little place in the New Deal–style scheme that the premier proposed for British Columbia.

The Liberals' slogan of "Work and Wages" expressed the essence of Pattullo's promise for the province. In numerous speeches and policy documents, the party outlined a program based on Pattullo's boundless faith in British Columbia and his belief in the ability of the government to revive the economy through stimulation of demand and active coordination of economic activity.

Pattullo was never shy about declaring his faith in BC, thundering in reply to the Tolmie government's budget speech in 1933 that "so long as there is an atom of fertility in the soil of British Columbia, so long as there is an ounce of mineral in her mountains, so long as there is a fish in the sea, so long as there is a fowl in the air, I will, to the capacity of our resources, see to it that our people shall not want for the means of subsistence."[57] His confidence in British Columbia went beyond its natural resources to its people, and he deplored the waste of human resources he saw around him. The finances of the government, or the "national credit" as Pattullo liked to say, should be used for the purpose of expanding purchasing power through the creation of a program of public works. If the nation was at war, then the national credit would be used to finance the war, he said prophetically: why not finance a war on unemployment? He proposed a National Economic Council and similar provincial councils, designed to coordinate the work of industry, bring production and consumption closer, help find markets for private enterprise, and consider questions of wages and hours of work. The province should renegotiate the terms of its loans in order to pay off its debts at more affordable rates. The federal government should bring in unemployment insurance, and some degree of state health insurance should be established. The rest of the platform was a variety of smaller, more concrete measures – studying the education system, encouraging tourist traffic by improving the highways, giving the Peace River some sort of access to the coast, and moving as many people as possible onto the land, so as to give them a chance to produce their own food.[58]

The similarity of this platform to the New Deal policies of Franklin D. Roosevelt's Democratic Party was hardly lost on Pattullo. "The new President of the United States seems to be a man of action," he noted, commenting dryly that, "when I heard his Inaugural Address, I thought that he must have been reading the platform of the Liberal Party of British Columbia and speeches of leaders of liberal thought in this Province."[59]

Pattullo's new policies reflected a shift away from the sort of liberalism characteristic of the Progressive era. Pattullo and the Liberal Party had earlier drawn on a "new liberalism" that, among other things, stressed the impact of the material environment on the individual. In other words, individuals could be reformed through changes in their environment. This idea provided room to consider the impact of the natural environment on social and economic development. Ultimately, the environment – social, material, and natural – could and should be subject to rational management by experts in order to create a better environment and so a better individual.[60]

Thus, soldiers could be rehabilitated through countryside resettlement, the Oliver government held, and a better society could be created through constructing a better (social and natural) environment. The Oliver government had engaged in a whole range of such progressive social reform measures: the regulation of wages and hours of work, the creation of a Department of Labour and of a Workmen's Compensation Board, public health measures, and the establishment of mothers' and old-age pensions.[61] For the Oliver government, land settlement had been about protecting the liberal individual from industrial capitalism, giving him the independence and security that could come only from owning and working land.

Pattullo's platform was an indication that the popularity of these goals was coming to an end. The New Deal variant of liberalism was about working with large capitalism, not limiting it or working towards alternatives to it. It accepted that most people would make their living in wage work, and aimed to make enough of such work available while protecting the individual through such measures as unemployment insurance. Most crucially for the argument made here, New Deal thought largely rejected the link between people and their natural environments. For Pattullo, everything had changed. In 1934, he wrote to Mackenzie King, thanking him for a charming visit to Kingsmere and noting its capacity to induce reflection. "My house where I now am stands alone on the rocks overlooking the sea, which at the moment merely murmurs its message," Pattullo wrote, and "I think that I should take this opportunity to write you a few impressions." He wrote mostly of policy prescriptions for which he clearly hoped to win King's support, but at one point the letter took a broader view of the state of the world as Pattullo saw it. "Scientific discovery and invention have made possible and brought about a higher standard of living for an ever increasing number of our people," Pattullo wrote. He continued, "It is useless to say that we must get back to the old days of the simple life. The great majority of our people simply will do nothing of the kind ..., [n]or do I think that there is any reason why they should. A higher standard of living having been made possible there should follow opportunity for an ever increasing percentage of our people to rise to these standards, not for the purpose of over-indulgence but for the greater enjoyment of the daily pursuit, for leisure and for cultural development."[62]

For Pattullo, architect of the most ambitious of the 1920s land settlement projects, the old dream was over. That dream had been one of anchoring the old values in the new society, of making modern the old days of the simple life. Yet the experiment had largely failed; in the meantime, industry had grown in BC, and the dominance of monopoly capitalism in North American economic, social, and cultural life could not be denied.

The memory of the soldier settlements changed. Pattullo remained fond of referring to them (in particular the South Okanagan project) during his days in opposition. But now they appeared to be more public works and less attempts to fashion a preferred way of life.[63] The acceptance by the Liberals of large-scale industrial capitalism became even more apparent as Pattullo, in power, pared down his program to concentrate on using the national credit for public works. There was little place in this scheme for back-to-the-land, now that land settlement largely no longer held the promise of a better world. Pattullo continued to refer to back-to-the-land occasionally, though always in the minimalist sense: it was better than starving in the city. Meanwhile, to the extent that it could afford to do so, the government concentrated on relief projects that had little to do with farming, such as the Young Men's Forestry Training Camps and Placer Miner Training. Government money went into public works such as the building of the Pattullo Bridge and UBC's Chancellor Boulevard. A victim of the legacy of the 1920s, and of a lack of money and a change in philosophy, organized land settlement as government policy was dead.

This is not to say that all talk of going back to the land disappeared. Various small projects were carried out over the years of the Depression. One example was what newspapers referred to as a "Quiet Back to the Land." There was a "noticeable turning to the land" in the early years of the Depression, according to Vancouver's *Province*. The Colonization Commissioner claimed that more people than ever before left the city in 1932 to settle on lands in various parts of the province. In the Fraser Valley, the *Province* reported, land was being cleared and houses built, and some farmers with large farms were subdividing them into small farms. The paper even reported approvingly on the settlement of Japanese families in the Fraser Valley, noting that the families "go in for intensive cultivation and their gardens are beauty spots."[64] At the same time, and in conjunction with the Dominion, the BC government was running a scheme of farm homes for boys. Poor youths would be paid five dollars per month to work for farmers who could not otherwise afford help.[65]

The BC government's one continuing farm-based relief project demonstrated its abandonment of the ideal of the independent farmer and its concern with the rights of the worker. In the winter of 1934, the new government tried to place single, unemployed men as farm labourers. Concerned with the possibility of replacing people already working on farms, the government specified that the relief workers were to work only on jobs outside of the normal routine of the farm. Few farmers took up this offer. Then, in the fall of 1936, the government tried again, signing on to a farm labour plan initiated by the Canadian Department of Labour. Canada and the province would jointly pay each man $7.50 per month. But the men rebelled. Jack Phillips of the Single Unemployed Association threw Pattullo's election promise back at him, demanding "work and wages [–] work for which we are fitted, at the wages which we deserve." The government responded by saying that any who refused the offer would be considered to be not serious about finding work; the men stated that they would go to work in the woods, but not on farms.[66]

The City of Vancouver, meanwhile, instituted a number of farm-related relief schemes over the latter part of the Depression. Starting in 1933, the Community Garden League distributed packets of seeds to relief recipients and arranged for empty lots in the neighbourhood of Kerrisdale to be used as garden land. The city donated twelve-and-a-half cents per recipient, and the league distributed seeds to between three thousand and five thousand people. Like the settlement schemes of the 1920s, this one depended on expert help and surveillance – seeds were distributed in April, and garden league members inspected the gardens in the summer. In the Vancouver suburb of Burnaby, a parallel organization distributed packets of carrots, parsnips, peas, beans, lettuce, turnips, cabbage, and beets.[67]

In another case, back-to-the-land intersected with the cooperative movement in the form of the Economic Security Co-operative Association, which aimed to create a community settlement for unemployed Vancouver men at Sayward on northern Vancouver Island. The association had 150 acres of cleared land available to it for free at Sayward, supplied by one J.E. Armishaw. The association was renting livestock from Armishaw, including eighty sheep. The site also featured a vacant sawmill. The association hoped to sell products to other cooperatives in Britain. When the group approached the city, it had already secured the support of the provincial Minister of Labour and the province's Administrator of Relief, who had promised $500 to refurbish the mill, money for transportation to the island, and the continuation of relief payments for eight months (four months' worth of which would be distributed up front as a lump sum payment). The city agreed to distribute its relief payments in the same way. With this backing, the settlers proceeded to the island. They soon found that their seed money was inadequate; by September, the city had agreed to advance them the remainder of their relief money. By November, though, the group had disintegrated. Several settlers stayed on, fortified by food relief payments from the city and the province, while the remainder were shipped back home by the province.[68]

This was to be one of the last stabs at back-to-the-land settlement. The legacy of the 1920s and the sheer difficulty of establishing farms in British Columbia had discouraged the adoption of back-to-the-land as a viable strategy for dealing with the Depression. It had become clear that the province was turning away from agriculture. As Pattullo indicated in his letter to Mackenzie King, and as suggested by the preference of the unemployed Vancouver men for forest labour over farm labour, the easy equation of industry and wage work with lack of virtue and moral decline was coming to an end. This was not just a British Columbian phenomenon. The terrible rural poverty of the Depression, the dust storms, and the rootless, desperate farmers of the prairies eroded much of the faith in agriculture's ability to anchor an alternative modernity to the industrial world. By the time of the Second World War the idea that agriculture was somehow central to the image of British Columbia had largely faded.[69] With it, at last, went the old colonial policy of land resettlement.

Yet as the country descended into war, and the Depression came to an end, Vancouver became involved in one final settlement scheme. In 1940, a "Citizens Advisory Council," apparently separate from the city and the province but ultimately operating with their blessing, set up the Salt Spring Island Community Farm, on the most populated of the Gulf Islands, in Georgia Strait between Victoria and Vancouver. Designed for single "unemployables" around the age of fifty, it was just as hierarchical, but more communal, than the liberal individualistic community settlements it followed. A central farmhouse featured a kitchen, a sitting room, staff bedrooms, and five dormitory rooms for the men, all fully wired for electricity. The house was surrounded by blacksmith and carpentry shops, a barn, poultry sheds, pig runs, and twenty acres of cropped land. The farm was worked like a factory. Each man had a job – fencing, plowing, wood-cutting, shake-splitting. The purpose of the farm was to give these men a better form of life than they would have had unemployed in the city. The farm was to pay for itself, ultimately, or at least to be cheaper than keeping men on relief. "Waste land" was being "brought into productivity," and "in the process of farm and land rehabilitation, men whose outlook was hopeless are being rehabilitated also."[70]

While looking forward, then, to a final acceptance of proletarianization and the centrality of wage work, and also, perhaps, to the communal land settlements of the 1960s, the Salt Spring Island farm also looked back to old values of rehabilitation and the virtues of the countryside, to the positives of the interaction between humans and the land. At its heart, the farm was designed to be a refuge for those battered by the interwar years. Some of the men were as young as forty-five, young enough to have been among the returned men of 1919. They were men who, "because of inability through sickness (generally resultant from many years on Relief), precedence of youth over age, lack of training, and various similar reasons, would never, in all probability, be absorbed into Private Industry again."[71] They differed from the mostly young settlers of Merville and the other communities of the 1920s, a reserve army of left-over labour rather than the cutting edge of a new age. No longer vanguards of a new age, they were instead relics of the interwar period. And like the ideals of this period, like the dream of transcending the dominance of industrial capitalism with a new life on the land, the men were expected to silently fade away.

Conclusion

SOME OF THE SOLDIER SETTLERS NEVER LEFT MERVILLE. The Clarks, as we saw in Chapter 3, stayed until 1962. The Hodgins lived there well into the 1980s. For their children, Merville was home. Jack Hodgins was born in the area in 1938 and grew up in Merville; the memory of the stories told around his family's kitchen table led to his decision to become a writer and, eventually, to become Vancouver Island's best known novelist. In 1998, Hodgins published *Broken Ground,* the story of a Vancouver Island soldier settlement called Portuguese Creek. Portuguese Creek is Merville thinly disguised, from the intricacies of blasting stumps to the great fire, including fictionalized versions of actual people and memories of the war that brought them all to a rough settlement in the Vancouver Island bush.[1]

On Saturday, 23 March 1968, Peter and Jennie Sprout represented one family of the seven remaining original settler families when their friends, children, ten grandchildren and two great-grandchildren gathered to help them celebrate fifty years of marriage.[2] A few years after this, Merville's second era of settlement began with the arrival of another settler group. Like the soldier settlers fifty years before, this group was trying to make good at farming. But unlike the returned men and their families, these settlers were trying to leave behind the larger society. These back-to-the-landers, refugees from the modernity of the 1960s, delighted in and celebrated their rustic lifestyle, chronicling their community's exploits in the pages of the *Gumboot Gazette.*[3]

Residents of the Comox Valley were not the only British Columbians to have such idealists in their midst. Communes sprang up all over the province in the 1970s, from Vancouver Island to the Kootenays, the Okanagan Valley, and the Cariboo. They had names such as Bar None Farm, Harmony Farmstead Co-op, Earth Seed, and Centre of the World Beautiful. They got advice from the "Tribes" column in the radical Vancouver weekly *The Georgia Straight,* and discussed issues at meetings of the British Columbia Coalition of Intentional Co-operative Communities, or in the newsletter *Open Circle.* Some settlements were small affairs consisting of, in the words of author and former commune-kid Justine Brown, "a motley group of cabins, a geodesic dome or an old converted school bus with chickens scratching on the roof and a clump of dope-smoking longhairs nodding within."[4] Others were more serious, such as the Marxist-Leninist CEEDS (Community Education and Economic Development Society) collective. Admirers of Native society but opposed to antimodernist idealizations of pre-contact culture, the people of CEEDS attempted to engage with contemporary Native people. Though this attempt met with problems, their more successful experiments in organic farming survive to this day.[5]

The highly political, revolutionary CEEDS group was a contrast to less engaged groups and to New Age spiritualist groups such as the Emissaries of the Divine Light, who set up shop near 100 Mile House, northwest of Kamloops.[6] Ultimately, the commune movement is too diverse to allow for succinct summary here. Though occupying some of the same land as the settlers of the 1920s and 1930s, this was a different movement, often motivated by disgust with or dread of the contemporary world. American academic and commune dweller Judson Jerome wrote in 1974 that "when we moved to the commune where we now live, Downhill Farm, my wife and I had a sense that it was just in time, that we were getting ourselves and our children out just ahead of a tidal wave of infection."[7] People such as Jerome and the CEEDS collective dreamed of an entirely new world, not a better form of modern life. Many of the commune dwellers were looking more for escape than anything else – if not escape from the larger society, then often from a counterculture that seemed to have gone wrong.[8]

The goal of escaping the city, of a better life lived closer to nature, brought together the soldier settlers of the 1920s and the back-to-the-landers of the 1970s. But the goal of 1920s rural settlement to bring humans and nature closer together within modernity – of building a new, modern form of rural life, or what I have called an alternative modernity – separates the early settlers from the later groups. Like the planners, intellectuals, engineers, and songwriters whom Richard White examined in his history of the Columbia River, those involved with BC's interwar resettlement project did not believe that the interests of humans and nature were inherently opposed. Americans, White argues, have more often believed that humans and nature are not inherently opposed and that, in building dams and laying out settlements, they were working with nature, not against it. Reflecting the ideas of such thinkers as Lewis Mumford, interwar engineers and planners saw themselves as building a society that would bring together human technology and the natural world.[9] Similarly, Michel Girard has argued that the federal government's Canadian Commission of Conservation (1909-21) understood the world as a set of systems, economic (as well as social and political) and ecological; the commission's goal was to bring these systems into sync.[10] "By all means," said F.N. Sinclair, Chief Engineer on the Sumas Project, of his reclamation plans, "let us aid nature, not oppose it."[11]

From our current vantage point, such an idea is hard to appreciate. As we have seen, in BC the belief in the possibility of an alternative, rural modernity was lost in the shift to Pattullo's New Deal. New Dealers rejected the formation of an alternative to industrial capitalism in favour of working with it to secure better results for the worker and society. The experience of the 1920s, in any case, convinced many in BC's bureaucracy and political class that there were limits to the land's capacity to provide, and that these limits had been reached in British Columbia. The distressed condition of established farms during the Great Depression only reinforced this conviction. Nor were these isolated developments. The problems of BC's rural areas were a small part of a much larger phenomenon, a point most spectacularly illustrated by the images that emerged during the 1930s from the continent's central plains – great, rolling clouds of black dust descending on towns, destitute farmers driving "Bennett Buggies" (cars with the engine removed and a horse attached, named after the prime minister), people gathered in collections of shacks (referred to in the US as Hoovervilles). Clearly, there was nothing romantic about farm life under industrial capitalism. The life of the independent family farmer was one of uncertainty, whereas the wartime and postwar economy could offer security to factory and office workers. A further blow to countryside ideals was the very fact that the country had been held up as a morally superior alternative to liberal capitalism. As such, it was embraced by all sorts – new liberals like Pattullo but also, fatally, by fascism, one of the two great alternatives to liberal capitalism in the interwar years. Despite the fact that a number of those sympathetic to fascism thought and wrote about agriculture and its place in modern life, the connection between the two was loose and adventitious. But with the defeat of fascism and the revelations of the horrors of the Nazi regime, ideas associated with them died a quick and inevitable death.[12]

The success of liberal capitalism in the postwar era of high modernism built a bigger wall than ever between the natural environment and much of the North American middle class. Steady work in industry and the professions, suburban homes, and high-speed highways contributed to making nature into an other, an image on a screen or a place to visit on holidays.[13] The steady growth of the Canadian and American national, provincial, and state parks systems has, as well, been the result of and a contributor to the idea that the true nature exists somewhere else, in wilderness, a place where there are no other humans and no evidence of their presence. The problem with this, as William Cronon has pointed out, is that it makes dealing with the human relationship with nature into a problem of preserving the most representative examples of wilderness. This means that the nature encountered by the average middle-class inhabitant of a city or a town – fields, trees, air, the Great Lakes – is not really nature, and so is not in need of attention. Nature is removed from daily life, and with it goes a consciousness of how daily activities impinge on nature. Further, so complete has been the victory of the wilderness ideal that contemporary critiques of the human relationship with nature tend implicitly to accept its terms. Those who do not demonstrate the sort of affection for untouched nature and suspicion of modernity that characterizes contemporary wilderness advocates – such as BC's proponents of an alternative modernity, or White's dam builders – are suspect.[14] From our point of view, their actions all too easily appear as simple resource extraction, and their ideas of bringing together human and natural systems seem naïve or manipulative.

Yet the consequences of this shift, for agriculture at least, have been serious. No longer idealized as a way of connecting humans with nature, agriculture has become largely an industrial activity, a process of maximizing production through the application of ever-more sophisticated products (such as chemical fertilizers or patented, genetically modified seeds) to the soil, using ever-more complex and expensive means of production (heavy farm machinery). The Green Revolution, the common name for the improvements in agricultural knowledge and techniques that have brought increased food supplies to the developing world, depends on such processes. Industrial agriculture is also tied closely to large-scale agro-capitalism. Farmers now depend on expensive farm equipment and on seeds that have been genetically altered so as to never reproduce, forcing the farmer to purchase new seed stocks every year. Meanwhile, oil-based fertilizers and pesticides slowly poison the soil.[15]

The land settlement enthusiasts of the 1920s believed in living in and working with nature. Interwar planners and engineers did not see nature as purely a set of resources to be exploited. This is not to say that their vision was not flawed. Their beliefs were based on a cultural ideal rooted in more easily farmed places such as England; this ideal fit poorly with the environmental conditions of most of British Columbia. These beliefs were founded on a scientific view of nature in which humans could manage and order the environment relatively un-problematically. Thus, proponents of the alternative modernity aimed at the conversion of existing landscapes into what they thought of as the proper countryside. This goal did not and could not allow them to work within the possibilities of the existing natural order. Colin Duncan has argued that a proper environmental ethic must foster respect for biodiversity, existing ecological complexity, and, in general, the particularities of places.[16] Dedication to a pre-ordained cultural ideal of the countryside does not allow for proper attention to such things, while new developments in ecology, stressing the constant presence of change within the natural world, cast doubt on the entire goal of orderly management. We clearly saw the "disorderly" character of nature, and the difficulties with imposing a rationally managed, orderly state, in the case of the Sumas Reclamation Project. The Vedder River cut itself a new channel in 1890, turning to flow into the lake and increasing its size. Floods on the Fraser were unpredictable in size and timing, and impossible to fully control.

The presence of Europeans and their landscapes is a very recent development in British Columbia. The provincial state's encouragement of resettlement was based on its perceived need to establish European-style settlement patterns in the mostly forbidding landscape of the western mountain cordillera. The landscapes created by land settlement planners and engineers were based on an imported cultural ideal and on economic and political needs. The way in which nature was understood was filtered through contemporary political ideologies and cultural constructs. The result was the transformed valley of the South Okanagan, the abandoned benchland farms near Creston, the draining of Sumas Lake, and the Merville fire. The landscapes of the alternative modernity were a direct result of the place of the environment in new liberalism.

Environmental philosophers have suggested that creating a functioning and sustainable relationship with nature may depend on moving beyond modern ethics, which has concentrated on creating rules for interaction between individuals. Environmental ethics, some suggest, may need to concentrate instead on character and virtues, guiding not individual behaviour in specific situations but suggesting a moral attitude towards the world and a way that attitude could be expressed.[17] If this is true, then the promises of the alternative modernity ideal are more important than its flaws. Inherent in the idea of creating an alternative rural modernity was a transcendence of the human/nature dichotomy that lies at the heart of the wilderness ideal. The example of the alternative modernity ideal suggests the possibility of an alternative path, a way around the intractable wars between environmentalists and capital. If the particular formulation for living in nature was flawed, then the idea of building a relationship between modern society and the natural world remains important and hopeful.

The projects of the Land Settlement Board and the Ministry of Lands inevitably left legacies, some significant, some quirky. The literature alone is impressive. Merville turned out Jack Hodgins, while Camp Lister can claim some credit for Earle Birney. As isolated pieces of farmland, Merville and Camp Lister have nurtured those unable or unwilling to fit into mainstream society. Merville became home to the back-to-the-land settlers of the 1970s; an even more isolated Camp Lister is now home for polygamous Mormons. Sumas Lake has not returned, and few now know that it ever existed. The Vedder Canal system is part of the BC government's Fraser Valley flood control system, its original purpose little known by the thousands of daily travelers on the Trans-Canada Highway, which passes through the former lakebed.

The southern Okanagan Valley today is a green agricultural landscape, dotted with wineries. The main canal is a little difficult for visitors to find, but once located, it can be followed easily enough. From its head under MacIntyre Bluff, it runs south and slightly east, cutting under the highway and then snaking across the dry lands just north of Oliver. Nearer town, it runs across the top of a driving range and through a golf course, at one point bridged by golf-cart paths. Residents of the valley still rely on "the ditch" (the name given to the canal by Julie Cancella in her celebratory local history) to keep the southern Okanagan green and productive. In less arable, un-irrigated lands, the original semi-desert landscape remains. Since the 1920s, the attitude of North American society towards these dry lands has changed. Now considered valuable as being unique in

Canada, a portion of them was set aside by the BC government in 2001 as the South Okanagan Grasslands Protected Area. This park, in the hills overlooking the irrigation area, is dedicated – ironically enough – to preserving the grassland environment that the South Okanagan project had sought to transform. The valley is a living symbol of the problems and possibilities inherent in creating a countryside in British Columbia.

Appendix

The following table gives some information on the background and fates of early soldier settlers at Merville. The table was compiled from biographies in Reta Blakely Hodgins, ed., *Merville and Its Early Settlers 1919-1985* (Merville, BC: Merville Community Association, 1985). The data are, unfortunately, too spotty to be the basis for any definite conclusions. As well, the biographies are only of people whom Hodgins and her assistants (working in Merville in the 1980s), could track down. Thus, the results reflect the experiences of people whose farms succeeded past the initial settlement phase (which I have set as ending in 1924). It is nevertheless interesting that the number of male settlers with no previous farming experience (seven) is almost as high as the number of those with previous experience (nine). Perhaps the LSB did have some success in helping people to establish themselves as farmers, and perhaps it would have been more successful if economic, political, and environmental circumstances had been better.

Name	Ethnicity	Birthplace	Previous farm experience	Married before arrival	Wife's farm experience	Farm lasted past 1924	Work in addition to farming
Adey, C.H.	Scottish	Scotland		Yes, Isabella		His son, Frank, took over the farm	Worked in the blacksmith shop
Barr, Andrew	Scottish	Scotland		Yes		Yes	
Beaumont, Joseph	English	England	Yes	Yes, Ada		Yes, until 1927, when he sold due to war injuries	Comox Logging and Railway Company
Bennett, Alfred E.	English	England		Yes, Ellen (second wife)		No, left to farm at Little River	Clearing the land and building outhouses
Beston, John	Irish	Ireland	Yes	No		Yes, until 1948	Smith Horace Sawmills
Biss, Lewis G.				No		Yes, until 1925, when he moved to Comox	Comox Logging and Railway Company, and blacksmith shop
Blackstock, John	Scottish	Scotland		Never married		Yes	Roadwork
Blunt, Maxwell C.	English	New Zealand	Yes, farmhand in Vancouver	No, soon after, Nora		No, moved to Courtenay in 1921	Garage owner and boxer
Clark, Edward	Welsh	Wales		Yes		Yes	Roadwork
Clifford, Jonathan	English	England	Yes, dairy farming	Yes, Mable		Yes	Animal caregiver for the Land Settlement Board
Currie, Alexander		Nova Scotia	None	Yes		Yes	
Egan, Frank	Scottish	US	None	Yes, Mary		Yes, until 1925	
Fraser, John C.	Scottish	Scotland		No		Yes	Comox Logging and Railway Company (repairing railway cars)
Garoz, C.				Yes		Yes	Roadwork

Name	Ethnicity	Birthplace	Previous farm experience	Married before arrival	Wife's farm experience	Farm lasted past 1924	Work in addition to farming
Graham, Archibald	Scottish	Scotland		Yes, Agnes	None	Yes	Road foreman
Gray, Arthur	English	England		Yes, Ethel	None	Yes, despite his death in 1922	His widow opened a tea room to support her family
Howard, John				No		Yes, moved to Comox in 1935	
Hughes, Fred	English	England		Yes		Yes	Road boss
Hunter, William	Scottish	Scotland		Yes, Annie		Yes, moved to Courtenay in 1936	Building contractor and carpentry
Isener, Dickey M.		Nova Scotia	Yes, farmhand in Nova Scotia	Yes, Mary		Yes	Catering dances
Kettle, C.			None	No			
Kings, Alfred "John"	English	England		Yes, Gladys "Nina"		Yes	Carpentry
Knott, Ernest	English	England		Yes		Yes	Fireman and clearing brush
Linton, Oliver	English	England	Yes, farmhand in Regina	Yes		No, destroyed in the fire of 1922	
MacIntosh, George	Scottish	Scotland		Yes, Jessie		Yes, until 1945, when he had a stroke	
Mathers, James	Irish	Ireland		Yes, Martha		Yes	President of the Courtenay Legion
McIntyre, Peter	Scottish	Scotland		Yes, Olive	None	No, destroyed in the fire of 1922	
Mitchell, Andrew	Scottish	Scotland	None	Yes		Yes	

Mitchell, George T.				Yes	None	Yes	Clearing land for highway, and machinist's helper
Muir, James	English	England	None	Yes, Elizabeth		Yes, until a 1927 house fire	Construction in the Comox Valley
Paquette, Frederick	French	Quebec		Yes, Nellie		Yes	
Pattison, Duncan		Alberta	Yes, owned a farm in Alberta	Yes, Elizabeth		Yes	
Pearce, Leonard	English	England		Yes, Isabella	Yes	Yes	
Poulton, Edward	English	England		Yes		Yes	Helped build the school and local businesses
Reid, James	Scottish	Scotland		No, married Miriam Mathers in 1929	Yes, on her father's farm in Merville	Yes	Comox Co-operative Creamery director
Robertson, J.K.	Scottish	Scotland		Yes, Agnes		Yes	
Sedgewick, James R.	English	England		Yes, Harriet		Yes	Comox Logging and Railway Company
Sprout, Peter N.		Alberta	None	Yes, Ada		Yes	Comox Co-operative Creamery director
Thomas, Felix T.	English	England	Yes, family farm in England	Yes, Dorothy		No, lost their farm in the 1922 fire. Moved to Courtenay	Auctioneer
Thomson, Robert D.	Scottish	Scotland	None	Never married		Yes, with the help of his nephew, John	
Trebett, J.	English	England		Yes		Yes, moved to Grantham but returned	
Wainwright, W.J.	English	English		No, soon after, Gertrude		No, moved in the summer of 1922	Comox Logging and Railway Company

Name	Ethnicity	Birthplace	Previous farm experience	Married before arrival	Wife's farm experience	Farm lasted past 1924	Work in addition to farming
White, Ernest A.	English	England		No, married Dorothy in 1924	None	Yes	Comox Logging and Railway Company, BC Telephone, BC Hydro, and harvesting for his neighbours
Wilson, Arthur H.	English	London	Yes, owned a farm in Saskatchewan	No, soon after, Betsie		Yes	Building contractor
Yates, James	English	England		Yes, Helen		Yes	Blacksmith

Notes

Foreword: Soldiers' Fields

1 Lawrence Binyon, "For the Fallen," available at http://www.bbc.co.uk/religion/ remembrance/poetry/wwone.shtml (accessed 12 March 2007).
2 John McCrae, "In Flanders Fields," available at http://www.bbc.co.uk/religion/ remembrance/poetry/wwone.shtml (accessed 12 March 2007).
3 "In defense of liberty and our country": inscription, on the Liberty Memorial Tower in Downtown Kansas City, Missouri; "Their ideal is our legacy": inscription, above the entrance arch of the Delville Wood Memorial, Longueval, France; "preserving the memory": Commonwealth War Graves Commission (see http://www.cwgc.org/content.asp?menuid=1&submenuid=4&id=4&menuname=History&menu=sub; accessed 20 February 2007). The War Graves Commission maintains some 2,500 sites commemorating, individually, over one million of the 1.7 million servicemen and women who died in two world wars.
4 The "for evermore" line from Ecclesiasticus is inscribed on a monument, designed by Edward Luytens, that is erected in all Commonwealth War Graves Commission cemeteries containing more than one thousand graves. Rupert Brooke, "The Soldier," War Sonnets, V, available at: http://www.oucs.ox.ac.uk/ltg/projects/jtap/tutorials/ intro/brooke/vsoldier.html (accessed 12 March 2007).
5 Chris Maclean and Jock Phillips, *The Sorrow and the Pride: New Zealand War Memorials* (Wellington, NZ: Historical Branch, GP Books, 1990).
6 "Dulce et decorum" is used derisively by Wilfred Owen in his poem with that title to question the "ardent zeal" of those who repeat this lie: available at http://www.warpoetry.co.uk/owen1.html (accessed 12 March 2007). The "for the good of the whole" quotation is taken from Matthew Henry, "Making New Zealanders through Commemoration: Assembling Anzac Day in Auckland, 1916-1939," *New Zealand Geographer* 62 (2006): 3-12.

7 Eric Pawson, "The Memorial Oaks of North Otago: A Commemorative Landscape," in Geoff Kearsley and Blair Fitzharris, eds., *Glimpses of a Gaian World: Essays in Honour of Peter Holland* (Dunedin: School of Social Sciences, University of Otago, 2004), 115-31.

8 Siegfried Sassoon, "On Passing by the New Menin Gate," available at http://www.aftermathww1.com/sassoon3.asp (accessed 12 March 2007).

9 Victoria Parliamentary Debates, 5 October 1916, vol. 144, p. 1838, cited in Simon A. Copley, "A Comparative Study of Soldier Settlement in South Australia and Victoria, 1943-1950," BA (Hons) thesis, Flinders University of South Australia, [1978] 1979, excerpts available at http://www.slsa.sa.gov.au/saatwar/collection/Z333.3194C784b_1.htm# (accessed 12 March 2007).

10 Raymond Evans, "A Gun in the Oven: Masculinism and Gendered Violence," in K. Saunders and R. Evans, eds., *Gender Relations in Australia: Domination and Negotiation* (Sydney: Harcourt Brace Jovanovich, 1992), 203.

11 Christopher Turnor, *Land Settlement for Ex-Service Men in the Overseas Dominions: Report of the Royal Colonial Institute* (London: Saint Catherine Press, 1920). See also Kent Fedorowich, *Unfit for Heroes: Reconstruction and Soldier Settlement in the Empire between the Wars* (Manchester: University of Manchester Press, 1995); and Douglas G. Marshall, "Soldier Settlement in the British Empire," *The Journal of Land and Public Utility Economics* 22, 3(1946): 259-65.

12 Quoted in J.M. Powell, *An Historical Geography of Modern Australia: The Restive Fringe* (Cambridge; Melbourne; Sydney: Cambridge University Press, 1988), 93. See also Powell's "The Debt of Honour: Soldier Settlement in the Dominions, 1915-1940," *Journal of Australian Studies* 8 (1981): 64-87, and his "Australia's 'Failed' Soldier Settlers, 1914-23: Towards a Demographic Profile," *Australian Geographer* 16 (1985): 225-29.

13 Massey quoted in Powell, *The Restive Fringe,* 90.

14 The estimate is derived from A.J. Hannan, "Land Settlement of Ex-Service Men in Australia, Canada and the United States," *Journal of Comparative Legislation and International Law,* 3rd ser., 2, 3 (1920): 225-37.

15 A.H. McClintock, ed., "Finance, Public," in *An Encyclopaedia of New Zealand* (Wellington: R.E. Owen, 1966). For studies of New Zealand soldier settlement, see C. Miller and Michael Roche, "New Zealand's 'New Order': Town Planning and Soldier Settlement after the First World War," *War and Society* 21, 1 (2003): 63-81; and various works by Michael Roche, viz: "Empire, Land and Duty: Soldier Settlement in New Zealand 1915-1924," in Lindsay Proudfoot and Michael Roche, eds., *(Dis)Placing Empire* (Aldershot: Ashgate, 2005), 135-53; "Houses Not Farms: Housing Loans for Soldier settlement in Palmerston North, New Zealand 1918-1931: Inverting the Rural Mythology," in *The 21st Century City: Past/Present/Future: Proceedings from the 7th Australasian Urban History/Planning History Conference, Deakin University, Geelong, 12-14 February* (Geelong: School of Architecture and Building, Deakin University, 2004), 334-49; "Coldstream Soldier Settlement in the 1920s and 1930s: A Lowland Farm Landscape and the 'Third Phase of Pastoralism' in Canterbury," in Geoff Kearsley and Blair Fitzharris, eds., *Glimpses of a Gaian World: Essays in Honour of Peter Holland* (Dunedin: School of Social Sciences, University of Otago, 2004), 133-50; "Soldier Settlement in New Zealand after World War I: Two Case Studies," *New Zealand Geographer* 58, 1 (2002): 23-33; and "Awapuni Soldier Settlement, A World War I Soldier Settlement in the Manawatu, 1919-1952," Occasional Paper 1/01, 2001 (Palmerston North, New Zealand: Geography Programme, School of People Environment and planning, Massey University), available at http://geography.massey.ac.nz/staff/roche/Awapuni.pdf.

16 Tom Brooking with Terry Hearn, "Breaking Up the Great Estates," in Malcolm McKinnon, eds., *The Historical Atlas of New Zealand* (Auckland: David Bateman and the Historical Branch of the Department of Internal Affairs, 1997); Copley, "A Comparative Study."

17 Debates continue, however: Stephen Garton, *The Cost of War: Australians Return* (Melbourne: Oxford University Press, 1996) argued that critics exaggerated the "failure" of soldier settlements (141). More recently, Murray Johnson argued in a PhD thesis (reported in part in "'Promises and Pineapples': Post-First World War Soldier Settlement at Beerburrum, Queensland, 1916-1929," *Australian Journal of Politics and History* 51, 4 [2005]: 496-512) that even the 1929 Australian Royal Commission Report had erred in estimating the persistence rate of Queensland's soldier settlers at 60 percent; by Johnson's calculations, the figure was probably below 40 percent. See also Monica Keneley, "Land of Hope: Soldier Settlement in the Western District of Victoria 1918-1930," *Electronic Journal of Australian and New Zealand History* (2000), available at http://www.jcu.edu.au/aff/history/articles/keneley2.htm (accessed 12 March 2007); and Marilyn Lake, *The Limits of Hope: Soldier Settlements in Victoria, 1915-1938* (New York: Oxford University Press, 1987).

18 Johnson, "Promises and Pineapples," 498.

19 Donald T. Griffith, "Land Settlement Proposals for Veterans: World Wars I and II," *The Journal of Land and Public Utility Economics* 21, 1 (1945): 74.

20 Ibid.

21 Donald G. Marshall, "Soldier Settlement in Agriculture," *The Journal of Land and Public Utility Economics* 20, 3 (1944): 270; see also Griffith, "Land Settlement Proposals"; W.A. Hartman, *State Land Settlement Problems and Policies* USDA Technical Bulletin 357 (May 1933); and Roy. J. Smith, "The California State Land Settlements at Durham and Delhi," *Hilgardia, California Agricultural Experimental Station*, Bull. 5, (October 1943): 489-91.

22 Province of British Columbia, *The Provincial Returned Soldiers Commission of British Columbia* (Victoria: 1917), 7, cited in Paul M. Koroscil, "Soldier Settlement and Development in British Columbia, 1915-1930," *BC Studies* 54 (Summer 1982): 66.

23 Canada, *Soldier Settlement on the Land, Report of the Soldier Settlement Board, March 31, 1921* (Ottawa: King's Printer, 1921), 10.

24 Koroscil, "Soldier Settlement and Development," 70.

25 Loans bore 5 percent interest; those for stock and equipment were repayable in six annual instalments, those for lands and buildings in twenty-five annual instalments. Loans for new-purchased farms were limited to $4,500 for land, $2,000 for stock and equipment, and $1,000 for permanent improvements. Applicants who already owned land were allowed no more than $5,000 in loans. After 1919, soldier settlers on unproductive (i.e., hitherto undeveloped) lands were allowed two years free of interest on advances for stock and equipment up to $2,000 to tide them over the initial period of low productivity. By amendments to policy in 1920, preferential treatment was afforded settlers going on raw land.

26 Canada, *Soldier Settlement on the Land*, 128-50, quotes from 141.

27 Quoted in Koroscil, "Soldier Settlement and Development," 69.

28 For more on these matters, see David Demeritt, "Visions of Agriculture in British Columbia," *BC Studies* 108 (Winter 1995-96): 29-59.

29 Philip Corrigan and Derek Sayer, *The Great Arch: English State Formation as Cultural Revolution* (Oxford, UK; New York, NY: Blackwell, 1985); James C. Scott, *Seeing Like*

a State: How Certain Schemes to Improve the Human Condition Have Failed (New Haven: Yale University Press, 1998); Ian McKay, "The Liberal Order Framework: A Prospectus for a Reconnaissance of Canadian History," *Canadian Historical Review* 81, 4 (2000): 617-45.

30 Richard White, *The Organic Machine: The Remaking of the Columbia River* (New York: Hill and Wang, 1995); Donald Worster, *Rivers of Empire: Water, Aridity and the Growth of the American West* (New York: Oxford University Press, 1985).

INTRODUCTION

1 By the state, I mean not just the government but the constellation of institutions associated with the government and involved in the administration and regulation of society. In the case of this book, that includes the linked institutions of the cabinet and legislature of British Columbia, the Ministry of Agriculture and the Ministry of Lands, and various boards and quasi-state bodies. I also do not mean a state in the sense of the junior level of government in the US federal system. In Canada, of course, the equivalent junior level of government is called a province. For a brief discussion of the difficulties inherent in defining the state, see Allan Greer and Ian Radforth, "Introduction," in Greer and Radforth, eds., *Colonial Leviathan: State Formation in Mid-Nineteenth-Century Canada* (Toronto: University of Toronto Press, 1992), 9-11.

2 On the use of the term resettlement, see the "Note on Terminology" on p. xxix.

3 Ian McKay, "The Liberal Order Framework: A Prospectus for a Reconnaissance of Canadian History," *Canadian Historical Review* 81, 4 (2000): 620-23. An earlier, influential use of the concept is Tina Loo, *Making Law, Order, and Authority in British Columbia, 1821-1871* (Toronto: University of Toronto Press, 1994).

4 Canadian liberal reformers were thus opposed to the large grants of land made to crown and clergy in the colony of Upper Canada after 1791, and the Lower Canada rebels spoke the language of liberty and individual rights in opposing the aristocratic political order of Lower Canada in 1837. On liberal opposition to feudal rights generally, see Cheryl Greenberg, "Twentieth-Century Liberalisms: Transformations of an Ideology," in Harvard Sitkoff, ed., *Perspectives on Modern America* (New York: Oxford University Press, 2001), 56-57; Stuart Hall, "Variants of Liberalism," in James Donald and Stuart Hall, eds., *Politics and Ideology* (Philadelphia: Open University Press, 1986), 38-39; and Karl Polanyi, *The Great Transformation* (Boston: Beacon Press, 1957 [1944]), 178-81.

5 Loo, *Making Law*, 52-53. For further discussions of liberalism, see Anthony Arblaster, *The Rise and Decline of Western Liberalism* (New York: Blackwell, 1984); Fernande Roy, *Progrès, harmonie, liberté: le libéralisme des milieux d'affaires francophones de Montréal au tournant du siècle* (Montreal: Boréal, 1988); and Patrick Joyce, *The Rule of Freedom: Liberalism and the Modern City* (New York: Verso, 2003).

6 McKay, "Liberal," 641.

7 The concept of landscape has a long history (and a large body of literature) in cultural and historical geography, but here I echo more recent works that stress the way in which power and ideology is inscribed in, and reflected by, particular landscapes. Classic texts include Denis Cosgrove, *Social Formation and Symbolic Landscape* (Madison,

WI: University of Wisconsin Press, 1998); and James S. Duncan, *The City as Text: The Politics of Landscape Interpretation in the Kandyan Kingdom* (New York: Cambridge University Press, 1990). See as well David Ley, "Styles of the Times: Liberal and Neo-Conservative Landscapes in Inner Vancouver, 1968-1986," *Journal of Historical Geography* 13, 1 (1987): 40-56. For excellent introductions, see Ian D. Whyte, *Landscape and History Since 1500* (London: Reaktion Books, 2002), 9-25; and the entry for landscape in R.J. Johnston, et al., eds., *The Dictionary of Human Geography,* 4th ed. (Malden, MA: Blackwell, 2000), 429-31.

8 Cited in Cole Harris, *The Resettlement of British Columbia* (Vancouver: UBC Press, 1998), 98-102. Compare Harris' maps illustrating First Nations movement across the land (70) with the maps of property (87-88); note on the later maps the small Indian reserves.

9 McKay, "Liberal," 642.

10 Richard White, *The Organic Machine: The Remaking of the Columbia River* (New York: Hill and Wang, 1995), particularly 30-81. See also Robert Gottlieb, *Forcing the Spring: The Transformation of the American Environmental Movement* (Washington, DC: Island Press, 1993), particularly 15-105; Mike Davis, *City of Quartz: Excavating the Future in Los Angeles* (New York: Vintage Books, 1992), 376-82; and James Murton, "What J.W. Clark Saw in British Columbia, or, Nature and the Machine: A Photo Essay," *BC Studies* 142/143 (Summer/Autumn 2004): 129-52.

11 Thomas Dunlap, *Saving America's Wildlife: Ecology and the American Mind* (Princeton: Princeton University Press, 1988); Thomas R. Dunlap, "Ecology, Culture, and Canadian National Parks Policy: Wolves, Elk, and Bison as a Case Study," in Rowland Lorimer, et al., eds., *To See Ourselves / To Save Ourselves: Ecology and Culture in Canada* (Montreal: Association for Canadian Studies, 1991), 139-47; Alan MacEachern, *Natural Selections: National Parks in Atlantic Canada, 1935-1970* (Montreal and Kingston: McGill-Queen's University Press, 2001); George Warecki, *Protecting Ontario's Wilderness: A History of Changing Ideas and Preservation Politics, 1927-1973* (New York: Peter Lang, 2000); John F. Reiger, *American Sportsmen and the Origins of Conservation,* 3rd ed. (Corvallis, OR: Oregon State University Press, 2001 [1975]); Peter Gillis, *Lost Initiatives: Canada's Forest Industries, Forest Policy, and Forest Conservation* (Toronto: Greenwood Press, 1986); Janet Foster, *Working for Wildlife: The Beginning of Preservation in Canada,* 2nd ed. (Toronto: University of Toronto Press, 1998); and Matthew Evenden, *Fish Versus Power: An Environmental History of the Fraser River* (New York: Cambridge University Press, 2004).

12 Tina Loo, "People in the Way: Modernity, Environment, and Society on the Arrow Lakes," *BC Studies* 142/143 (Summer/Autumn 2004): 161-96; and Tina Loo, "Making a Modern Wilderness: Conserving Wildlife in Twentieth-Century Canada," *Canadian Historical Review* 82, 1 (2001): 92-121. See also Arn Keeling and Robert McDonald, "The Profligate Province: Roderick Haig-Brown and the Modernizing of British Columbia," *Journal of Canadian Studies* 36 (Fall 2001): 7-23.

13 Neil S. Forkey, "Victorian Dreams, Progressive Realities: The Commission of Conservation Critiques Old Ontario's 'Colonization' Policy," paper presented at the Themes and Issues in North American Environmental History Conference, Toronto, 1998; Michel F. Girard, *L'écologisme retrouvé: Essor et déclin de la Commission de la conservation du Canada* (Ottawa: University of Ottawa Press, 1994); and Barry Potyondi, *In Palliser's Triangle: Living in the Grasslands, 1850-1930* (Saskatoon, SK: Purich Publishing, 1995).

14 H.V. Nelles, *The Politics of Development: Forests, Mines, and Hydro-Electric Power in Ontario, 1849-1941* (Toronto: Macmillan of Canada, 1974); and Trevor J. Barnes, et al., "Stormy Weather: Cyclones, Harold Innis, and Port Alberni, BC," *Environment and Planning A* 33 (2001): 2127-47.
15 Donald Worster, *Rivers of Empire: Water, Aridity and the Growth of the American West* (New York: Oxford University Press, 1985), 51-60, 282-84.
16 This debate is summarized in Leslie A. Pal, *Interests of State: The Politics of Language, Multiculturalism, and Feminism in Canada* (Montreal and Kingston: McGill-Queen's University Press, 1993).
17 James C. Scott, *Seeing Like a State: How Certain Schemes to Improve the Human Condition Have Failed* (New Haven, CT: Yale University Press, 1998), 2-7, 201, 221, 304-6.
18 On this last point, see Colin A.M. Duncan, "On Identifying a Sound Environmental Ethic in History: Prolegomena to Any Future Environmental History," *Environmental History Review* 15, 2 (1991): 10.
19 This phrase is used by Brett McGillivray, *Geography of British Columbia: People and Landscapes in Transition* (Vancouver: UBC Press, 2000), 6.
20 *The National Dream: Building the Impossible Railway,* Episode 5 ("The Railway General"), videocassette, James Murray, prod., Eric Till and James Murray, dirs. (Toronto: CBC Enterprises, 1974).
21 Much of the preceding draws on McGillivray, *Geography,* Chapter 1.
22 Harris, *Resettlement,* 161-93.
23 Douglas negotiated treaties, as was standard British practice, with the Lekwammen people living around Victoria and with a few other Vancouver Island peoples. He then quickly abandoned the practice, for reasons debated by historians. On the mainland, no treaties were signed. See Cole Harris, *Making Native Space: Colonialism, Resistance, and Reserves in British Columbia* (Vancouver: UBC Press, 2002).
24 Loo, *Making Law,* 34-53.
25 Ibid., 113-33.
26 Christopher Clarkson, "Property Law and Family Regulation in Pacific British North America, 1862-1873," *Histoire sociale/Social History* 30, 60 (1997): 386-92, 414-16; and Adele Perry, *On the Edge of Empire: Gender, Race, and the Making of British Columbia, 1849-1871* (Toronto: University of Toronto Press, 2001), throughout. Perry does not deal with liberalism directly but discusses, on pp. 126 and 137, the position of the *British Colonist* newspaper (Victoria), a mouthpiece for liberal reform, on land laws and the importation of white women.
27 The US and Canadian governments were heavily involved in the late-nineteenth- and early-twentieth-century resettlement of the prairies – for instance, through the negotiation of land cessions with Native peoples, land laws favouring settlement over grazing, massive irrigation and settlement projects, and the active recruitment of settlers.
28 J.I. Little, *Nationalism, Capitalism, and Colonization in Nineteenth-Century Quebec: The Upper St. Francis District* (Montreal and Kingston: McGill-Queen's University Press, 1989); Neil Forkey, *Shaping the Upper Canadian Frontier: Environment, Society, and Culture in the Trent Valley* (Calgary: University of Calgary Press, 2003); Peter W. Sinclair, "Agricultural Colonization in Ontario and Quebec: Some Evidence from the Great Clay Belt, 1900-45," in Donald H. Akenson, ed., *Canadian Papers in Rural History,* vol. 5 (Gananoque, ON: Langdale Press, 1986), 105-12. On New Brunswick, see Béatrice Craig, "Agriculture and the Lumberman's Frontier in the Upper St. John Valley, 1800-70," *Journal of Forest History* 32, 3 (1988): 125-37.

29 Debate on the Quebec colonization movement has tended to pit those who see the movement as an ideological project of conservative Catholic elites to preserve old Quebec versus those who see colonization as an economic phenomenon associated with a growing forest industry. See Christian Morissonneau, *La terre promise: Le mythe du Nord québécois* (Montreal: Hurtubise HMH, 1978); and Normand Séguin, *Agriculture et colonisation au Québec: Aspects historiques* (Montreal: Boréal Express, 1980). In *Nationalism*, J.I. Little takes a middle path, noting the usefulness of colonization (to *all* Quebec elites, not just conservative Catholics), in preserving the social structure. Further, Little counters Séguin, arguing that forest companies had no interest in having settlers live near to their operations, and that settlers could survive only in a mixed agri-forest economy. My analysis here bears out Little's conclusions about the tension between settlers and forest companies, and about the dependence of settlers on a forest economy (see Chapter 3).

30 Cole Harris and David Demeritt, "Farming and Rural Life," in Harris, *Resettlement*, 226. See also David Demeritt, "Visions of Agriculture in British Columbia," *BC Studies* 108 (1995-96): 29-59.

31 Jason Patrick Bennett, "Apple of the Empire: Landscape and Imperial Identity in Turn-of-the-Century British Columbia," *Journal of the Canadian Historical Association* 9 (1998): 63-92.

32 Harris and Demeritt, "Farming and Rural Life," 249. Harris develops the discussion on European colonialism in BC more broadly in the rest of the book, focusing particularly on changing land uses and European introductions (from steamboats to pathogens), which allowed Europeans to reshape the land into an environment more suited to them and less suited to the First Nations.

33 Harris and Demeritt, "Farming and Rural Life," 223-25.

34 R.W. Sandwell, "The Limits of Liberalism: The Liberal Reconnaissance and the History of the Family in Canada," *Canadian Historical Review* 84, 3 (2003): 423-50.

35 See Little, *Nationalism*; Craig, "Agriculture"; Séguin, *Agriculture*; and R.W. Sandwell, *Contesting Rural Space: Land Policy and the Practices of Resettlement on Saltspring Island, 1859-1891* (Montreal and Kingston: McGill-Queen's University Press, 2005), especially Chapters 5 and 6, 104-58.

36 Technology made possible this reliance on the nuclear family by reducing the number of labourers needed. Harriet Friedmann, "World Market, State and Family Farm: Social Bases of Household Production in the Era of Wage Labour," *Comparative Studies in Society and History* 20 (1978): 547-48; also discussed in Sandwell, "Limits," 435.

37 Sandwell, "Limits," 435.

38 McKay, "Liberal," 634-39.

39 Ibid., 624.

40 Ibid., 623-34 (quotation is from 623). See also Roy, *Progrès*, Chapter 4; and Hall, "Variants," 38-42.

41 Polanyi, *Transformation*, 178-81.

42 Andrew Dobson, *Green Political Thought*, 2nd ed. (New York: Routledge, 1995), 5-11; John Gray, *Beyond the New Right: Markets, Government and the Common Environment* (New York: Routledge, 1993), 124-29, 176-77; and Robyn Eckersley, *Environmentalism and Political Theory: Toward an Ecocentric Approach* (Albany, NY: State University of New York Press, 1992), 23-24.

43 James T. Kloppenberg, *Uncertain Victory: Social Democracy and Progressivism in European and American Thought, 1870-1920* (New York: Oxford University Press, 1986).

210

Notes to pages 13-14

John Dewey, Kloppenberg argues, participates in both the earlier philosophical rethinking and the later effort to create a politics out of the work of the philosophers of the *via media.*

44 Ibid., 132. Kloppenberg's argument is summarized in 3-11 and 410-14.
45 Ibid., 299.
46 Barry Ferguson, *Remaking Liberalism: The Intellectual Legacy of Adam Shortt, O.D. Skelton, W.C. Clark, and W.A. Mackintosh, 1890-1925* (Montreal and Kingston: McGill-Queen's University Press, 1993), 237-38 (for the quotation, see 237); Kloppenberg, *Uncertain,* 298-348; Peter Weiler, *The New Liberalism: Liberal Social Theory in Great Britain, 1889-1914* (New York: Garland Publishing, 1982), 13-24. "Neo-conservative" is something of a misnomer, its use necessary because of the popular meaning of liberal in the US (and, to a lesser extent, Canada). Among North American academics and Europeans generally, the "neo-conservatives" are known by the more revealing name of "neo-liberal." Stuart Hall argues that neo-liberals represent the classical, laissez-faire arm of liberalism that swung towards the conservative parties. The values of the neo-liberals and the values of the conservatives (such as tradition, community, and hierarchy) were fused, if a bit incongruously, and a new political entity emerged in the form of Margaret Thatcher's Conservative Party. See Hall, "Variants," 66-67.
47 See Weiler, *The New Liberalism,* 75-94; Hall, "Variants," 66; and David Blaazer, *The Popular Front and the Progressive Tradition: Socialists, Liberals, and the Quest for Unity, 1884-1939* (New York: Cambridge University Press, 1992), 13-17.
48 Kloppenberg, *Uncertain,* 311; Daniel T. Rodgers, "In Search of Progressivism," *Reviews in American History* 10, 4 (1982): 123-26. Richard L. McCormick, *The Party Person and Public Policy: American Politics from the Age of Jackson to the Progressive Era* (New York: Oxford University Press, 1986), 269-72, lists a variety of characteristics for the progressive movement, as above, but later suggests that the concerns with social consciousness, etc., are the centre of the movement (280-81). Edward A. Stettner, *Shaping Modern Liberalism: Herbert Croly and Progressive Thought* (Lawrence, KS: University Press of Kansas, 1993); David Seideman, *The New Republic: A Voice of Modern Liberalism* (New York: Praeger Publishers, 1986); and Eldon J. Eisenach, *The Lost Promise of Progressivism* (Lawrence, KS: University Press of Kansas, 1994) support Kloppenberg's argument that certain progressives, forming a distinct group, were directly influenced by "new liberal" ideas.
49 Ferguson, *Remaking Liberalism,* 240-46. The still-classic histories of evangelical reform are Richard Allen, *The Social Passion: Religion and Social Reform in Canada, 1914-28* (Toronto: University of Toronto Press, 1971); and Ramsay Cook, *The Regenerators: Social Criticism in Late Victorian Canada* (Toronto: University of Toronto Press, 1985), though Cook's secularization thesis on the relationship between the rise of Christian social science and the decline of adherence to the tenets of Christianity in Canadian society has generated wide debate. See also Mariana Valverde, *The Age of Light, Soap, and Water: Moral Reform in English Canada, 1885-1925* (Toronto: McClelland and Stewart, 1991). For the technical/Keynesian argument, see Doug Owram, *The Government Generation: Canadian Intellectuals and the State, 1900-45* (Toronto: University of Toronto Press, 1986).
50 Ferguson, *Remaking Liberalism,* particularly 3-42, 62-90. Ferguson points out that Shortt et al. have been dismissed as "continentalists" for this stand. But Ferguson argues that these so-called continentalists held that, because Canada had economic

and state structures and a geography that differed from those in the US, Canada's interests differed from those of its southern neighbour as well.

51 Ibid., 188-201.

52 Girard, *L'écologisme*, 1-8, 51-80.

53 Ibid., 29, emphasis added. See also pp. 28-32. In the US, "Country Life" reformers attempted to bring progressive reform to the farm. Girard's discussion of the Commission of Conservation suggests that we might see their efforts to modernize farming and rural life as part of a more general effort to better incorporate nature into human systems. On the Country Life movement in the US, see David Danbom, *Born in the Country: A History of Rural America* (Baltimore: Johns Hopkins University Press, 1995); David Danbom, *The Resisted Revolution: Urban America and the Industrialization of Agriculture, 1900-1930* (Ames, IA: Iowa State University Press, 1979); and William L. Bowers, *The Country Life Movement in America, 1900-1920* (Port Washington, NY: Kennikat, 1974). In Canada, Country Life never became a government-sponsored program as it did in the US: see Demeritt, "Visions," 47-57, and David C. Jones, "'There Is Some Power about the Land': The Western Agrarian Press and Country Life Ideology," *Journal of Canadian Studies* 17 (1982): 96-108. Country Life shared some common concerns with the back-to-the-farm or back-to-the-land movement, but was more comfortable with modern urban life and was much more widespread. In North America, few people appear to have left the city to return to the farm, though back-to-the-land spawned manifestos by lawyer Bolton Hall (*A Little Land and a Living* [New York: The Arcadie Press, 1908]); supportive articles in mainstream publications such as Toronto-based *Saturday Night*; and a settlement of small farms in San Ysidro, California. The idea was potent, however, inspiring the soldier settlements studied here and re-surfacing in the Great Depression and again in the 1970s. The movement in the early twentieth century is covered in Paul K. Conklin, *Tomorrow a New World: The New Deal Community Program* (Ithaca, NY: Cornell University Press, 1959); David Shi, *The Simple Life: Plain Living and High Thinking in American Culture* (New York: Oxford University Press, 1985); and Danbom, *Resisted*, 36-38. For short summaries of both these movements see James Murton, "Country Life Movement," and "Back to the Farm," in John D. Buenker and Joseph Buenker, eds., *The Encyclopedia of the Gilded Age and Progressive Era* (Armonk, NY: M.E. Sharpe, 2005).

54 Ferguson, *Remaking Liberalism*, 199-201.

55 Forkey, "Victorian Dreams," 9. See 1-9.

56 Paul M. Koroscil, "Soldiers, Settlement and Development in British Columbia, 1915-1930," *BC Studies* 54 (Summer 1982): 63-87.

57 Ibid., 85-87.

58 Harris and Demeritt, "Farming and Rural Life," 219-49.

CHAPTER 1: LIBERALISM AND THE LAND

1 See Hilton Young, "Lister as I knew it," n.d. [but from internal references, must be post-1965], British Columbia Archives (hereafter BCA), Library Collection, pp. 1-2; Committee from the Courtenay-Comox Board of Trade and the Comox Agricultural Association to Barrow, Minister of Agriculture, 25 January 1923, BCA, Land Settlement

Board papers (hereafter LSB papers), GR-929, vol. 41, file 2; "Premier Oliver on Budget," 1920, BCA, Thomas Dufferin Pattullo papers (hereafter T.D. Pattullo papers), MS-003, vol. 9, file 11, p. 162.

2 Army and Navy Veterans in Canada (Victoria) to Premier John Oliver, 5 April 1919, BCA, Premier's papers, GR-441, vol. 206, file 9. The Premier indicates a broader knowledge of the story, and the story itself is mentioned in various newspaper accounts.

3 Victoria newspapers reported on the homecoming of the *Asia* for weeks before its arrival, and the men were greeted with a reception on landing in Victoria. See "*S.S. Empress of Asia* is bringing troops here from Liverpool," *Victoria Times*, 3 January 1919, 1; "City to honor all returning soldiers," *The Colonist* (Victoria) 7 January 1919, 7; "Arrangements made for big reception," *Victoria Daily Times*, 22 January 1919; and "Welcome to troopship Empress of Asia," *Victoria Daily Times*, 24 January 1919.

4 Margaret A. Ormsby, "The History of Agriculture in British Columbia," *Scientific Agriculture* [precursor to the *Canadian Journal of Agricultural Science*] 20, 1 (1939): 61-63.

5 This discussion assumes the (to me) obvious point that North American Native peoples reworked the environment in order to fulfill their subsistence needs. William Denevan is a major figure in the attempt to abolish the myth of Native people as natural environmentalists. See William Denevan, "The Pristine Myth: The Landscape of the Americas in 1492," *Annals of the Association of American Geographers* 82, 3 (1992): 369-85.

6 In their recent history of BC, *British Columbia: Land of Promises* (Don Mills, ON: Oxford University Press, 2005), Patricia E. Roy and John Herd Thompson make the distinction between coastal and interior peoples while noting the great diversity of BC's First Nations (12-19).

7 Jean Barman, *The West beyond the West: A History of British Columbia*, rev. ed. (Vancouver: UBC Press, 1996), 14-17; John Lutz, "After the Fur Trade: The Aboriginal Labouring Class of British Columbia, 1849-1890," *Journal of the Canadian Historical Association* 3 (1992): 71, 74.

8 Cole Harris with David Demeritt, "Farming and Rural Life," in Harris, *The Resettlement of British Columbia: Essays on Colonialism and Geographical Change* (Vancouver: UBC Press, 1997), 219; John Lutz, "'Relating to the Country': The Lekwammen and the Extension of European Settlement, 1843-1911," in R.W. Sandwell, ed., *Beyond the City Limits: Rural History in British Columbia* (Vancouver: UBC Press, 1999), 19-21. Lekwammen is the contemporary name for the peoples that Governor James Douglas called the Songhees. At the time of contact, however, these people did not see themselves as belonging to one single group.

9 Harris and Demeritt, "Farming and Rural Life," 220-22, 231, 249.

10 Lutz, "After the Fur Trade," 73-81, 92.

11 Ibid., 86-91. Also on the potlatch, see Douglas Cole and Ira Chaikin, *An Iron Hand upon the People: The Law against the Potlatch on the Northwest Coast* (Vancouver: Douglas and McIntyre, 1990).

12 Lutz, "After the Fur Trade," 91-93. In 1881, there were 29,000 Native people and only 23,798 non-Native people in BC; by 1891, the Native population had dropped to 26,000, while the non-Native population had grown to 72,123. These figures are estimates compiled by Lutz from the Canada census and other primary and secondary sources. In particular, Lutz notes, the 1891 census did not separate populations based on race, so the figure for non-Native peoples is the total provincial population, minus an estimate of the Native population. See the table and explanation in Lutz, 93.

13 Margaret A. Ormsby, *British Columbia: A History* (Toronto: Macmillan of Canada, 1958), 101-3, 107; see also Ormsby, "History," 62.
14 Christopher Clarkson, "Property Law and Family Regulation in Pacific British North America, 1862-1873," *Histoire sociale/Social History* 30, 60 (1997): 386-89, 414-16.
15 Clarkson, "Property Law," 390-92; Adele Perry, *On the Edge of Empire* (Toronto: University of Toronto Press, 2001), 124-31; R.W. Sandwell, "Negotiating Rural: Policy and Practice in the Settlement of Saltspring Island, 1859-91," in Sandwell, ed., *Beyond the City Limits,* 84-85.
16 To acquire land by pre-emption, the pre-emptor simply staked a claim to a set acreage – up to 160 or 320 acres, depending on where the pre-emption took place, and accounting for shifts in the legislation over time.
17 Robert E. Cail, *Land, Man, and the Law: The Disposal of Crown Lands in British Columbia, 1871-1913* (Vancouver: UBC Press, 1974), 245; Sandwell, "Negotiating," 85-87.
18 David Demeritt, "Visions of Agriculture in British Columbia," *BC Studies* 108 (1995-96): 40; R.W. Sandwell, "Peasants on the Coast? A Problematique of Rural British Columbia," in Donald H. Akenson, ed., *Canadian Papers in Rural History,* vol. 5 (Gananoque, ON: Langdale Press, 1986), 226-80.
19 Demeritt, "Visions," 42.
20 Harris, *Resettlement,* 69-73.
21 Oliver Rackham, chronicler of the English countryside, notes that as most European food plants derive from semi-arid areas in the present-day Middle East, the draining of wetlands (or land "reclamation") is a common and ancient practice in European agriculture. Perhaps because it is such a basic and necessary practice, the term "reclamation" – as US historian David Igler notes – carries overtones of rescue and redemption, of saving the land from its current state and imposing regulation and order. Igler notes further that reclamation was responsible for the transformation of more land in the American West than any other process. Oliver Rackham, *The History of the Countryside* (London: Weidenfeld and Nicholson, 1995), 374-94; David Igler, *Industrial Cowboys: Miller and Lux and the Transformation of the Far West, 1850-1920* (Los Angeles: University of California Press, 2001), especially Chapters 4 (particularly 93-97) and 5.
22 Demeritt, "Visions," 43.
23 Harris and Demeritt, "Farming and Rural Life," 240-41.
24 Sandwell, "Negotiating," 90-101; Sandwell, "Peasants," 226-80.
25 Demeritt, "Visions," 43; Harris and Demeritt, "Farming and Rural Life," 227-31.
26 In the Okanagan valley, much of the farmland sits on level patches of ground atop cliffs that rise up from the lake. These are called benchlands.
27 J.T. Bealby, *Fruit Ranching in British Columbia,* 2nd ed. (London: Adam and Charles Black, 1911), 217. The quotation is cited in Demeritt, "Visions," 36.
28 *Fruit Magazine* 2, 2 (November 1910); *Man-to-Man Magazine* [continued by *British Columbia Magazine*] 6, 8 (September 1910).
29 Demeritt, "Visions," 33-39; Jason Patrick Bennett, "Apple of the Empire: Landscape and Imperial Identity in Turn-of-the-Century British Columbia," *Journal of the Canadian Historical Association* 9 (1998): 67-85. See also Jean Barman, *Growing Up British in British Columbia: Boys in Private School* (Vancouver: UBC Press, 1984).
30 Demeritt, "Visions," 38-39; Bennett, "Apple," 87-90.
31 Noted in Harris and Demeritt, "Farming and Rural Life," 233. But see Ian MacPherson, "Creating Stability Amid Degrees of Marginality: Divisions in the Struggle for

Orderly Marketing in British Columbia, 1900-1940," in Akenson, ed., *Canadian Papers in Rural History,* vol. 5, 309-33.

32 Nelson Riis, "The Walhachin Myth: A Study in Settlement Abandonment," *BC Studies* 17 (Spring 1973): 14; Ken Favrholdt, "Domesticating the Dry Belt: Agricultural Settlement in the Hills around Kamloops, 1860-1960," in Sandwell, ed., *Beyond the City Limits,* 102-19.

33 On the land companies, see Paul M. Koroscil, "Boosterism and the Settlement Process in the Okanagan Valley, British Columbia, 1890-1914," in Akenson, ed., *Canadian Papers in Rural History,* vol. 5 (Gananoque, ON: Langdale Press, 1986), 73-102.

34 Barman, *West,* 143-44; Justine Brown, *All Possible Worlds: Utopian Experiments in British Columbia* (Vancouver: New Star Books, 1995), 53-58.

35 Brown, *All Possible Worlds,* 24-25; the constitution is reproduced in Cliff Kopas, *Bella Coola* (Vancouver: Mitchell Press, 1970), 246-47.

36 Brown, *All Possible Worlds,* 23.

37 Ibid., 31.

38 This account is drawn from J. Donald Wilson, "Matti Kurikka: Finnish-Canadian Intellectual," *BC Studies* 20 (1973-74): 50-65; J. Donald Wilson, "'The police beat them up just to keep warm': A Finnish-Canadian Communist Comments on Environmental Depredation and Capitalist Exploitation in Early 20th-Century British Columbia," *Labour/Le Travail* 44 (1999): 191-204; and Brown, *All Possible Worlds,* 29-34.

39 Kent Fedorowich, *Unfit for Heroes: Reconstruction and Soldier Settlement in the Empire between the Wars* (New York: St. Martin's Press, 1995), 5-12, 16.

40 "Memorandum: Re South African War Land Grants. File 102548," 18 September 1931, in *Book of Applications under South African War Land Grant,* British Columbia, Department of Lands (records relating to the South African War Land Grant Act), GR-1396.

41 British Columbia, "Report of the Royal Commission on Agriculture," *Sessional Papers* 2 (1914), L13. This discussion as a whole draws on L8-L39.

42 British Columbia, "Royal Commission on Agriculture," L9.

43 William Rayner, *British Columbia's Premiers in Profile* (Surrey, BC: Heritage House, 2000), 116-18; Ormsby, *British Columbia,* 392-94.

44 On Shortt as a new liberal reformer of government, see Barry Ferguson, *Remaking Liberalism: The Intellectual Legacy of Adam Shortt, O.D. Skelton, W.C. Clark, and W.A. Mackintosh* (Montreal and Kingston: McGill-Queen's University Press, 1993), 118-35.

45 "Mr. Chairman," speech, n.d., BCA, T.D. Pattullo papers, MS-003, vol. 65, file 1a, pp. 185-90.

46 Pattullo suggested the name for the new board, that it be concerned with selecting the best land for settlement and then fostering community settlements, and that it take over the work of the Agricultural Credit Commission. All these suggestions were implemented. See Pattullo to Minister of Agriculture, 13 December 1916, BCA, Premier's papers, GR-441, vol. 336, file 8.

47 "The first regular meeting of the Land Settlement Board," press release, BCA, LSB papers, GR-929, vol. 13, file 8.

48 Clippings Book 1, n.s., n.d., University of British Columbia Special Collections (hereafter UBCSC), South Vancouver Ratepayers Protective Association Fonds.

49 Premier's Speech on Address, 14 February 1919, BCA, T.D. Pattullo papers, MS-003, vol. 9, file 11. On Oliver, see Ormsby, *British Columbia,* 398-99, 407.

50 For more on Smith, see Chapter 2.
51 Joseph Herbert, "The Man behind the Apple Show," *Opportunities Magazine* 2, 5 (1910): 15.
52 "The Editor's Ambition," *Fruit Magazine* 4 (1911). Though I have found no instances of Smith calling explicitly for white settlement, his views on race are suggested by his protest against reports that Col. Sam Hughes, Minister of Militia, was planning to create a "Hindoo regiment" in Vancouver. "Knowing Col. Hughes to be a staunch Canadian first and last," Smith said, "we were not disposed to credit the report." See "Canadian Defenders," *Fruit Magazine* 4 (1911).
53 "Press Interview, Release Monday, 17 September 1917," press release, 1917, BCA, LSB papers, GR-929, vol. 13, file 8.
54 "At the Regular Meeting of the Land Settlement Board ... January 9th, 1918," 7 [sic] January 1918, and "Copy of Reports ...," BCA, LSB papers, GR-929, vol. 8, file 3. On Sumas and the South Okanagan, see Chapters 4 and 5. The southern Okanagan Valley was, in the end, developed by the Ministry of Lands, not the LSB.
55 "Copy of Reports as at November 30th, 1917, Received by the Chairman from the Directors of the Land Settlement Board, December 3rd, 1917," BCA, LSB papers, GR-929, vol. 8, file 3, p. 12. See also the reports contained in GR-929, vol. 8, file 5.
56 Paul M. Koroscil, "Soldiers, Settlement, and Development in British Columbia, 1915-1930," *BC Studies* 54 (1982): 70-72.
57 See "Office Staff – Land Settlement Board," n.d., BCA, LSB papers, GR-929, vol. 13, file 5; "The activities of the Land Settlement Board ...," 5 November 1919, BCA, LSB papers, GR-929, vol. 13, file 9; and British Columbia, "Annual Report of the Land Settlement Board of British Columbia for the Year 1919," *Sessional Papers* 2 (1920), M59-M66. See also the attachment to Chairman, Land Settlement Board, to F.C. Wade, Agent-General for BC (London), 19 November 1919, BCA, LSB papers, GR-929, vol. 9, file 3; Director, Land Settlement Board to C.W. Whitney-Griffiths, Esq., Secretary, Advisory Board, Farmers' Institutes, Department of Agriculture [BC], 28 April 1921, BCA, LSB papers, GR-929, vol. 9, file 4; and Superintendent to Bonavia, 30 December 1920, BCA, LSB papers, GR-929, vol. 9, file 4. Development Areas 3 and 4 were discontinued after a short time. Only Merville and Camp Lister were ever developed.
58 Robin Fisher, *Duff Pattullo of British Columbia* (Toronto: University of Toronto Press, 1991), 136-37.
59 This portrait of Pattullo's early life is from Fisher, *Pattullo*, Chapter 1, 3-29.
60 Fisher, *Pattullo*, 135-36.
61 Ibid., 142-43.
62 Pattullo to Jack Strickland, c/o *The Province* (Vancouver), 3 January 1945, BCA, T.D. Pattullo papers, MS-003, vol. 65, file 12.
63 "Mr. Chairman," speech, n.d., BCA, T.D. Pattullo papers, MS-003, vol. 65, file 1a, pp. 187, 188.
64 James T. Kloppenberg, *Uncertain Victory: Social Democracy and Progressivism in European and American Thought, 1870-1920* (New York: Oxford University Press, 1986), 349-54.
65 The LSB conducted the survey by sending questionnaires to military hospitals and asking hospital staff to survey the men and return the results. Of 1,108 soldiers undergoing treatment in BC, 728 were interviewed: 291 wanted to farm; 236 of those 291 were pronounced by the hospitals to be physically fit for farming; 239 had experience

farming; 112 of the 291 were married; 36 had $500 to $1000 in investment capital; and 8 had more than $1000 in investment capital. See Chair, LSB, to E.D. Barrow, Minister of Agriculture, 27 June 1918, BCA, LSB papers, GR-929, vol. 12, file 11. Original questionnaire and correspondence from military hospitals is in GR-929, vol. 10, file 4.

66 "Premier Oliver on Budget," 1920, BCA, T.D. Pattullo papers, MS-003, vol. 9, file 11, p. 163.

67 On the conference, see the correspondence between Oliver and the Dominion government collected in British Columbia, "Correspondence re Dominion Conference," *Sessional Papers* 2 (1919), M15-M20. Walker and Kirchner's impressions are mentioned in "Premier Oliver on Budget," 1920, BCA, T.D. Pattullo papers, MS-003, vol. 9, file 11, p. 162. On the re-establishment of First World War veterans, see Desmond Morton and Glenn Wright, *Winning the Second Battle: Canadian Veterans and the Return to Civilian Life, 1915-1930* (Toronto: University of Toronto Press, 1987).

68 British Columbia, "Report of the Superintendent of British Columbia Soldier Settlement," *Sessional Papers* 2 (1919), N17-N18. The report does not indicate precisely how large some of these parcels were.

69 J.A. Calder to John Oliver, 8 January 1919, British Columbia, *Sessional Papers* 2 (1919), M19.

70 Oliver to Meighen, 5 June 1919, BCA, Premier's papers, GR-441, vol. 199, file 17.

71 Government of Canada [unsigned] to Lt. A.F. Walker, 15 March 1919, BCA, Premier's papers, GR-441, vol. 199, file 17; Province of British Columbia, *Journals of the Legislative Assembly* (1919), 111. Walker's correspondent did not specify what was communistic about the BC government's plans, but one could imagine that the elements of central planning and cooperation contained within the letter prompted the comment by Meighen, who was as staunch a classical liberal as could be found.

72 A.A. McLean, Comptroller, Royal North West Mounted Police (Ottawa) to Tolmie, 26 December 1919, and S/Sgt J.G. Jones to 'E' Division, Vancouver, RNWMP, 8 December 1919, UBCSC, Simon Fraser Tolmie Fonds (hereafter Tolmie Fonds), vol. 27, file 28; John Oliver to Arthur Meighen, 9 December 1920, UBCSC, Tolmie Fonds, vol. 26, file 28.

CHAPTER 2: SOLDIERS, SCIENCE, AND AN ALTERNATIVE MODERNITY

1 This portrait of Frederick Moore Clement is based on his memoir: *My Thoughts Were on the Land: Autobiography of Fred Clement, Virgil, Ontario* (White Rock, BC: n.p., 1969), 1-7.

2 Peter McArthur, *In Pastures Green* (Toronto: J.M. Dent and Sons, 1916), 37, 117-20, 39-42.

3 David Demeritt notes that, before the present Point Grey site was approved for the Provincial University, the soil was tested to make sure it was possible to establish a farm there. Demeritt, "Visions of Agriculture in British Columbia," *BC Studies* 108 (1995-96): 52 n. 82. Here, Demeritt is citing Cole Harris, "Locating the University of British Columbia," *BC Studies* 32 (1976-77): 106-25.

4 F.F. Wesbrook, "The Provincial University in Canadian Development," address delivered at the inauguration of the first president of the University of Manitoba, at Winnipeg, 19 November 1913, University of British Columbia University Archives (hereafter UBCUA), Frank F. Wesbrook Fonds, vol. 1, file 14, p. 7.

5 See the finding aid for the Leonard S. Klinck Fonds (hereafter Klinck fonds), UBCUA. Macdonald College is now part of McGill University.

6 Clement, *My Thoughts*, 20.

7 Ibid., 17-20 (quotation is from 20).

8 Michael Bunce, *The Countryside Ideal: Anglo-American Images of Landsape* (New York: Routledge, 1994). The quote is from McArthur, *In Pastures Green*, 117.

9 Raymond Williams, *The Country and the City* (London: Chatto and Windus, 1973), 124-34.

10 Jackson Lears makes this point in *Fables of Abundance: A Cultural History of Advertising in America* (New York: Basic Books, 1994), 9-13.

11 Robert Browning, "Home Thoughts, From Abroad," quoted in Bunce, *Countryside*, 40. This paragraph is based on pp. 40-55.

12 Michael G. Dalecki and C. Milton Coughenour, "Agrarianism in American Society," *Rural Sociology* 57, 1 (1992): 49; and Demeritt, "Visions," 40-41.

13 Bunce, *Countryside*, 31, 57. Sarah Hale as the founder of Thanksgiving was discussed by Peter Stevens at the annual New Frontiers in Graduate History conference, March 2001, York University, Toronto, ON.

14 Demeritt, "Visions," 40; H.V. Nelles, *The Politics of Development: Forests, Mines, and Hydro-Electric Power in Ontario, 1849-1941* (Toronto: Macmillan of Canada, 1974), 39-47; Richard Mackie, "The Colonization of Vancouver Island, 1849-1858," *BC Studies* 96 (1992-93): 3-40.

15 British Columbia, Bureau of Provincial Information, *Bulletin No. 10: Land and Agriculture in British Columbia* (1903), 109.

16 "Editorial," *Fruit Magazine* 6, 4 (1913): 145.

17 William Cronon argues that, though Wordsworth experienced sublime terror in the wilderness of the Alps, whereas John Muir found God in Yosemite, both reactions were "in fact pages from the same holy book": nature as cathedral. The wilderness ideal as a cultural phenomenon, then, is connected with the countryside ideal that sees nature as a Wordsworthian principle of creation. BC boosters did not have to stretch very far to bring together wilderness and country life. Cronon also sees wilderness as a cultural formation of modernity, emerging in the United State in the 1890s, out of nostalgia for the vanished frontier. William Cronon, "The Trouble with Wilderness, or, Getting Back to the Wrong Nature," in William Cronon, ed., *Uncommon Ground: Rethinking the Human Place in Nature* (New York: W.W. Norton, 1996), 71-79 (quotation is from 76). Tina Loo also argues for the wilderness ideals' origins in modernity, pointing to wilderness as an escape for tired businessmen and to the modern techniques of "rational planning and marketing" used to create the wilderness experience for many. Tina Loo, "Making a Modern Wilderness: Conserving Wildlife in Twentieth-Century Canada," *Canadian Historical Review* 82, 1 (2001): 92-121.

18 British Columbia, Bureau of Provincial Information, *Land and Agriculture*, 51.

19 This was an established tactic of particular Anglophone Canadian nationalists, such as those who argued that Canadians would form a hardy, northern race that would inevitably achieve leadership of the British Empire. See Carl Berger, *Sense of Power: Studies in the History of Canadian Imperialism, 1867-1914* (Toronto: University of Toronto Press, 1970), 49-77, 128-52.

20 British Columbia, Bureau of Provincial Information, *Land and Agriculture*, 51, 26, 55, 98.

21 *Fruit Magazine* 3, 2 (May 1911): 49-50.

22 W.G. Capelle (Winnipeg) to LSB, 21 December 1920, BCA, LSB papers, GR-929,

vol. 15, file 3; and Land Settlement Board and W.A. Wright (Denison, KS) to Chair LSB, 24 September 1921, BCA, LSB papers, GR-929, vol. 17, file 10. It should be noted that these letters did not mention race, concentrating instead on the possibility of escaping prairie winters.

23 British Columbia, Bureau of Provincial Information, *New BC* (1908), 41.

24 *Man-to-Man Magazine: An Index to Opportunity* [continued by *British Columbia Magazine*] 6 (1910); and Canadian Pacific Railway, *Southern British Columbia. The Garden of Canada. Kootenay, Boundary, Okanagan and Columbia River Districts. Brief Description of Their Wonderful Natural Resources and Scenic Beauties* (1909), 51.

25 "Burton, BC: A Land of Opportunity," *Fruit Magazine* 2, 3.

26 British Columbia, Bureau of Provincial Information, *Bulletin No. 23: Handbook of BC, Canada – Its Position, Advantages, Resources, Climate, Mining, Lumbering, Fishing, Farming, Ranching, and Fruit-Growing,* 7th ed. (1913), 9.

27 George Altmeyer, "Three Ideas of Nature in Canada," in Chad and Pam Gaffield, eds., *Consuming Canada: Readings in Environmental History* (Toronto: Copp Clark, 1995), 98.

28 D.C. Ireland, "A Voice from the City," *Westward Ho! Magazine* 2 (March 1908): 52, quoted in Altmeyer, "Three Ideas," 99.

29 Archibald Lampman, *Comfort of the Fields,* Raymond Souster, ed. (Sutton West, ON: Paget Press, 1979), 94-95.

30 Robert Craig Brown, "Introduction," in John MacDougall, *Rural Life in Canada* (Toronto: University of Toronto Press, 1973), ix.

31 MacDougall, *Rural Life,* 115-20, 133-39, 189-97.

32 Ibid., 181.

33 Rev. R.G. MacBeth, *Land in British Columbia* (London: William Stevens, 1920), 20.

34 At least, he does not mention his family in the collection of columns published as *In Pastures Green.* It is possible that McArthur did not want to splash his family's affairs across the pages of the *Toronto Globe,* but the fact that he could write columns on farming without discussing work in the home is telling.

35 MacDougall, *Rural Life,* 39-41. MacDougall presents statistics for only Ontario, New Brunswick, and Nova Scotia.

36 Ibid., 128.

37 Steam donkeys were steam engines mounted on skids, used in logging to yard trees.

38 MacBeth, *Land,* 17, 22. MacBeth does not name Merville specifically, but mentions returned soldiers clearing a ten-thousand-acre tract. Merville was the only returned-settler project of this size.

39 McArthur, *In Pastures Green,* vii, 94.

40 Ibid., 122.

41 Demeritt, "Visions," 47-57 (quotation is from 48); David Danbom, "Romantic Agrarianism in Twentieth-Century America," *Agricultural History* 65, 4: 4. On the Country Life movement, see also David Danbom, *The Resisted Revolution: Urban America and the Industrialization of Agriculture, 1900-1930* (Ames, IA: Iowa State University Press, 1979); David C. Jones, "'There Is Some Power about the Land': The Western Agrarian Press and Country Life Ideology," *Journal of Canadian Studies* 17 (1982): 96-108; and William L. Bowers, *The Country Life Movement in America, 1900-1920* (Port Washington, NY: Kennikat, 1974).

42 McArthur, *In Pastures Green,* 41, 92-93.

43 From Ishbel Robertson Currier, "A Brief Biography of James Wilson Robertson by Ishbel Robertson Currier," typescript, n.d., University of British Columbia Special Collections (hereafter UBCSC), James Wilson Robertson Fonds, vol. 1, file 34. The address from which this quote is taken was delivered in 1910.
44 Agnes C. Laut, "The New Spirit of the Farm," *Outing Magazine* 52, 1 (April 1908): 7. This was the first in a series of articles that continued in the May and September 1908 issues. Laut's articles were likely once part of the British Columbia Legislative Library, as they are held in the BCA's library collection, a significant portion of which was once part of the Legislative Library.
45 Currier, "Brief Biography," 5-6.
46 Michel F. Girard, *L'écologisme retrouvé: Essor et déclin de la Commission de la conservation du Canada* (Ottawa: University of Ottawa Press, 1994), 139-40.
47 "'Showing Us,' by a Canadian. Maxwell Smith, of Vancouver, Editor of *Fruit Magazine,* Discusses the Strictly Apple Show (From the Portland 'Oregonian' of December 15, 1910). Address Delivered at the Recent Meeting of the Oregon State Horticultural Society in Portland," *Fruit Magazine* 7, 4 (January 1911): 294.
48 "The masses of our youth" cartoon, *Fruit Magazine* 4 (1912): 207.
49 "Outline of course on 'The Scientific Basis of Agriculture,'" 1916, UBCUA, Klinck Fonds, vol. 3, file 41a; "The Evolution of Agriculture," paper read before the Vancouver Institute, 5 February 1917, UBCUA, Klinck Fonds, vol. 4, file 6.
50 British Columbia, "Reports of the Department of Agriculture. Eighth Report, 1913," *Sessional Papers* 2 (1915), R5-R9, R19.
51 British Columbia, "Reports of the Department of Agriculture, 1913," R6.
52 See Desmond Morton and Glenn Wright, *Winning the Second Battle: Canadian Veterans and the Return to Civilian Life, 1915-1930* (Toronto: University of Toronto Press, 1987), 100, 35.
53 Morton and Wright, *Winning,* 14.
54 Kent Fedorowich, *Unfit for Heroes: Reconstruction and Soldier Settlement in the Empire between the Wars* (New York: St. Martin's Press, 1995), 12. Most of the preceding paragraph draws on pp. 5-12. On the US, see David Shi, *The Simple Life: Plain Living and High Thinking in American Culture* (New York: Oxford University Press, 1985), 223.
55 Fedorowich, *Unfit,* 25-45, 144-90; and David Danbom, *Born in the Country: A History of Rural America* (Baltimore: Johns Hopkins University Press, 1995), 181. See also Paul M. Koroscil, "Soldiers, Settlement, and Development in British Columbia, 1915-1930," *BC Studies* 54 (1982): 63-87; and John McDonald, "Soldier Settlement and Depression Settlement in the Forest Fringe of Sakatchewan," *Prairie Forum* 6, 1 (1981): 35-55. The literature on soldier settlement has focused on the failure of the programs to establish working farms. Fedorowich sees soldier settlement as both conservative (in that it hearkens back to old practices and to rural society) and innovative (in that it tries to establish a new yeoman class). All point to hamfisted over-management by the state as a key cause of failure. While I generally agree with these conclusions, I argue here that the role of the environment and the role of the state's relationship to the environment need to be explored in order to enable a fuller understanding of the shortcomings of soldier settlement.
56 British Columbia, *Report of the Provincial Returned Soldiers' Aid Commission (British Columbia),* 1916, J3-J4.
57 John Helyer to Premier Oliver, 29 October 1918, BCA, Premier's papers, GR-441, vol. 190, file 9.

58 L. Curtis, "Influx of Britishers after the War," n.d., n.s., BCA, Premier's papers, GR-441, vol. 168, file 1.
59 Thos. E. Sedgwick to the Premier, 28 November 1916, BCA, Premier's papers, GR-441, vol. 176, file 9.
60 "Memorandum prepared by R.E. Gosnell, with reference to the natural resources of British Columbia ...," memo, 1917, BCA, Premier's papers, GR-441, vol. 336, file 9; Director of Elementary Agricultural Education to H.E. Young, 8 December 1915, Committee Reports to the Provincial Returned Soldiers' Aid Commission, BCA, Returned Soldiers' Aid Commission papers (hereafter RSAC papers), GR-1315, reel B2517.
61 Canadian National Reconstruction Groups, *The Problems of National Reconstruction: A Summary by the Standing Committee on Plans and Propaganda of the Canadian National Reconstruction Groups* (Montreal, 1918), 51-52.
62 Canadian National Reconstruction Groups, *Problems,* 9-10.
63 Military Hospitals Commission, *The Soldier's Return: from 'Down and Out' to 'Up and In Again': A Little Chat with Private Pat* (Ottawa, 1917), 3, quoted in Morton and Wright, *Winning,* 101.
64 That is, it would seem, working with engines.
65 John Kyle, Vocational Officer for BC, Military Hospitals Commission, "Report on Vocational Training in British Columbia," Military Hospitals Commission Reports, March 1917, BCA, RSAC papers, GR-1315, p. 7, reel B2517.
66 Director to Young, 8 December 1915, Committee Reports, BCA, RSAC papers, GR-1315, p. 9, reel B2517.
67 Great War Veterans Association, "Land Settlement," n.d. [but after May 1919], BCA, RSAC papers, GR-1315, series 50-G-69, reel B2515.
68 "Proposed Method of Finding Employment for a Large Number of Returned Soldiers," Committee Reports, BCA, RSAC papers, GR-1315, p. 1, reel B2517.
69 "The ex-serviceman ...," n.d. [about 1918], n.s. [a previous letter from J.R. Pyper to Robertson, Chairman, RSAC, February 1923, identifies this as "Dr. Wacis' report"], BCA, RSAC papers, GR-1315, reel B2515, p. 1.
70 Village Centres Council for Curative Treatment and Training of Disabled Men, *Third Annual Report, 1921* (Eastcott, Kingston Hill, Surrey, England, 1922), 8. Included in BCA, RSAC papers, GR-1315, series 50-G-78, B2515.
71 "Proposed Method ...," Committee Reports, BCA, RSAC papers, GR-1315, p. 2, B2517.
72 "Outline of Short Courses in Agriculture ... 1918-19," n.d., UBCUA, Klinck Fonds, vol. 4, file 14.
73 "Agricultural Instruction for Returned Soldiers. Short Courses at the University Proposed," n.d., UBCUA, Klinck Fonds, vol. 4, file 14.
74 "UBC Buildings and Facilities: Chronological Index," at UBC Library Special Collections Website, http://www.library.ubc.ca/spcoll/ubc_arch/chrono.html/, accessed 5 July 2001; "Buildings and Grounds of The University of British Columbia, Vancouver, BC," map, UBCUA, Pamphlet Series, Faculty of Agricultural Sciences Fonds, vol. 57, file 21.
75 British Columbia, *Report of the Provincial Returned Soldiers' Aid Commission,* 1916, J4-J14.
76 "Proposed Method ...," Committee Reports, BCA, RSAC papers, GR-1315, B2517, p. 2; A. Carmichael, "A Land Settlement Plan for Returned Soldiers," 21 December 1915, Committee Reports, BCA, RSAC papers, GR-1315, reel B2517, pp. 2-3; and Commit-

tee on Immigration and Committee on Agriculture to Victoria Board of Trade, 4 October 1915, Committee Reports, BCA, RSAC papers, GR-1315, reel B2517, p. 4.

77 Carmichael, "Land Settlement," p. 7; Director to Young, 8 December 1915, Committee Reports, BCA, RSAC papers, GR-1315, reel B2517, pp. 4-5; Deputy Minister, Agriculture, to Young, 5 January 1916, Committee Reports, BCA, RSAC papers, GR-1315, reel B2517, pp. 3-4.

78 Carmichael, "Land Settlement," p. 4; Director to Young, p. 8; Committee on Immigration and Committee on Agriculture to Victoria Board of Trade, p. 2; W.J. Elliot to James Speakman (Calgary), 9 December 1915, Committee Reports, BCA, RSAC papers, GR-1315, reel B2517, p. 3; Deputy Minister, Agriculture, to Young, p. 7.

79 Director to Young, p. 4; Deputy Minister, Agriculture, to Young, pp. 6-7.

80 Carmichael, "Land Settlement," p. 6; Director to Young, p. 6; Deputy Minister Agriculture to Young, p. 7.

81 "Recommendation of the Provincial Commission to the Provincial Government," n.d., Committee Reports, BCA, RSAC papers, GR-1315, reel B2517. This report was the basis for the report on land settlement that appeared in the Returned Soldiers' Aid Commission's public report, *Report of the Returned Soldiers' Aid Commission*, 1916.

82 Director to Young, p. 12.

83 W.H.K. to A. Speakman, M.P., 30 May 1922, BCA, LSB papers, GR-929, vol. 13, file 6. On Kirchner, see Chapter 1.

84 James C. Scott, *Seeing Like a State: How Certain Schemes to Improve the Human Condition Have Failed* (New Haven, CT: Yale University Press, 1998). I discuss Scott's argument in the Introduction.

85 Clement James Freeman to John Oliver, 17 June 1918, and Premier to Freeman, 19 June 1918, BCA, Premier's papers, GR-441, vol. 189, file 2.

CHAPTER 3: STUMP FARMS

1 Names of settlers in this chapter have been changed, as required by the terms of my research agreement with the BC Archives.

2 "Merville – A Retrospect," typescript, c. 1960, Clippings File: Merville, Courtenay District Museum and Archives (hereafter CDMA).

3 See Reta Blakely Hodgins, ed., *Merville and its Early Settlers 1919-1985*, (Merville, BC: Merville Community Association, 1985), 111, 69; also "Community Record," 1919, BCA, LSB papers, GR-929, vol. 41, file 2. Curry is listed as being single in "Store Credits – Development Area No. 1," 5 June 1920, BCA, LSB papers, GR-929, vol. 41, file 2, which also lists "Married Men with Families at Camp," indicating that families stayed behind at either Headquarters or Merville while the men went onto their lots. This would match Lily Clark's recollection that she spent two years in the town (see Hodgins, *Merville*, 111, and "Merville – A Retrospect"). The acreages appear in "Recapitulation Merville Farm Costs Nov. 30, 1922," BCA, LSB papers, GR-929, vol.41, file 2. The locations of Little's, Curry's, and Clark's farms can be seen on "Development Area Merville-Courtenay," map, BCA, LSB papers, GR-929, vol. 29, file 2.

4 "Merville – A Retrospect."

5 Ibid.

6 British Columbia, "Report of the Royal Commission on Agriculture," *Sessional Papers* 2 (1914).

7 Richard Somerset Mackie, *Island Timber: A Social History of the Comox Logging Company, Vancouver Island* (Victoria, BC: Sono Nis Press, 2000), 9-17, 26; Cole Harris, *Making Native Space: Colonialism, Resistance, and Reserves in British Columbia* (Vancouver: UBC Press, 2002), 111-12, 328.

8 Mackie, *Island Timber,* 26-49.

9 The idea of placing farmers on logged-off lands was pursued with great energy in Washington State, resulting in a promotional magazine, government pamphlets, conferences, an association, and a debate between loggers and settlement advocates over the proper use of forest lands. See *Logged-Off Farms Magazine,* 1912-1914; State of Washington, Statistics and Immigration Bureau, *The Logged-Off Lands of Western Washington,* by H.F. Giles, Deputy Commissioner (Olympia: Boardman, 1911); and State of Washington, Office of Commissioner of Public Lands, *Vacant Logged-Off Lands,* by Clark V. Savidge, Commissioner (Olympia: F.M. Lamborn Public Printer, 1922).

10 See "Vancouver and Gulf Islands. Physical Features," [1918], BCA, LSB papers, GR-929, vol. 9, file 4.

11 M.H. Nelems to Maxwell Smith, Chairman, LSB, 31 December 1918, BCA, LSB papers, GR-929, vol. 42, file 4.

12 P.A. Boving, "Report Regarding 4000 to 5000 Acres 'Logged Off Forest Land' & about 300 Acres 'Indian Reserve,' Near Courtenay, BC, Inspected November 13-16, 1918," 23 January 1919, BCA, LSB papers, GR-929, vol. 42, file 4. It is not clear precisely what lands he inspected, but they were located "about three miles North of Courtenay, and East of the Island Highway," which would place them in the Kitty Coleman area. M.H. Nelems, Chairman, LSB, to Barrow, 10 February 1919, BCA, Land Settlement Board, GR-1047, file 1, states that Boving's was the only soil report. The LSB did not appear to make an effort to acquire the Indian reserve lands, despite Boving's report that they were "well adapted for agricultural purposes."

13 Boving, "Report."

14 Ibid.

15 Nelems to Barrow, 10 February 1919. The two other reports are preserved as Nelems to Smith, 31 December 1918, BCA, LSB papers, GR-929, vol. 42, file 4; and Thos. P. MacKenzie, Commissioner of Grazing, to Chairman, LSB, 2 January [1919], BCA, LSB papers, GR-929, vol. 42, file 4. Nelems took over from Maxwell Smith as chairman of the LSB on 7 February 1919. His tenure was short; W.S. Latta, who had been on the *Asia,* became acting chair in October 1919. See "Index to Orders-in-Council," BCA, LSB papers, GR-929, vol. 8, file 9.

16 It is not entirely clear when the lands were actually purchased. The second annual report of the LSB, issued in January 1919, states that the land was purchased on 18 December 1918. See British Columbia, "Annual Report of the Land Settlement Board of British Columbia for the Year 1918," *Sessional Papers* 2 (1919), M37. Yet Nelems wrote to the Minister of Agriculture on 10 February 1919, urging purchase (see preceding footnote). The LSB must have purchased the land at some point in the winter of 1918-19, as they were surveying and settling the land by spring.

17 R.P. Bishop, "Land Settlement Board. Report on Reconnaissance of Logged Off Lands Near Courtenay," 10 May 1919, BCA, LSB papers, GR-929, vol. 43, file 11 (quotations are from pp. 6 and 16). The E & N was a branch line of the CPR. It ran from Victoria in the south to Courtenay, and never was extended north of this point.

18 Bishop to Chairman, LSB, 1 September 1919, BCA, LSB papers, GR-929, vol. 43, file 8.

19 Bishop to Chairman, LSB, 22 October 1919, BCA, LSB papers, GR-929, vol. 43, file 8.
20 Bishop to Chairman, LSB, 18 November 1919, BCA, LSB papers, GR-929, vol. 43, file 9.
21 Boving to Nelems, 16 September 1919, BCA, LSB papers, GR-929, vol. 43, file 8.
22 Mackie, *Island Timber,* 93-113.
23 Chairman, LSB, to Barrow, 23 April 1919, BCA, LSB papers, GR-929, vol. 42, file 4; and "Report on Development Area No. 1 – Merville," n.d. [1922-24 from the file], BCA, LSB papers, GR-929, vol. 41, file 2.
24 "Report on Development Area No. 1 – Merville," n.d.
25 Thus, LSB records that list the Merville settlers generally include only the male property holders. For example, two records included in GR-929, vol. 41, file 2, list settlers without mentioning women: "Nominal Role, Merville, From June 30, 1921" and "Community Record, May-June-July" (1919). The effects of this attitude on the successes and failures of the project are discussed below.
26 Christopher Clarkson, "Property Law and Family Regulation in Pacific British North America, 1862-1873," *Histoire sociale/Social History* 30, 60 (1997): 386-416; and Adele Perry, *On the Edge of Empire: Gender, Race, and the Making of British Columbia, 1849-1871* (Toronto: University of Toronto Press, 2001), 124-31.
27 Bishop to Chairman, LSB, 13 February 1920, BCA, LSB papers, GR-929, vol. 43, file 9.
28 I have found no discussion of the intricacies of blasting stumps, but given the size of the stumps (considered below), the fact that they could not have been of a standard size or shape, and the difficulties of working with blasting powder, this is likely a fairly accurate representation. I am influenced by novelist Jack Hodgins' vivid description of the skill and danger involved in blasting stumps in his novel about Merville: *Broken Ground: A Novel* (Toronto: McClelland and Stewart, 1998), 13-16, 53-65. In *Seeing Like a State: How Certain Schemes to Improve the Human Condition Have Failed* (New Haven, CT: Yale University Press, 1998), James C. Scott notes the way in which modern planning can break down in the face of ecological complexity (see 262-306, also throughout). Labour historians have noted that the industrial de-skilling process has not been able to entirely separate the work process from the necessity for specific skills. Loggers, in particular, have been able to maintain considerable independence in their work due to their knowledge of the forest. See Ian Radforth, "Logging Pulpwood in Northern Ontario," in Craig Heron and Robert Storey, eds., *On the Job: Confronting the Labour Process in Canada* (Montreal and Kingston: McGill-Queen's University Press, 1986), 245-80; and Richard Rajala, "The Forest as Factory," *Labour/Le Travail* 32 (1993): 73-104.
29 On logging procedures of the time, see Rajala, "Forest," and Mackie, *Island Timber,* throughout.
30 "Report on Development Area No. 1 – Merville," n.d.
31 Chairman, LSB, to Premier, 30 August 1919, BCA, LSB papers, GR-929, vol. 13, file 5.
32 "Report on Development Area No. 1 – Merville," n.d.; see also LSB to C.E. Whitney-Griffiths, 8 March 1923, BCA, LSB papers, GR-929, vol. 41, file 2.
33 Mackie, *Island Timber,* 162-77.
34 LSB to C.E. Whitney-Griffiths, 8 March 1923.
35 See Chapter 1.
36 "Report on Development Area No. 1 – Merville," n.d.; see also "Notes on Situation in Development Areas," 17 February 1920, BCA, LSB papers, GR-929, vol. 41, file 3; and F. Furk, Cost Accountant, "Courtenay Development Area No. 1, Statement of Affairs

224 Notes to pages 86-91

as at December 31, 1919," BCA, LSB papers, GR-929, vol. 42, file 4. Acreage amounts are from Furk.

37 "Report on Development Area No. 1 – Merville," n.d.; and Furk, "Courtenay ... Dec 31, 1919."

38 Anonymous, "Reflections on Merville from the Grantham Side," quoted in Reta Blakely Hodgins, ed., *Merville,* 7.

39 "Report on Development Area No. 1 – Merville," n.d., and "Merville – A Retrospect."

40 Much of this section is derived from "Report on Development Area No. 1 – Merville," n.d., and other sources as noted.

41 "Report on Developmnet Area No. 1 – Merville," n.d.

42 Ibid.

43 See Chapter 4.

44 LSB, Director (R.D. Davies) to Min of Agriculture, memo, Mar 23, 1920, BCA, Bruce A. McKelvie papers, MS-001, vol. 5, file G.

45 LSB [W.S. Latta], "Instructions to Superintendent, Development Area No. 1," [11 or 12 May] 1920, BCA, McKelvie papers, MS-001, vol. 6, file G.

46 "Report on Development Area No. 1 – Merville," n.d.

47 Ibid.

48 Ibid. The report here paraphrases instructions given to Halley.

49 Ibid.; LSB [W.S. Latta] to R.D. Davies, memo, 28 May 1920, BCA, LSB papers, GR-929, vol. 41, file 4.

50 K.G. Halley to Col. Latta, LSB, private report, 31 June 1920, BCA, LSB papers, GR-929, vol. 41, file 4. This section and the following paragraph are from K.G. Halley, Supervisor, to LSB, report, 30 June 1920, BCA, LSB papers, GR-929, vol. 41, file 4.

51 "Notes on Situation in Development Areas," 17 February 1920, BCA, LSB papers, GR-929, vol. 41, file 3.

52 Halley to Latta, 6 July 1920; Latta to Halley, 21 August 1920; Halley to Latta, 25 August 1920; all in BCA, LSB papers, GR-929, vol. 41, file 4.

53 Halley to Latta, 15 June 1920; C.S.R. Cowan, Assistant Forester, to Latta, 7 July 1920; Halley to Latta, 25 August 1920; all in BCA, LSB papers, GR-929, vol. 41, file 4.

54 Merville Branch of the Ladies Auxiliary of the Great War Veterans' Association to Canadian Patriotic Fund, 15 July 1920, BCA, Returned Soldiers' Aid Commission (hereafter RSAC), GR-1315, series 50-F-2, reel B2514.

55 Halley to Latta, 28 September 1920, BCA, LSB papers, GR-929, vol. 41, file 5.

56 Halley to Latta, 4 November 1920, BCA, LSB papers, GR-929, vol. 41, file 1; reply (probably from Latta) is LSB to Halley, 8 November 1920, BCA, LSB papers, GR-929, vol. 41, file 1. The need to secure power suggests that there was no electricity in the town centre.

57 Halley to Latta, monthly report, 6 December 1920, BCA, LSB papers, GR-929, vol. 41, file 1.

58 Halley to Latta, monthly report, 1 January 1921, BCA, LSB papers, GR-929, vol. 41, file 1.

59 Halley to Latta, monthly report, 5 March 1921, BCA, LSB papers, GR-929, vol. 41, file 1.

60 Halley to Latta, monthly report, 6 February 1921 and 5 March 1921, BCA, LSB papers, GR-929, vol. 41, file 1; S.H. Hopkins, District Representative, to Halley, 14 February 1921, BCA, LSB papers, GR-929, vol. 41, file 1.

61 Director, LSB, to Halley, 28 April 1921, BCA, LSB papers, GR-929, vol. 41, file 6.

62 Halley to Davies, Director, LSB, 6 May 1921, BCA, LSB papers, GR-929, vol. 41, file 6.

63 Latta to Davies, 21 May 1921, BCA, LSB papers, GR-929, vol. 41, file 6.

64 Director, LSB, to Latta, 25 July 1921, BCA, LSB papers, GR-929, vol. 41, file 6. His fellow committee members were the local MLA and a settler.

65 Latta to Davies, 21 May 1921, BCA, LSB papers, GR-929, vol. 41, file 6.

66 Cole Harris with David Demeritt, "Farming and Rural Life," in Harris, *The Resettlement of British Columbia: Essays on Colonialism and Geographical Change* (Vancouver: UBC Press, 1997), 227.

67 Accountant to Latta, 9 September 1925, BCA, LSB papers, GR-929, vol. 42, file 3.

68 See various reports in BCA, LSB papers, GR-929, vol. 41, file 7.

69 District Representative to Davies, 19 October 1921, BCA, LSB papers, GR-929, vol. 41, file 7.

70 In other words, progress loans were loans made as a percentage of the value of the improvement work to be done. Halley would estimate the value of planned improvements on a particular farm, and then loan the owner a percentage of that value. Therefore, those with few or no improvements to make had no access to progress loans.

71 Averages are from District Representative to Davies, 19 October 1921, BCA, LSB papers, GR-929, vol. 41, file 7; figures on Little, Clark, and Curry are from "Recapitulation Merville Farm Costs Nov 30, 1922," BCA, LSB papers, GR-929, vol. 41, file 2.

72 This exchange is included in a collection of letters between Halley, Curry, and LSB accountant Sonley, BCA, LSB papers, GR-929, vol. 41, file 1.

73 Little's sales are noted in a series of letters written by G.B. Capes, Latta, and Sonley (3 and 10 September, 11 October, and 2 November 1921), and in Accountant to LSB, Merville, 10 November 1921; all in BCA, LSB papers, GR-929, vol. 47, file 1. The first quote is taken from Clifford to Sonley, 28 November 1921, BCA, LSB papers, GR-929, vol. 47, file 2. Little's comments are taken from Clifford to Sonley, 28 November 1921, BCA, LSB papers, GR-929, vol. 47, file 2.

74 Latta to Davies, 19 October 1921, BCA, LSB papers, GR-929, vol. 41, file 7.

75 Halley to Latta, 30 January 1922, BCA, LSB papers, GR-929, vol. 41, file 8; see also Halley to Sonley, 16 January 1922, BCA, LSB papers, GR-929, vol. 47, file 3.

76 LSB to Halley, memo, 9 February 1922, and Halley to Latta, 13 February 1922, BCA, LSB papers, GR-929, vol. 41, file 8.

77 J.W. Trebett to LSB, 16 January 1922, BCA, LSB papers, GR-929, vol. 47, file 3.

78 Clifford to Sonley, February 1922, and LSB to Clifford, 28 March 1922, BCA, LSB papers, GR-929, vol. 47, file 3; LSB to Clifford, 26 April 1922, and Halley to Latta, 11 May 1922, BCA, LSB papers, GR-929, vol. 47, file 4.

79 Halley to Latta, 11 May 1922, BCA, LSB papers, GR-929, vol. 47, file 4.

80 Settlers' Representatives to Director, LSB, 22 February 1922, BCA, LSB papers, GR-929, vol. 41, file 8.

81 Secretary, Merville Community Association, to Halley, 3 April 1922, BCA, LSB papers, GR-929, vol. 47, file 4.

82 "Report on Development Area No. 1 – Merville," n.d.

83 This account of the Merville fire is based primarily on "Fire of July 6, 1922," Clippings File: Merville, CDMA; "The Merville Fire – 1922, from the diary of Geoffrey Bernard Capes," in Hodgins, *Merville*, 248-54; and "Cyclone of Fire Sweeps Merville Area," *Comox Argus*, 13 July 1922, 1. The *Comox Argus* was accessed via clippings in the

Courtenay and District Museum and Archives clippings files and in Land Settlement
Board clippings relating to the Merville fire. As well, newspaper editions published
during July and August of 1922 were scanned for details of the fire.

84 "Merville – A Retrospect."
85 Capes, "Merville Fire," in Hodgins, *Merville,* 248-49.
86 Some details here are from Coroner's Inquest, "Merville Fire Trial," 7 July 1922,
   CDMA, Comox Logging and Railway Fonds (hereafter CLR Fonds), box 21, file 1,
   part 2, p. 3; and Hodgins, *Merville,* 69.
87 Wayne's fate is from Hodgins, *Merville,* 69. Capes phoned from Courtenay. I have
   found no mention of phones in Merville, though as it was only three miles from
   Courtenay and on the highway, it is possible that phone service existed in the town
   centre. Cole Harris reports that by 1911 there were twenty thousand telephones in BC,
   but most were in Vancouver; see Harris, *Resettlement,* 177.
88 "Merville – A Retrospect."
89 "Report on Development Area No. 1 – Merville," n.d.
90 Untitled table of settlers with losses and board's offers of assistance; "List of Settlers
   Burnt Out at Merville"; and "Estimate of Replacements Required – Merville Fire
   1922"; all found in BCA, LSB papers, GR-929, vol. 42, file 1.
91 "Cyclone," *Comox Argus,* 13 July 1922, 3, 7. See also "Relief Camp is Running Smoothly,"
   Comox Argus, 20 July 1922.
92 "Merville," entry in table of fire statistics, Annual Report of Forest Fires, BCA,
   Department of Lands, Forests Branch, GR-315.
93 Supervisor of Assessors and Agencies to Premier, 2 August 1922, BCA, Supervisor of
   Assessors and Agencies, GR-879, vol. 3, file D.
94 "Merville Resurgent," editorial, *Comox Argus,* 13 July 1922.
95 "Seeding Down," "The Relief Camp," "Fire-Sufferers Voice Requests," and "Provide
   Concert for Fire Victims," *Comox Argus,* 27 July 1922.
96 "Relief Camp is Closing Down," *Comox Argus,* 3 August 1922.
97 "Fire-fighting," *Comox Argus,* 3 August 1922.
98 "Merville Soil," 3 August 1922; "'Carry On' at Merville," 17 August 1922; and "Small
   Damage Done to Merville Soil," 24 August 1922; all in *Comox Argus.*
99 "Report on Development Area No. 1 – Merville," n.d.; LSB to Minister of Agriculture,
   30 August 1922; "Soil Report by W. Newton: Merville Burnt-over Area," 25 July 1922;
   "Untitled table of settlers with losses"; all in BCA, LSB papers, GR-929, vol. 42, file 1.
100 Oliver to Latta, 12 July 1922, BCA, LSB papers, GR-929, vol. 42, file 1.
101 LSB to Colonel F.A. Robertson, Chairman, BC Returned Soldier Commission, 1
   August 1922, BCA, LSB papers, GR-292, vol. 42, file 1.
102 Supervisor to Premier, 2 August 1922, BCA, Supervisor of Assessors and Agencies,
   GR-879, vol. 3, file D.
103 On this phenomenon, see Stephen Pyne, *Fire in America: A Cultural History of Wildland and Rural Fire* (Princeton, NJ: Princeton University Press, 1982), 204.
104 Supervisor to Premier, 2 August 1922. See also "Bevan Mill is Wiped Out," *Comox
   Argus,* 20 July 1922, 1.
105 Coroner's Inquest, 7 July 1922, CDMA, CLR Fonds, vol. 21, file 1, part 2, pp. 5-7.
106 The case is *Peter McIntyre v. Comox Logging and Railway Company,* Supreme Court of
   British Columbia, Vancouver, BC. This account is drawn from "Statement of Claim,"
   17 May 1923; "Reasons for the Judgement of the Honourable Mr. Justice D.A. McDonald," Vancouver, BC, 27 March 1924; and "Statement of Fact," enclosed with Davis,

Marshall, MacNeill and Pugh, Davis, Lawson, Ralston and Hossie, Barristers, Solicitors, and c. to R.J. Filberg (Headquarters, BC), 11 August 1922; all in CDMA, CLR Fonds, vol. 21, file 1, part 2.

107 Snags are dead trees supported upright by living trees.

108 Comox Logging and Railway Company, "Report on Merville Forest Fire of July 6th, 1922," 1923, CDMA, CLR Fonds, vol. 2, file 2, part 1, pp. 14-15.

109 On the problematic relationship of logging, railways, and land settlement, see Pyne, *Fire in America*, 199-204, 210-11.

110 See Dorothy M. Bishop to *Victoria Daily Colonist*, 19 December 1922, BCA, Supervisor of Assessors and Agencies, GR-879, vol. 3, file E; "Relief Committee Sending Cheques: Merville Sufferers Should Now Be in Receipt of Funds Given on Their Behalf," clipping, n.d., n.s., BCA, Supervisor of Assessors and Agencies, GR-879, vol. 3, file G; and "Merville and District Relief Committee Statement of Receipts and Disbursements," 26 February 1923, BCA, Supervisor of Assessors and Agencies, GR-879, vol. 3, file H.

111 Shopkeeper to Barrow, Minister of Agriculture, 29 January 1923, BCA, LSB papers, GR-929, vol. 45, file 2.

112 See Committee from the Courtenay-Comox Board of Trade and the Comox Agricultural Association to Barrow, 25 January 1923, BCA, LSB papers, GR-929, vol. 41, file 2 (the government's resentment is apparent in comments pencilled on the letter); British Columbia, "Annual Report of the Land Settlement Board for the Year 1922," *Sessional Papers* 2 (1924), Z7, which contains the quote; and "Report on Development Area No. 1 – Merville," n.d.

113 "Report on Development Area No. 1 – Merville," n.d.

114 See a series of vouchers in BCA, LSB papers, GR-929, vol. 46, files 6-7. Little's advance is noted in LSB to LSB, Courtenay, 19 March 1923, BCA, LSB papers, GR-929, vol. 46, file 7.

115 Capes to Latta, 13 March 1923, BCA, LSB papers, GR-929, vol. 42, file 2.

116 Halley to Latta, 16 April 1923; Halley to Latta, 23 April 1923; LSB to Halley, 26 April 1923; LSB to LSB, Courtenay, 26 April 1923; Capes to Latta, 24 April 1923; LSB to Halley, 28 May 1923; LSB to Capes, 28 May 1923; all in BCA, LSB papers, GR-929, vol. 42, file 2. The LSB was dissolved in the 1970s.

117 "Memorandum for Lieut.-Col. R.D. Davies," 7 January 1924, BCA, LSB papers, GR-929, vol. 42, file 2. The quote is from "Operation of the Provincial Land Settlement Board in Regard to Soldier Settlement," n.s., n.d. [but likely 1923 from the context], BCA, LSB papers, GR-929, vol. 41, file 2.

118 "Unimproved Farms – Merville," n.d. [but likely 1924] and "Improved Farms – Merville," 1924, BCA, LSB papers, GR-929, vol. 42, file 7.

119 Hodgins, *Merville*, 111.

120 "Report on Development Area No. 1 – Merville," n.d., pp. 28-29.

121 Ann Simpson to Latta, 4 April 1924; LSB to Ann Simpson, 18 August 1924; and Ann Simpson to LSB, 22 August 1924. The number of settlers is included in a handwritten note of information phoned in to the Premier's office, 16 September 1924. All of this material is in BCA, LSB papers, GR-929, vol. 42, file 2.

122 *McIntyre v. Comox Logging*, reasons for judgment of the Honourable Mr. Justice D.A. McDonald, Vancouver, 27 May 1924, CDMA, CLR Fonds, box 2, series 2, file 13, part 1.

123 "List of Properties for Sale – Merville," 1 April 1925, BCA, LSB papers, GR-929, vol. 42, file 8.

124 "Report on Merville Settlers. February 1926," BCA, LSB papers, GR-929, vol. 42, file 7.
125 Hodgins, *Merville*, 69.
126 "Memorandum – To the Honourable the Minister of Lands," 1 February 1929, BCA, McKelvie papers, MS-001, vol. 6, file H.
127 "Land Purchasers at Merville as at December, 1944," BCA, LSB papers, GR-929, vol. 29, file 2.
128 Hodgins, *Merville*, 112.
129 "Merville – A Retrospect," 1.

CHAPTER 4: CREATING ORDER AT SUMAS

1 Laura Cameron, *Openings: A Meditation on History, Method, and Sumas Lake* (Montreal and Kingston: McGill-Queen's University Press, 1997), 46; F.N. Sinclair, "A History of the Sumas Drainage and Dyking District," typescript, n.d., BCA, Library Collection.
2 W.L. Blatchford, Secretary, "Minutes of the Sumas Dyking Meeting ...," 24 November 1919, BCA, LSB papers, GR-929, vol. 50, file 8.
3 See Chapter 1.
4 "Proceedings of the Agriculture Committee of the Legislative Assembly of the Province of British Columbia, Held at the Parliament Buildings, Dec 3rd, 1925 ...," BCA, LSB papers, GR-929, vol. 48, file 10, p. 9.
5 C. Cartwright, "Report on Sumas Reclamation Project," 18 October 1919, BCA, LSB papers, GR-929, vol. 48, file 5. On the 1948 flood, see W.R. Derrick Sewell, *Water Management and Floods in the Fraser River Basin* (Chicago: Department of Geography, University of Chicago, 1965), 15-16.
6 Sinclair, "A History of the Sumas Drainage and Dyking District," n.d.
7 "The Sumas Reclamation Project," pamphlet, BCA, Library Collection, p. 2. Reprinted from *Agricultural Journal*, November 1922.
8 Cartwright, "Report," 18 October 1919, BCA, LSB papers, GR-929, vol. 48, file 5.
9 Cameron, *Openings*, 23, 44, 50-51; Barbara Beldam, "Sumas Prairie – A Mosaic of Memories," in Millicent A. Lindo, ed., *Making History: An Anthology of British Columbia* (Victoria: n.p., 1974), 32-33.
10 From Jody R. Woods, "Sumas Lake Transformations," in Keith Thor Carlson, ed., *A Stó:lō Coast Salish Historical Atlas* (Vancouver: Douglas and McIntyre, 2001), 104.
11 Imbert Orchard, *Floodland and Forest*, Sound Heritage Series no. 37 (Victoria: PABC Sound and Moving Image Division, 1983," quoted in Cameron, *Openings*, 23. Generally see Cameron, *Openings*, 16-40, 50-51; Brian Thom and Laura Cameron, "Changing Land Use in *Solh Temexw* (Our Land): Population, Transportation, Ecology, and Heritage," in Keith Thor Carlson, ed., *You Are Asked to Witness: The Stó:lō in Canada's Pacific Coast History* (Chilliwack, BC: Stó:lō Heritage Trust: 1997), 173.
12 Keith Thor Carlson, "Indian Reservations," in Carlson, *Stó:lō Atlas*, 94-95.
13 Quoted in Cameron, *Openings*, 57.
14 "Sumas Reclamation," pamphlet, p. 2; W.S. Latta, Director, LSB, "Record of Events – Sumas," 31 December 1926, BCA, LSB papers, GR-929, vol. 48, file 3; Cameron, *Openings*, 53-57. Cole Harris sees Sproat as supporting and attempting to work out an independent role for Native people within colonial society, an attempt that eventually

failed. See Harris, *Making Native Space* (Vancouver: UBC Press, 2002), 98-166.

15 "Sumas Reclamation," pamphlet, 2; W.S. Latta, Director, LSB, "Record of Events – Sumas," 31 December 1926, BCA, LSB papers, GR-929, vol. 48, file 3.

16 See Latta, "Record ... Sumas," 4-5; "Sumas Reclamation," pamphlet, p. 2; Sinclair, "History," 4; "Skeleton Outline of the History of the Sumas Dyking Project, with reference to the Statutes affecting the same," BCA, LSB papers, GR-929, vol. 50, file 8, p. 2. On BC Electric's attempt, see also Henry Ewert, *The Story of the B.C. Electric Railway* (North Vancouver, BC: Whitecap Books, 1986), 72, and the map inside the front cover.

17 Pattullo to Barrow, 18 August 1917, BCA, Premier's papers, GR-441, vol. 190, file 3.

18 Names of landowners in this chapter have been changed, in accordance with my research agreement with the BC Archives. Jakob Zink to M. Smith, Chair, LSB, 16 October 1917, BCA, LSB papers, GR-929, vol. 50, file 1. See also Chairman, LSB, to John Wilson, Sumas, 11 October 1917; and R.A. Heluk to LSB, 10 December 1917; both in BCA, LSB papers, GR-929, vol. 50, file 1.

19 "Minutes," 4 February 1918, BCA, LSB papers, GR-929, vol. 50, file 2.

20 Cameron, *Openings,* 67-68.

21 Sinclair, "History," 5; LSB, Reports, BCA, LSB papers, GR-929, vol. 49, file 5.

22 F.N. Sinclair, "Sumas Reclamation Project Final Report," 5 July 1919, BCA, LSB papers, GR-929, vol. 48, file 5.

23 Oliver was Minister of Agriculture when the act passed.

24 John Oliver to Minister of Lands, 25 July 1917, BCA, LSB papers, GR-929, vol. 50, file 1.

25 W.E. Payne, Vancouver Board of Trade, to Oliver, 10 August 1918, and Vancouver Board of Trade to Maxwell Smith, 17 August 1918, BCA, LSB papers, GR-929, vol. 50, file 3.

26 "Reclamation Scheme Adds Whole County to Producing Area," *Vancouver Daily World,* n.d. [clipping – between 1920 and 1923 from the context], BCA, J.W. Jones papers, MS-023, vol. 7, file 3.

27 "Dyking of Sumas Area Approved," 1919, n.s., BCA, J.W. Jones papers, MS-023, vol. 7, file 3. By "property," Oliver was likely referring to the lakelands, whose sale was intended to recoup much of the costs of the scheme. Still, his use of the term speaks to the extent to which Oliver conceived of private property as the legitimate basis of activity.

28 For landowners that worried about costs, see Jacob Zink to Maxwell Smith, Chairman, LSB, 16 October 1917, and T.M. Hall to Maxwell Smith, 11 October 1917, BCA, LSB papers, GR-929, vol. 50, file 1. The budget figure is from "Minutes of the Meeting of the Property Owners of the Sumas Dyking District ...," 27 March 1920, BCA, LSB papers, GR-929, vol. 51, file 3. Though the plan for the reclamation was approved at the initial meeting at which Oliver issued his warning, the lowest bid proved to be higher than the engineers' estimate. This higher figure was then approved at the 1920 meeting.

29 Director, LSB, to Minister of Agriculture, memo, 24 August 1921, and Chief Engineer, Sumas Dyking District, "Report for the Land Settlement Board on the Sumas Dyking District ...," 22 June 1921, BCA, LSB papers, GR-929, vol. 49, file 2. See also Director, LSB, "Report for the Hon, the Minister of Ag, on the Sumas Reclamation Project," n.d., BCA, LSB papers, GR-929, vol. 49, file 3; and F.N. Sinclair, Chief Engineer, Sumas to LSB, progress report, 6 January 1920, BCA, LSB papers, GR-929, vol. 49, file 2.

30 Blatchford, Secretary, Sumas Dyking Advisory Board, to Davies, 16 June 1921, and Director, LSB, to Blatchford, 6 July 1921, BCA, LSB papers, GR-929, vol. 51, file 9.

31 Latta, "Record ... Sumas," 17. See also Director, LSB, "Report on Sumas Reclamation Project for Month of October, 1921"; Director, LSB, "Progress Report for the Month of November," n.d.; and F.N. Sinclair to LSB, "Progress Report for November," 16 December 1921; all in BCA, LSB papers, GR-929, vol. 49, file 3.

32 Latta, "Record ... Sumas," 18; "Sumas Reclamation," pamphlet, p. 6; "Report by Chief Engineer on Sumas Reclamation Project to May 31, 1923 ...," BCA, LSB papers, GR-929, vol. 49, file 6.

33 "Report on Sumas River Dam," 26 November 1923, BCA, LSB papers, GR-929, vol. 49, file 6; "Sumas Report," 1923, BCA, LSB papers, GR-929, vol. 49, file 6; and G.P. Moe, Construction Engineer, "Sumas River Dam Sumas Dyking District," 12 October 1922, BCA, LSB papers, GR-929, vol. 49, file 5.

34 "Report by Chief ... to May 31, 1923," BCA, LSB papers, GR-929, vol. 49, file 6.

35 "Land Settlement Board," BCA, LSB papers, GR-929, vol. 8, file 8; and "Minutes of meeting of Sumas Dyke Commission held in the office of the Land Settlement Board on May 9, 1924," BCA, LSB papers, GR-929, vol. 49, file 8. The sturgeon and duck stories are in Cameron, *Openings*, 74.

36 "P.C. 1229" and "Agreement for the sale of Dominion Lands in British Columbia (Sumas Drainage Project)," 8 August 1923, BCA, Commission on Dyking, Drainage, and Irrigation (1946), GR-680, vol. 3, file 2.

37 C. Tice, Chief Agronomist to Col. Davies, memo, 28 April 1924, BCA, LSB papers, GR-929, vol. 53, file 1.

38 "Minutes of meeting of Sumas Dyke Commission, 18 January 1924, Chilliwack," BCA, LSB papers, GR-929, vol. 49, file 8.

39 "Minutes of meeting of Sumas Dyke Commission, July 2, 1924," BCA, LSB papers, GR-929, vol. 49, file 8.

40 Latta, "Record ... Sumas," 25.

41 Ibid., 31.

42 LSB to T.L. Hughes, LSB Chilliwack, 16 March 1925, and "Record of Proceedings of the Commissioners of the Sumas Drainage, Dyking, and Development District October 27, 1925," BCA, LSB papers, GR-929, vol. 49, file 9.

43 "Lake Land Development Account," 14 January 1926, BCA, LSB papers, GR-929, vol. 55, file 6.

44 LSB to Rowberry, Chilliwack, 14 January 1926, BCA, LSB papers, GR-929, vol. 55, file 6.

45 "Farm Lands for Sale in the Sumas Drainage and Dyking District, situated in the Lower Fraser Valley British Columbia," 1923 [date inferred from textual evidence. The finding aid notes that the pamphlets are from 1923-24], BCA, LSB papers, GR-929, vol. 48, file 1.

46 "Sumas Reclaimed Lands," pamphlet, n.d. [probably 1927], BCA, Library Collection.

47 See Inspector of Dykes to Wm. Atkinson, Minister of Agriculture, 9 December 1930, BCA, Inspector of Dykes, GR-1569, vol. 6, file 4. See also Sumas Commissioner, "Re: Sumas Lands," n.d.; Sumas Commissioner to Hans Hannesen, 13 June 1927; and Sumas Commissioner to R.S. Hanna, 16 May 1927; all in BCA, Inspector of Dykes, GR-1569, vol. 9, file 1. See also Commissioner Sumas to Barrow, Minister of Agriculture, 18 October 1927, BCA, LSB papers, GR-929, vol. 53, file 6.

48 "Government to Sell 8,700 Acre Block at Sumas," clipping, n.s., n.d., and "Offer Made for Sumas Acreage," clipping, n.s., n.d., BCA, J.W. Jones papers, MS-023, vol. 7, file 1. The agreement between the real estate company of Fell and Scharfe and the

government – and the Order-in-Council authorizing it – are in BCA, LSB papers, GR-929, vol. 49, file 10. Acreages are from "Amount of Land Sold in the Sumas Drainage, Dyking, and Development District up to 1st Nov. 1930," handwritten, and the report for 31 December 1930, BCA, Inspector of Dykes, GR-1569, vol. 9, file 2.

49 "Sumas Drainage, Dyking, and Development District, Balance Sheet and Statements as at 1928," and "Sumas Drainage, Dyking, and Development District, Balance Sheet and Statements as at 1929," BCA, Inspector of Dykes, GR-1569, vol. 6, file 4.

50 "Sumas Project as at December 31, 1932" balance sheet, BCA, LSB papers, GR-929, vol. 29, file 16.

51 R.L. Maitland to J.W. Jones, 25 January 1927, BCA, J.W. Jones papers, MS-023, vol. 3, file 1.

52 "Proceedings of the Agriculture Committee, of the Legislative Assembly of the Province of British Columbia, Held at the Parliament Buildings," BCA, LSB papers, GR-929, vol. 48, files 7-10. Participants are listed by last name only in the transcripts of the hearings. I assume that the "Mr. Blackman" acting on behalf of the owners is the same Henry Blackman, Esq., K.C. [King's Counsel], who appeared as part of another commission investigating financial problems of area landowners in 1928. See "In the Matter of the Sumas Dyking District Relief Act 1928. Minutes of ... the Sumas Relief Commission Constituted Under Sumas Dyking District Relief Act, 1928," BCA, Sumas Dyking District Relief Commission, GR-1089.

53 The canal took over twenty-seven of the forty-nine acres of the Aylechootlook reserve. The LSB argued that, as the remaining twenty-two acres were now so much more valuable, nothing was owed to the band. In the end, the board agreed to purchase the land that the canal ran through for a total of $188.72, or $7 per acre. See Cameron, *Openings*, 72 and n. 122.

54 "Proceedings of the Agriculture Committee, of the Legislative Assembly of the Province of British Columbia, Held at the Parliament Buildings, Dec. 3rd, 1925," BCA, LSB papers, GR-929, vol. 48, file 10, pp. 1-14; the quote is from p. 14.

55 "Sumas Reclaimed Lands," pamphlet, 1924, BCA, LSB papers, GR-929, vol. 48, file 1.

56 "Proceedings of the Agriculture Committee of the Legislative Assembly of the Province of British Columbia, Held at the Parliament Buildings ... – Testimony of E.D. Barrow," 7 December 1925, BCA, LSB papers, GR-929, vol. 48, file 8, pp. 108-16.

57 "Proceedings of the Agriculture Committee ...," 7 December 1925, pp. 75-79.

58 "Proceedings of the Agriculture Committee ...," 8 December 1925, BCA, LSB papers, GR-929, vol. 48, file 9, p. 129.

59 "Proceedings of the Agriculture Committee ...," 8 December 1925, p. 170.

60 "Proceedings of the Agriculture Committee ...," 7 December 1925, pp. 79-80. For other farmer's assertions that dairying is more profitable, see pp. 86 and 97.

61 "Proceedings of the Agriculture Committee ...," 7 December 1925, p. 87. On the other crops, see p. 93, and "Proceedings of the Agriculture Committee ...," 8 December 1925, p. 124.

62 On the inability of small farmers in Washington State to compete with the prairies, see Richard White, "Poor Men on Poor Lands: The Back-to-the-Land Movement of the Early Twentieth Century," in G. Thomas Edwards and Carlos A. Schwantes, eds., *Experiences in a Promised Land: Essays in Pacific Northwest History,* (Seattle: University of Washington Press, 1986), 287-303.

63 Cole Harris with David Demeritt, "Farming and Rural Life," in Harris, *The Resettlement of British Columbia* (Vancouver: UBC Press, 1997), 241.

64 "Proceedings of the Agriculture Committee ...," 7 December 1925, p. 103.

65 "Proceedings of the Agriculture Committee ...," 8 December 1925, p. 147.

66 "Proceedings of the Agriculture Committee ...," 8 December 1925, p. 152, and 7 December 1925, p. 79. In *Openings*, Laura Cameron's major point is the variety of stories that can be told about a place like Sumas Lake. In discussing the draining of the lake, however, she builds an argument on the "discord" surrounding the project, a discord she suggests may lie in a conflict between the local and the provincial. In doing so, she misses the essential agreement between the landowners and the government, as expressed in these hearings. She quotes Conover's opposition to the dike but not his convictions about its success. Cameron therefore misses the ways in which environmental and racial attitudes could unite local farmers and the state. See Cameron, *Openings*, 26-27, 38.

67 "Proceedings of the Agriculture Committee ...," 10 December 1925, BCA, LSB papers, GR-929, vol. 48, file 7, pp. 189-201.

68 Inspector of Dykes to Hon. E.T. Kenney, Minister of Lands, 2 March 1946, BCA, Commission on Dyking, Drainage, and Irrigation (1946), GR-680, vol. 3, file 2.

69 Inspector to Kenney, 2 March 1946, BCA, Commission on Dyking, Drainage, and Irrigation (1946), GR-680, vol. 3, file 2.

70 "'Public Inquiries Act' (Chapter 131, RSBC, 1936). Inquiry before Frederick Moore Clement, Sole Commissioner, to determine how much each of the improved districts under the 'water act,' 1939, and of the districts under the 'Drainage, Dyking and Development Act,' 1905, that are indebted to the province can pay annually in respect of its indebtedness," BCA, Commission on Dyking, Drainage, and Irrigation (1946), GR-680, vol. 1, pp. 262-67, 308-15, and throughout.

71 On Scott, see Introduction herein.

CHAPTER 5: ACHIEVING THE MODERN COUNTRYSIDE

1 Pattullo, Minister of Lands, to Maxwell Smith, Chairman, Land Settlement Board, 19 February 1918, BCA, LSB papers, GR-929, vol. 12, file 11; Robin Fisher, *Duff Pattullo of British Columbia* (Toronto: University of Toronto Press, 1991), 137-38.

2 Chair, Land Settlement Board, to Minister of Lands, 26 February 1918, BCA, LSB papers, GR-929, vol. 12, file 11.

3 Smith to John Oliver, Premier, 18 September 1918, BCA, Premier's papers, GR-441, vol. 339, file 14.

4 Fisher, *Duff Pattullo*, 131-32.

5 See Richard White, *The Organic Machine: The Remaking of the Columbia River* (New York: Hill and Wang, 1995), 30-58.

6 Donald Worster, *Rivers of Empire: Water, Aridity and the Growth of the American West* (New York: Oxford University Press, 1985), 191-256.

7 That is, a view that nature was important only to the extent that it was directly useful to human enterprises.

8 Worster, *Rivers*, 3-60, 243-56.

9 White, *Organic*, ix-xi, 59-113. White's point is not to defend the damming of the Columbia, but to condemn a view of humans and nature that insists on keeping the two separate.

10 Mark Fiege, *Irrigated Eden: The Making of an Agricultural Landscape in the American*

West (Seattle and London: University of Washington Press, 1999), 3-80, 171-209 (the quote is from 172).

11 "Development Area No. 2 ... Land Settlement Board of British Columbia," BCA, LSB papers, GR-929, vol. 38, file 3.

12 Report on Lot 17, Registered Map No. 1494, BCA, LSB papers, GR-929, vol. 38, file 3.

13 Hilton Young, "Lister as I Knew It," typescript, n.d., BCA, Library Collection, 4-5, 15.

14 Young, "Lister," 11.

15 "Notes on the Creston Area," February 1922, BCA, LSB papers, GR-929, vol. 38, file 1.

16 W.S. Latta for LSB, "Recommendations Re New System at Camp Lister," n.d., and "Notes on the Creston Area," February 1922, BCA, LSB papers, GR-929, vol. 38, file 1.

17 LSB to Rowberry, Area Supervisor, 28 July 1920, BCA, LSB papers, GR-929, vol. 38, file 8.

18 "Notes on the Creston Area," February 1922, BCA, LSB papers, GR-929, vol. 38, file 1; Young, "Lister," 6.

19 LSB to Rowberry, 28 July 1920, BCA, LSB papers, GR-929, vol. 38, file 8.

20 "Fruit Trees, Camp Lister, May 15th, 1922," BCA, LSB papers, GR-929, vol. 38, file 1.

21 "Notes on the Creston Area," February 1922.

22 Young, "Lister," 6-7; Creston. Account Book, 1919-22, BCA, LSB papers, GR-929, vol. 101; Creston. Account Book, 1920, BCA, LSB papers, GR-929, vol. 102; LSB to A.H. Rowberry, Superintendent of Development Area, 28 July 1920, BCA, LSB papers, GR-929, vol. 38, file 8. Shiplap is boards cut to notch together when their edges are overlaid, forming a waterproof exterior shell for a house.

23 Elspeth Cameron, *Earle Birney: A Life* (Toronto: Viking, 1994), 27-28.

24 Young, "Lister," 10.

25 Ibid., 6, 9.

26 W.S. Latta to R.D. Davies, 11 May 1922, BCA, LSB papers, GR-929, vol. 38, file 11.

27 Young, "Lister," 10.

28 Cameron, *Earle Birney,* 28-29.

29 Ibid., 30-31.

30 LSB [likely W.S. Latta, from initials WSL on letter] to Minister of Agriculture, 26 October 1922, and LSB [likely W.S. Latta] to Minister of Agriculture, 24 October 1922, BCA, LSB papers, GR-929, vol. 38, file 1.

31 "November 1923 instalment of interest," BCA, LSB papers, GR-929, vol. 38, file 7.

32 LSB [likely W.S. Latta] to Davies, memo, 8 July 1922, and Latta to Davies, 11 May 1922, BCA, LSB papers, GR-929, vol. 38, file 11.

33 Chairman, Publicity Committee, Creston Board of Trade, to Superintendent, LSB, 30 October 1920, BCA, LSB papers, GR-929, vol. 38, file 9.

34 R.P. Bishop to Davies, 26 February 1920, BCA, LSB papers, GR-929, vol. 38, file 16. Bishop summarizes the district water engineer's views in his report to the LSB.

35 See "Development Area No. 2," pamphlet, vol. 38, file 3; and District Representative, LSB, to Frank C. Overman, 21 July 1921, vol. 39, file 1; both in BCA, LSB papers, GR-929.

36 Director, LSB, to Bishop, 9 March 1920, and LSB to Assistant Comptroller of Water Rights Branch, 7 October 1920, BCA, LSB papers, GR-929, vol. 38, file 16. For the LSB's defence of its claim, see LSB to Water Rights Branch, 18 May 1922; Assistant to Comptroller, Water Rights Branch, to LSB, 26 March 1925; and Comptroller to LSB, 11 June 1926; all in BCA, LSB papers, GR-929, vol. 38, file 16.

37 LSB to R.D. Todd, c/o LSB, Lister, 14 August 1922, BCA, LSB papers, GR-929, vol. 38, file 16.

38 W.J. Biker, District Engineer, "Department of Lands, Water Rights Branch, Report of Proposed Irrigation Scheme for Soldier Settlement Area at Lister to E.A. Cleveland, Comptroller of Water Rights, Victoria, BC District Engineer's Office, Nelson, BC, January, 1923," BCA, LSB papers, GR-929, vol. 38, file 16.
39 Biker, "Proposed Irrigation Scheme."
40 Director, LSB, to Minister of Agriculture, 2 May 1929, BCA, LSB papers, GR-929, vol. 38, file 16; Cameron, *Earle Birney*, 34; and Young, "Lister," 13, 16-17.
41 Dennis A. Demarchi, "An Introduction to the Ecoregions of British Columbia," Wildlife Branch, Ministry of Environment, Lands, and Parks, Government of British Columbia, 1996, 29-30; Richard Cannings, "Natural History of British Columbia," in Daniel Francis, ed., *Encyclopedia of British Columbia* (Madeira Park, BC: Harbour Publishing, 2000), 487-90.
42 "The Southern Okanagan Irrigation Project at Oliver, BC," n.d., BCA, Water Rights Branch, GR-0884, vol. 1, file 22.
43 June Ryder, "Physical Geography of BC: Overview," in *Encyclopedia of British Columbia*, 554-57.
44 Julie Cancella, *The Ditch: Lifeline of a Community* (Oliver, BC: Oliver Heritage Society Museum and Archives, 1986), 6-7; A.O. Cochrane, Cochrane and Ladner to J.W. Jones, 15 March 1919, BCA, J.W. Jones papers, MS-023, vol. 2, file 2.
45 These studies are in BCA, Lands Branch papers, O Series Correspondence Files (hereafter "O" Files), GR-1441, file 7850#1. Elwood Mead was a progressive reformer and advocate of land settlement and irrigation. He went on to become head of the California Land Settlement Board and its soldier settlement program in 1915. He also proposed a soldier settlement program to the US Congress. In 1924, he became head of the US Bureau of Reclamation, where he supervised the construction of the Hoover and Grand Coulee Dams, among other projects. Mead's role in soldier settlement is discussed briefly in David Danbom, *Born in the Country: A History of Rural America* (Baltimore: Johns Hopkins University Press, 1995), 181; and in David Shi, *The Simple Life: Plain Living and High Thinking in American Culture* (New York: Oxford University Press, 1985), 223. Donald Worster is critical of Mead's record in *Rivers*, 182-88. On Mead as a proponent of a modern countryside, see Donald Pisani, "Reclamation and Social Engineering in the Progressive Era," *Agricultural History* 57 (1983): 46-63.
46 Latimer to the Southern Okanagan Land Company, n.d., BCA, Lands Branch papers, "O" Files, GR-1441, file 07850#1. Latimer's name does not appear on this document, but he is identified as the author in W.T. Shatford to Southern Okanagan Land Company, n.d., in the same file.
47 Elwood Mead to the Southern Okanagan Land Company, 10 October 190[-?], BCA, Lands Branch papers, "O" Files, GR-1441, file 07850#1.
48 Shatford to Southern Okanagan Land Company, n.d., BCA, Lands Branch papers, "O" Files, GR-1441, file 07850#1.
49 W.T. Shatford to F.R.E. DeHart, Director, Land Settlement Board, 15 February 1918, BCA, Land Settlement Board, GR-1047, file 1.
50 For the development of the Okanagan, see Chapter 1. It would appear that, in purchasing the land, Pattullo pulled the rug out from under the LSB. The LSB's representative for the Okanagan, F.R.E. DeHart, originally discussed the sale of the lands with Shatford (see previous footnote). In a note attached to a copy of the letter from Shatford to DeHart, however, DeHart complains that "when Hon. Pattullo put deal

through it was not refered [sic] to the Board or my-self in whose district these lands are located." For the Shatford letter with DeHart's attached note, see BCA, J.W. Jones papers, MS-023, vol. 2, file 2. There is no date on the note, but as the Ministry of Lands purchased the land in December 1918, the date is likely sometime in 1919.

51 See Chapter 1. The relationship of the South Okanagan Irrigation Project to the problems of the land companies is developed in the section "Humans and Nature in the Irrigated Landscape," p. 151 herein.

52 "Buys Big Tract in Southern Okanagan," clipping, n.d., n.s., and "Engineer is Named in Development of Okanagan Property," clipping, n.d., n.s., BCA, J.W. Jones papers, MS-023, vol. 7, file 4. Later, Pattullo would claim that he "personally" conceived and directed the project. In reality, the project drew on existing plans, as noted, and Pattullo left most decisions to his officials. Yet his interest in and willingness to protect the project is quite obvious. He personally toured and selected the site. He appears periodically throughout the project's correspondence, demanding details on key points. When the viability of the town of Oliver was threatened by the Premier's unwillingness to move local government offices there, Pattullo engaged in a cordial debate with Oliver over the issue. In later years, when the project was critiqued as an expensive failure, Pattullo vigorously defended it. His favourite story concerned the project's main diversion dam. Opposition critics liked to say that, while it was known as the Pattullo Dam, South Okanagan residents were more likely to say "damn Pattullo!" Pattullo suggested that a brass plaque with the dam's name be attached to the dam itself, so that everyone would know who was responsible. See "Mr. Pattullo's Address over CNRV," 9 October 1931, BCA, Thomas Dufferin Pattullo papers (hereafter T.D. Pattullo papers), MS-003, vol. 65, file 1a, p. 65. Pattullo's argument with the premier is in Premier to Minister of Lands, 23 April 1921; Pattullo to Prime Minister [of BC], 19 May 1921; Premier to Pattullo, 7 June 1921; and Pattullo to Oliver, 8 June 1921, BCA, Premier's papers, GR-441, vol. 345, file 6. For examples of direct management of the project, see Comptroller, Water Rights, to Minster of Lands, 18 December 1918; and T.D. Pattullo to Duncan C. Scott, 23 July 1919; all in BCA, Lands Branch papers, "O" Files, GR-1441, 07850#1. The dam story is in "Premier Pattullo's Radio Address," 8 November 1935, BCA, T.D. Pattullo papers, MS-003, vol. 65, file 1b, p. 168.

53 British Columbia, "Report of the Superintendent of British Columbia Soldier Settlement," *Sessional Papers* 2 (1919), N17-N21.

54 Clark's early career is taken from his obituary: "Funeral Here of Major Clark," *Victoria Times,* 26 October 1936.

55 "A Short History of the Development of Irrigation in British Columbia," n.d., n.s., BCA, Water Rights Branch, GR-884, vol. 1, file 7.

56 "Engineer is Named in Development of Okanagan Property," clipping, n.d., n.s., BCA, J.W. Jones papers, MS-023, vol. 7, file 4.

57 "That under the authority of ...," BCA, Lands Branch papers, "O" Files, GR-1441, file 011012, p. 122.

58 Oliver was presumably named after the premier, though I did not find any discussion on the subject.

59 "Southern Okanagan Irrigation ...," BCA, Water Rights Branch, GR-884, vol. 1, file 22.

60 Ernest A. Cleveland, "Irrigation in British Columbia. A Review of Irrigation in the Province from the Earliest Undertaking to the Present Extensive Systems," paper read

before the British Columbia Professional Meeting of the Engineering Institute of Canada, Vancouver, BC, 16 July 1922, BCA, Water Rights Branch, GR-0884, vol. 1, file 8, p. 7.

61 Cleveland, "Irrigation," pp. 1-10 (quotation is from p. 9).

62 Ibid., 9-14.

63 E.A. Cleveland to Minister of Lands, 15 November 1922, BCA, Premier's papers, GR-441, vol. 223, file 1.

64 Daniel B. Botkin, *Our Natural History: The Lessons of Lewis and Clark* (New York: Grosset/Putnam, 1995). On Sumas, see Chapter 4.

65 Worster, *Rivers*, 191-256; Fiege, *Irrigated Eden*, 171-209.

66 See the bound report "Southern Okanagan Irrigation Project at Oliver, BC," BCA, Water Rights Branch (South Okanagan Irrigation Project), GR-1288.

67 "Government Irrigation Project: Opportunities for Home-seekers," pamphlet, 1921, BCA, Library Collection.

68 Ibid.

69 Clark to Mr. Helmer, Dominion Experimental Station (Summerland, BC), 8 February 1922; Clark to R. Simpson (Oliver, BC), 10 February 1922; Clark to W.G. Wilkins, Sales Agent (Oliver), 10 February 1922; and Clark to Mr. Latimer, Project Engineer (Oliver), 10 February 1922; all in BCA, Lands Branch papers, "O" Files, GR-1441, file 013744.

70 Preserved as the John William Clark Collection, BCA, accession 198210-004.

71 Howard B. Leighton, "The Lantern Slide and Art History," *History of Photography* 8 (1984): 107-18; and Library of Congress and Frances Loeb Library, Graduate School of Design, Harvard University, "Lantern Slides: History and Manufacture," *American Landscape and Architectural Design, 1850-1920,* available at http://memory.loc.gov/ ammem/award97/mhsdhtml/lanternhistory.html/, accessed 2 October 2003.

72 Clark to J.M. Gibbon, 21 February 1922; Clark to Gibbon 20 March 1922, telegram; Clark to Helmer, 21 March 1922; all in BCA, Lands Branch papers, "O" Files, GR-1441, file 013744. On Clark's expedition to India, see correspondence in BCA, T.D. Pattullo papers, MS-003, vol. 14, file 16. "Round the World on Lantern Screen," *Victoria Times,* 22 November 1922, and "Major J.W. Clarke [sic] Talks About India," *The Daily Colonist* (Victoria), 14 February 1923, describe illustrated lectures given at the Kiwanis Club and at a Victoria high school, though these were not actually on the topic of the South Okanagan project.

73 J.W. Clark, "Illustrated Lecture on British Columbia Featuring Oliver and the Okanagan Valley," 7 November 1928, and "Illustrated Lecture on British Columbia Featuring the Okanagan Valley," 23 April 1929, BCA, John William Clark collection, "Lantern Slide Lectures: Okanagan," box 1.

74 For a more extended treatment of Clark's shows, see James Murton, "What J.W. Clark Saw in British Columbia, or, Nature and the Machine: A Photo Essay," *BC Studies* 142/143 (Summer/Autumn 2004): 129-52.

75 Cancella, *The Ditch,* 16.

76 "Southern Okanagan ....," n.d., BCA, Water Rights Branch, GR-0884, vol. 1, file 22. Petition to the Hon. T.D. Pattullo, Minister of Lands, 1 March 1927, BCA, Lands Branch papers, "O" Files, GR-1441, 7850#7, mentions that nine hundred acres are served by pumps.

77 "Government Irrigation Project," 1921.

78 T.D. Pattullo to Premier Oliver, 13 January 1921, BCA, Premier's papers, GR-441, vol. 345, file 6.
79 "Land Sale at Oliver Meets Fair Response," clipping, n.d., *Penticton Herald,* and "Auction Sale of S. Okanagan Land," clipping, n.d., *The Colonist* (Victoria); both in BCA, J.W. Jones papers, MS-023, vol. 2, file 2.
80 Cleveland to Minister of Lands, 15 November 1922, BCA, Premier's papers, GR-441, vol. 223, file 1.
81 "Land Sale ...," n.d., BCA, J.W. Jones papers, MS-023, vol. 2, file 2.
82 J.W. Clark to Wm. Donald, Provincial Demonstration Plot, 10 June 1919; "Layritz Nurseries. Sold to Mr. F.H. Latimer, Penticton, BC," invoice, 7 May 1919; "The Brackman-Ker Milling Co. Limited ... sold to Provincial Government, Water Rights Branch ...," invoice, 7 May 1919; and "Southern Okanagan Lands Project. Demonstration Plot," diagram, n.d.; all in BCA, Lands Branch papers, "O" Files, GR-1441, file 0010817.
83 F.H. Latimer, Project Engineer, to Comptroller of Water Rights, 26 July 1924, BCA, Premier's papers, GR-441, vol. 242, file 10.
84 All of these developments are mentioned in Cleveland to Minister of Lands, 15 November 1922, BCA, Premier's papers, GR-441, vol. 223, file 1.
85 E.A. Cleveland to Premier, 4 February 1924, BCA, Premier's papers, GR-441, vol. 239, file 2.
86 Travelling Auditor to Comptroller-General, 20 January 1925, BCA, Premier's papers, GR-441, vol. 274, file 2.
87 Premier to Minister of Lands, marked confidential, 6 March 1925, and Frank T. Shutt, Dominion Chemist, Central Experimental Farm (Ottawa) to Capt. G. Hill Wilson (Oliver), 16 March 1924, BCA, Premier's papers, GR-441, vol. 246, file 2. On the soils in this area, see British Columbia, *Report of the Royal Commission on the Tree Fruit Industry of British Columbia,* 1958, 137-39.
88 Premier to Minister of Lands, 6 March 1925.
89 "Cut is Made in Oliver Land Price," *The Province* (Vancouver), 4 April 1925, 1. I have cited this from a typed copy of the original story, which appears in BCA, J.W. Jones papers, MS-023, vol. 5, file 3. Pattullo's address to the settlers is mentioned in Earle to Comptroller of Water Rights, 3 March 1925, BCA, Lands Branch papers, "O" Files, GR-1441, file 058996.
90 J. [surname unknown] to Captain Grant, Secretary, Oliver Growers' Co-operative Association, 14 October 1925, and J. [surname unknown] to Frank Eraut, Manager of the Oliver Cannery, 14 October 1925, BCA, Lands Branch papers, "O" Files, GR-1441, file 0065122.
91 Deputy Minister of Lands to Albert Millar, 20 October 1925, BCA, Lands Branch papers, "O" Files, GR-1441, file 04009.
92 "The Construction Work ...," n.d. [late 1925 or early 1926 from the context], BCA, Lands Branch papers, "O" Files, GR-1441, file 058996. An intercrop is a crop grown between rows of orchard trees, in this case as a way for the farmer to make a living while the fruit trees matured.
93 Lyle MacDougall to Minister of Lands, 12 September 1928, BCA, Lands Branch papers, "O" Files, GR-1441, file 7850#7.
94 "Duty of water" refers to the amount of water required for a particular type of crop to grow.
95 "Petition to the Hon. T.D. Pattullo, Minister of Lands," 1 March 1927, and G. Hill-Wilson

to Pattullo, 25 February 1927, accompanying petition, BCA, Lands Branch papers, "O" Files, GR-1441, file 7850#7.

96 W.H. Gaddes and M.T. Penrose to F.P. Burden, 6 December 1928, BCA, Premier's papers, GR-441, vol. 277, file 12; and Petition from Oliver settlers to the Premier, Minister of Lands, and Minister of Mines, 26 February 1930, BCA, Premier's papers, GR-441, vol. 304, file 2.

97 "Southern Okanagan Lands Project: Summary of Acreage, Dec., 1928," BCA, Lands Branch papers, "O" Files, GR-1441, file 7850#7.

98 Cancella, *The Ditch*, 21.

99 See British Columbia, "Royal Commission on Tree Fruit Production," 1958, 275-76.

100 F.H. Latimer, "Fairview/Osoyoos Irrigation Project," Nov 1907, vol. 3, file 4, and "South Okanagan," summary report, n.s., n.d. [probably 1924], vol. 6, file 2; both in BCA, J.W. Jones papers, MS-023. "Soldiers Land Act 1918 to v. 57," table, 1 August 1928, file 7850#11, p. 78, and "Balance Sheet as at March 31st, 1928 ...," file 7850#14A; both in BCA, Lands Branch papers, "O" Files, GR-1441. Though the balance sheets indicate that sales up to 1928 were in the neighbourhood of $400,000 for lots sold for fruit growing, over $300,000 in principal was still owed on these lots, not to mention interest costs. Figures on land sales are only approximate as any lands completely paid off would not appear on this statement. However, there were likely few of these.

101 Cleveland to F.H. Cunningham, Chief Inspector Dominion Fisheries, 21 November 1919; Cunningham to Cleveland, 11 December 1919; J. McHugh, Resident Engineer, Dominion Fisheries, to Cleveland, 27 February 1920; Cleveland to McHugh, 11 March 1920; all in BCA, Lands Branch papers, "O" Files, GR-1441, file 7850#1. McHugh to Cleveland, 20 March 1920; F.H. Latimer to Cleveland, 2 April 1920; Provincial Fisheries Department to BC Land Settlement Board, 5 June 1922; and H. Earle to Comptroller, Water Rights, 11 February 1927; all in BCA, Lands Branch papers, "O" Files, GR-1441, file 011012#12.

102 E.R. Bucknell, Assistant Entomologist, Dominion Entomological Branch, to Cleveland, 11 October 1923; Cleveland to Latimer, 30 October 1923; Latimer to Cleveland, 9 May 1924; all in BCA, Lands Branch papers, "O" Files, GR-1441, file 7850#5. R. Simpson, Nursery Manager, to Earle, 30 June 1925, and J.W. Clark to Earle, 31 July 1925, BCA, Lands Branch papers, "O" Files, GR-1441, file 58996.

103 Earle to Comptroller, Water Rights, 16 March 1927; Earle to Comptroller, Water Rights, 7 May 1927; and Earle to Comptroller, Water Rights, 7 August 1928; all in BCA, Lands Branch papers, "O" Files, GR-1441, file 58996.

104 "Notes on High Water in Okanagan Lake, 1921," 16 June 1921, and J. McDonald, Superintendent of Construction, to Comptroller, Water Rights [Cleveland], 30 August 1921, BCA, Lands Branch papers, "O" Files, GR-1441, file 7850#2.

105 My source for this section is Cancella, *The Ditch*, 22-26.

106 D.W. Hodsdon, Project Manager to Superintendent of Lands, 5 May 1951, BCA, Lands Branch papers, "O" Files, GR-1441, file 7850#14A.

CHAPTER 6: PATTULLO'S NEW DEAL

1 Mrs. W.P. Brown to Lands Department, 22 July 1932, BCA, Lands Branch papers, O Series Correspondence Files (hereafter "O" Files), GR-1441, file 0106628.

2 The classic account of the ecological roots of the dust bowl is Donald Worster, *Dust Bowl: The Southern Plains in the 1930s* (Toronto: Oxford University Press, 1979). Prairie farmers replaced perennial grasses with monocultures of grains, which, when harvested, left the soil bare and without plant roots to stabilize it. This problem was exacerbated by the Depression, when destitute farmers failed to put in a crop. On similar farming practices and the roots of the dust bowl in Palliser's Triangle, see Barry Potyondi, *In Palliser's Triangle: Living in the Grasslands, 1850-1930* (Saskatoon, SK: Purich Publishing, 1995).

3 John Herd Thompson and Allen Seager, *Canada 1922-1939: Decades of Discord* (Toronto: McClelland and Stewart, 1985), 195-96.

4 G.C. Goodison to Col. Latta, 28 February 1933, and Otto Wohlleben to Col. Latta, 1 September 1933, BCA, Lands Branch papers, "O" Files, GR-1441, 0130607.

5 Frank Garner Smith to Col. Latta, 4 June 1937, BCA, Lands Branch papers, "O" Files, GR-1441, file 0115281.

6 R.J. and L. Smith to Dr. Gaddes, 28 November 1933, BCA, Lands Branch papers, "O" Files, GR-1441, file 0109741.

7 J. Sherwin to Mayor Wells Gray, New Westminster, 2 September 1933, BCA, Lands Branch papers, "O" Files, GR-1441, file 0109741.

8 W.H. Gaddes, Chairman, BC Government Relief Land Settlement Committee, to Wells Gray, 13 September 1933; Gaddes to D. Sutherland, District Agriculturalist, Smithers, BC, 13 September 1933; Gaddes to J. Hinchcliffe, Minister of Lands, 13 October 1933; Wells Gray to Hinchcliffe, 6 October 1933; Wells Gray to Gaddes, 6 October 1933; and J. Sherwin to Wells Gray, 29 September 1933; all in BCA, Lands Branch papers, "O" Files, GR-1441, file 0109741.

9 Dawn Bowen, "'Forward to a Farm': The Back-to-the-Land Movement as a Relief Initiative in Saskatchewan during the Great Depression," PhD diss., Department of Geography, Queen's University, Kingston, 1998. Bowen offers detailed analysis of two communities formed in northern Saskatchewan, and the environmental and social factors that conditioned their success and failure. She points to underfunding as the schemes' major problem, and argues that the schemes saved money and that settlers benefited from their contact with the land. In doing so, Bowen supports the conclusions of contemporary supporters. My analysis, however, challenges some of these conclusions for the case of BC, as will be seen.

10 This is not to say that agricultural settlement and development came to an end in BC entirely. The resettlement of the prairie lands of the Peace River region, in the northeast corner of the province, took place after the Second World War.

11 Bruce A. McKelvie, "Memorandum on Re-Settlement of Bush Farm Lands in BC," 4 December 1929, Unversity of British Columbia Special Collections (hereafter UBCSC), Simon Fraser Tolmie Fonds (hereafter Tolmie Fonds), vol. 7, file 17. Agricultural experts were fond of counselling a switch to mixed farming in this period. See John Herd Thompson, *The Harvests of War: the Prairie West, 1914-1918* (Toronto: McClelland and Stewart, 1978); Barry Potyondi, *Palliser's Triangle*, 100-10; and Bowen, "Forward."

12 W.H. Gaddes to Hon. S.F. Tolmie, 9 November 1928, UBCSC, Tolmie Fonds, vol. 6, file 4. The remainder of the paragraph is from Gaddes, Colonization Commissioner, to Tolmie, report, 17 January 1930, UBCSC, Tolmie Fonds, vol. 10, file 13.

13 Jean Barman, *The West beyond the West: A History of British Columbia*, rev. ed. (Toronto: University of Toronto Press, 1996), 247.

14 Margaret Ormsby, *British Columbia: A History* (Toronto: Macmillan, 1958), 442-43.

15 Thompson and Seager, *Decades*, 214-215, 351. Alberta had a decline of 61 percent and Manitoba, 49 percent. The national average was 48 percent. For complete figures, see *Decades*, Table 14, p. 351.

16 Sydney Hutcheson, *Depression Stories* (Vancouver: New Star Books, 1976), 34, 45, 59-60 (quoted in Barman, *West*, 249).

17 I have not read about this migration but know of it because my grandfather was faced with this choice. Living in Victoria, he could go no further west, and that, combined with bleak personal circumstances, pushed him to move to the prairies.

18 Lougheed to Tolmie, 11 May 1931, UBCSC, Tolmie Fonds, vol. 7, file 17.

19 Ormsby, *British Columbia*, 446-47.

20 Ibid., 444.

21 N.S. Lougheed, Minister of Lands, to Tolmie, 12 June 1931, vol. 7, file 17; and Gaddes to Tolmie, 20 April 1932, vol. 6, file 4; both in UBCSC, Tolmie Fonds. The government eventually took up the idea of subsidizing prospectors. It set up the Placer Mining Training School to train young men to make their living panning for gold. Some of these men, mostly from Vancouver and Victoria, graduated and went out to seek their fortune. See Lesley Cooper, "More Than Mere Survival: Placer Gold and Unemployment in 1930s British Columbia," MA thesis, Department of History, University of Victoria, Victoria, BC, 1995.

22 James Struthers, *No Fault of Their Own: Unemployment and the Canadian Welfare State, 1914-1941* (Toronto: University of Toronto Press, 1983), 8-9, 156-57. Bowen, "Forward," 229-42, counters that Struthers' argument downplays Canadians' genuine attachment to the land. She fails, however, to distinguish between the use of rural ideals and an actual experience of agriculture, arguing that Canada was a "nation of farmers," despite the fact that many no longer farmed. But she is correct to say that Struthers places undue emphasis on the cynicism of back-to-the-land supporters.

23 "Speech by the Honorable T.D. Pattullo at the Hotel Vancouver. Vancouver, BC, September 24th, 1931," UBCSC, Tolmie Fonds, vol. 21, file 25.

24 Tolmie to N.S. Lougheed, 16 November 1931, UBCSC, Tolmie Fonds, vol. 7, file 22.

25 This discussion is based on S.L. Howe, Provincial Secretary, to Premier, 25 July 1931, UBCSC, Tomie Fonds, vol. 12, file 25, which contains the memo that begins, "The Prime Minister and the Members of the Executive Council of British Columbia have the honour to submit, for the consideration of the Right Honourable the Prime Minister of Canada, the conclusions they have reached after their examination of the existing situation."

26 Lougheed to Tolmie, 12 June 1931, UBCSC, Tolmie Fonds, vol. 7, file 17.

27 Lougheed to Tolmie, 8 April 1931, UBCSC, Tolmie Fonds, vol. 21, file 11. This estimate did not include grazing lands.

28 "Send Surplus Population Back to Land, Says Lougheed," *The Province* (Vancouver), 23 November 1932; and "Urges Faith in Province: Hon. N.S. Lougheed Visions Bright Future for Last Great West," *The Colonist* (Victoria), 11 March 1933.

29 These schemes are in vol. 17, file 21, and especially vol. 17, file 22; both in UBCSC, Tolmie Fonds.

30 Tolmie to Hon. G.D. Robertson, Minister of Labour, c/o Premier of Saskatchewan, 19 June 1931, UBCSC, Tolmie Fonds, vol. 12, file 20.

31 "Suggestions Dealing with the Problem of Unemployment Submitted to the House

Committee on Unemployment by F.C. Brown, Managing-Director, Canada Western Cordage Co., Ltd.," 1932, UBCSC, Tolmie Fonds, vol. 12, file 25.

32 Joseph Smith and A.M. Robertson to Tolmie, 29 February 1932, and G.R. Bates to Tolmie, 2 May 1932, UBCSC, Tolmie Fonds, vol. 7, file 22.

33 W.B.T. Frank, Secretary, Maple Grove Conservative Association, to M. Manson, MLA, 23 May 1932; O.T. Jackson, Secretary, Matsqui Agricultural and Horticultural Association and Farmers' Institute, to Tolmie, 29 June 1932; quotation from "Copy of a Resolution passed by Langley Farmers' Institute at a meeting held at Fort Langley, BC, on May 21st, 1932"; and Secretary-Treasurer, British Columbia School Trustees' Association, report, 20 May 1932; all in UBCSC, Tolmie Fonds, vol. 7, file 22.

34 Gaddes to Tolmie, 10 March 1932; Gaddes to Tolmie, 30 March 1932; Gaddes to Tolmie, 5 April 1932; Gaddes to Secretary, Prime Minister's Office, 16 February 1932; and "Comments on Capt. F.C. Brown's Suggestion for Relief of Unemployment," in Gaddes to Tolmie, 23 April 1932, UBCSC, Tolmie Fonds, vol. 7, file 22.

35 H. Cathcart, Deputy Minister of Lands, to Premier, 13 November 1931, and Cathcart to Premier, memo, 18 May 1933, UBCSC, Tolmie Fonds, vol. 7, file 21.

36 "Memorandum of Agreement ... between ... the Province of British Columbia ... and City of Vancouver," 16 January 1933, City of Vancouver Archives (hereafter CVA), Social Service Department Fonds, series 449 (Vancouver Social Service Department, Director), loc. 106-A-6, file 8; British Columbia, "Report of the Operations of the BC Government Relief Land Settlement Committee for the Year Ended December 31st, 1933," *Sessional Papers*, 1934, X13.

37 See the minutes of the BC Government Relief Land Settlement Committee meetings for 12 May, 14 May, 16 May, 24 November, and 2 December 1932, and for 1 February 1933; all in BCA, Land Settlement Board, GR-929, vol. 7, file 1; and W.S. Latta, Secretary, BC Government Relief Land Settlement Committee, "BC Government Relief Land Settlement Plan, 1932," 30 November 1933 and Latta, "BC Government Relief Land Settlement Plan, 1932: Recommendations," 2 December 1933, BCA, Lands Branch papers, "O" Files, GR-1441, file 0109741.

38 Latta, "BC Government Relief Land Settlement Plan, 1932."

39 Minutes, 10 February to 9 May 1933, BCA, Land Settlement Board, GR-929, vol. 7, file 1. The Vancouver names are from "Relief Land Settlement Plan," table, 8 December 1934, CVA, Social Service Department Fonds, loc. 106-A-6, file 8. Vancouver names are pseudonyms, as required by my research agreement. The New Westminster names are from "Record of Families. BC Government Relief Land Settlement Plan, 1932," June 1933, BCA, Lands Branch papers, "O" Files, GR-1441, file 0109741.

40 See BCA, Lands Branch papers, "O" Files, GR-1441, files 0130607#1, 0130607#2, and 0130607#3. The three files comprise 1,153 pages, including ten letters from 1937 at the end of the file. The figure of 1,054 enquiries is from "To Spend $600 on Families," clipping, n.s., n.d., BCA, Lands Branch papers, "O" Files, GR-1441, file 0106628.

41 Minutes, 6 July, 10 August, and 17 October 1933, BCA, Land Settlement Board, GR-929, vol. 7, file 1; British Columbia, "Report of the Operations of the BC Government Relief Land Settlement Committee for the Year Ended December 31st, 1933," *Sessional Papers*, 1934, X14; and "Summary of Reports on BC Government Relief Land Settlement Scheme," attached to Warner Loat, Alderman, and W.R. Bone, Relief Officer, to W.W. Smith, Chairman, Relief and Unemployment Committee, 27 August 1934, CVA, Social Service Department Fonds, loc. 106-A-6, file 8.

42 British Columbia, "BC Government Relief Land Settlement Plan, 1932," report, 14

January 1935, 6 January 1936, and 7 January 1937, *Sessional Papers* for 1935, 1936 and 1937; Loat and Bone to Smith, 27 August 1934, CVA, Social Service Department Fonds, loc. 106-A-6, file 8.

43 "Re Relief Land Settlement Plan, 1932," 15 November 1939, BCA, Lands Branch papers, "O" Files, GR-1441, file 0125406.

44 "Back to the Land," clipping, n.d., reprinted from *New Outlook*, BCA, Lands Branch papers, "O" Files, GR-1441, file 0106628.

45 "Relief Families Leave for Land under New Plan," *The Province* (Vancouver), 4 April 1933.

46 For these difficulties, see A.F. Pears, Road Superintendent, Department of Public Works, to Latta, 25 September 1933, BCA, Lands Branch papers, "O" Files, GR-1441, file 0109741.

47 See BCA, Lands Branch papers, "O" Files, GR-1441, file 0115281.

48 Ormsby, *British Columbia,* 444; and Robin Fisher, *Duff Pattullo of British Columbia* (Toronto: University of Toronto Press, 1991), 221.

49 Ormsby, *British Columbia,* 447-48; and Fisher, *Duff Pattullo,* 221-24.

50 Ormsby, *British Columbia,* 448-52; and Fisher, *Duff Pattullo,* 223-38.

51 G.S. Pearson, Minister of Labour, to the Premier, 19 November 1934, BCA, Premier's papers, GR-1222, vol. 127, file 9.

52 E.W. Griffith, Administrator to Hon. J. Hinchcliffe, Minister of Lands, 2 November 1933, BCA, Lands Branch papers, "O" Files, GR-1441, file 0115073.

53 Pearson to Norman McL. Rogers, Minister of Labour, 10 June 1936, and Rogers to Pearson, 29 June 1936, BCA, Lands Branch papers, "O" Files, GR-1441, file 0125406.

54 "Memorandum of Agreement ... between ... the Dominion of Canada ... and ... the Province of British Columbia ...," 31 December 1936, BCA, Lands Branch papers, "O" Files, GR-1441, file 0125406.

55 Griffith to Pearson, 8 March 1938, BCA, Premier's papers, GR-1222, vol. 145, file 11.

56 Pearson to Premier, 19 November 1934, BCA, Premier's papers, GR-1222, vol. 127, file 9.

57 "Mr. Pattullo's Speech on the Debate in Reply to the Speech from the Throne," 27 February 1933, BCA, Thomas Dufferin Pattullo papers (hereafter T.D. Pattullo papers), MS-003, vol. 53, file 22.

58 "Mr. Pattullo's Speech on the Debate in Reply to the Speech from the Throne," 27 February 1933 and "Mr. Pattullo's Reply to the Budget Speech," 16 March 1933; "A Brief Synopsis of Liberal Policy," August 1933; all in BCA, T.D. Pattullo papers, MS-003, vol. 53, file 12.

59 "Mr. Pattullo's Reply to the Budget Speech," 16 March 1933.

60 See Introduction and Chapter 1.

61 See "Mr. Chairman ...," speech on social legislation, n.d. [post 1928], BCA, T.D. Pattullo papers, MS-003, vol. 65, file 1a.

62 Pattullo to Right-Honourable W.L. Mackenzie King, Leader of the Opposition, 9 August 1934, BCA, T.D. Pattullo papers, MS-003, vol. 55, file 2.

63 For example, see "Mr. Pattullo's Address over CNRV, Vancouver, BC," 9 October 1931, vol. 65, file 1a, and "Premier Pattullo's Radio Address," 8 November 1935, vol. 65, file 1b; both in BCA, T.D. Pattullo papers, MS-003.

64 "A Land Policy," *The Province* (Vancouver), 24 July 1933, and "Back-to-Land Move Reached High Mark During Past Year," *The Province* (Vancouver), 1 January 1933.

65 "Farm Homes for BC Boys is Approved," clipping, 30 October 1932, CVA, Major Matthews Collection, loc. 503-C-2, p. 173.

66 Pearson to Norman Rogers, 10 June 1936; "BC Single Jobless Will Go to Farms," clipping, 30 September 1936; "Province Promises Relief for Workless Who Go On Farms," clipping, 28 October 1936; "Single Jobless Vote to Reject Farm Job Plan," clipping, 28 October 1936; "Jobless Rebel Against Order to Go Farming," clipping, 15 December 1936; all in CVA, Major Matthews Collection, loc. 503-C-6.

67 "Garden Seeds for Relief Recipients," clipping, 18 March 1933, and "Tax Sale Lands for Gardens," clipping, 19 March 1933, CVA, Major Matthews Collection, loc. 503-C-4; "Vegetable Seeds to Be Distributed," clipping, 29 March 1935, and "Hundreds Apply For Free Seeds Today as Distribution Starts," clipping, 2 April 1935, CVA, Major Matthews Collection, loc. 503-C-5.

68 E.W. Griffith, Administrator, Unemployment Relief Branch, Province of BC, to Alderman L.D. McDonald, Chairman, Relief Committee, City of Vancouver, 11 April 1935; "Sayward Valley Plan Under Way," clipping, n.s.; W.L. Woodford, City Clerk to Bone, Relief Officer, City of Vancouver, 16 April 1935; Bone to Deputy Mayor Alderman C.E. Tisdall, 10 September 1935; Griffith to Bone, 14 November 1935; Bone to Tisdall, 16 November 1935; Bone to Griffith, 18 November 1935; Woodford to Bone, 26 November 1935; all in CVA, Social Service Department Fonds, all in loc. 106-A-5, file 11.

69 Cole Harris with David Demeritt, "Farming and Rural Life," in Harris, *The Resettlement of British Columbia* (Vancouver: UBC Press, 1997), 245.

70 Acting City Clerk to Bone, Social Service Administrator, 3 July 1940, and memo attached to Bone to J.A. Ward, Esq., Trade School Regulations, Administration Office, 10 July 1940, CVA, Social Service Department Fonds, loc. 106-A-7, file 4; and "Outline and Progress to Date of the Salt Spring Island Community Farm," 31 May 1940, CVA, Office of the Mayor Fonds, series 483 (Correspondence Files), loc. 34-A-5, file 13.

71 "Outline and Progress," ibid.

CONCLUSION

1 Jack Hodgins, *Broken Ground: A Novel* (Toronto: McClelland and Stewart, 1998) and Jack Hodgins, *A Passion for Narrative: A Guide for Writing Fiction* (Toronto: McClelland and Stewart, 1993).

2 "Friends gather to honor couple on 50th wedding anniversary," clipping, n.s., n.d. [1968], Courtenay District Museum and Archives (hereafter CDMA), Clipping Files: Merville. The figure of seven original families may or may not be accurate; it depends on the source of the reporter's information and the definition of an original family.

3 Clipping Files: Merville (CDMA) contains copies of the *Gumboot Gazette*. Local people told me that it was the paper of the back-to-the-landers.

4 Justine Brown, *All Possible Worlds: Utopian Experiments in British Columbia* (Vancouver: New Star Books, 1995), 61-76 (the quotes and names of the communes are on 63).

5 Brown, *All Possible Worlds*, 66-71. See http://www.jnweb.com/ceeds/.

6 Ibid., 71-76.

7 Judson Jerome, *Families of Eden: Communes and the New Anarchism* (New York: Seabury Press, 1974), x.

8 Brown, *All Possible Worlds*, 61; Robert Gottlieb, *Forcing the Spring: The Transformation of the American Environmental Movement* (Washington, DC: Island Press, 1993), 102-3.

9 Richard White, *The Organic Machine: The Remaking of the Columbia River* (New York: Hill and Wang, 1995), particularly 48-88.

10 Michel F. Girard, *L'écologisme retrouvé: Essor et déclin de la Commission de la conservation du Canada* (Ottawa: University of Ottawa Press, 1994), 1-8, 29.

11 F.N. Sinclair, "Sumas Reclamation Project Final Report," 5 July 1919, BCA, Land Settlement Board, GR-929, vol. 48, file 5.

12 Colin A.M. Duncan, *The Centrality of Agriculture: Between Humankind and the Rest of Nature* (Montreal and Kingston: McGill-Queen's University Press, 1996), xv. On fascism as the alternative for those opposed to liberal capitalism in the interwar years, see Eric Hobsbawm, *The Age of Extremes: The Short Twentieth Century, 1914-1991* (London: Michael Joseph, 1994).

13 Alexander Wilson, *The Culture of Nature: North American Landscape from Disney to the Exxon Valdez* (Toronto: Between the Lines, 1991), throughout.

14 William Cronon, "The Trouble with Wilderness, or, Getting Back to the Wrong Nature," in William Cronon, ed., *Uncommon Ground: Rethinking the Human Place in Nature* (New York: W.W. Norton, 1996), 69-84.

15 An excellent short introduction to major developments in twentieth-century world agriculture is J.R. McNeill, *Something New under the Sun: An Environmental History of the Twentieth-Century World* (New York: W.W. Norton, 2000), 212-27.

16 Colin A.M. Duncan, "On Identifying a Sound Environmental Ethic in History: Prolegomena to Any Future Environmental History," *Environmental History Review* 15, 2 (1991): 15-23.

17 Joseph R. Des Jardins, *Environmental Ethics: An Introduction to Environmental Philosophy* (Belmont, CA: Wadsworth Publishing, 1993), 150-52.

Bibliography

ARCHIVAL AND MANUSCRIPT COLLECTIONS

British Columbia Archives (Victoria)

Government Records (Major Collections)

Lands Branch papers, O Series Correspondence Files ("O" Files), GR-1441
Land Settlement Board papers, GR-929
Premier's papers, GR-441
Returned Soldiers' Aid Commission papers, GR-1315

Government Records (Minor Collections)

Commission on Dyking, Drainage and Irrigation (1946), GR-680
Department of Lands, Forest Branch, GR-315
Department of Lands (Records relating to the South African War Land Grant Act),
    GR-1396
Inspector of Dykes, GR-1569
Land Settlement Board, GR-1047
Premier's papers, GR-1222
Provincial Secretary, GR-527
Supervisor of Assessors and Agencies, GR-0879
Sumas Dyking District Relief Commission, GR-1089
Surveys and Land Records Branch, GR-1088
Water Rights Branch, GR-884
Water Rights Branch (South Okanagan Irrigation Project), GR-1288

Private Manuscripts

Bruce A. McKelvie papers, MS-001

J.W. Jones papers, MS-023
Thomas Dufferin Pattullo papers, MS-003

Visual Records Collection

Gen. File, Selected Photographs
John William Clark, Photographs, 198210-004

University of British Columbia Library, Special Collections Division (Vancouver)

James Wilson Robertson Fonds
Simon Fraser Tolmie Fonds
South Vancouver Ratepayers Protective Association Fonds

University of British Columbia, University Archives (Vancouver)

Faculty of Agricultural Sciences Fonds
Frank F. Wesbrook Fonds'
Leonard S. Klinck Fonds

City of Vancouver Archives (Vancouver)

Major Matthews Collection
Office of the Mayor Fonds
Social Service Department Fonds

Courtenay and District Museum and Archives (Courtenay, BC)

Clippings File: Merville
Comox Logging and Railway Company Fonds

OTHER SOURCES

Abbott, Philip. "Thoreau, Nature and the Redemption of Liberalism." *The Journal of Politics* 47 (1985): 182-208.
Abrams, Philip. "Notes on the Difficulty of Studying the State." *Journal of Historical Sociology* 1 (1988): 58-89.
Agnew, John S. "The Devaluation of Place in Social Science." In John S. Agnew and James S. Duncan, eds., *The Power of Place: Bringing Together Geographical and Sociological Imaginations*, 9-29. Boston: Unwin Hyman, 1989.
Agnew, John S. and James S. Duncan. "Introduction." In John S. Agnew and James S. Duncan, eds., *The Power of Place: Bringing Together Geographical and Sociological Imaginations*, 1-8. Boston: Unwin Hyman, 1989.
Allardyce, Gilbert. "'The Vexed Question of Sawdust': River Pollution in Nineteenth-Century New Brunswick." In Chad Gaffield and Pam Gaffield, eds., *Consuming Canada: Readings in Environmental History*, 119-30. Toronto: Copp Clark, 1995.
Allen, Richard. *The Social Passion: Religion and Social Reform in Canada, 1914-28*. Toronto: University of Toronto Press, 1971.

Bibliography247

Altmeyer, George. "Three Ideas of Nature in Canada." In Chad Gaffield and Pam Gaffield, eds., *Consuming Canada: Readings in Environmental History,* 96-118. Toronto: Copp Clark, 1995.

Artibise, A.F., and G.A. Stelter. "Conservation Planning and Urban Planning: The Canadian Commission of Conservation in Historical Perspective." In Chad Gaffield and Pam Gaffield, eds., *Consuming Canada: Readings in Environmental History,* 152-69. Toronto: Copp Clark, 1995.

Barman, Jean. *The West beyond the West: A History of British Columbia.* Vancouver: UBC Press, 1996.

Barnes, Trevor J., Roger Hayter, and Elizabeth Hay. "Stormy Weather: Cyclones, Harold Innis, and Port Alberni, BC." *Environment and Planning A* 33 (2001): 2127-47.

Bartholomew and Associates. *A Plan for the City of Vancouver, British Columbia, Including Point Grey and South Vancouver and a General Plan of the Region.* Vancouver: Vancouver Town Planning Commission, 1929.

Bauman, Zygmunt. *Postmodern Ethics.* Cambridge, MA: Blackwell, 1993.

Bennett, Jason Patrick. "Apple of the Empire: Landscape and Imperial Identity in Turn-of-the-Century British Columbia." *Journal of the Canadian Historical Association* 9 (1998): 63-92.

Berger, Carl. *The Sense of Power: Studies in the Ideas of Canadian Imperialism, 1867-1914.* Toronto: University of Toronto Press, 1970.

Blaazer, David. *The Popular Front and the Progressive Tradition: Socialists, Liberals, and the Quest for Unity, 1884-1939.* New York: Cambridge University Press, 1992.

Botkin, Daniel. *Our Natural History: The Lessons of Lewis and Clark.* New York: Grosset/Putnam, 1995.

Bowen, Dawn Suzanne. "'Forward to a Farm': The Back-to-the-Land Movement as a Relief Initiative in Saskatchewan during the Great Depression." PhD diss., Department of Geography, Queen's University, Kingston, 1998.

Bowers, William L. *The Country Life Movement in America, 1900-1920.* Port Washington, NY: Kennikat, 1974.

British Columbia. "Annual Report of the Land Settlement Board of British Columbia for the Year 1918." *Sessional Papers* 2, 1919.

–. "Annual Report of the Land Settlement Board of British Columbia for the Year 1919." *Sessional Papers* 2, 1920.

–. "Annual Report of the Land Settlement Board of British Columbia for the Year 1922." *Sessional Papers* 2, 1924.

–. "BC Government Relief Land Settlement Plan, 1932." *Sessional Papers,* 1935, Y13.

–. "BC Government Relief Land Settlement Plan, 1932." *Sessional Papers,* 1936, EE11.

–. "BC Government Relief Land Settlement Plan, 1932." *Sessional Papers,* 1937, O12.

–. "Correspondence re/ Dominion Conference." *Sessional Papers* 2, 1919.

–. *Journals of the Legislative Assembly,* 1919.

–. "Report of the Operations of the BC Government Relief Land Settlement Committee for the Year Ended December 31st, 1933." *Sessional Papers,* 1934, X13-X14.

–. *Report of the Returned Soldiers' Aid Commission (British Columbia),* 1916.

–. *Report of the Royal Commission on the Tree Fruit Industry of British Columbia,* 1958.

–. "Report of the Superintendent of British Columbia Soldier Settlement." *Sessional Papers* 2, 1919.

–. "Reports of the Department of Agriculture. Eighth Report, 1913." *Sessional Papers* 2, 1915.
British Columbia. Bureau of Provincial Information. *Bulletin No. 10: Land and Agriculture in British Columbia*, 1903.
–. *Bulletin No. 23. Handbook of BC Canada. Its Position, Advantages, Resources, Climate, Mining, Lumbering, Fishing, Farming, Ranching, and Fruit-Growing.* 7th ed. 1913.
–. *New B.C.*, 1908.
British Columbia Magazine (continues from *Westward Ho! Magazine* and *Man-to-Man Magazine*). Vancouver, 1907 and 1910.
Brown, Justine. *All Possible Worlds: Utopian Experiments in British Columbia.* Vancouver: New Star Books, 1995.
Bunce, Michael. *The Countryside Ideal: Anglo-American Images of Landscape.* New York: Routledge, 1994.
Burchell, Graham, Colin Gordon, and Pete Miller, eds. *The Foucault Effect: Studies in Governmentality.* Chicago: University of Chicago Press, 1991.
Cail, Robert E. *Land, Man, and the Law: The Disposal of Crown Lands in British Columbia, 1871-1913.* Vancouver: UBC Press, 1974.
Cameron, Elspeth. *Earle Birney: A Life.* Toronto: Viking, 1994.
Cameron, Laura. *Openings: A Meditation on History, Method, and Sumas Lake.* Montreal and Kingston: McGill-Queen's University Press, 1997.
Canadian National Reconstruction Groups. *The Problems of National Reconstruction: A Summary by the Standing Committee on Plans and Propaganda of the Canadian National Reconstruction Groups.* Montreal, 1918.
Canadian Pacific Railway. *Southern British Columbia: The Garden of Canada. Kootenay, Boundary, Okanagan and Columbia River Districts. Brief Description of Their Wonderful Natural Resources and Scenic Beauties*, 1909.
Cancella, Julie. *The Ditch: Lifeline of a Community.* Oliver, BC: Oliver Heritage Society Museum and Archives, 1986.
Cannings, R. "Natural History of British Columbia." In Daniel Francis, ed., *Encyclopedia of British Columbia*, 487-90. Madeira Park, BC: Harbour Publishing, 2000.
Careless, J.M.S. *Frontier and Metropolis: Regions, Cities, and Identities in Canada before 1914.* Toronto: University of Toronto Press, 1989.
Carlson, Keith Thor. "Indian Reservations." In Keith Thor Carlson, ed., *A Stó:lō Coast Salish Historical Atlas*, 94-95. Vancouver: Douglas and McIntyre
Clarkson, Christopher. "Property Law and Family Regulation in Pacific British North America, 1862-1873." *Histoire sociale/Social History* 30, 60 (1997): 386-416.
Clement, Frederick Moore. *My Thoughts Were on the Land: Autobiography of Fred Clement, Virgil, Ontario.* White Rock, BC: n.p., 1969.
Conkin, Paul K. *Tomorrow a New World: The New Deal Community Program.* Ithaca, NY: Cornell University Press, 1959.
Cook, Ramsay. "1492 and All That: Making a Garden Out of a Wilderness." In Chad Gaffield and Pam Gaffield, eds., *Consuming Canada: Readings in Environmental History*, 62-80. Toronto: Copp Clark, 1995.
–. "Cabbages Not Kings: Towards an Ecological Interpretation of Early Canadian History." *Journal of Canadian Studies* 25, 4 (1990-91): 5-16.
–. "Canada: An Environment without a History?" Paper presented at conference, Themes and Issues in North American Environmental History, Toronto, 1998.
–. *The Regenerators: Social Criticism in Late Victorian Canada.* Toronto: University of

Toronto Press, 1985.

Cooper, Lesley. "More Than Mere Survival: Placer Gold and Unemployment in 1930s British Columbia." MA thesis, Department of History, University of Victoria, Victoria, 1995.

Corrigan, Philip, and Derek Sayer. *The Great Arch: English State Formation as Cultural Revolution*. New York: Blackwell, 1985.

Cosgrove, Denis. *Social Formation and Symbolic Landscape*. Madison, WI: University of Wisconsin Press, 1998.

Craig, Béatrice. "Agriculture and the Lumberman's Frontier in the Upper St. John Valley, 1800-70." *Journal of Forest History* 32, 3 (1988): 125-37.

Cronon, William. *Changes in the Land: Indians, Colonists, and the Ecology of New England*. New York: Hill and Wang, 1983.

-. "Introduction: In Search of Nature." In William Cronon, ed., *Uncommon Ground: Rethinking the Human Place in Nature*, 23-56. New York: W.W. Norton, 1996.

-. *Nature's Metropolis: Chicago and the Great West*. New York: W.W. Norton, 1991.

-. "The Trouble with Wilderness, or, Getting Back to the Wrong Nature." In William Cronon, ed., *Uncommon Ground: Rethinking the Human Place in Nature*, 69-90. New York: W.W. Norton, 1996.

Dalecki, M.G., and C.M. Coughenour. "Agrarianism in American Society." *Rural Sociology* 57, 1 (1992): 48-64.

Danbom, David. *Born in the Country: A History of Rural America*. Baltimore: Johns Hopkins University Press, 1995.

-. *The Resisted Revolution: Urban America and the Industrialization of Agriculture, 1900-1930*. Ames, IA: Iowa State University Press, 1979.

-. "Romantic Agrarianism in Twentieth-Century America." *Agricultural History* 65, 4 (1991): 1-12.

Davis, Mike. *City of Quartz: Excavating the Future in Los Angeles*. New York: Vintage Books, 1992.

-. *The Ecology of Fear: Los Angeles and the Imagination of Disaster*. New York: Metropolitan, 1998.

Davison, J. Robert. "Turning a Blind Eye: The Historian's Use of Photographs." *BC Studies* 52 (1981-82): 16-38.

Demarchi, D.A. *An Introduction to the Ecoregions of British Columbia*. Victoria: Wildlife Branch, Ministry of Environment, Lands and Parks, Government of British Columbia, 1996.

Demeritt, David. "Visions of Agriculture in British Columbia." *BC Studies* 108 (1995-96): 29-59.

Denevan, William. "The Pristine Myth: The Landscape of the Americas in 1492." *Annals of the Association of American Geographers* 82, 3 (1992): 369-85.

Des Jardins, Joseph R. *Environmental Ethics: An Introduction to Environmental Philosophy*. Belmont, CA: Wadsworth Publishing, 1993.

Dobson, Andrew. *Green Political Thought*. New York: Routledge, 1995.

Duncan, Colin A.M. *The Centrality of Agriculture: Between Humankind and the Rest of Nature*. Montreal and Kingston: McGill-Queen's University Press, 1996.

-. "On Identifying a Sound Environmental Ethic in History: Prolegomena to Any Future Environmental History." *Environmental History Review* 15, 2 (1991): 5-30.

Duncan, James S. *The City as Text: The Politics of Landscape Interpretation in the Kandyan Kingdom*. New York: Cambridge University Press, 1990.

Duncan, James S., and David Ley. "Introduction: Representing the Place of Culture." In James S. Duncan and David Ley, eds., *Place/Culture/Representation*, 1-21. New York: Routledge, 1993.

Dunlap, Thomas. "Ecology, Culture, and Canadian National Parks Policy: Wolves, Elk, and Bison as a Case Study." In Rowland Lorimer, ed., *To See Ourselves / To Save Ourselves: Ecology and Culture in Canada*, 139-47. Montreal: Association for Canadian Studies, 1991.

–. *Saving America's Wildlife: Ecology and the American Mind*. Princeton: Princeton University Press, 1988.

Eckersley, Robyn. *Environmentalism and Political Theory: Toward an Ecocentric Approach*. Albany, NY: State University of New York Press, 1992.

Eisenach, Eldon J. *The Lost Promise of Progressivism*. Lawrence, KS: University Press of Kansas, 1994.

Eksteins, Modris. *Rites of Spring: the Great War and the Birth of the Modern Age*. Toronto: Lester and Orpen Dennys, 1994.

Evenden, Matthew. "Remaking Hells Gate: Salmon, Science, and the Fraser River, 1938-1948." *BC Studies* 127 (2000): 47-82.

Ewert, Henry. *The Story of the BC Electric Railway*. North Vancouver, BC: Whitecap Books, 1986.

Favrholdt, Ken. "Domesticating the Drybelt: Agricultural Settlement in the Hills around Kamloops, 1860-1960." In R.W. Sandwell, ed., *Beyond the City Limits: Rural History in British Columbia*, 102-19. Vancouver: UBC Press, 1999.

Fedorowich, K. *Unfit for Heroes: Reconstruction and Soldier Settlement in the Empire between the Wars*. New York: St. Martin's Press, 1995.

Ferguson, Barry. *Remaking Liberalism: The Intellectual Legacy of Adam Shortt, O.D. Skelton, W.C. Clark, and W.A. Mackintosh*. Montreal and Kingston: McGill-Queen's University Press, 1993.

Fiege, Mark. *Irrigated Eden: The Making of an Agricultural Landscape in the American West*. Seattle and London: University of Washington Press, 1999.

Fisher, Robin. *Contact and Conflict: Indian-European Relations in British Columbia, 1774-1890*. Vancouver: UBC Press, 1977.

–. *Duff Pattullo of British Columbia*. Toronto: University of Toronto Press, 1991.

Forkey, Neil S. "Damning the Dam: Ecology and Community in Ops Township, Upper Canada." *Canadian Historical Review* 79, 1 (1998): 68-99.

–. *Shaping the Upper Canadian Frontier: Environment, Society, and Culture in the Trent Valley*. Calgary: University of Calgary Press, 2003.

–. "Victorian Dreams, Progressive Realities: The Commission of Conservation Critiques Old Ontario's 'Colonization' Policy." Paper presented at conference, Themes and Issues in North American Environmental History, Toronto, 1998.

Foster, Janet. *Working for Wildlife: The Beginning of Preservation in Canada*. Toronto: University of Toronto Press, 1998.

Foster, John Bellamy. *Marx's Ecology: Materialism and Nature*. New York: Monthly Review Press, 2000.

Freeden, Michael. *The New Liberalism: An Ideology of Social Reform*. Oxford: Clarendon Press, 1978.

Girard, Michel F. *L'écologisme retrouvé: Essor et déclin de la Commission de la conservation du Canada*. Ottawa: University of Ottawa Press, 1994.

Glacken, Clarence. *Traces on the Rhodian Shore: Nature and Culture in Western Thought from Ancient Times to the End of the Eighteenth Century.* Berkeley: University of California Press, 1967.

Gottlieb, Robert. *Forcing the Spring: the Transformation of the American Environmental Movement.* Washington, DC: Island Press, 1993.

Gould, Peter C. *Early Green Politics: Back to Nature, Back to the Land, and Socialism in Britain, 1880-1900.* New York: Harvester Press/St. Martin's Press, 1988.

Gray, John. *Beyond the New Right: Markets, Government, and the Common Environment.* New York: Routledge, 1993.

Greenberg, Cheryl. "Twentieth-Century Liberalisms: Transformations of an Ideology." In Harvard Sitkoff, ed., *Perspectives on Modern America*, 55-79. New York: Oxford University Press, 2001.

Hall, Stuart. "Variants of Liberalism." In James Donald and Stuart Hall, eds., *Politics and Ideology*, 34-69. Philadelphia: Open University Press, 1986.

Hannah, Matthew G. *Governmentality and the Mastery of Territory in Nineteenth-Century America.* New York: Cambridge University Press, 2000.

Harpstead, Milo I., and Francis D. Hole. *Soil Science Simplified.* Ames, IA: Iowa State University Press, 1980.

Harris, Cole. *Making Native Space: Colonialism, Resistance, and Reserves in British Columbia.* Vancouver: UBC Press, 2002.

–. *The Resettlement of British Columbia: Essays on Colonialism and Geographical Change.* Vancouver: UBC Press, 1997.

Harrison, Peter. "Subduing the Earth: Genesis 1, Early Modern Science, and the Exploitation of Nature." *Journal of Religion* 79, 1 (1999): 86-109.

Hays, Samuel P., ed. "Forum: Environmental History, Retrospect and Prospect." *Pacific Historical Review* 70, 1 (2001): 55-111.

Hobsbawm, Eric. *The Age of Extremes: The Short Twentieth Century, 1914-1991.* London: Michael Joseph, 1994.

Hodgins, Jack. *Broken Ground: A novel.* Toronto: McClelland and Stewart, 1998.

–. *A Passion for Narrative: A Guide for Writing Fiction.* Toronto: McClelland and Stewart, 1993.

Hodgins, Reta Blakely, ed. *Merville and Its Early Settlers, 1919-1985.* Merville, BC: Merville Community Association, 1985.

Igler, David. *Industrial Cowboys: Miller & Lux and the Transformation of the Far West, 1850-1920.* Los Angeles: University of California Press, 2001.

Jackson, Kenneth T. *Crabgrass Frontier: The Suburbanization of the United States.* New York: Oxford University Press, 1985.

Jasen, Patricia. *Wild Things: Nature, Culture, and Tourism in Ontario, 1790-1914.* Toronto: University of Toronto Press, 1995.

Jerome, Judson. *Families of Eden: Communes and the New Anarchism.* New York: Seabury Press, 1974.

Jezierski, John V. "Henry G. Peabody and the Detroit Publishing Company in British Columbia." *BC Studies* 122 (1999): 77-84.

Joyce, Patrick. *The Rule of Freedom: Liberalism and the Modern City.* New York: Verso, 2003.

Keeling, Arn, and Robert McDonald. "The Profligate Province: Roderick Haig-Brown and the Modernizing of British Columbia." *Journal of Canadian Studies* 36 (Fall 2001): 7-23.

Kloppenberg, James T. *Uncertain Victory: Social Democracy and Progressivism in European and American Thought, 1870-1920.* New York: Oxford University Press, 1986.

Koroscil, Paul M. "Boosterism and the Settlement Process in the Okanagan Valley, British Columbia, 1890-1914." In Donald H. Akenson, ed., *Canadian Papers in Rural History,* vol. 5, 73-102. Gananoque, ON: Langdale Press, 1986.

–. "Soldiers, Settlement, and Development in British Columbia, 1915-1930." *BC Studies* 54 (1982): 63-87.

Lampman, A. *Comfort of the Fields.* Ed. R. Souster. Sutton West, ON: Paget Press, 1979.

Laut, Agnes C. "The New Spirit of the Farm." *Outing Magazine* (April, May, and September 1908).

Leighton, Howard B. "The Lantern Slide and Art History." *History of Photography* 8, 2 (1984): 107-18.

Ley, David. "Styles of the Times: Liberal and Neo-Conservative Landscapes in Inner Vancouver, 1968-1986." *Journal of Historical Geography* 13, 1 (1987): 40-56.

Library of Congress and Frances Loeb Library, Graduate School of Design, Harvard University. "Lantern Slides: History and Manufacture," 1999, http://memory.loc.gov/ammem/award97/mhsdhtml/lanternhistory.html/.

Little, J.I. *Nationalism, Capitalism, and Colonization in Nineteenth-Century Quebec: The Upper St. Francis District.* Montreal and Kingston: McGill-Queen's University Press, 1989.

Logged-Off Farms Magazine (continues from *Little Logged-Off Lands*), 1912-14.

Loo, Tina. *Making Law, Order, and Authority in British Columbia, 1821-1871.* Toronto: University of Toronto Press, 1994.

–. "Making a Modern Wilderness: Conserving Wildlife in Twentieth-Century Canada." *Canadian Historical Review* 82, 1 (2001): 92-121.

–. "People in the Way: Modernity, Environment, and Society on the Arrow Lakes." *BC Studies* 142/143 (Summer/Autumn 2004): 161-96.

Lutz, John. "After the Fur Trade: The Aboriginal Labouring Class of British Columbia, 1849-1890." *Journal of the Canadian Historical Association* 3 (1992): 69-93.

–. "'Relating to the Country': The Lekwammen and the Extension of European Settlement, 1843-1911." In R.W. Sandwell, ed., *Beyond the City Limits: Rural History in British Columbia,* 17-32. Vancouver: UBC Press, 1999.

MacBeth, Rev. R.G. *Land in British Columbia.* London: William Stevens, 1920.

MacDougall, John. *Rural Life in Canada.* Reprint, with an introduction by Robert Craig Brown. Toronto: University of Toronto Press, 1973 [1913].

MacEachern, Alan. *Natural Selections: National Parks in Atlantic Canada, 1935-1970.* Montreal and Kingston: McGill-Queen's University Press, 2001.

–. "Rationality and Rationalization in Canadian National Parks Predator Policy." In Chad Gaffield and Pam Gaffield, eds., *Consuming Canada: Readings in Environmental History,* 197-212. Toronto: Copp Clark, 1995.

Mackie, Richard Somerset. "The Colonization of Vancouver Island, 1849-1858." *BC Studies* 96 (Winter 1992-93): 3-40.

–. *Island Timber: A Social History of the Comox Logging Company, Vancouver Island.* Victoria, BC: Sono Nis Press, 2000.

MacPherson, Ian. "Creating Stability amid Degrees of Marginality: Divisions in the Struggle for Orderly Marketing in British Columbia, 1900-1940." In Donald H.

Akenson, ed., *Canadian Papers in Rural History,* vol. 5, 309-33. Gananoque, ON: Langdale Press, 1986.

Marsh, Jan. *Back to the Land: The Pastoral Impulse in England, from 1880 to 1914.* London: Quartet Books, 1982.

McArthur, Peter. *In Pastures Green.* Toronto: J.M. Dent and Sons, 1916.

McCormick, Richard L. *The Party Person and Public Policy: American Politics from the Age of Jackson to the Progressive Era.* New York: Oxford University Press, 1986.

McDonald, John. "Soldier Settlement and Depression Settlement in the Forest Fringe of Sakatchewan." *Prairie Forum* 6, 1 (1981): 35-55.

McEvoy, Arthur. *The Fisherman's Problem: Ecology and Law in the California Fisheries, 1850-1980.* New York: Cambridge University Press, 1986.

McGillivray, Brett. *Geography of British Columbia: People and Landscapes in Transition.* Vancouver: UBC Press, 2000.

McKay, Ian. "The 1910s: The Stillborn Triumph of Progressive Reform." In Ernest Forbes and Del Muise, eds., *The Atlantic Provinces in Confederation,* 192-222, 549-54. Toronto/Fredericton, NB: University of Toronto Press/Acadiensis Press, 1993.

–. "The Liberal Order Framework: A Prospectus for a Reconnaissance of Canadian History." *Canadian Historical Review* 81, 4 (2000): 617-45.

–. *The Quest of the Folk: Antimodernism and Cultural Selection in Twentieth-Century Nova Scotia.* Montreal and Kingston: McGill-Queen's University Press, 1994.

McKillop, A.B. *Matters of Mind: The University in Ontario, 1791-1951.* Toronto: University of Toronto Press, 1994.

Morissonneau, Christian. *La terre promise: Le mythe du Nord québécois.* Montreal: Hurtubise HMH, 1978.

Morton, Desmond, and Glenn Wright. *Winning the Second Battle: Canadian Veterans and the Return to Civilian Life, 1915-1930.* Toronto: University of Toronto Press, 1987.

Murton, James. "What J.W. Clark Saw in British Columbia, or, Nature and the Machine: A Photo Essay." *BC Studies* 142/143 (Summer/Autumn 2004): 129-52.

Nash, Robert. "Wilderness and Man in North America." In J.G. Nelson and R.C. Scace, eds., *The Canadian National Parks: Today and Tomorrow,* vol. 1, 66-93. Calgary, AB: University of Calgary, 1968.

Nelles, H.V. *The Politics of Development: Forests, Mines and Hydro-Electric Power in Ontario, 1849-1941.* Toronto: Macmillan of Canada, 1974.

Odum, Eugene P. *Ecology and Our Endangered Life Support Systems.* Sunderland, MA: Sinauer Associates, 1993.

Oke, T.R., M. North, O. Slaymaker, and D.G. Steyn. "Primordial to Prim Order: A Century of Environmental Change." In Graeme Wynn and Timothy Oke, eds., *Vancouver and Its Region,* 146-70. Vancouver: UBC Press, 1992.

Opportunities Magazine. 1910.

Ormsby, Margaret. *British Columbia: A History.* Toronto: Macmillan, 1958.

–. "The History of Agriculture in British Columbia." *Scientific Agriculture* 20, 1 (1939): 61-63.

Osborn, Matt. "Sowing the Field of British Environmental History." H-Environment Historiography Series in Global Environmental History, 2001, http://www2.h-net.msu.edu/~environ/historiography/.

Osborne, Brian S., and Susan E. Wurtele. "The Other Railway: Canadian National's Department of Colonization and Agriculture." *Prairie Forum* 20, 2 (1995): 231-53.

Owram, Doug. *The Government Generation: Canadian Intellectuals and the State, 1900-45.* Toronto: University of Toronto Press, 1986.

Pal, Leslie A. *Interests of State: The Politics of Language, Multiculturalism, and Feminism in Canada.* Montreal and Kingston: McGill-Queen's University Press, 1993.

Perry, Adele. *On the Edge of Empire: Gender, Race, and the Making of British Columbia, 1849-1871.* Toronto: University of Toronto Press, 2001.

Pisani, Donald. "Reclamation and Social Engineering in the Progressive Era." *Agricultural History* 57 (1983): 46-63.

Polanyi, Karl. *The Great Transformation.* Boston: Beacon Press, 1944.

Potyondi, Barry. *In Palliser's Triangle: Living in the Grasslands, 1850-1930.* Saskatoon, SK: Purich Publishing, 1995.

Pyne, Stephen J. *Fire in America: A Cultural History of Wildland and Rural Fire.* Princeton, NJ: Princeton University Press, 1982.

Rackham, Oliver. *The History of the Countryside.* London: Weidenfeld and Nicolson, 1995.

Radforth, Ian. "Logging Pulpwood in Northern Ontario." In Craig Heron and Robert Storey, eds., *On the Job: Confronting the Labour Process in Canada,* 245-80. Montreal and Kingston: McGill-Queen's University Press, 1986.

Rajala, Richard. "The Forest as Factory." *Labour/Le Travail* 32 (1993): 73-104.

Rayner, William. *British Columbia's Premiers in Profile.* Surrey, BC: Heritage House, 2000.

Reiger, John F. *American Sportsmen and the Origins of Conservation.* Corvallis, OR: Oregon State University Press, 2001 [1975].

Riis, Nelson. "The Wallachin Myth: A Study in Settlement Abandonment." *BC Studies* 17 (1973): 14.

Rodgers, Daniel T. "In Search of Progressivism." *Reviews in American History* 10, 4 (1982): 113-32.

Ross, W. McGregor. *Kenya from Within: A Short Political History.* London: George Allen and Unwin, 1927.

Roy, Fernande. *Progrès, harmonie, liberté: Le libéralisme des milieux d'affaires francophones de Montréal au tournant du siècle.* Montreal: Boréal, 1988.

Roy, Patricia E., and John Herd Thompson. *British Columbia: Land of Promises.* Don Mills, ON: Oxford University Press, 2005.

Runte, Alfred. *National Parks: The American Experience.* Lincoln, NE: University of Nebraska Press, 1997.

Ryder, June. "Physical Geography of BC: Overview." In Daniel Francis, ed., *Encyclopedia of British Columbia,* 549-59. Madeira Park, BC: Harbour Publishing, 2000.

Sandwell, R.W. *Contesting Rural Space: Land Policy and the Practices of Resettlement on Saltspring Island, 1859-1891.* Montreal and Kingston: McGill-Queen's University Press, 2005.

–. "Introduction: Finding Rural British Columbia." In R.W. Sandwell, ed., *Beyond the City Limits: Rural History in British Columbia,* 3-14. Vancouver: UBC Press, 1999.

–. "The Limits of Liberalism: The Liberal Reconnaissance and the History of the Family in Canada." *Canadian Historical Review* 84, 3 (2003): 423-50.

–. "Negotiating Rural: Policy and Practice in the Settlement of Saltspring Island, 1859-91." In R.W. Sandwell, ed., *Beyond the City Limits: Rural History in British Columbia,* 83-101. Vancouver: UBC Press, 1999.

–. "Peasants on the Coast? A Problematique of Rural British Columbia." In Donald H. Akenson, ed., *Canadian Papers in Rural History,* vol. 5, 226-80. Gananoque, ON: Langdale Press, 1986.

–. "Rural Reconstruction: Towards a New Synthesis in Canadian History." *Histoire sociale/Social History* 27, 53 (1994): 1-32.

Schmitt, Peter J. *Back to Nature: The Arcadian Myth in Urban America*. New York: Oxford University Press, 1969.

Schwartz, Joan M. "The Past in Focus: Photography and British Columbia, 1858-1914." *BC Studies* 52 (1981-82): 5-15.

Scott, James C. *Seeing Like a State: How Certain Schemes to Improve the Human Condition Have Failed*. New Haven, CT: Yale University Press, 1998.

Seager, Allen. "The Resource Economy, 1871-1921." In Hugh J.M. Johnston, ed., *The Pacific Province: A History of British Columbia*, 205-52. Vancouver: Douglas and McIntyre, 1996.

Séguin, Normand, ed. *Agriculture et colonisation au Québec: Aspects historiques*. Montreal: Boréal Express, 1980.

Seidman, David. *The New Republic: A Voice of Modern Liberalism*. New York: Praeger Publishers, 1986.

Sekula, Allan. *Photography against the Grain: Essays and Photo Works 1973-1983*. Halifax, NS: The Press of the Nova Scotia College of Art and Design, 1984.

–. "Photography between Labour and Capital." In Benjamin H.D. Buchloch and Robert Wilkie, eds., *Mining Photographs and Other Pictures: A Selection from the Negative Archives of Sheddon Studio, Glace Bay, Cape Breton, 1948-68*, 193-268. Halifax, NS/Sydney, NS: Press of the Nova Scotia College of Art and Design/University College of Cape Breton Press, 1983

Sewell, Derrick W.R. *Water Management and Floods in the Fraser River Basin*. Chicago: Department of Geography, University of Chicago, 1965.

Shi, David. *The Simple Life: Plain Living and High Thinking in American Culture*. New York: Oxford University Press, 1985.

Shore, Marlene. *The Science of Social Redemption: McGill, the Chicago School, and the Origins of Social Research in Canada*. Toronto: University of Toronto Press, 1987.

Sinclair, Peter W. "Agricultural Colonization in Ontario and Quebec: Some Evidence from the Great Clay Belt, 1900-45." In Donald H. Akenson, ed., *Canadian Papers in Rural History*, vol. 5, 105-12. Gananoque, ON: Langdale Press, 1986.

Slaymaker, O., M.J. Bovis, M. North, T.R. Oke, and J. Ryder. "The Primordial Environment." In Graeme Wynn and Timothy Oke, eds., *Vancouver and Its Region*, 17-37. Vancouver: UBC Press, 1992.

Steinberg, Theodore. *Nature Incorporated: Industrialization and the Waters of New England*. Amherst, MA: University of Massachusetts Press, 1991.

–. *Slide Mountain, or, the Folly of Owning Nature*. Los Angeles: University of California Press, 1995.

Stettner, Edward A. *Shaping Modern Liberalism: Herbert Croly and Progressive Thought*. Lawrence, KS: University Press of Kansas, 1993.

Stewart, Mart A. "Environmental History: Profile of a Developing Field." *History Teacher* 31, 3 (1998): 351-68.

Steyn, D.G., M.J. Bovis, M. North, and O. Slaymaker. "The Biophysical Environment Today." In Graeme Wynn and Timothy Oke, eds., *Vancouver and Its Region*, 267-89. Vancouver: UBC Press, 1992.

Struthers, James. *No Fault of Their Own: Unemployment and the Canadian Welfare State, 1914-1941*. Toronto: University of Toronto Press, 1983.

Tagg, John. *The Burden of Representation: Essays on Photographies and Histories*. London: Macmillan Education, 1988.

Thom, Brian, and Laura Cameron. "Changing Land Use in Solh Temexw (Our Land): Population, Transportation, Ecology, and Heritage." In Keith Thor Carlson, ed., *You Are Asked to Witness: The Stó:lō in Canada's Pacific Coast History*, 163-80. Chilliwack, BC: Stó:lō Heritage Trust, 1997.

Thomas, Keith. *Man and the Natural World: Changing Attitudes in England, 1500-1800.* London: A. Lane, 1983.

Thomas, John L. *A Country in the Mind: Wallace Stegner, Bernard DeVoto, History, and the American Land.* New York: Routledge, 2000.

Thompson, John Herd. *The Harvests of War: The Prairie West, 1914-1918.* Toronto: McClelland and Stewart, 1978.

Thompson, John Herd, and Allen Seager. *Canada, 1922-1939: Decades of Discord.* Toronto: McClelland and Stewart, 1985.

Urry, John. *The Tourist Gaze: Leisure and Travel in Contemporary Societies.* London: Sage, 1990.

Valverde, Mariana. *The Age of Light, Soap, and Water: Moral Reform in English Canada, 1885-1925.* Toronto: McClelland and Stewart, 1991.

Village Centres Council for Curative Treatment and Training of Disabled Men. *Third Annual Report, 1921.* Eastcott, Kingston Hill, Surrey, England, 1922.

Warecki, George. *Protecting Ontario's Wilderness: A History of Changing Ideas and Preservation Politics, 1927-1973.* New York: Peter Lang, 2000.

Washington, State of. *The Logged-Off Lands of Western Washington,* 1911.

–. *Vacant Logged-Off Lands,* 1922.

–, Office of Commissioner of Public Lands. *Vacant Logged-Off Lands,* by Clark V. Savidge, Commissioner. Olympia: F.M. Lamborn Public Printer, 1922.

–, Statistics and Immigration Bureau. *The Logged-Off Lands of Western Washington,* by H.F. Giles, Deputy Commissioner. Olympia: Boardman, 1911.

Weiler, Peter. *The New Liberalism: Liberal Social Theory in Great Britain, 1889-1914.* New York: Garland Publishing, 1982.

White, Richard. "American Environmental History: The Development of a New Historical Field." *Pacific Historical Review* 54 (1985): 297-335.

–. "'Are You an Environmentalist or Do You Work for a Living?': Work and Nature." In William Cronon, ed., *Uncommon Ground: Rethinking the Human Place in Nature,* 171-85. New York: W.W. Norton, 1996.

–. "Environmental History: Watching a Field Mature." *Pacific Historical Review* 70, 1 (2001): 103-11.

–. *The Organic Machine: The Remaking of the Columbia River.* New York: Hill and Wang, 1995.

–. "Poor Men on Poor Lands: The Back-to-the-Land Movement of the Early Twentieth-Century." In G. Thomas Edwards and Carlos Schwantes, eds., *Experiences in a Promised Land: Essays in Pacific Northwest History,* 287-303. Seattle: University of Washington Press, 1986.

Whyte, Ian D. *Landscape and History Since 1500.* London: Reaktion Books, 2002.

Williams, Raymond. *The Country and the City.* London: Chatto and Windus, 1973.

Wilson, Alexander. *The Culture of Nature: North American Landscape from Disney to the Exxon Valdez.* Toronto: Between the Lines, 1991.

Wilson, J.D. "Matti Kurikka: Finnish-Canadian Intellectual." *BC Studies* 20 (1973-74): 50-65.

–. "'The police beat them up just to keep warm': A Finnish Canadian Communist Comments on Environmental Depredation and Capitalist Exploitation in Early 20th-Century British Columbia." *Labour/Le Travail* 44 (1999): 191-204.

Woods, Jody R. "Sumas Lake Transformations." In Keith Thor Carlson, ed., *A Stó:lō Coast Salish Historical Atlas*, 104-5. Vancouver: Douglas and McIntyre, 2001.

Worster, Donald. *Dust Bowl: The Southern Plains in the 1930s*. Toronto: Oxford University Press, 1979.

–. "The Ecology of Order and Chaos." *Environmental History Review* 14, 1-2 (1990): 1-18.

–. *Rivers of Empire: Water, Aridity, and the Growth of the American West*. New York: Oxford University Press, 1985.

–. "Transformations of the Earth: Towards an Agroecological Perspective in History." *Journal of American History* 76 (March 1990): 1087-1106, 1142-47.

Wrigley, C.C. "Kenya: The Patterns of Economic Life, 1902-1945." In Vincent Harlow and E.M. Chilver, eds., assisted by Alison Smith, *History of East Africa*, vol. 2, 209-64. Oxford: Clarendon Press, 1965.

Wynn, Graeme. "'Images of the Acadian Valley': The Photographs of Amos Lawson Hardy." *Acadiensis* 15, 1 (1985): 59-83.

Index

Printed and bound in Canada by Friesens

Set in Adobe Garamond by Robert and Shirley Kroeger,
  Kroeger Enterprises

Copy editor: Jillian Shoichet

Proofreader: Sarah Munro

Cartographer: Eric Leinberger